# EYEWITNESS COMPANIONS

# Mythology

## PHILIP WILKINSON &
## NEIL PHILIP

> "AS PAN GU SLEPT, HIS BODY
> BECAME THE MOUNTAINS
> AND HIS BLOOD, THE RIVERS."

Chinese myth: *Pan Gu and Nü Wa's Creation*

# "THEY ROWED BACK OUT INTO THE DEEP OCEAN, AND WERE NEVER SEEN AGAIN."

Irish myth: *The Voyage of Bran*

LONDON, NEW YORK,
MUNICH, MELBOURNE, DELHI

| | |
|---|---|
| **Managing Editor** | Debra Wolter |
| **Managing Art Editor** | Karen Self |
| **Production Controller** | Inderjit Bhullar |
| **DTP** | John Goldsmid |
| **Art Director** | Bryn Walls |
| **Publisher** | Jonathan Metcalf |

Produced for Dorling Kindersley by

**cobaltid**

The Stables, Wood Farm, Deopham Road,
Attleborough, Norfolk NR17 1AJ
www.cobaltid.co.uk

**Editors**
Marek Walisiewicz, Kati Dye,
Louise Abbott, Jamie Dickson, Sarah Tomley

**Art Editors**
Paul Reid, Lloyd Tilbury, Pia Ingham,
Claire Oldman, Annika Skoog

First published in 2007 by
Dorling Kindersley Limited
80 Strand, London WC2R 0RL
A Penguin Company

2 4 6 8 10 9 7 5 3 1

Text copyright © 2007 Philip Wilkinson and Neil Philip

A CIP catalogue record for this book is
available from the British Library.

ISBN 978-1-40531-820-4

Colour reproduction by GRB, Italy.
Printed and bound in China by Leo.

See our complete catalogue at
**www.dk.com**

# CONTENTS

# EVERY HUMAN SOCIETY HAS ITS MYTHOLOGY, A BODY OF SACRED STORIES ABOUT THE GODS AND MATTERS OF COSMIC SIGNIFICANCE, FROM THE CREATION TO WHAT HAPPENS AFTER DEATH. PEOPLE HAVE BEEN TELLING THESE STORIES FOR THOUSANDS OF YEARS, TO HELP THEM MAKE SENSE OF THE WORLD AND THEIR LIVES.

Across the cultures of the world there are seemingly countless myths and numberless gods and goddesses. The Hindu myths of India alone are said to involve thousands of deities. The variety of these myths is fascinating, their stories endlessly entertaining, and they have inspired artists and writers across the centuries. And they are still relevant to us today. Many people read myths for the light they throw onto life, relationships, and the ways of the world. Above all, myths provide unique insights into the ideas, religions, values, and cultures of the people who first told them. Understand their mythology and you understand their world.

**Precious artefacts** such as the Bronze Age disc of Phaistos from Crete give us glimpses of ancient civilizations.

## A DUAL APPROACH

This book is a guide to many of the most interesting and influential of the myths of the world. The main body of the book explores myth geographically, with chapters on the mythologies of the continents from Europe to Oceania, and with one chapter devoted to the especially influential Classical myths of Ancient Greece and Rome. Complementing this is a Who's Who of mythology, a series of brief biographies of gods and goddesses, detailing their origins, characters, and deeds.

## SOURCING THE STORIES

The retellings of myths in this book rely on two different kinds of sources. In some cases, ancient writers left accounts of their peoples' myths, and these texts provide sources for cultures such as Classical Greece and India. Where there are no ancient texts we rely on the work of folklorists and anthropologists who have studied the people, visited them, and written down the stories that make up their oral traditions. The majority of African, North American, and Oceanic myths have come to us in this way.

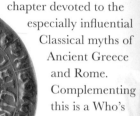

**Mythologies merge** at the tomb-sanctuary of King Antiochus I in Turkey, where monumental stone figures depict both Greek and Persian deities.

# *I*NTRODUCING MYTHOLOGY

**M**YTHS ARE SACRED STORIES. They tell of the creation of the world; the emergence of gods and the first men and women; the adventures of heroes and the audacity of tricksters; the nature of heaven and the Underworld; and of what will happen when time comes to an end. Every human culture has its own myths that are passed on from one generation to the next.

The sacred quality of myth is its most central characteristic. Often the full version of a myth, or its inner meaning, may be known only to priests, shamans, or initiates into a particular cult. Sometimes the myth may be told only at a particular time of year, or in the course of a particular ceremony, or to a designated group. Among the Australian Aboriginal peoples, myths may be the secret knowledge of the men, or the women, or of one moiety, or division, of the people. A myth may even be the private property of a particular family or individual.

**The first stories** recorded in myth are likely to have been prompted by the natural world surrounding early peoples.

## MYTH AND RELIGION

Myth is an essential element of all religions. Myths set out as stories form beliefs about the nature of the divine, the nature of humanity, and the covenant between the two. While in casual parlance the word "myth" means something fictitious, in essence all myths are means of exploring fundamental reality. Myths are stories that tell us the truth about ourselves.

## FLEXIBLE TRUTHS

Myths are ambiguous and subtle. They contain many meanings. They are not fixed, but flexible: they adapt to changed circumstances and new knowledge. This innate flexibility of myth – first remarked on by the

anthropologist Raymond Firth in his studies on Tikopia, one of the Solomon Islands – mimics scientific method in the way it adjusts theories to fit the facts rather than ignoring facts that do not fit the theory.

An example of this flexibility can be seen in the mythology of the Achumawi of California, as told to C. Hart Merriam in 1928 by Istet Woiche. Merriam had enormous admiration for this old myth-teller, the Speaker and Keeper of the Laws of the Madesiwi band. He wrote: "As our acquaintance grew... I came to regard him as a remarkably learned man." When Istet Woiche learned that the Earth spins on its axis and circles the sun – not part of the traditional lore of the Achumawi – he considered it carefully and decided that it must be true, reasoning that: "If the world did not travel, there would be no wind." He incorporated this new knowledge into his mythology, assigning the task of setting the world turning to World's Heart, one of the two pre-existing deities of the Madesiwi.

**Storytelling** and the maintenance of myth and ritual was the province of elders and wise men and women.

**Prehistoric art** often suggests that the artists were recording legendary stories and events.

Myths are a fusion of the creative, spiritual, and social impulses of humankind. The stories have many functions: some religious, some aesthetic, and some practical. Essentially, each society's myths act as a pattern-book for every aspect of that society's culture.

## MYTH AND METAPHOR

Myths, like poems, work through metaphor. They fold the world over on itself, until points that were distant and distinct from each other touch and merge, and these equivalences show us who we really are. The descent of the Sumerian goddess Inanna to the Underworld, for example, can be read by a modern reader as a psychologically exact and poetically alive depiction of a woman's initiation into her female power. The Pima of southwestern North America have a myth in which the god Buzzard creates a miniature cosmos, just like our world. Each myth is like this miniature cosmos, presenting a world of meanings. In the words of the anthropologist Maya Deren: "Myth is the facts of the mind made manifest in a fiction of matter."

# MYTHS IN CONTEXT

Myths are sacred stories about the great issues of life and death, but they are also tied in with the social structure and values of a society – its ideas about family, about gender relations, about law and order, and about cooking, hunting, and agriculture.

## PATHWAY TO THE SACRED

Myths provide both a pathway into the world of the sacred, and a guide to how to live in the world of daily reality. For a society that identifies itself completely with its mythology, every action in this world has an echo in that of the gods. In a culture that is utterly steeped in myth – such as that of the Warao people in the Orinoco Delta region of

**Rituals and re-enactments** of the sacred stories bind societies together: ritual artefacts become prized possessions, imbued with magic.

Venezuela – every aspect of life, however mundane, is infused with a sense of the sacred.

## AN ENTRANCE TO SOCIETY

The truth of the Warao's mythology lies in the way it binds the people into the complex eco-niche in which they live. When a Warao baby is born, it enters a lifelong bond of mutual respect and responsibility with the Warao gods. The baby's first cry carries across the world to the mountain home of Ariawara, the god of origin, and the god's own welcoming cry echoes back. Three days after the birth, Hahuba, the snake of being, who lies coiled in the waters around the world and breathes in time with the tides, sends a balmy breeze to embrace the new arrival. Already, the baby is part of the balance between natural and supernatural that is the warp and weft of Warao daily life.

## THE WORLD IN MICROCOSM

Peoples such as the Warao are perfectly attuned to their environment. On one level their myths are exciting stories about sacred beings in the creation-time, and on another, they are a

**Tribal rivalry** in Indian society is mirrored in myths that tell of heroes among legendary families who outshine one another in acts of bravery.

detailed guide to the delicately balanced ecology of the world in which they live.

When researching the mythology of the Ifugao people on Luzon Island in the Philippines, Roy Franklin Barton gave up trying to count the Ifugao gods after he reached 1,500. These deities – the 70 gods of reproduction, the five arthritis-afflicters, and so on – are beings with little meaning to anyone except the Ifugao themselves. The intensely local nature of Ifugao myth means that it is not useful for drawing generalizations about the world, but in its own specific context it codifies and explains every aspect of Ifugao life.

pair in marriage; Domidicus, who led the bride home; Domitius, who installed her; Manturna, who kept her there; Virginiensis, who untied her girdle; Subigus, who subdued her to her husband's will; Prema, who held her down; and Pertunda, who enabled penetration. As St Augustine ironically pleaded, "Let the husband have something to do too."

> ## "WE LIVE BY MYTH AND INHABIT IT AND IT INHABITS US. WHAT IS STRANGE IS HOW WE REMAKE IT."
>
> Michael Ayrton, *The Midas Consequence*

## MANAGING HUMAN AFFAIRS
Like the Ifugao, the Romans had a god or goddess for every purpose. A Roman husband needed the help of eight gods just to consummate his marriage: Jugatinus, who joined the

## TEMPLATES FOR DAILY LIFE
Myths, then, are not simply stories. They offer social cohesion; act as charters for behaviour, even in the marriage bed; perform and maintain a fine calibration of each society – its values and structures, and its relationship with its environment; and create the spiritual underpinning for custom, ritual, and belief.

# IN THE BEGINNING

Almost every human society presents an account of how the world, people, and animals were created. Creation myths typically tell of a primal world of empty space or undifferentiated water or ice being shaped by a creator, or of a cyclical battle between order and chaos.

## THE GREAT I AM!

The most common theme in creation myths across cultures is the will of a creator god, who separates the Earth from the heavens, shapes the landscape, and creates people from clay, twigs, sweat – even from his own fleas. In Ancient Egyptian myth, this god was Ra, or Amun-Ra – also called Nebertcher, the Lord without Limit – who brought himself into being simply by saying "I am!" before setting the forces of creation in motion by an act of masturbation. The notion of willing the world into existence is present in the myth of the Keres of the American southwest, whose Thinking Woman wove the universe from her own thoughts.

## CREATION FROM WATER

The emergence of existence from a watery abyss is a feature of Egyptian myth, where a mound of land emerges from the ocean of Nun, while the Babylonian creation myth tells of the

**Ra, the creator sun god** of Egyptian mythology, is often represented in human form with a pharaoh's crown, sailing his sacred barque across the sky.

birth of all things from the union of sweet and salt water. In many cultures, an agent of transformation must bring soil up from the primal depths to form the land. The Ainu, the indigenous people of Japan, tell how the creator Kotan-kor-kamuy sent a water wagtail down from heaven to bring earth from the bottom of the primal flood in order to make land; among the Native North Americans, the "earth-diver" takes the form, variously, of a beaver, mink, muskrat, loon, turtle, or duck. Sometimes this figure is a co-creator, who attempts to spoil the world, as in the Siberian myth of Ulgan and Erlik. When Erlik came up from his dive to the bottom of the ocean he kept some mud in his mouth, hoping to make his own world once he had seen how it was done. When Ulgan ordered the mud to expand, Erlik nearly choked, and the mud he spat out made the boggy patches of the Earth.

**Amaterasu the sun goddess** and Susano the storm god are the children of the Japanese creator gods Izanami and Izanagi. Creation is often followed by the procreation of elemental deities to control various aspects of the new cosmos.

## FORCES OF NATURE

In many mythologies, the forces of nature themselves combine to bring the world into being. The Himalayan creation myth of the Singpho tells how in the beginning there was no Earth or sky, just cloud and mist. From this, a cloud-woman was born. She in turn gave birth to two snow-children, who had a mud-girl and a cloud-boy. These two also married, and their son was the wind. His breath was so strong that he blew his cloud-father up and away, and dried up his mud-mother, so that they became the sky and the Earth.

Such a creation myth could readily be related to natural phenomena, but others are far more abstract and intellectual. According to the Juaneño and Luiseño Indians of California, in the beginning there was nothing at all, just empty space. In that empty space, two clouds formed. One was called Vacant, and the other was called Empty. Vacant stretched herself out, and became the Earth; Empty rose up as high as he could, and became the sky. From this sister and brother everything in the world was born. One Polynesian creation myth is so detailed in its account of creation it even celebrates the birth of the dust of the air, from the union of "Small thing" and "Imperceptible thing".

## CYCLES OF CREATION

In Hindu belief, the god Brahma is the source of all space-time, and creation works in a continuous cycle. When Brahma wakes, the world comes into being for a "day" which lasts more than four billion years; when Brahma sleeps, the whole illusion of the world dissolves back into nothingness. This concept of a series of new creations can be found in many other mythologies, such as those of Mesoamerica. Even the end of all things, as in the Norse battle of Ragnarok, the twilight of the gods, can turn out simply to be a new beginning.

# "MYTHS ARE PUBLIC DREAMS; DREAMS ARE PRIVATE MYTHS."

Joseph Campbell, anthropologist

**With their proximity** to the heavens, mountains, from the Himalayas to the American Rockies, feature in many creation myths.

# THE COSMOS

The creation of the sun, the moon, and the stars is part of almost all mythologies. By observing the dance of the stars and the pathways of the planets, we measure time. The changing face of the night sky has led to myths of the world's ages, and of power battles in the heavens.

## THE ETERNAL RETURN

One of the key features of many mythologies is the contrast between the straight line of time as we experience it and the circle of mythological time, which embodies what one historian of religions, Mircea Eliade, called "the myth of eternal return". Myths and rituals are a way of entering the eternal present of this mythological time and accessing its creative power.

## THE WORLD TREE

Many cosmologies envisage a universe with a number of layers, joined together by a central axis or "world tree". The Vikings located Niflheim, the world of the dead, at the bottom of the cosmos, the mortal world Midgard in the middle, and Asgard, the world of the gods, on top. Connecting these, and the realms of the elves, giants, and dwarves, was the world tree, Yggdrasil.

## THE SKY MILL

One of the central concepts of early mythology was the sky mill, which turned on the cosmic pillar or world tree. The millstone of the celestial equator ground out the ages of the world. One of the names given to the Inca high god, Viracocha, translates as "the bearer of the mill". The Incas, noticing the astronomical phenomenon of precession (the "wobble" in the Earth's rotation that causes the equinoxes to move through the constellations), feared that the stars and the sun were at war, and tried to tie them together to prevent disaster by performing rituals at the Hitching-Post of the Sun at Machu Picchu. There they pleaded with Viracocha: "May the world not turn over."

**A classic pose for the** Hindu god Vishnu, showing the deity resting on the cosmic serpent Shesha, who holds the entire universe within his hood.

# "OUR PEOPLE WERE MADE BY THE STARS."

Young Bull, a Pitahawirata Pawnee

## MODELLING THE COSMOS

The Pawnee of the Great Plains of North America believe that they were made by the stars, and that, at the end of the world, they will turn into stars. This cosmic mythology is reflected in the architecture of the Pawnee earth lodge, which, like the Lakota sweat lodge, is a miniature model of the universe. The lodges are built with posts in the northeast, northwest, southwest, and southeast to represent the four gods who hold up the heavens. The entrance faces east, to allow the building to "breathe", and the buffalo-skull altar of Tirawa, the creator, lies in the west.

**For the Greeks,** the Omphalos Stone at Delphi marked the centre of the world; *omphalos* is Greek for navel.

## A LIVING VILLAGE

The Dogon of Mali in West Africa have one of the most intricate mythological systems ever recorded. Every single aspect of Dogon life is alive with myth. Each Dogon village, for instance, is regarded as a living person. It is built north-to-south, with a smithy at its head and shrines at its feet, because Amma, the creator, made the world from clay in the form of a woman lying in this position. The hut of the Hogon, or headman, is a model of the cosmos, and his movements are attuned to the rhythm of the universe. His pouch is "the pouch of the world"; his staff is "the axis of the world".

## THE SUN IS GOD

The reputed last words of the British painter J. M. W. Turner, "the sun is God", are reflected in all mythologies. The bronze Nebra sky disc, an astronomical artefact from around 1600 BCE, depicts the heavens as seen from the Mittelberg mountain in Germany. Probably used as a calendar, it shows the sun, the moon, the stars, the winter and summer solstices, and a golden ship in which the sun traversed the sky.

# THE FIRST BEINGS

All mythologies tell of how the first humans were made. But in many instances, humankind seems to emerge as a kind of afterthought, following on only once the main business of creation has been accomplished, either by the gods or by a preceding race of beings.

## MYTHICAL ANCESTORS

In Australia, Africa, and the Americas, many myths are concerned not with modern humans but with ancestral beings of the creation-time, who are part-human, part-animal. Their activities in the creation-time – for the Australian Aborigines, the Dreaming – shaped the world and established its laws. For instance, the mythological "history of the universe" of the Achumawi of California, recorded from Istet Woiche, covers 160 pages. Human beings only enter the story on page 159. Most of the book is taken up with the doings of a race known as the First People. It is only after a catastrophic flood that almost all of the First People turn into animals, and then the human race as we know it emerges.

## THE CREATIVE FLUX

These primal beings, with their raw powers of transformation and creation, are crucially important to the mythology and world view of many cultures. The understanding brought by a mythology such as the Achumawi's is that the world has been in a state of creative flux since the dawn of time, that everything in it is connected, and that human beings come in as a late addition to the mix.

## MYTHS OF THE ICE AGE

This same world-view probably once prevailed in Europe, as can be seen in the cave paintings of the Ice Age. These paintings of animals, humans, and animal-humans seem to relate to shamanic hunting rituals. They are

**The Mesoamerican eagle warrior** honours a member of a preceding race of animal-beings – a theme common to many cultures.

## "LET US MAKE MAN WITH AN IMAGINATION."

From Rabbi Nahman of Bratslav's alternative translation of *Genesis* 1:26

**Christianity's Adam and Eve** have many parallels in mythologies around the world, when the first people annoy the gods and are banished or transformed.

those gods with prayer and sacrifice. In both Classical Greek and Mayan mythology, three versions of humanity are created before the gods are, albeit somewhat grudgingly, satisfied with the result. The unsatisfactory prototypes may be destroyed or exiled by their exasperated creators, or transformed into animals. Sometimes humans originate almost by accident, as in the Slovenian myth in which God was so exhausted after creating the universe that a drop of sweat fell from his brow. That drop became the first man, who was fated to toil and sweat himself.

## BACK TO THE PRIMAL STATE

In the mythology of the Nuxalk (Bella Coola) of British Columbia, the supreme god, Alquntam, created the first human beings. These humans each chose a bird or animal "cloak" hanging in the House of Myths, and descended to Earth in that form. For the Nuxalk, the body was simply a "blanket of flesh". The spirit was immortal. When a person died, their spirit retraced the path of their ancestors until it reached the spot where the first ancestor descended to Earth. Then it took the ancestor's cloak and rose to live in the House of Myths.

mirrored in the rock art of the San (Bushmen) of southern Africa, whose living myths are preoccupied with the doings of the Early Race of animal-people. The San creator god retains the ability to transform himself into many different animal forms.

## TRIAL AND ERROR

The creation of human beings by the gods is sometimes the last in a series of attempts to make a race fit to nourish

**The shores of Tierra del Fuego,** where the Yamana people's human-animal ancestors settled. The women ruled over the men, until the men rebelled.

# HEROES AND TRICKSTERS

Mythology has two kinds of heroes. The first are people celebrated for great deeds, such as Heracles. The second brought humankind the gifts of culture, such as growing crops, making pots, or spinning cloth. The ambivalent tricksters may be such culture heroes, or even co-creators.

## CONTRARY CLOWNS

The importance of tricksters in mythology lies in the cultural recognition that life is at its core a paradox and a joke. This is evident, for instance, in the behaviour of the *heyoka* clowns of the Lakota, a nation of the American Midwest. *Heyoka* are people who, having dreamed of the mythical being called the Thunderbird, thereafter do everything contrarily.

**The Vodun trickster god** Legba must be propitiated with offerings of milk and eggs poured over him.

They wear their clothes inside out, walk backwards, and talk in opposites. The model for all *heyoka* is Iktomi, the Lakota trickster, who talks with the Thunderbird. Iktomi – originally Ska, god of wisdom – was condemned to wander the Earth armed with only his cunning, which continually entraps him in his own schemes. Iktomi can speak with every living thing, make himself invisible, and transform himself into an old man, the better to play tricks on humans.

## SPIDER AND HARE

The name Iktomi means Spider, and he is said to have a round body like a spider, and spider's legs but human hands and feet. Other Native American tricksters are Hare, Big Rabbit, Raven, Coyote, and Mink. In Africa, the trickster is usually Spider or Hare: the trickster figures Anansi the Ashanti spider-man and Hare were taken by slaves from Africa to the Caribbean and the USA, where in the southern states they became better known as Aunt Nancy, a figure who appears in Gullah folk tales, and Brer Rabbit, the cunning but sometimes conceited folk-hero of the stories of Uncle Remus.

## GREEK TRICKSTERS

A number of Greek gods, including Hermes and Dionysus, exhibit trickster characteristics. Even the great hero Heracles is sometimes depicted as a trickster, as in the Roman story in which (as Hercules) he and his mistress Omphale dress up in each other's clothes to fool the lecherous Faunus (*see p.92*). A vase painting depicting the myth of Heracles's attempted theft of the

**Raven the trickster** is common to the myths of northerly tribes on both the North American and Siberian landmasses.

Delphic altar shows Heracles as a trickster trying to lure Apollo down from the roof of a temple with a tray of tempting fruit; in Heracles's other hand he holds his club, ready to attack.

## LOKI'S TRICKS

The Norse god Loki is a trickster who is at once one of the gods of Asgard – Odin the All-father is his foster-brother

The Hero Twins in both Mayan and southwestern Native American myth blend both bravery and trickery in their battles with monsters who blight the world. It is the cunning of Odysseus that wins the Trojan War for the Greeks, and it is the courage of the wily Maui-of-a-Thousand-Tricks of Polynesian myth that makes him try to conquer death, and die in the attempt.

> "DISORDER BELONGS TO THE TOTALITY OF LIFE, AND THE SPIRIT OF THIS DISORDER IS THE TRICKSTER."

Karl Kerényi, "The Trickster in Relation to Greek Mythology" in Paul Radin's *The Trickster*

– and one of the giants who are the gods' mortal enemies. Loki's tricks cost the gods dear, but also gain them their greatest treasures, and he is tolerated by them until he goes too far, causing the death of Odin's beloved son, Balder the Beautiful. After Loki taunts the gods by revealing all their shameful secrets (for instance, that the giant Hymir's daughters used the mouth of the sea god Njörd as a chamber-pot), the gods hunt him down and bind him to a rock using the entrails of his son Narvi, and arrange for poison to drip from a snake on to his face.

## DUAL NATURES

The trickery of heroes and the heroism of tricksters mean that these figures often share characteristics.

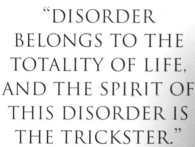

**Heracles possessed** the great physical strength of a hero, but his character was flawed by greed, lust, and a violent temper.

# THE GREAT FLOOD

The Biblical story of Noah's Ark is simply the best-known of many world myths in which an angry god destroys and cleanses the world with water or flames. The parallels between Noah's story and earlier Mesopotamian myths recorded in the *Epic of Gilgamesh* are striking.

## A NEW START

In many mythologies the world in its primal state consists solely of ocean. The action of the gods in flooding it therefore returns it to its pristine condition, enabling a fresh start. In the mythology of the Chewong of Malaysia, the creator Tohan turns the world over every now and then, drowning all the people except those he has warned, and then creates a new Earth on the underside. Flood myths are found right across the world, even (though sparsely) in sub-Saharan Africa and continental Europe. The Hindu myth of Manu and the flood is the best-known of a host of Asian variants.

**In Hindu myth,** the god Vishnu takes the form of a fish – Matsya – to save the mortal Manu from the deluge.

## BIBLICAL INFLUENCES

Some indigenous flood myths have fused so closely with the Biblical story of the flood that it is hard to separate the influences. In Western Australia, for example, the story of Noah has been superimposed upon the local landscape. Building on their own flood traditions, the Aboriginal people believe that Noah's ark landed just south of the Fitzroy River, and that its remains can still be seen there.

In Peru, the Inca creator Viracocha, displeased with his first attempt at humanity – a race of giants – destroyed them with a flood which turned them to stone. The Incas pointed to ancient statues such as those at Tiahuanaco (a sacred site in what is now Bolivia) as evidence of this early race.

## THE FLOOD AS PUNISHMENT

The concept of the flood as punishment recurs in the Classical story of Atlantis (*see box*). In Ancient Greek myth, Zeus sent a flood to punish the arrogance of

# "ATLANTIS DISAPPEARED IN THE DEPTHS OF THE SEA."

Plato, *Timaeus*

In Greek myth, Deucalion and Pyrrha threw stones over their shoulders to recreate humankind. These stones were said to be the bones of Mother Earth.

the very first humans. The Titan Prometheus warned Deucalion, his son, of the coming catastrophe. Deucalion built a chest, and took refuge in it with his wife Pyrrha. For nine days and nights they were tossed by the waters, until they came to ground at Mount Parnassos. When the rains stopped, Deucalion made a sacrifice to Zeus, who in turn offered Deucalion a wish. Deucalion wished for more people. On the instructions of Zeus, Deucalion and Pyrrha threw stones over their shoulders: those that Deucalion threw became men, and those that Pyrrha threw became women.

## SOLE SURVIVORS

Repopulation of the Earth after inundation often requires such ingenious means, particularly when, as in Slavonic and Mesopotamian myth, only a single individual – a man – survives. One such story of the Huichol, a group indigenous to central Mexico, tells of a flood that only one man and his faithful bitch escaped. Spying on her, the man saw that she was able to transform herself into woman's form.

He threw her dog-skin on the fire, and she whined until he bathed her in nixtamal water (maize grains soaked in an alkaline solution), whereupon she became a true woman. They married, and became the ancestors of humanity.

### THE MYTH OF ATLANTIS

The mythical island of Atlantis was shaped into a place of wonder by the god Poseidon for his mortal love Cleito. Their sons ruled the Mediterranean wisely, but in time the divine blood grew thinner, and the people of Atlantis succumbed to mortal passions and wanted power for themselves. Poseidon, in sorrow and anger, stirred up the sea until a huge wave engulfed Atlantis and the island sank beneath the water.

# DEATH AND BEYOND

Why we die, and what happens to us when we do, are questions
that have been addressed in many myths. Heroic figures descend to
the Underworld seeking answers to such questions from the gods of
death – who may also, like the voodoo god Gédé, be lords of life.

## SECRETS OF THE HEREAFTER

The myths of ancient Sumer are
intimately meshed in questions of
mortality and immortality. After the
death of his friend Enkidu, the hero
Gilgamesh searches for the secret
of eternal life, and nearly wins it.
The goddess Inanna descends to the
Underworld and is stripped of all she
holds dear before rising again as the
Great Goddess of heaven and Earth.

## THE SEARCH FOR CERTAINTY

So compelling is the issue of what lies
beyond death that it can change the
course of history. In 627, the English
king Edwin of Northumbria held a
council to decide whether or not to
convert to Christianity. One of his
followers compared the life of a man
to the flight of a sparrow through a
banqueting hall. Who knew what

happened in the darkness before or
after? Christianity offered an answer.
Edwin agreed, and so did Coifi, the
high priest of the old gods, who
himself initiated the destruction of
the old pagan temples.

## THE FINAL JUDGMENT

The Egyptians conceived of the
afterworld as a narrow valley with a river
running through it, separated from this
world by a mountain range. The
magician Setne visited the seven halls
of this afterworld. In the fifth hall, those
accused of crimes were standing at the
door and pleading for mercy. The
seventh hall was the Hall of the Two
Truths, where the sins of the dead were
weighed against the feather of Ma'at.

The idea of a difficult journey after
death to a place of final judgment is not
confined to "great" civilizations. The
Guarayú of Bolivia tell how the soul of
the deceased has the choice of a wide,
easy path and a narrow, dangerous one.
Choosing the narrow path, the soul
endures many perils before joining
Tamoi, the Grandfather, in his paradise.
One test is to walk past a magic tree
without listening to its voices; this tree
knows every secret of the soul's past life.

## THE MOON

The moon is a powerful symbol of
death and rebirth in many mythologies.
The Digueño of California say
that Frog was angry at the
Maker, Tu-chai-pai, and
spat poison into the pool
where the Maker drank.
The Maker did not drink
the poison, but was so
heartbroken that he

**Many Underworlds** have a "gatekeeper". The Greeks
had Charon and the Egyptians, Aken; the bridge to the
Norse Hel (*above*) is guarded by the giantess Modgud.

**Underworlds such as** the Greek Hades may be visited by heroes intent on rescuing a comrade or lover – a common theme in myth.

decided to die. He told the people, "I shall die with the moon." When the moon had shrunk to a crescent, the Maker died and turned into six stars. Ever since, all creatures must die.

## THE CURSE OF IMMORTALITY

The Greek myth of the Sibyl of Cumae warns against wishing for immortality. Apollo fell in love with the young seer and offered her whatever she desired. She asked for as many years of life as she could hold grains of sand. Apollo granted her request but, when she then rejected him, withheld the gift of eternal youth. She withered away, ending her days hung up in a jar like an insect. Whenever she was asked what she wanted, she replied: "I want to die."

**The Egyptian Field of Reeds** is comparable to the Romans' Elysian Fields – a final resting-place for the heroic and good that offers an immortality of heavenly bliss.

# THE END OF THE WORLD

Just as most mythologies describe the beginning of the world at the moment of creation, so most predict the end of the world in some final cataclysm, in which the props holding up the sky will give way, or the world will be consumed by fire or subsumed by flood.

## PREVENTING THE END

The Native American peoples of California celebrate elaborate annual rituals whose purpose is "world renewal". The New Year festival of ancient Babylon had the same purpose – keeping the forces of chaos at bay and allowing the god Marduk to establish universal order for the coming year. Implicit in rituals such as these is the idea that without concerted effort the world will slip back into a primal chaos; that it can be uncreated just as easily it was created. For example, when Jasper Blowsnake – a key source for ethnographers recording the mythology of the Winnebago

nation – was initiated into the sacred medicine rite of his tribe, he was told: "Keep it absolutely secret. If you disclose it this world will come to an end. We will all die." Similarly, when Edward S. Curtis photographed the sacred turtle drums of the Mandan, their keeper, Packs Wolf, told him: "Do not turn them over; if you do, all the people will die."

## COMING CATASTROPHES

Across the world – from the Hmong of Laos to the Toba of the Gran Chaco in South America – there are myths of world catastrophes that happened in the past, and warnings of others that await us in the future. As the poet Robert Frost wrote: "Some say the world will end in fire,/Some say in ice. From what I've tasted of desire/I hold with those who favor fire."

## THE MEANING OF TIME

The Mayan *Book of Chilam Balam* states that "All moons, all years, all days, all winds, reach their completion and pass

**Ragnarok,** the last cataclysmic battle in Norse mythology, will mark the end of this world.

away." The Maya believed that time kept the gods trapped within the stars. This notion is reflected in Zoroastrian mythology, where time was devised as a means of trapping the evil spirit Ahriman within creation, and bringing about his eventual downfall.

## A TIRED GOD

An Ancient Egyptian drinking song speaks of "millions and millions of years to come" in the land of dead; but the Egyptians did not think that eternity would last forever. A day would come when the sun god Ra would tire and bring this world to an end. Then he would be reunited with Osiris in the primal waters of Nun. All this was promised to Osiris by Ra when Osiris was first given charge of the Underworld. Ra said, "I will destroy all creation. The land will fold into endless water, as it was in the beginning. I will remain there with Osiris, after I have changed myself back into a serpent that men cannot know, that the gods cannot see."

## THE COSMIC SERPENT

This serpent is the true original form of Ra, containing the elemental forces of both creation and chaos. It will sleep in

**The Zoroastrian god** Ahura Mazda has parallels with the Hindu Siva in that he may both create and destroy the world.

the cosmic ocean, its head in its tail, until it wakes once more from slumber to create the world anew. To the creator, each cycle of human history is no more than a day, and all human hopes and dreams of eternal life last only until

nightfall, when the universe will collapse in on itself, and return to the purity of the primal nothingness.

## A NEW CREATION

The Hindu concept of each cycle of creation being simply a day and night for Brahma is close to the Ancient Egyptian model. Even worlds that will end in battle and conflagration, such as that of the Norse gods, who will be vanquished in the battle of Ragnarok, quietly recreate themselves on the far side of disaster. The Vikings said that only two people, Lif and Lifthrasir, would survive to repopulate this fresh new world.

## THE FIFTH WORLD

In the mythology of the Hopi, whose pueblo Oraibi is the oldest inhabited settlement in North America, this world, the fourth in a series of seven, is now entering its "end-time". Their prophecies foretell that when a blue star appears and its spirit, Saquasohuh, descends to Earth to dance in the plaza, this fourth world will come to its end. The fifth world that will replace it is already emerging. The signs can be read, they say, in the Earth itself.

# THE CLASSICAL WORLD

T HE CLASSICAL WORLD is the umbrella term we use for the sophisticated civilization that began in Ancient Greece and was taken over and developed by the Romans. Greek and Roman writers recorded huge numbers of myths, relating stories of their gods and goddesses to every aspect of life, from the weather and the harvest to the foundation of their principal cities.

The Ancient Greeks had one of the richest of all mythologies, involving scores of gods and goddesses. The writings that relate these life-affirming stories span more than a millennium, from the early poets Homer and Hesiod, who probably lived in the 8th or 7th centuries BCE, to the dramatists and poets who flourished in Athens during its 5th-century BCE heyday.

When the Romans conquered most of Europe a few centuries later, they adopted many of the Greek myths. They added gods and goddesses of their own, and characters from the myths of conquered peoples. Most of the Classical gods and goddesses took human form and displayed human traits: love, jealousy, anger, and warmongering are recurring themes. But they were also very powerful, and the Greeks and Romans believed that the gods had a huge influence over life. Most governed a particular aspect of the cosmos or of existence – Ares ruled over battle; Aphrodite was the goddess of love – but many, like Athena, the goddess of war, wisdom, and crafts, had more varied roles.

## PEOPLE AND GODS

Ancient Greece was not a single country but a series of separate city-states, and each of these had its own patron deities (*see pp.52–3*). Athena was the goddess of Athens, for example, while Zeus ruled supreme at Olympia. Each city built temples to its deity and usually held regular festivals in his or her honour. These embraced both the arts, with competitions for poets and playwrights, and sport, from discus-throwing to wrestling.

The Greeks did not look to their gods for moral leadership or guidance in how to live. The gods were too capricious and even amoral for that. But people did believe that by making offerings or sacrifices to a particular deity they would get the god on their side and benefit from protection as they went about their daily lives.

### CLASSICAL POETS

A few figures stand out as key sources for Classical mythology. The earliest are two Greek epic poets: Homer, whose *Iliad* and *Odyssey* tell the stories of the Trojan War and the adventures of Odysseus; and Hesiod, whose *Theogony* covers the origins of the world and the genealogy of the gods. The *Library of Mythology*, by the later writer Apollodorus, covers many of the Greek myths. The most important Roman writer is Virgil, whose *Aeneid* recounts the story of the hero Aeneas and the foundation of Rome.

**Virgil, writing in the** 1st century BCE, modelled his works on the *Odyssey* and *Iliad* of Homer.

They selected the deity carefully – before going on an ocean voyage, for example, an ancient Greek would make an offering to the sea god Poseidon.

The seriousness with which the gods' powers were taken is illustrated in Homer's poem the *Iliad*, which frequently attributes the changing fortunes of the two sides in the Trojan War to the influence of the gods looking down from their home on Mount Olympus.

**Mythologies** often merged in the Classical world, as this Egyptian motif on an Ancient Greek necklace pendant demonstrates.

## A LASTING INFLUENCE

The deities were so important in Greece and Rome that much of what survives from the Classical era is connected to their mythology. This includes temples where the gods were worshipped, theatres where plays were staged in their honour, treasuries where offerings were collected, and objects decorated with mythological scenes.

**The Sanctuary of Athena** is part of the temple complex at Delphi in Greece. It was dedicated to the goddess Athena, in her role as the guardian of wisdom and spiritual consciousness.

After the decline of Rome in the 5th century CE, the popularity of Classical myths diminished. Interest in them revived in Europe during the Renaissance period, beginning early in the 15th century. Artists began to paint mythological subjects again, and Classical poets were translated into modern European languages.

Classical mythology has been popular ever since, both in the arts and in other fields. For example, pioneer psychoanalyst Sigmund Freud coined the phrase "Oedipus complex" after the legendary sexual transgressions of Oedipus, king of Thebes. In a similar way, Classical mythology has even reached the business world, with some management consultants describing a business with one dominant leader as having a "Zeus culture". The myths of Greece and Rome live on.

# THE PRIMAL EGG

📖 Creation
🏛 Ancient Greece
🏛 The cosmos

✍ Pliny, *Natural History*; Apollonius
   of Rhodes, *Argonautica*

In the beginning there was nothing but a swirling void called Chaos. Eventually, out of the nothingness, a creator force emerged. Some say this force was Gaia, Mother Earth; some say it was a goddess called Eurynome, who took the form of a dove. Gaia or Eurynome laid a great egg, from which emerged Uranus, the sky; Ourea, the mountains; Pontus, the sea, and many other parts of the cosmos.

**The goddess Eurynome,** impregnated by the wind serpent, took the form of a dove to lay the Universal Egg, which contained the entire material world.

Gaia and Uranus made love, and the earliest creatures to inhabit the Earth were born. First came the Cyclopes, giant creatures that looked like people but had only one eye, in the middle of their foreheads. Uranus disliked the Cyclopes and thought they might usurp his power, so he banished them to the Underworld.

Gaia and Uranus later produced six huge and powerful children who grew up to rule the Earth, and became known as the Titans (*see below*). The descendants of these Titans were to become some of the most important and enduring gods in Classical culture: the gods of Mount Olympus.

# THE BIRTH OF THE TITANS

📖 The first beings;
   origin of the gods
🏛 Ancient Greece

🏛 The cosmos; Earth
✍ Hesiod, *Theogony*

Gaia and Uranus bore a race of children called the Titans. Among them was Cronos, who became their leader. The Titans were giants of incredible strength. They settled down with female Titans (Titanesses), and began to rule the Earth.

Soon the Titans and Titanesses began to have children, some of whom were destined to become the most powerful gods and goddesses. Eos,

goddess of the dawn, and Helios, the sun god, were the children of Hyperion. Cronos, king of the Titans, had many children with his wife Rhea. The offspring of Cronos and Rhea became the gods of Mount Olympus, also called the Olympians (*see p.40*), and they were to become as powerful a race as the Titans themselves.

**The Titan Atlas,** descendant of Uranus (sky) and Gaia (Earth), was so strong that he could bear the world on his shoulders.

# THE FIRST HUMANS

📖 Origins of humanity
🏳 Ancient Greece
🏛 Earth

✍ Hesiod, *Works and Days*; Hesiod, *Theogony*;
Aeschylus, *Prometheus Bound*

The gods made two botched attempts to create
people to inhabit the Earth before the human race
as we know it was created by the Titan
Prometheus, acting on a request from the god
Zeus. Prometheus then took on a guardian role,
helping humans on several occasions when they
fell foul of the gods. This enraged the gods, and
the Titan spent many years suffering a terrible
punishment after he made Zeus angry.

### KEY CHARACTERS

**ZEUS** • *king of the gods,
son of Cronos and Rhea*
**PROMETHEUS** • *a second-
generation Titan, son of
Iapetos and Clymene*

## PLOT SYNOPSIS

The first two attempts to create humans
produced the peaceful Golden Race, who
had no children and died out, and the
Silver Race, who were banished to the
Underworld by Zeus because they were
evil. Then Prometheus fashioned the
Bronze Race from clay, who thrived.

### A TRICK PLAYED ON ZEUS

On one occasion, the people sacrificed a
bull to Zeus. They could keep some of it
and offer some to the god, but they could
not agree on which parts. Prometheus
helped them by dividing the meat
into two: one portion was the good

meat, wrapped in bull's hide; the other
just bones covered in tasty-looking fat.
Zeus chose the second, and was so angry
when he discovered the trick that he
refused to give fire to humanity. But
Prometheus stole it from Zeus and took
it to Earth, showing everyone how to
use it. Furious, Zeus punished him by
chaining him to a rock, where a great
eagle pecked away at his liver. Zeus
renewed the liver every day, causing
endless torture, until finally Prometheus
was rescued by the hero Heracles.

**RELATED MYTHS ▸** The first humans (*p.115*)
• Pan Gu and Nü Wa's creation (*pp.172–3*)

**The Prometheus myth** continues to fascinate
modern artists: this is Paul Manship's *Prometheus*
statue at the Rockefeller Plaza in New York, USA.

# WAR OF THE GODS AND TITANS

- Wars of the gods
- Ancient Greece
- Greece; Crete; the cosmos

- Hesiod, *Theogony*; Apollodorus, *Library of Mythology*

The first rulers of the universe were the Titans, the offspring and descendants of Uranus and Gaia. A race of giant immortals, they wielded enormous power, but did not rule in harmony. The real trouble began when Cronos, the chief Titan, began to have children with his wife Queen Rhea. Their offspring (the gods and goddesses) fought a long and bitter war against the older Titans before finally achieving victory under their leader Zeus.

> **KEY CHARACTERS**
>
> **CRONOS** • *king of the Titans*
> **RHEA** • *queen of the Titans*
> **AMALTHEA** • *a goat-nymph*
> **ZEUS** • *king of the gods*
> **POSEIDON** • *god of the sea*
> **HADES** • *god of the Underworld*
> **TYPHON** • *a monster*

## PLOT SYNOPSIS

### THE CHILDREN OF RHEA

Cronos, king of the Titans, took the Titaness Rhea as his queen. Soon the couple began to have children. But there was a problem. Cronos had been told by an oracle that one of his children would kill him. To prevent this, each time a baby was born, Cronos took the child and swallowed it. This happened five times, so when she gave birth for the sixth time, Rhea decided to deceive her husband. She hid her baby, Zeus, and wrapped a stone in swaddling clothes. Cronos took the stone and swallowed it, and Rhea secretly sent Zeus to Crete, where he was brought up by a faithful goat-nymph called Amalthea and nourished on honey supplied by Cretan bees.

**Cronos,** king of the Titans, ate five of his children but was ultimately dethroned by his son, Zeus.

### ZEUS RESCUES HIS SIBLINGS

Amalthea died as Zeus was nearing adulthood, and he had her skin made into a magically strong shield. Zeus had learned about his parentage and how his father had treated his siblings, and

now decided that he would return to Greece and take his revenge.

Back in Greece Zeus met Metis, a cunning Titaness who told him that it was not too late to rescue his siblings. Metis gave Zeus a drug, which he in turn administered to Cronos the Titan, causing him to vomit up his five other children: the gods Poseidon and Hades, and the goddesses Hestia, Demeter, and Hera. Then Zeus freed the Cyclopes, a race of one-eyed giants sent to the Underworld by Uranus and kept there by Cronos. They also wanted to take their revenge on the Titans.

### THE GREAT BATTLE

Under the leadership of Zeus, the gods and goddesses, together with the Cyclopes, declared war on Cronos and the Titans. The struggle lasted for ten years, and the hugely powerful Titans seemed invincible. But the Cyclopes were skilled craftsmen who produced some mighty weapons for the gods. They forged a thunderbolt for Zeus;

a great trident for Poseidon, which could create earthquakes and sea-storms; and a magical helmet for Hades that made him invisible when he put it on. By using these powerful weapons the young gods eventually managed to defeat the Titans.

**Both male and female** gods and Titans participated in the war (sometimes known as the Titanomachy), depicted on the Great Altar of Zeus, Pergamon.

## DIVISION OF THE SPOILS

When the fighting was over, the gods ruled the cosmos, and decided to divide up power between them. Unable to think of any other way to determine who should rule which part of the universe, they decided to draw lots. Zeus became ruler of the sky, Poseidon was made god of the sea, and Hades, king of the Underworld. The defeated Titans were imprisoned in Tartarus, a deep region of the cosmos, deeper even than the Underworld and peopled by dreadful monsters. One of the Titans, Atlas, was punished by being given the job of holding the heavens on his shoulders.

**Gods and men** were privileged to borrow Hades's magical helmet.

## GIANTS AND MONSTERS

Gaia, mother of the Titans, was furious when her children were imprisoned in Tartarus, so she started another war. She rallied together another group of her children, the giants, and took them to war and the battle began all over again. Once more the Olympian gods were victorious, but then Zeus was forced to fight one last battle – with the monster Typhon. The battle ended when Zeus cornered him in Sicily and hurled Mount Etna at the monster's head. The fire that erupts from Etna was sometimes said to come from the thunderbolts Zeus had used in this last fight. Zeus's struggle for power was now over, and he reigned supreme over the universe.

**RELATED MYTHS ▶** The war between the gods (*p.116*)

# THE GODS OF OLYMPUS

Greek mythology has a huge cast of characters, from the early race known as the Titans to the mortal heroes whose adventures are recounted by writers such as Homer and Apollonius. But the most important group are the Olympians – the gods and goddesses said to live on Mount Olympus. The Greeks believed that these supreme deities influenced nearly everything that happened on Earth.

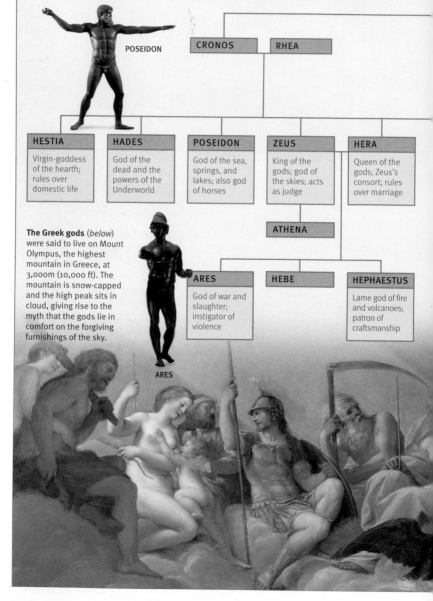

POSEIDON

CRONOS — RHEA

| HESTIA | HADES | POSEIDON | ZEUS | HERA |
|--------|-------|----------|------|------|
| Virgin-goddess of the hearth; rules over domestic life | God of the dead and the powers of the Underworld | God of the sea, springs, and lakes; also god of horses | King of the gods; god of the skies; acts as judge | Queen of the gods; Zeus's consort; rules over marriage |

ATHENA

**The Greek gods** (*below*) were said to live on Mount Olympus, the highest mountain in Greece, at 3,000m (10,000 ft). The mountain is snow-capped and the high peak sits in cloud, giving rise to the myth that the gods lie in comfort on the forgiving furnishings of the sky.

| ARES | HEBE | HEPHAESTUS |
|------|------|------------|
| God of war and slaughter; instigator of violence | | Lame god of fire and volcanoes; patron of craftsmanship |

ARES

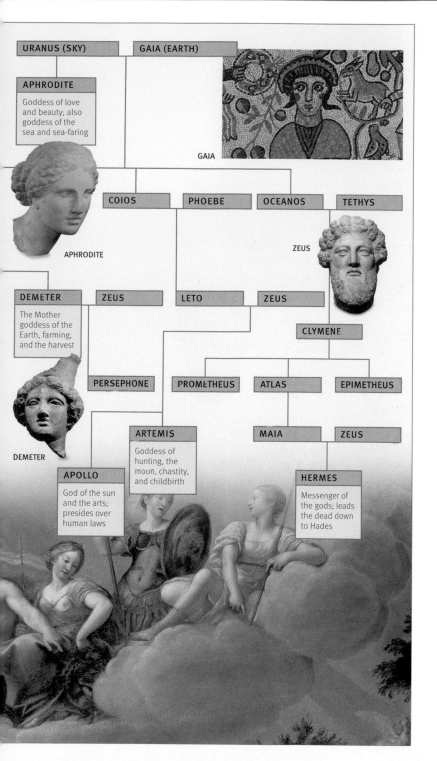

**URANUS (SKY)**

**GAIA (EARTH)**

**APHRODITE**

Goddess of love and beauty; also goddess of the sea and sea-faring

GAIA

APHRODITE

**COIOS**

**PHOEBE**

**OCEANOS**

**TETHYS**

ZEUS

**DEMETER**

The Mother goddess of the Earth, farming, and the harvest

**ZEUS**

**LETO**

**ZEUS**

**CLYMENE**

DEMETER

**PERSEPHONE**

**PROMETHEUS**

**ATLAS**

**EPIMETHEUS**

**ARTEMIS**

Goddess of hunting, the moon, chastity, and childbirth

**MAIA**

**ZEUS**

**APOLLO**

God of the sun and the arts; presides over human laws

**HERMES**

Messenger of the gods; leads the dead down to Hades

# THE LOVES OF ZEUS

📖 Loves of the gods
🗺 Ancient Greece
🏛 Mount Olympus; Greece

✍ Hesiod, *Theogony*; Apollodorus, *Library of Mythology*

Zeus, son of Cronos and Rhea, became king of the gods after leading them in their overthrow of the Titans. The name Zeus means "sky", and as the sky god he controlled the weather and used the thunderbolt as his weapon. Hera, the goddess of marriage and childbirth, was his sister as well as his wife. But Zeus had many other sexual conquests, and made Hera extremely jealous as a result. The lovers of Zeus were both human and divine.

**KEY CHARACTERS**

**ZEUS** • *king of the gods*
**HERA** • *a goddess, the wife and sister of Zeus*
**ZEUS'S LOVERS** • *various goddesses, nymphs, and humans*

## PLOT SYNOPSIS

### ZEUS AND METIS

Zeus's first passion was for the sea-nymph Metis ("thought"), and although the wise nymph changed her shape into many different forms trying to escape him, he succeeded in making love to her. When Metis became pregnant, Gaia, the Earth goddess, prophesied that she would give birth first to a girl, and then to a boy who would become the ruler of heaven. Fearing this, Zeus swallowed Metis and her unborn child, thus acquiring her wisdom. The child, the goddess Athena, was born from Zeus's head.

ZEUS

### CONQUESTS AND MARRIAGE

Besides Metis, Zeus had many divine lovers who bore him children. Themis, a Titaness, gave birth to the Hours and the Fates; Euronyme, a sea-nymph, gave birth to the Graces; and Mnemosyne, another Titaness, was the mother of the nine Muses. These transitory unions were eclipsed by the long-lasting partnership Zeus enjoyed with his sister Hera. She bore him three children: Ares, the god of war; Hebe, the cup-bearer of the gods; and Eileithuia, goddess of childbirth. A fourth child, Hephaestus, the lame "smith to the gods", is said to be Hera's alone, although some say Zeus fathered him secretly, taking the form of a cuckoo.

### MARITAL ROWS

As befits a god often termed "the gatherer of clouds", Zeus's marriage was a stormy one. Hera once left him, but Zeus won her back with a trick. He ordered a statue of a woman to be made and covered with a bridal veil, to look like a real woman. He then introduced this woman as his new wife. Hera was

**The Temple of Hera** at Paestum, Italy, was a place of pilgrimage for childless couples and the setting for sacred rites celebrating marriage.

furious, and rushed to the scene to attack the statue, only for her anger to turn to laughter when she discovered the ruse. On another occasion when Hera defied him, Zeus bound her with chains and suspended her with anvils hanging from her feet.

### JEALOUS WIFE
Zeus's sexual appetite caused Hera terrible jealousy, and she pursued his lovers relentlessly. When the goddess Leto was pregnant with Apollo and Artemis, Hera forbade any land from sheltering her; she had to flee across the world until she found the floating island of Delos. Hera turned Zeus's lovers Callisto into a bear and Io into a cow.

### A MASTER OF DISGUISE
Zeus would transform himself to seduce a woman he desired. He slept with Alcmene in the guise of her husband Amphitryon, fathering the hero Heracles. For Europa he turned himself into a bull. When Danaë was shut in a bronze chamber, Zeus came to her as a shower of gold. To seduce Semele, however, he simply disguised himself as a mortal.

**Zeus impregnated** the Greek princess Danaë in the form of a shower of gold. The result of the union was a son, the Greek hero Perseus.

### LEDA AND THE SWAN
Leda was the beautiful wife of Tyndareos, king of Sparta. As she lay on the river bank one day, Zeus came to her in the form of a swan, seeking help as it escaped from an eagle (Zeus's symbolic bird). Leda, taking pity on the swan, embraced the bird, and Zeus took her by surprise. Leda then became the only human to lay an egg, from which were hatched Helen (the great beauty who would later be blamed for the fall of Troy) and the twin boys Castor and Pollux (*see p.89*). Ultimately the tragic lives of her children led Leda to take her own life.

---

### THE CHILDREN OF ZEUS

The Greeks believed that three sets of Zeus's children had a huge impact on the lives of humans. The Fates controlled human destiny, spinning and measuring the thread of each human life, and cutting it at the time of death. The Graces influenced the joy of life, and the Muses controlled human art and creativity.

**The three Graces** embodied beauty, grace, and generosity.

# THE AFFAIRS OF APHRODITE

📖 Loves of the gods
🏴 Ancient Greece
🏛 Mount Olympus; Greece; the Underworld

✒ Homer, *Odyssey*; Apollodorus, *Library of Mythology*

Cronos, king of the Titans, attacked his father Uranus, whose blood dripped into the sea, mixed with the sea foam, and gave birth to Aphrodite, goddess of love. A magic girdle made her irresistibly attractive to both gods and mortals. Zeus made her marry his son, Hephaestus, but he was lame and unattractive and so she took many lovers. Some of her affairs caused amusement, but they could also lead to disasters, such as the Trojan War.

### KEY CHARACTERS

**APHRODITE** • *goddess of love*
**HEPHAESTUS** • *god of fire*
**ARES** • *god of war*
**ADONIS** • *a handsome youth*

## PLOT SYNOPSIS

### APHRODITE AND ARES
One of Aphrodite's lovers was Ares, the god of war. When her husband Hephaestus found out about the affair, he decided to teach the couple a lesson. A skilled metalworker, he made a net of bronze wire and suspended it from the ceiling above Aphrodite's bed. When the couple next went to bed together, Hephaestus released the net, catching them red-handed. Then Hephaestus invited all the other gods to come and laugh at the lovers, squirming around like fish in a net.

### APHRODITE AND ADONIS
Adonis was a handsome young man who was loved by both Aphrodite and the goddess Persephone, wife of Hades, king of the Underworld (*see p.54*). When Adonis chose Aphrodite instead of her, Persephone was furious, and told Ares – who was still in love with Aphrodite – about the affair.

**The goddess Aphrodite** rose from the waves in a shell, reputedly at Paphos in Cyprus, which became her cult centre.

Jealous Ares sent a wild boar to attack and kill Adonis, who consequently arrived in the Underworld – much to the delight of Persephone. However, Aphrodite did not want to lose Adonis, so she appealed to Zeus to let him return to Earth. Zeus considered both sides and decided on a compromise: each year Adonis was to stay in the Underworld for six months with Persephone, but he would be allowed to return to Aphrodite for the remaining half of the year.

### OTHER LOVES
Aphrodite had numerous other lovers, including the god Hermes, with whom she had a son called Hermaphroditus, who had the physical attributes of both sexes. She also had an affair with the Trojan prince Anchises, who was father of the hero Aeneas (*see p.80*). She is said to have had affairs with the gods Zeus, Pan, and Dionysus, one of whom was reputedly the father of her son Priapus, the god of fertility.

# THE JEALOUSY OF AMPHITRITE

- 📖 Loves of the gods
- 🏛 Ancient Greece
- 🏛 The sea

- ✍ Apollonius, *Argonautica*;
  Tzetzes, *On Lycophron*

Like Zeus, Poseidon had a ravenous sexual appetite. He was married to the sea-nymph Amphitrite, and they had one child, Triton, who, like a merman, was half-human and half-fish. Poseidon also had many affairs, fathering other children who became sea-monsters or minor gods of the sea. Amphitrite tired of her husband's unfaithfulness, and wrought a vicious revenge on one of his lovers, the beautiful nymph Scylla.

### KEY CHARACTERS

**POSEIDON** • *god of the sea*
**AMPHITRITE** • *a sea-nymph, married to Poseidon*
**SCYLLA** • *a sea-nymph turned sea-monster*

## PLOT SYNOPSIS

Scylla began life as a beautiful sea-nymph who caught the eye of Poseidon. However, her fate was sealed when Poseidon's wife Amphitrite discovered her husband's passion for the nymph and vowed to put an end to the affair.

Amphitrite dropped some herbs into the water where Scylla bathed. As a result, her rival was transformed into a monster, as six dog's heads sprang up from around her body, barking and grabbing at

**The nymph Amphitrite** was drawn by dolphins to her wedding with the sea god Poseidon.

anything that passed by. Unsurprisingly, Poseidon's passion for his lover cooled rapidly, and he soon returned to his wife.

Scylla joined the terrifying sea-monster Charybdis (another of Poseidon's offspring, this time with Gaia) at the straits of Messina and the pair became one of the most feared hazards to ships at sea. Homer's *Odyssey* relates how six of Odysseus's companions were killed when passing through these dangerous straits.

### THE TEMPLE OF POSEIDON AT SOUNION

Sounion sits at the tip of a cape sticking out into the Aegean in southeastern Attica in Greece, surrounded on three sides by sea. Although dedicated to Poseidon, Zeus and Athena were also worshipped there. The Greeks made offerings to Poseidon to protect them from storms. The temple was destroyed when the Persians and Greeks fought in the early 5th century BCE, but was quickly rebuilt, and its ruins survive today.

**The Temple of Poseidon** at Cape Sounion, just outside Athens in Greece, is first mentioned in Homer's epic poem the *Odyssey*.

**Olympus, home of the gods,** depicted in a ceiling fresco by Giulio Romano in the Room of the Giants, Palazzo del Te, Mantua, Italy. At the top of the picture, the supreme god Zeus brandishes his thunderbolts; at the bottom, his brother Poseidon wields his trident.

# APOLLO AND THE ORACLES

📖 Revenge
🏴 Ancient Greece
🏛 Delphi, Greece

✍ Apollodorus, *Library of Mythology*;
*Homeric Hymn to Apollo*

Apollo, the god of the sun and the arts, was the son of Zeus and a Titaness called Leto. Zeus's wife Hera was jealous when she found out about her husband's affair with Leto, and so sent a monstrous serpent-monster, the Python, in pursuit of the Titaness. When he grew up, Apollo took his revenge on the Python for harassing his mother. He hunted the creature, finally caught it at Delphi, and killed it.

The Python had devastated the land and villages of Delphi for many years, so in thanks to Apollo the people built a temple to him, commemorating his victory over the serpent.

Apollo in turn bestowed the temple's priestess, known as the Pythia, with the power of prophecy. Many Greeks came to Apollo's temple at Delphi to consult this oracle and find out what the future held in store for them.

# THE FATE OF DAPHNE

📖 Rivalry between the gods;
transformation
🏴 Ancient Greece

🏛 Greece
✍ Apollodorus, *Library of Mythology*;
Ovid, *Metamorphoses*

Apollo, a skilful archer, once chose to make fun of the love god Eros by deriding his attempts at archery. Angered by this, Eros planned his revenge. His quiver contained two types of arrow: gold-tipped ones that made their target fall hopelessly in love, and lead-tipped ones that made the victim abhor anything romantic.

### EROS'S REVENGE
Eros shot the gold-tipped arrow at Apollo and made the god fall in love with the nymph Daphne, whom he wounded with the lead-tipped arrow, preventing her from ever feeling love.

So began a hopeless mismatch. Apollo took off in pursuit of the dismayed Daphne through the mountains. As she ran from him, she prayed to Zeus to be transformed so that Apollo could not catch her. Her prayers were answered, and she was turned into a laurel tree.

**Apollo declared** the laurel tree sacred because of his love for Daphne, and from this point on he always wore a wreath of laurel leaves in his hair.

# APOLLO'S LYRE

📖 Crime and reconciliation
🗡 Ancient Greece
🏛 Arcadia, Greece

✍ Apollodorus, *Library of Mythology*;
*Homeric Hymn to Hermes*

Apollo was the owner of a herd of cattle and tended them carefully, but his attention once wandered from them while he was conducting a love affair with the youth Hymenaeus. Noticing that the cattle were neglected, the young god Hermes – who, like Apollo, was one of Zeus's sons – decided to steal them and drove the beasts away to Pylos, where he hid them in a cave. Unfortunately for him, Apollo had the gift of prophecy, so was able to see where his cattle were hidden and quickly went in pursuit of the thief. When he caught up with Hermes, the young god showed Apollo a stringed

**The ancient Greek lyre** was to figure in many myths, including that of Orpheus in the Underworld (*see p.57*).

instrument that he had made by stretching animal intestines across the shell of a tortoise. As Hermes played the instrument, Apollo was so entranced by the music that he agreed to let Hermes keep his cattle in return for the instrument – which came to be known as a lyre.

# THE MUSIC CONTEST

📖 Contest and punishment
🗡 Ancient Greece
🏛 Phrygia (in modern Turkey)

✍ Apollodorus, *Library of Mythology*;
Diodorus Siculus, *Library of History*

Marsyas was a satyr (part-goat, part-man), and he was famous as a musician. He invented the double flute and enchanted all who heard him with his music. He was so confident of his ability that he decided to prove his excellence once and for all by challenging Apollo to a musical contest. Apollo agreed, on one condition: that the winner could punish the loser in any way he chose. Marsyas accepted the condition and the competition began. At first they played

**When Apollo** flayed Marsyas (seated), it was said there flowed such a "river of blood" that it became a real river.

with equal beauty – no-one among the spectators could decide who was the winner. But then Apollo laid down a fresh challenge: the pair should play their instruments upside-down. This was an unfair challenge as the lyre was far simpler to play this way than the flute, and Apollo won easily. As punishment he decided to tie Marsyas to a pine tree and skin him alive.

# POSEIDON AND THE FLOOD

📖 Rivalry between the gods
🏴 Ancient Greece
🏛 Mount Olympus; the Acropolis

✍ Herodotus, *History*; Pausanias, *Guide to Greece*

Poseidon was the god of the sea and, together with Zeus and the Underworld god Hades, was one of the three greatest deities of Ancient Greece. He had huge power, and his ability to summon up earthquakes and storms at sea made mortals tremble at his strength. If thwarted or defeated, he would unleash a terrible flood – which is precisely what happened when he got involved in a dispute over which deity should have power over Athens.

### KEY CHARACTERS

**POSEIDON** • god of the sea, first-generation Olympian, son of Cronos and Rhea
**ATHENA** • goddess of war and wisdom, daughter of Zeus and Metis, born directly from Zeus's head

## PLOT SYNOPSIS

### RIVALS FOR ATHENS

The gods vied for power over Greece's largest city and its surrounding area, known as Attica. Athena and Poseidon were especially keen to be named patron deity of the city, and to decide which one of them would win the title, they declared that they would compete to provide the people there with the greatest gift.

### THE GODS CREATE THEIR GIFTS

Poseidon went to the Acropolis (the hill overlooking Athens) and struck the ground with his trident, whereupon a spring of salt water began to flow. Athena made a much more useful gift, the first olive tree, planting it on the Acropolis. But to make the final decision fair,

**POSEIDON**

Zeus called together all the gods to hear evidence, including testimony from Cecrops, king of Attica, who confirmed that Athena's tree was indeed the first olive ever seen on the Acropolis. Athena won the day, and has been the goddess of Athens ever since.

### THE GREAT FLOOD

Poseidon was furious at the other gods' decision and brought down his trident on the Aegean Sea with an almighty crash. A great wave rose up and cascaded over the plain of Eleusis where Athens stood. Although flooded for a long time, the city finally recovered, and the Athenians could once more enjoy food, oil, and wood from Athena's olive trees.

# THE WRATH OF ATHENA

📖 Ill-starred love;
gifts from the gods
🏛 Greece
🏚 Ancient Greece
🖾 Callimachus, *The Bathing of Pallas*

Athena was beautiful but, unlike most of the other gods and goddesses of Ancient Greece, she was a virgin, and very modest. One day a man called Tiresias, enraptured by her beauty, followed the goddess to the spring where she went to bathe. He watched and saw her naked body as she entered the water, but Athena caught sight of him and exploded with anger. She clapped her hands over Tiresias's eyes, and made him blind. One of the nymphs who attended Athena took pity on Tiresias and pleaded with the goddess to give him something in compensation for his blindness. Athena, who in the end became sorry for the pain she had caused her admirer, gave Tiresias the gift of prophecy.

## AN ALTERNATIVE VERSION

In some versions of the myth, Athena is bathing with Tiresias's mother, Chariclo, with whom she is in love. Tiresias, who is hunting with dogs nearby, happens upon the women when he goes to the river to drink. Athena is furious at being discovered and blinds him, only to compensate him with the gift of prophecy for his mother's sake.

# THE WEAVING CONTEST

📖 Contest and punishment;
transformation
🏛 Lydia, Greece
🏚 Ancient Greece
🖾 Ovid, *Metamorphoses*

Arachne was a young woman who was famous as the most talented weaver and embroiderer alive. People said that she must have learned her skill from Athena, who was the goddess of cloth-makers and embroiderers, but the girl insisted that she had learned from no-one. When Athena heard of Arachne's boast, she disguised herself as an old woman and suggested that Arachne show greater modesty. The woman replied with insults, at which point Athena revealed herself and challenged Arachne to an embroidery contest. Athena produced an image depicting the gods of Olympus and their victories over mortals; Arachne's work showed the loves of the gods. Athena saw that the woman's work was as good as her own, and in fury, struck Arachne with her weaving shuttle and tore up the embroidery. In despair after the goddess's abusive treatment, Arachne decided to hang herself, but at the last moment the goddess relented and turned Arachne into a spider – which can spin and weave beautifully, forever.

**The myth claims** Arachne as the origin of the spinning spider, which is *arachnes* in Greek.

# MYTHS AND THE GREEK CITY-STATES

In the Classical period Greece was made up of a number of small independent city-states. More prominent cities, such as Athens and Sparta, increased their power by colonizing their neighbours and by founding colonies on nearby islands, the coast of Asia Minor (modern Turkey), and southern Italy. Everywhere they went, the Greeks built temples to their gods, which formed a focus for their lives.

## CULT CENTRES

Some places had a special significance for the gods and goddesses, and became famous all over Greece. One notable example was the sanctuary of Demeter and her daughter Persephone at Eleusis, near Athens. The story tells how Demeter came to Eleusis searching for her missing daughter and established a series of secret rites there.

Another example of a mythological event leading to the creation of a temple was at Brauron, east of Athens. Agamemnon was about to sacrifice his daughter Iphigenia to Artemis, when the goddess took pity on her and let her escape to Brauron, where she arrived with her brother Orestes, carrying Artemis's statue. The temple and cult of Artemis were founded there as a result.

## LOCAL GODS AND GODDESSES

Several other sites had close links with a specific god. Epidaurus was the main home of Asclepius, the god of medicine, Athens was identified with the goddess Athena, Olympia with Zeus, Argos with Hera, and Delphi with Apollo. Poseidon, god of the sea, was especially venerated in Corinth, but had many temples in coastal locations, to ward off treacherous storms that threatened to destroy ships and sailors.

**Athena** presided over her sisterhood, the Athenai, in Athens, but was also worshipped in Sparta.

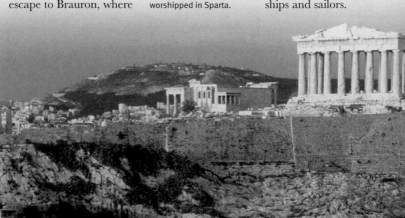

## SANCTUARIES

Prominent deities such
as Apollo and Zeus
attracted devotees from
far and wide, and their
major temples, such as
that of Apollo at Delphi and the
shrine of Zeus at Olympus, were
developed into elaborate cult centres.
Buildings erected in their sacred
precincts included theatres and
stadia. There were also treasuries,
where important gifts were left by
people from the different city-states.
The great sanctuary at Delphi had
around a dozen treasuries, built by
the citizens of places such as Athens,
Megara, and Syracuse.

## GAMES

Major cult centres, including Delphi
and Olympia, became the home of
elaborate festivals in honour of their
gods. These events could attract
people from all over Greece and
were milestones in the Greek
calendar. They often took the form
of competitive games, and the most
famous of these were the games in
honour of Zeus at Olympia, the
precursors of the modern Olympics.

## THE FESTIVALS OF ATHENS

The city of Athens staged a number
of festivals. The Panathenaea, which
included horse races and arts
contests, was held in honour of
Athena. The Athenians also held
several festivals dedicated to
Dionysus, god of the theatre,
featuring competitions for plays.
The surviving works of major Greek
writers from Aeschylus to
Aristophanes were originally written
for the grandest annual festival,
known as the Great Dionysia.

**The Parthenon in Athens** takes its name from
one of Athena's titles, Athena Parthenos –
Athena the virgin. It is her most famous temple.

# DEMETER AND PERSEPHONE

📖 Fertility
🏛 Ancient Greece
🏛 Eleusis, Greece; the Underworld

✍ *Homeric Hymn to Demeter*, Pausanias, *Guide to Greece*

Demeter was the Olympian goddess of the Earth, plants, and agriculture. She had just one child, Persephone, who was said to have been born after Demeter had an affair with Zeus. The beautiful Persephone did not think of love or marriage because she was too busy helping her mother ripen the harvest every year. But when Hades, god of the Underworld, fell in love with her, it seemed the entire natural order would be thrown off course.

**KEY CHARACTERS**

**DEMETER** • *Olympian goddess of the Earth, daughter of Cronos and Rhea*
**PERSEPHONE** • *daughter of Demeter and Zeus*
**HADES** • *god of the Underworld*

## PLOT SYNOPSIS

### THE ABDUCTION
Zeus's brother Hades fell in love with Persephone and wanted to take her to the Underworld. The god knew that if he asked Demeter's permission, he would be refused, because the Earth goddess needed her daughter to help her make the plants fertile.

Hades waited until Persephone was on her own picking flowers one day, and then he ripped open the earth in front of her. Reaching out of the ground, Hades grabbed the astonished Persephone and dragged her into the Underworld.

Persephone was said by some to have eaten pomegranate seeds in the Underworld, sealing her fate.

### DEMETER'S DISTRESS
When she realized that her daughter had disappeared, Demeter was distraught. She searched the world for Persephone, until she reached Eleusis, where she lay exhausted on a stone slab known from then on as the Joyless Stone.

### THE NEW ORDER
With Demeter's attention elsewhere, the crops failed to ripen and all the plants on Earth started to shrivel and die. Zeus saw that if this state of affairs was allowed to continue, the Earth and its people would soon perish. But Hades would not give up Persephone. So Zeus came up with a compromise: Persephone would spend half the year on Earth, helping her mother to grow and ripen plants, and half the year in the Underworld with Hades, forcing the Earth to suffer winter – a temporary death.

### THE TEMPLE AT ELEUSIS
The goddess Demeter founded a temple to her daughter Persephone at Eleusis, near Athens, which became the centre of a religious cult thought "to hold the entire human race together". Any Greek-speaker, male or female, free or enslaved, could be initiated into the Mysteries of Eleusis. These rites took place every autumn, and celebrated the birth in the Underworld of a miraculous son to Persephone, named Brimos, the Strong One.

**RELATED MYTHS ▶** The vanishing god (*p.152*) • Storm versus sun (*p.182*) • Daughter of the sun (*p.198*)

# THE MADNESS OF DIONYSUS

- 📖 Revenge of the gods
- 🏴 Ancient Greece
- 🏛 The Mediterranean; Asia;
  North Africa; Thebes in Boeotia, Greece
- 📖 Apollodorus, *Library of Mythology*

Dionysus was the son of Zeus and the mortal princess Semele, and he was the god of wine and the theatre. As an adult he travelled the world, conquering countries such as India and gathering an exotic group of followers. Wherever they travelled, Dionysus and his friends taught people how to make wine – and how to enjoy it in drunken orgies and dances in which the participants became caught up in a mad frenzy.

### KEY CHARACTERS

**ZEUS** • *king of the gods*
**HERA** • *queen of the gods*
**SEMELE** • *princess of Thebes*
**DIONYSUS** • *god of wine and the theatre*
**PENTHEUS** • *king of Thebes*
**AGAVE** • *Pentheus's mother*

## PLOT SYNOPSIS

### A CHILD RESCUED
Hera, jealous of her husband Zeus's affair with Semele, ordered the Titans to take Semele's child Dionysus and tear him apart. This they did, but one Titaness, who was the child's grandmother, took pity on him and made him whole again.

### DIONYSUS ON HIS TRAVELS
When he grew up, Dionysus went travelling with Silenus, a wise but drunken old satyr. As they journeyed, they attracted all kinds of followers, including a terrifying group of women called Maenads. They were famous for secret rituals, which involved working themselves up into an insane frenzy of hectic and sometimes violent dancing.

**The Dionysia** (*see also p.53*) was a three-day festival of drinking and outrageous behaviour. Apollodorus describes Dionysus as "discoverer of the grapevine".

### THE DEATH OF PENTHEUS
On returning to the Mediterranean, Dionysus and his group caused all kinds of trouble with their drunken rites. At Thebes the queen mother, Agave, joined the Maenads in their secret rituals. Her son, King Pentheus, complained to Dionysus about their behaviour; in response he advised him to spy on the Maenads. But when Pentheus did this, the Maenads discovered him, as Dionysus had foreseen. They captured the king, and in a mad trance they set upon him, tearing him limb from limb.

**A faun drinks wine** directly from a wineskin during a Dionysian orgy in this image from a Greek red-figure vase from the Classical period.

# THE RESCUE OF ALCESTIS

- 📖 Faithfulness unto death
- 📿 Ancient Greece
- 🏛 Thessaly, Greece; the Underworld

- ✍ Strabo, *Geography*;
  Servius on Virgil's *Eclogues*

Apollo granted a special favour to Admetus, king of Pherae in Thessaly. He persuaded the Fates that Admetus should not die at his appointed time if he could find someone to die in his place. The only person who loved Admetus enough to die in his stead was his wife Alcestis. But when the faithful Alcestis actually died, Admetus was distraught. He realized that he missed his courageous and beautiful wife greatly and was full of remorse that he had condemned her to death. The situation was saved by Heracles, who volunteered to travel down to the Underworld, fight with Thanatos, the god of death, and bring back Alcestis. When she returned she was younger and even more beautiful than before.

**In *Alcestis* by** the Greek playwright Euripides, Alcestis on her deathbed makes Admetus swear that he will not remarry.

# HADES AND THE NYMPHS

- 📖 Loves of the gods
- 📿 Ancient Greece
- 🏛 The Underworld; Earth

- ✍ Strabo, *Geography*;
  Servius on Virgil's *Eclogues*

The god Hades was the Olympian brother of Zeus and Poseidon, and ruler of the Underworld, which the Greeks also called the Kingdom of Hades, or simply "Hades" for short.

The Greeks believed the Underworld to be either at the centre of the Earth or beyond Ocean – the great river that flowed around the earthly lands. The Kingdom of Hades was famous for leading to two dark regions, Tartarus and Erebus, where souls were sent to be punished. Tartarus was said to be as far beneath the Earth as the Earth was

from heaven, and it was commonly used by the gods as a place in which to dispose of their enemies.

When Hades left his Underworld kingdom to visit the surface of the Earth, he was sometimes overwhelmed by lust for unfortunate nymphs. Luckily his wife Persephone was usually able to prevent him from acting on his desires. When he pursued the nymph Menthe, she transformed her into a sprig of mint; when Hades fell in love with another nymph, Leuce, Persephone changed her into a poplar tree.

# ORPHEUS IN THE UNDERWORLD

📖 Failed rescue
📍 Ancient Greece
🏛 Thrace, Greece

✍ Hyginus, *Fabulae*;
Pausanias, *Guide to Greece*

The hero Orpheus, prince of Thrace, was the greatest musician of the ancient world. People said that his singing voice and the music he made with his lyre were so harmonious that even the rocks and trees responded. When his wife Eurydice died, Orpheus planned to use his skill as a musician to bring her back to life. His story involved heroic daring but ended in tragedy. It has inspired many artists – and especially composers – ever since.

**KEY CHARACTERS**

**ORPHEUS** • son of King Oeagrus of Thrace
**EURYDICE** • wife of Orpheus
**HADES** • god of the Underworld, brother of Zeus and Poseidon

## PLOT SYNOPSIS

### THE POWER OF MUSIC
When Orpheus's beloved wife Eurydice died as the result of a snake bite, the hero decided to undertake a perilous journey to the Underworld to win her back. When he arrived he sang and played to Hades and Persephone, who were moved by his eloquent music.

**Funerary stele** from the 4th century, showing Orpheus taming wild animals with the beauty and power of his music.

Immediately Eurydice was forced to stop. Hades snatched her back into the Underworld and Orpheus was forced to continue alone.

### DON'T LOOK BACK
Hades said that Orpheus could take his wife back to the land of the living on one condition: as he led her from the Underworld he must not look back at her. The couple began their journey, but eventually Orpheus could not resist a glimpse at his beloved wife.

### THE MUSIC CONTINUES
Orpheus never remarried. He died a terrible death: his body was torn apart by drunken Maenads, angry at his lack of interest in the female sex. Miraculously, his head floated to the island of Lesbos, singing as it went.

**RELATED MYTHS ▸** Daughter of the Sun (*pp.198–9*) • Izanami and Izanagi (*pp.180–1*)

### THE FERRYMAN OF THE STYX

The Greeks believed that the journey to the Underworld involved crossing the river Styx. Souls were ferried across in a rickety boat by Charon, in return for one or two obols (copper coins that the deceased's relatives placed under the tongue or on the eyes of the dead person). Charon usually refused to ferry the living, saying his boat was unsafe, but a few heroes – such as Heracles and Orpheus – persuaded him with bribery or trickery.

*"...this mighty man, a broad-chested hero, supreme of all creatures, shall rise among the stars to a throne in heaven..."*

Theocritus, *Idyll* XXIV

# THE LABOURS OF HERACLES

- 📖 Heroic deeds
- 🏛 Ancient Greece
- 🏛 The Mediterranean; the Underworld
- ✍ Apollodorus, *Library of Mythology*; Pausanias, *Guide to Greece*

**Heracles** possessed miraculous strength from birth; as a baby he strangled two huge snakes that were placed in his cradle. He was also phenomenally tall and wielded a legendary club, which he was said to have made himself.

## BEHIND THE MYTH

Heracles, perhaps the greatest hero of Ancient Greece, was the son of Zeus and Alcmene, the daughter of the king of Argos. Zeus's wife Hera resented the child, because he reminded her of her husband's infidelity, so Zeus agreed to call him Heracles ("glory of Hera") in compensation.

Half-man and half-god, Heracles grew up to have remarkable strength and a love of adventure. But his existence continued to offend Hera, especially when he married and had children, so one day she took her revenge by driving him into an insane frenzy, during which he killed his wife Megara and their children, tragically believing them to be his enemies.

The gods decided that Eurystheus, king of Mycenae, should decide on a series of punishments for these acts. So the king thought up a series of 12 near-impossible tasks, which, to everyone's astonishment, Heracles eventually completed.

### INSPIRATIONAL TALES

The 12 tasks of Heracles feature in many poems and plays from the Classical period. The Romans, who called the hero Hercules, also loved his story. Euripides tells his story in his play *Children of Heracles*, and the Roman writer Seneca wrote two plays about him. Much later, Shakespeare was to mention him in more than 30 of his plays. Heracles also plays an important role in many other myths, including the stories of the death of Alcestis (*see p.56*) and the Golden Fleece (*see p.76*). But unlike other Classical heroes such as Odysseus and Aeneas, Heracles has no single epic devoted to his deeds.

### KEY CHARACTERS

**HERACLES** • son of Zeus
**MEGARA** • Heracles's wife
**HERA** • Zeus's sister and consort
**EURYSTHEUS** • king of Mycenae
**DIOMEDES** • king of Thrace
**HIPPOLYTA** • queen of the Amazons
**ATLAS** • a Titan giant
**THE HESPERIDES** • Atlas's daughters

## PLOT SYNOPSIS

### THE MONSTERS OF GREECE

For his first four tasks, Heracles was ordered to kill or capture several fantastic beasts that lived in various places in the northern Peloponnese.

First he went to Nemea to kill a fearsome lion with a skin so tough that no weapon could pierce it. Heracles strangled and skinned the Nemean lion, afterwards using the hide as his cloak.

His second task was to kill the Hydra that lived at Lerna, a many-headed monster who grew two heads each time one head was cut off. He overcame the beast by beheading it and cauterizing the wounds, preventing regrowth.

The third labour was to capture the Ceryneian hind, a deer sacred to the goddess Artemis. Heracles chased it until it was exhausted, then caught it and took it back to Eurystheus.

The fourth beast that Heracles had to deal with was the Erymanthian boar, which the hero trapped in a snowdrift.

**As Heracles cut off** each of the heads of the Lernaean Hydra, his companion (and nephew) Iolaus swiftly cauterized the wound.

### CLEANSING AND CLEARING

The next two labours involved both sheer hard work and ingenuity. First Eurystheus commanded Heracles to clean out the gigantic heaps of dung that fouled the huge stables of Augeas, king of Elis, which he did by diverting two rivers to wash all the filth away.

For his sixth labour he cleared Lake Stymphalis, northwest of Mycenae, of monstrous birds that lived there, using a bow and a sling, and special castanets given to him by the goddess Athena.

### HERACLES TRAVELS EAST

Heracles then travelled southeast to Crete, to capture a great bull said to be the father of the Minotaur. From there the hero journeyed northeast to Thrace, where his task was to round up a group of fearsome man-eating mares that belonged to the local king, Diomedes. In order to gain access to the creatures, Heracles had to kill Diomedes, whom he then fed to the mares to satisfy their hunger. The horses then proved easy for Heracles to control and he led them on

# "HE WILL FULFIL 12 TASKS, THEN TAKE HIS PLACE ABOVE"

Theocritus, *Idyll* XXIV

board ship before taking them back to Eurystheus as ordered. The Mycenaean king then sent the hero to steal the girdle of Hippolyta, queen of the almost-invincible Amazon women, but Heracles succeeded yet again.

## AT THE EDGE OF THE WORLD

Despairing of finding an impossible task for Heracles, the king sent him to the very edge of the world to steal a herd of cattle belonging to the giant herdsman Geryon. When he returned, successful once more, Eurystheus sent him to Mount Atlas to retrieve the golden apples of the Hesperides, the daughters of the Titan Atlas, who held the world on his shoulders. Atlas offered to fetch the apples for Heracles if the hero took the world on his shoulders for a moment. But when Atlas returned with the apples he had to be tricked into taking the world back on to his shoulders again.

## IN THE UNDERWORLD

Heracles's last, successful labour was to capture the vicious three-headed dog Cerberus. His tasks complete, Heracles was finally freed from the terrible guilt of having killed his wife and children, and was granted immortality.

## HERACLES BECOMES IMMORTAL

Heracles had god-like strength but a human body. Some said that he finally faced death after shooting a centaur, Nessus, who was raping his wife. The dying centaur told his wife of a potion that, applied to Heracles's shirt, would make him faithful forever, but it was a trick and made Heracles's flesh catch fire. Heracles asked to be set upon a funeral pyre, but as the smoke reached Mount Olympus, Zeus ended the fire with a thunderbolt and took Heracles up to Olympus to be a god.

**Heracles, duped by the centaur** into wearing a deadly garment, is finally overwhelmed.

# THESEUS AND THE MINOTAUR

- Hero versus monster
- Ancient Greece
- Athens, Greece; Crete
- Plutarch, *Theseus*; Pausanias, *Guide to Greece*

The story of the Minotaur is the most famous myth featuring the great Athenian hero Theseus. Minos, king of Crete, kept the Minotaur, a flesh-eating monster with a bull's head and man's body, at the heart of an impenetrable labyrinth near his palace at Knossos. Every nine years Minos forced the people of Athens to send 14 young men and women as food for the beast; a black-sailed ship sailed to the island with its human cargo.

**KEY CHARACTERS**

**AEGEUS** • *king of Athens*
**THESEUS** • *son of Aegeus*
**MINOS** • *king of Crete*
**ARIADNE** • *daughter of Minos*
**THE MINOTAUR** • *a creature made by Poseidon*

## PLOT SYNOPSIS

### THE ATHENIANS SET OFF

Theseus volunteered to be one of those sent to Crete as food for the Minotaur, planning to kill the beast. King Aegeus, worried that his son would be harmed, asked him to hoist white sails on his return so that he could see instantly that his beloved son Theseus was safe.

### DEFEAT OF THE MINOTAUR

When the Athenians arrived on Crete, King Minos's daughter, Ariadne, fell in love with Theseus. She offered to help him in exchange for the promise of marriage, and gave Theseus a ball of twine. Tying one end of the twine at the entrance to the maze, Theseus entered, unwinding as he went. At the heart of the maze, he fought and killed the Minotaur.

### RETURN TO ATHENS

Following the twine out of the maze, Theseus rescued his fellow Athenians and set sail for home, taking Ariadne with him. But forgetting that he owed his success to her, he abandoned her on the island of Naxos. He was punished for his heartlessness, because his sailors forgot to hoist the white sails, and Aegeus, watching from the shore, assumed Theseus was dead and threw himself from the cliff, into a sea that was forever after called the Aegean.

**Theseus slays the Minotaur** in the labyrinth, which was built by Daedalus for Minos to contain the monster.

# THE CURSE OF HIPPOLYTUS

- 📖 Tragedy of passion
- 🏛 Ancient Greece
- 🏛 Athens, Greece

✍ Apollodorus, *Epitome*; Plutarch, *Theseus*; Pausanias, *Guide to Greece*

Phaedra, daughter of King Minos of Crete and the second wife of Theseus, nursed a secret passion for Hippolytus, Theseus's son by Hippolyta, queen of the Amazons. Phaedra sent a note to Hippolytus, confessing her love; but he, in return, visited her only to reproach her for this incestuous passion. When it became clear that she was being rejected, Phaedra grew angry and cried out, accusing Hippolytus of attacking her. In great despair, she hanged herself, leaving a note that accused Hippolytus

of terrible crimes. When Theseus read the note he turned against his son and asked the sea god Poseidon to punish him. And so one day, as Hippolytus was riding in his chariot, Poseidon sent a huge wave to overwhelm his horses and Hippolytus crashed to his death.

**Poseidon kills Hippolytus,** around whom a Greek cult venerating chastity grew up.

# IN DEFENCE OF ATHENS

- 📖 State foundation
- 🏛 Ancient Greece
- 🏛 Athens, Greece

✍ Apollodorus, *Epitome*; Plutarch, *Theseus*; Pausanias, *Guide to Greece*

After King Aegeus of Athens killed himself, his son Theseus took the throne in his place. He had to fight and ultimately execute many rivals, and was even accused of murder in the law courts (he was acquitted when he became the first person to plead justifiable homicide). Theseus then set about expanding the power of Athens, bringing many of the surrounding areas under Athenian rule and inviting those

regions to send delegates to a common council in Athens. He set up a proper constitution, minted the first coins, and agreed boundaries with his neighbours. He also reorganized the Isthmian Games of Corinth and instituted the festival of Panathenaea in honour of Athena. For these reasons, Theseus was seen as the true founder of the Athenian state.

**King Theseus of Athens,** depicted here in a bronze statuette that formed part of an ancient cauldron handle.

# PERSEUS SLAYS MEDUSA

📖 Hero versus monster
🏴 Ancient Greece
🏛 The island of Seriphos

🗡 Apollodorus, *Library of Mythology*

Princess Danaë, daughter of King Acrisius, had a child called Perseus with Zeus. Acrisius, worried about a prediction that he would be killed by his grandson, put Danaë and her son in a wooden chest and threw them into the sea. The chest floated to the island of Seriphos, where luckily they were rescued by the king, Polydectes. This king was later to be the instigator of Perseus's greatest adventure: the struggle to kill the gorgon Medusa.

**KEY CHARACTERS**

**PERSEUS** • *son of Zeus and Danaë*
**POLYDECTES** • *king of Seriphos*
**MEDUSA** • *a gorgon*
**ATHENA** • *goddess of war*
**HERMES** • *messenger of the gods*

## PLOT SYNOPSIS

Invited to dinner by King Polydectes, Perseus and his friends discussed what gifts they should bring to honour their host. Most decided to bring a horse, but Perseus, who had no horse, said he would bring instead the head of Medusa, a hideous Gorgon (*see right*).

### GIFTS FROM THE GODS
Perseus prayed for the help of the gods, who came to his aid. Nymphs gave him winged sandals and the helmet of Hades, which made the wearer invisible. Hermes gave Perseus a sickle made of adamant. Athena gave him her polished bronze shield.

### THE GORGONS

The three Gorgons, Euryale, Stheno, and Medusa, were monstrous creatures, with hands of bronze, wings of gold, scaled bodies, and tusks like those of a boar. Their hair was a mass of writhing snakes. Each Gorgon had a glance so powerful that anyone who looked at them was instantly turned to stone.

### MEDUSA'S DEFEAT
Perseus hunted out Medusa and waited until she fell asleep. Hovering above her in his winged sandals, he raised Athena's shield and took aim by looking at the Gorgon's reflection in its metal, so that he did not look at her directly. Then he brought down the sickle and decapitated her. Stowing the head in a bag he fled from the scene, chased by Medusa's sisters, but escaped by putting on Hades's helmet, and so becoming invisible.

# THE RESCUE OF ANDROMEDA

📖 Exploits of hero
🏹 Ancient Greece
🏛 Ethiopia

✍ Herodotus, *History*; Apollodorus, *Library of Mythology*

On his journey back to Seriphos after killing the Gorgon (*see opposite*), Perseus travelled through the land of Ethiopia, where he caught sight of a beautiful princess called Andromeda and fell in love with her. But as he soon discovered, there was trouble in Ethiopia, and it centred on Andromeda. Her parents had boasted that their daughter's beauty was greater than that of the sea-nymphs, or nereids, and in a fury, Poseidon had flooded the land. The people of Ethiopia had therefore decided to pacify

Poseidon by sacrificing Andromeda to a sea-monster. When Perseus asked for her hand in marriage, her father Cepheus agreed – if Perseus killed the monster first. He duly killed the beast and took Andromeda as his bride.

**Perseus flew to** Andromeda's aid using Hermes's winged sandals, lent to him by nymphs.

# THE DEATH OF ACRISIUS

📖 Exploits of hero; tragic fulfilment of prediction
🏹 Ancient Greece

🏛 Larissa, Thessaly, Greece
✍ Apollodorus, *Library of Mythology*

When he returned to Seriphos after killing the Gorgon (*see opposite*), Perseus found the king, Polydectes, trying to rape Danaë, his mother. Using the Gorgon's head, Perseus turned Polydectes to stone. He appointed the old king's brother Dictys as ruler, and left for his native Argos. On the way he stopped to take part in some games that were being held at Larissa in memory of the local king,

who had recently died. As Perseus took his throw of the discus, a mighty wind blew it off course and it killed an old man. It turned out that the old man was none other than his grandfather, Acrisius, whom he had never seen. An oracle that had predicted Acrisius would be killed by his grandson had been proved right.

**Perseus was a great athlete** and a keen discus-thrower, which finally led to the fulfilment of a prophecy.

# THE TRAGEDY OF OEDIPUS

📖 Tragedy of fate
🏛 Ancient Greece
🏛 Thebes in Boeotia, Greece

✍ Apollodorus, *Library of Mythology*;
Sophocles, *Oedipus the King*

As a baby, Oedipus was abandoned to die by his father Laius, king of Thebes, after an oracle predicted that the child would kill his father and marry his mother. The baby was rescued and brought up by the king and queen of Corinth. When he grew up, Oedipus consulted the oracle at Delphi, and the prediction was repeated. Believing the king and queen of Corinth to be his parents, he fled the court to embark upon a tragic journey.

### KEY CHARACTERS

**LAIUS** • *king of Thebes*
**JOCASTA** • *queen of Thebes*
**OEDIPUS** • *son of Laius and Jocasta*
**THE SPHINX** • *a hybrid creature with a woman's head and a lion's body*

## PLOT SYNOPSIS

### FULFILLING THE PROPHECY

On his travels Oedipus came to a narrow point in the road at the same time as a chariot coming the other way. Neither would give way: the argument escalated and Oedipus killed the other traveller. It was Laius; Oedipus had unwittingly killed his father.

Outside Thebes, Oedipus met the Sphinx, a monster who killed those who could not answer a riddle: "What goes on four legs in the morning, two at noon, and three in the evening?" Oedipus was the first person ever to answer correctly: "A human being, who crawls as a baby, walks upright as an adult, and uses a stick in old age."

### OEDIPUS THE KING

The people of Thebes were so impressed that they made Oedipus king and the widowed Queen Jocasta became his wife. He had unknowingly married his mother. When he later discovered the truth, his terrible shame led him to blind himself, while Jocasta hanged herself in despair.

**In a scene** from the 1967 film *Oedipus Rex*, Oedipus (played by Christopher Plummer) kisses his ill-fated mother Jocasta (played by Lilli Palmer).

# BELLEROPHON AND PEGASUS

📖 Tragic death of hero
📕 Ancient Greece
🏛 Lycia, Greece

✍ Apollodorus, *Library of Mythology*;
Homer, *Iliad*

As a young man, Bellerophon was falsely accused of seducing the wife of Proetus, king of Argos, and Proetus banished him. He sent him to Iobates, king of Lycia, with a letter telling the king to kill Bellerophon. But Iobates refused to kill a guest directly. Instead, he sent Bellerophon to slay the Chimaera, a fearsome monster, part-lion, part-goat, and part-snake, which was terrorizing his people. He assumed Bellerophon would perish in the struggle. But Athena helped Bellerophon by giving him the winged horse

Pegasus, so that he could swoop down on the Chimaera and kill it. As a result, Bellerophon and Iobates became friends. All went well until the hero became too ambitious and tried to fly to Mount Olympus, home of the gods, on Pegasus. Angered by Bellerophon's presumption, Zeus made the horse throw his rider, and Bellerophon was killed when he fell.

**Pegasus was born** when Medusa was killed (*see p.64*). Some say he sprang from Medusa's neck, others from the earth around her.

# THE 49 MURDERESSES

📖 Tragedy of suspicion
📕 Ancient Greece
🏛 Argos, Greece

✍ Apollodorus, *Library of Mythology*;
Pausanias, *Guide to Greece*

King Danaus of Egypt, who had 50 daughters, quarrelled with his brother Aegyptus, who had 50 sons. Fearing for the safety of his daughters, Danaus left Egypt and settled with his daughters in Argos, where he invited his nephews to stay with him. The nephews said that the quarrel was over and asked permission to marry Danaus's daughters, but the king was suspicious, as it seemed to him that the sons of Aegyptus were still his enemies. So he accepted the

offer, but gave each of his daughters – the Danaides – a dagger. Each bride was told to kill her husband on the wedding night. When they retired for the night, 49 of the women killed their husbands, cutting off their heads. Only one, Hypermnestra, relented, because her husband Lynceus had behaved nobly and kindly toward her. The 49 sisters who had obeyed their father were later forgiven and purified by the gods Athena and Hermes.

# GREEK PLAYWRIGHTS AND MYTHOGRAPHERS

The reason that so many Greek myths have endured is that the Ancient Greeks wrote about them copiously, telling and retelling the stories of the gods, goddesses, and heroes in poetry, prose, and drama. Some of these versions, especially the two epic poems of Homer – the *Odyssey* and the *Iliad* – and the plays of the Greek tragic dramatists, have become classics of world literature.

## THE EPICS OF HOMER

Homer was one of the earliest and greatest of the ancient poets. His birth date is uncertain, although scholars agree it was probably in the 8th or 7th century BCE. He is famous for two epics: the *Iliad*, which tells of events during the Trojan War; and the *Odyssey*, which deals with the adventures of the hero Odysseus on his journey back to Greece from Troy. These two epics, which may have started life as oral narratives that Homer organized, reworked, and wrote down, became famous in Ancient Greece and are still prized for their directness, characterization, and rich poetic language.

**Greek players** used masks to denote different characters or emotions.

## THE WORKS OF HESIOD

The other early poet who dealt extensively with myths was Hesiod. His *Theogony*, which was probably written in the 8th or 7th century BCE, tells the story of the creation of the cosmos, the birth of the gods, and Zeus's rise to power. Another poem, *Works and Days*, tells of Prometheus and the five ages of the world.

**The shadowy figure** of Orpheus leading his wife from the Underworld is an image that continues to haunt contemporary writers and audiences.

## THE PLAYWRIGHTS

The three great playwrights of Ancient Greece, Aeschylus (*c*.525–456 BCE), Sophocles (*c*.490–406 BCE), and Euripides (480–406 BCE), all used myths for their plots.

The three powerful plays of Aeschylus's *Oresteia* trilogy deal with the murder of the hero Agamemnon and the revenge of his son Orestes. He also wrote a play about Prometheus.

Sophocles's subjects included Oedipus, the Trojan War, Antigone, and Heracles. Euripides also wrote a number of "Trojan" plays as well as *The Madness of Heracles* and *Alcestis*.

**The Greek theatre** at Epidaurus, near Athens, is almost perfectly preserved.

These plays were originally acted as part of the great drama festivals at Athens during the city's heyday in the 5th century BCE, but were later seen all over the Greek world and beyond.

## LATER WRITERS

During the 4th century BCE, the Greek world and its culture expanded dramatically when Alexander the Great conquered large parts of Asia and the Mediterranean. This inspired many writers, including Apollonius of Rhodes (3rd century BCE), who wrote an epic poem called *Argonautica*, telling the story of Jason and the Golden Fleece. Later the poet Ovid (43 BCE–17 CE) retold a number of transformational myths in his *Metamorphoses*, while at some point in the first or second century CE the Athenian writer Apollodorus produced a book called *Library of Mythology*. This contained many of the Greek myths which were to be used frequently as source material by writers in the 16th and 17th centuries.

# THE JUDGMENT OF PARIS

- 📖 Rivalry of the gods
- 📖 Ancient Greece
- 🏛 Mount Ida, Troy (*see box, p.71*)

- ✍ Ovid, *Heroides*;
  Lucian, *Dialogues of the Gods*

There had long been rivalry between Greece and Troy, a city across the Aegean Sea in what is now northwestern Turkey. But the most serious conflict took place when the Trojan prince Paris, son of King Priam and Queen Hecuba, was asked to judge a kind of beauty contest between three of the Olympian goddesses. When Paris decided in favour of Aphrodite, goddess of love, he started a chain of events that led to the Trojan War.

**KEY CHARACTERS**

**PARIS** • *prince of Troy*
**HERA** • *queen of the gods*
**ATHENA** • *goddess of war and wisdom*
**APHRODITE** • *goddess of love*
**MENELAUS** • *king of Greece*
**HELEN** • *queen of Greece*

## PLOT SYNOPSIS

### THE THREE GODDESSES

When Eris, the goddess of strife, was not invited to the wedding of Thetis and Peleus, she arrived anyway, carrying a golden apple inscribed with the words, "For the fairest". Zeus asked prince Paris to judge who should have the apple: Hera, who promised Paris wealth and power; Athena, who offered him wisdom and success in war; or Aphrodite, who promised he would marry the most beautiful woman in the world. Paris chose Aphrodite.

**Foretelling the plot** of Sleeping Beauty, the uninvited guest Eris arrives with a "gift" that threatens to disrupt the natural order.

### THE ABDUCTION OF HELEN

Paris was later sent to Greece with instructions to secure the release of the Trojan princess Hesione, or to take a Greek princess if negotiations failed. When Paris arrived, he fell in love with Helen, reputedly the most beautiful woman in the world – but also the wife of the Greek king Menelaus. Helen also fell in love with Paris, and the two left Greece for Troy, leaving Hesione behind. Furious, Menelaus organized an army – led by his brother, the great soldier Agamemnon, and Odysseus – and went to Troy to get Helen back. The Trojan War (*see opposite*) had begun.

# THE TROJAN WAR

📖 War  
📕 Ancient Greece  
🏛 Troy (*see box, below*)

✍ Homer, *Iliad*

The war between Greece and Troy, which began when the Trojan prince Paris and the Greek queen Helen ran off together, lasted for ten years. There were many casualties, including several prominent heroes from both sides. The Greeks were finally victorious after smuggling their soldiers into the besieged city of Troy inside a wooden statue of a horse. Helen was reunited with her husband, King Menelaus, and taken back to Greece.

**KEY CHARACTERS**

**PARIS** • prince of Troy  
**HELEN** • queen of Troy  
**AGAMEMNON** • commander of the Greek army  
**ACHILLES** • Greek hero  
**AJAX** • commander of the Greek army  
**ODYSSEUS** • Greek hero

## PLOT SYNOPSIS

The war raged on for years. The Greek hero Achilles was famously killed by Paris, who rightly identified Achilles's only weak spot, and killed him with a single arrow shot through his heel. A second Greek hero, Ajax, committed suicide in shame when Agamemnon (the military leader) ruled that the wily strategist Odysseus was the more worthy to inherit Achilles's armour.

### THE TROJAN HORSE
Odysseus came up with the winning strategy. He told the Greeks to announce that they had lost the war, then leave a huge wooden horse – secretly filled with soldiers – as an offering to Athena by the gates of Troy.

As planned, once the horse was dragged into the city, the soldiers climbed out, opened the city gates, and let in the rest of the Greek army. The Greeks sacked the city and then sailed for home, victorious, with Queen Helen.

**Brad Pitt** plays Achilles, slain by Paris during the Trojan War, in the 2004 film *Troy*.

### WHERE WAS TROY?
The ancient city of Troy was located at the place now known as Hissarlik, in western Turkey. Today, the much-excavated site shows the remains of a city that was built and rebuilt many times. Even in its ruined state, it bears a telling similarity to the Troy of the *Iliad*. Its massive walls recall Homer's description of the place, as does the windswept site. The broad plain on which the city stands is a credible location for the relentless battles between the Greeks and the Trojans.

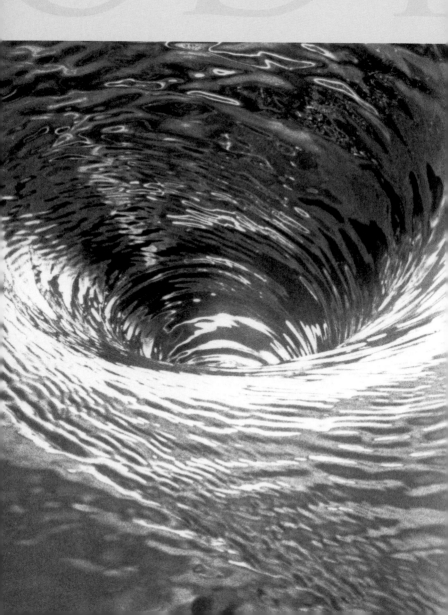

*"...the Sirens bewitch everybody that approaches them. There is no home-coming for the man who draws near them unawares..."*

Circe, from Homer's *Odyssey*

# THE ODYSSEY

- 📖 Epic journey
- 📍 Ancient Greece
- 🏛 The Mediterranean
- 📖 Homer, *Odyssey*

**In most accounts** Odysseus was the son of Laertes and Aticlea, the king and queen of Ithaca. However, some writers made him the son of Sisyphus, an infamous trickster, to account for his cunning and guile.

## BEHIND THE MYTH

The *Odyssey*, a great epic poem by Homer, recounts events that take place immediately after the Trojan War. The central character is Odysseus, a Greek who had played a major role in the war, fighting for ten years and ultimately coining the idea of a hollow wooden horse to help the Greeks enter Troy. The *Odyssey* recounts his long journey home. Throughout the poem Odysseus wins our sympathy. He is wise, brave, and always longing to get home to see his wife Penelope and his beloved son Telemachus.

## AN EVENTFUL JOURNEY

After the war, Odysseus sets sail from Troy to his home in Ithaca, one of the Ionian islands west of mainland Greece. This journey should be straightforward – across the Aegean Sea, around the southern Peloponnese, and then north to Ithaca. But Odysseus's voyage is dogged by mishaps and punctuated by fantastic adventures – meetings with gods, enchantresses, monsters, cannibals, and even a journey to the Underworld. This combination of events makes the *Odyssey* one of the greatest adventure stories of all time.

The misadventures that occur on Odysseus's journey involve the loss of his fleet of 12 ships and, eventually, all of the men who sail with him. Odysseus finally reaches Ithaca, to discover that many suitors are bankrupting him and harassing his wife Penelope. Athena, who has helped Odysseus throughout his journey, gives him a disguise so that he can see what is going on, dispose of the suitors, and be reunited with Penelope at last.

### KEY CHARACTERS

**ODYSSEUS** • *king of Ithaca*
**PENELOPE** • *Odysseus's wife*
**TELEMACHUS** • *son of Odysseus and Penelope*
**POLYPHEMUS** • *one of the Cyclopes*
**AEOLUS** • *god of the winds*
**CIRCE** • *demi-goddess and enchantress*
**CALYPSO** • *demi-goddess*
**NAUSICAA** • *princess of the Phaeacians*

## PLOT SYNOPSIS

After Odysseus left Troy, his ship was blown south to the land of the Lotus Eaters. Eating the exotic lotus fruit made his crew forget their past and want to stay forever, so Odysseus was forced to drag them back to their ships.

Their next port of call was the country of the Cyclopes, fearsome one-eyed giants. One of them, named Polyphemus, trapped Odysseus and his men in a cave, and began to devour them. Odysseus, who had told Polyphemus that his name was Outis (Greek for "no-one"), blinded the giant by putting out his eye with a stake. When Polyphemus cried for help he shouted: "Outis [No-one] is hurting me!'"so his fellow giants ignored him and the Greeks were able to escape.

### FICKLE WINDS

The Greeks then came to the floating island occupied by Aeolus, god of the four winds. To help Odysseus, Aeolus gave him the three adverse winds tied up in a bag; the only remaining wind would have blown all his ships straight to Ithaca. But thinking that the bag contained treasure, his men opened it, let out all the winds and blew the ship off-course – ultimately into the hands of another race of cannibal giants, the Laistrygonians, who destroyed all but one of Odysseus's ships.

### THE MAGIC OF CIRCE

Odysseus sailed on and came to the island of the sorceress Circe, who transformed Odysseus's men into pigs. Odysseus himself escaped by eating the protective herb moly, which Hermes had given to him. Realizing she had met her match, Circe transformed his

**Odysseus blinded Polyphemus,** and then he and his men escaped by tying themselves beneath the bellies of the giant's sheep, out of his reach.

> "I AM ODYSSEUS, LAERTES' SON. THE WHOLE WORLD TALKS OF MY STRATAGEMS, AND MY FAME HAS REACHED THE HEAVENS."
>
> Homer, *Odyssey*

## SHIPS IN ANCIENT GREECE

Greece was a mountainous country where land travel was difficult. Many ancient Greek cities were on the coast and their inhabitants travelled from one place to another by boat. For long journeys and for warfare, the Greeks used large ships that boasted huge square sails and banks of oars, so that they could move quickly whether or not there was a good wind. Ships like this could also ram enemy vessels at speed.

**Fir, cedar, and pine** were the chosen materials for Greek fighting ships; their keels may have been shielded with metal.

men back into their human form and told Odysseus to visit the Underworld, to find out more about his future. He did so, and was told by the ghosts that back in Ithaca, people were inside his home fighting over his possessions.

### PERILS AT SEA

Back aboard, Odysseus's next challenge was to sail past the Sirens, whose beautiful song was known to seduce sailors. He blocked his men's ears with wax, having ordered them to tie him to the mast so that he could hear the Sirens' music without being lured away.

Next he had to sail the narrow channel between the six-headed monster Scylla and the whirlpool Charybdis. The ship sailed through, but Odysseus steered slightly too close to Scylla, who killed some of his men.

### ODYSSEUS ALONE

The ship then called at Thrinacia, an island belonging to the sun god Helios, who kept his cattle there. Odysseus had been warned not to harm any of these animals, but his men went ahead and killed some. When they put to sea again, Zeus sent down a thunderbolt that

**Penelope was revered** for her fidelity and devotion: she waited many years for Odysseus's return.

smashed the ship to pieces and drowned all his men. Odysseus, the sole survivor, clung to the wreckage of his ship and was washed up on the island home of the goddess Calypso. She took a fancy to Odysseus, but he resisted her advances, made a raft, and set sail once more. Shipwrecked yet again, he was found by the beautiful princess Nausicaa, who was very like his beloved wife Penelope. Odysseus was tempted to stay, but eventually set sail once more for Ithaca.

### THE RETURN HOME

Odysseus arrived to find his house full of suitors vying for his wife's hand. She had cunningly refused to choose from among them until she had finished the cloth she was weaving, which she busily unravelled every night. Finally forced to choose, she announced that she would marry the man who could string her husband's great bow. Only Odysseus, in disguise, was able. Penelope recognized him, and Odysseus killed all the suitors with the help of his son, Telemachus.

**RELATED MYTHS ▶** The voyage of Bran (p.102) • Qayaq the wander-hawk (p.206)

# THE GOLDEN FLEECE

📖 Quest; epic journey
🏴 Ancient Greece

🏛 Various locations in the Mediterranean and on the Black Sea coast
✍ Apollonius of Rhodes, *Argonautica*

Jason was the rightful king of Iolcus in northeastern Greece, but his uncle Pelias had taken the throne when Jason was an infant. When he came of age, Jason demanded his rightful inheritance, but Pelias decreed that Jason could become his heir only if he stole the priceless Golden Fleece from Colchis, which lay on the far western shore of the Black Sea. Jason's journey to Colchis and his return home is one of the most famous Classical stories.

## KEY CHARACTERS

**JASON** • *heir to the kingdom of Iolcus*
**PELIAS** • *Jason's uncle*
**HERACLES** • *a Greek hero*
**PHINEUS** • *a prophet*
**AEËTES** • *king of Colchis*
**MEDEA** • *daughter of Aeëtes*

## PLOT SYNOPSIS

### THE ARGONAUTS

A fine ship was built for Jason's voyage to Colchis. Called the *Argo*, its hull was magical because it contained timbers that came from the sacred oak at the oracle of Zeus at Dodona. Once the vessel was finished, Jason recruited a crew – known as the Argonauts – made up of some of the greatest heroes of Greece; men such as Heracles, Orpheus, and Peleus. They set sail from Greece, heading toward the Hellespont.

Poster for *Jason and the Argonauts* (1963), showing the moment when the bronze giant Talos rises from the sea.

### THE VOYAGE OUT

The Argonauts' journey to Colchis was full of adventure. They stayed for a while on the Aegean island of Lemnos, where they fell for the charms of the all-female population. They lost Heracles in the land of the Mysians, when a sea-nymph seduced his friend Hylas and Heracles went off in pursuit. Next they encountered the blind prophet

Phineus, who offered to help them if they destroyed the Harpies – birds with women's heads who pecked at Phineus's eyes and deposited foul-smelling slime. Two of the Argonauts, Calais and Zetes, chased the Harpies away.

The Argonauts' next challenge was to sail through the Clashing Rocks at the entrance to the Black Sea. These rocks swung together and crushed anything that passed between them, but Phineus taught Jason how to negotiate them. He sent a bird between the rocks, the rocks clashed and opened, and the Argonauts rowed through at full speed before the great stones had a chance to shut again.

## FIRE-BREATHING BULLS

Aeëtes, king of Colchis, did not want to give up the Fleece, so when Jason arrived, he set the hero a challenge: he was to harness a pair of fire-breathing bulls, and use them to plough serpents' teeth into the soil. From these teeth would instantly spring up armed warriors. There seemed almost no chance of success. But Jason had the help of Aeëtes' daughter Medea, who had the gift of sorcery. She fell in love with Jason, and gave him the powers needed to accomplish the task. But Aeëtes still refused to give up the Fleece. Medea suggested that Jason

**The Argonauts** stopped off on the isle of Lemnos, where the women welcomed them with open arms. Jason fathered twins with the queen, and many other Argonauts fathered children.

**The *Argo* was built** at Pagasae (now Volos) on the east coast of Greece by a man called Argos, with the help of the goddess Athena (seated, on the left).

could overcome the serpent that guarded the Fleece by asking Orpheus to charm it to sleep with music from his lyre. The plan worked: Jason snatched the Fleece and sailed back to Iolcus, taking Medea with him.

## HOMEWARD BOUND

On the way home Jason encountered many of the monsters that Odysseus had met on his long journey (*see pp. 72–5*), such as the Sirens and Scylla and Charybdis. He also met new challenges, such as the bronze giant Talos, who hurled vast rocks at the *Argo* until Medea killed him with a stare. And so Jason returned with the Golden Fleece and claimed his throne.

# THE GREEK AND ROMAN GODS

According to legend, the city of Rome was founded in 753 BCE, and within 500 years it controlled the whole of Italy. The country then began to look beyond its borders, and in the 2nd century BCE the Romans conquered most of Europe, the eastern Mediterranean, and North Africa. As they annexed states, the Romans absorbed parts of the new cultures, including tales from the various mythologies.

## COMPOSITE GODS

When the Romans conquered a new territory, it was usually in their interests to allow the local people to carry on worshipping their own gods, but to give these gods a new, Roman "spin" – to emphasize the fact that the conquered race was now part of the Roman Empire. If a local deity had something in common with a Roman or Italian god, the two might be amalgamated under the Roman god's name. So Roman deities not only had features of earlier Italian gods, but might also acquire attributes from the gods of conquered races, especially Greece.

**The Trevi Fountain** in Rome is based on the mythological palace of the Roman sea god Neptune (the Greek Poseidon).

## THE SKY GOD JUPITER

Before Rome became powerful, the Etruscans were one of the most important Italian peoples. When the Romans conquered them, they assimilated some of their gods (*see pp.90–1*), and sometimes blended them with attributes from the Greek gods at the same time. A good example of this is the Etruscan god Tinia, the sky god or "thunderer", who was re-named Diospiter or Jupiter (the father of the sky) by the Romans, and worshipped as a god of thunder. After conquering Greece, the Romans added in attributes from the Greek sky god Zeus, to make Jupiter the supreme Roman god.

**Cupid orders** Mercury the messenger to announce his power to the universe.

| ROMAN AND GREEK COUNTERPARTS | | |
|---|---|---|
| **ROMAN NAME** | **ROLE** | **GREEK COUNTERPART** |
| Aesculapius | God of healing | Asclepius |
| Apollo | God of sun, art | Apollo |
| Bacchus | God of wine | Dionysus |
| Ceres | Goddess of harvest | Demeter |
| Cupid | God of love | Eros |
| Diana | Goddess of hunting | Artemis |
| Juno | Consort of Jupiter | Hera |
| Jupiter | Sky god; supreme god | Zeus |
| Mars | God of war | Ares |
| Mercury | God of finance; messenger | Hermes |
| Minerva | Goddess of wisdom | Athena |
| Neptune | God of the sea | Poseidon |
| Venus | Goddess of love | Aphrodite |
| Vesta | Goddess of the hearth | Hestia |
| Vulcan | God of fire | Hephaestus |

## THE RULING TRIUMVIRATE

For many years Rome was governed by a triumvirate (three rulers), and the Romans saw the gods in a similar way. Second to Jupiter in the godly hierarchy were two goddesses, Juno and Minerva. Juno, the sister and wife of Jupiter, was the Roman equivalent of the Greek Hera. She was the protector of women and the goddess of marriage and childbirth. Minerva, originally an Etruscan goddess of the crafts, was combined with the Greek goddess Athena to become goddess of wisdom as well as patron of artists and craft workers.

## OTHER ASSIMILATIONS

The Romans assimilated other Italian and Greek deities. Mercury was an old Italian god, the deity of trade and finance (his name is related to the word *mercator*, merchant). Mercury became identified with the Greek Hermes. Diana was an Italian goddess of hunting who was merged with the Greek Artemis to become one of the most popular deities of the empire. Some Roman gods came directly from the Greeks – for example, Apollo, who had no early Italian equivalent but built up a huge Roman following. However, the Romans were always keen to emphasize the moral superiority of their own gods over their Greek counterparts.

# AENEAS FOUNDS AN EMPIRE

📖 Journey and foundation
🏛 Various locations in and around
📭 Ancient Rome
the Mediterranean; Italy
✍ Virgil, *Aeneid*

The founding of Rome as a political and
geographical force started when the young Aeneas,
prince of Troy, left the scene of the Trojan War
and began a long journey. After many adventures
he arrived in Italy, took over the area of Latium
on the River Tiber, founded a new city, and began
Rome's long line of kings and emperors. His life
was set against a backdrop of struggles between
Venus, his mother, and the goddess Juno.

**KEY CHARACTERS**

**AENEAS** • *son of Anchises
and the goddess Venus*
**DIDO** • *queen of Carthage*
**THE CUMAEAN SIBYL** •
*a prophetess*
**LATINUS** • *king of Latium*
**LAVINIA** • *Latinus's
daughter*

## PLOT SYNOPSIS

### AENEAS LEAVES TROY
There were two
prophecies about Aeneas,
of which he was aware:
he would found a new
city, and he would destroy
the city of Carthage in
North Africa. And so
after defeat in the Trojan
War (*see p.71*), he decided
to leave Troy, taking with
him a band of followers,
and set sail for the
foretold new territory.
Crossing the Aegean and
Ionian seas, they arrived
in Sicily, home to the
Cyclopes, a race of
one-eyed giants. The sailors were lucky
to escape from the island with their
lives. They sailed south, but their ships
were then wrecked off the North
African coast by Juno, who was trying
to protect her city of Carthage.

**The wandering hero** Aeneas
travelled from Troy to become the
ancestor of the mighty Romans.

### LOVE IN CARTHAGE
Aeneas was washed up near the city,
where he met Dido, Carthage's queen.
Venus made the pair fall in love, so Dido
would forget her allegiance to Juno, but
Aeneas left Dido (*see opposite*) when he
realized that his destiny lay elsewhere.

### THE SIBYL AND THE
UNDERWORLD
Sailing next to Cumae,
on the west coast of Italy,
Aeneas met the Sibyl (*see
also p.88*), a prophetess
who guarded a cave at
the entrance to the
Underworld. Leading
Aeneas down into the
Underworld, the Sibyl
showed him a vision of
the future: the city of
Rome and the many
generations of Roman
heroes who would one
day be born.

### AENEAS IN LATIUM
When he landed in Latium, Aeneas
agreed a treaty with Latinus, the local
ruler, which included marriage to his
daughter Lavinia. This infuriated
Turnus, king of the Rutilians, to whom
Lavinia was betrothed. He declared
war, and the Trojans and people of
Latium fought the Rutilians for several
months, until Aeneas killed Turnus.
Aeneas brought the two sides together
under his leadership and founded the
city of Lavinium, which guided and
ultimately ceded to the power of Rome.

# DIDO AND AENEAS

📖 Love tragedy
📕 Ancient Rome
🏛 Carthage, North Africa

✍ Virgil, *Aeneid*

Dido was a former prophetess from Tyre who founded, then ruled, the city of Carthage on the coast of North Africa. Soon after the city was built, the Trojan hero Aeneas arrived with a large group of veterans from the Trojan War. It was love at first sight, and seemed a perfect match – Dido was a noble queen and leader; Aeneas, a hero who had fearlessly led his troops. But the affair distracted Aeneas from his destiny, with tragic consequences.

## KEY CHARACTERS

**AENEAS** • son of Anchises and the goddess Venus
**DIDO** • queen of Carthage, daughter of Mutto, the king of Tyre

## PLOT SYNOPSIS

### THE CURSE OF DIDO

Dido and Aeneas were living together as man and wife when a messenger of the gods came to remind Aeneas that his duty lay elsewhere. He decided to leave Dido, begging her to understand that his destiny was to found a new city, not become king of Carthage.

Dido decided to end her life. She had a funeral pyre built and, as she saw the Trojan ships disappearing across the sea, she cursed Aeneas, declaring that Carthage and Rome would always be enemies. She climbed on to the pyre and took her own life with a sword.

### VIRGIL'S AENEID

The epic poem the *Aeneid*, which tells the story of Aeneas, is the masterpiece of the great Roman poet Virgil (70–19 BCE). Virgil's patron was the emperor Augustus, so the poet told a story that went to the heart of Roman culture. He described the hero's journey and the role of Aeneas and his followers as ancestors of the Romans. He also justified the city's war with Carthage in the 3rd century BCE, which was seen as fulfilling Dido's declaration that the two cities would always be enemies.

**Telling tales of** his adventures, Aeneas first impressed, then won the love of Queen Dido.

# ROMULUS AND REMUS

📖 Sibling rivalry; city foundation    ✍ Livy, *History of Rome*; Ovid, *Fasti*
🏛 Ancient Rome
🏛 Northern and central Italy

The story of the twin brothers Romulus and Remus tells how the pair were abandoned by their grandfather to be washed away down a river before being rescued by a wolf. After their true identity is revealed by the gods, they regain their real status and ultimately found the city of Rome. With its theme of wolf-children, the story seems to reach back to an ancient tradition, paralleling many later European tales of abandoned infants.

### KEY CHARACTERS

**NUMITOR AND AMULIUS** • *joint rulers of Alba Longa*
**RHEA SILVIA** • *a Vestal virgin*
**ROMULUS AND REMUS** • *sons of Rhea Silvia and the god Mars*
**A SHE-WOLF**
**FAUSTULUS** • *a shepherd*

## PLOT SYNOPSIS

### THE ABANDONED TWINS

Two brothers – the law-maker Numitor and the soldier Amulius – ruled the city of Alba Longa in central Italy. The pair quarrelled and Amulius took over the city, imprisoning Numitor and forcing his daughter, Rhea Silvia, to join the Vestal virgins (preventing any dynastic threat). But the god Mars raped Rhea Silvia and she bore twin boys, Romulus and Remus. As punishment for breaking her vows, Rhea Silvia was buried alive and her children were condemned to be drowned in the Tiber.

### RESCUE AND REVOLT

Fortunately the river god saw the twins and ensured they were found and suckled by a she-wolf, who looked after them until they were discovered by Faustulus, a shepherd. He took them home to his wife, Acca Larentia, and the couple brought them up. On reaching adulthood, Mars told the twins of their real parentage.

Romulus and Remus called together all the farm workers of the region and staged a revolt, killing Amulius and reinstating Numitor.

After a while Alba Longa became overcrowded and Romulus and Remus decided to leave to found a new city on the banks of the River Tiber. But soon they quarrelled and Remus was killed, leaving the new town to be named Rome in honour of its ruler, Romulus.

**The she-wolf** was sacred to Mars, the boys' real father, and some said the god had sent the wolf to rescue them.

# THE RAPE OF THE SABINES

📖 Abduction and revenge
📑 Ancient Rome
🏛 Rome

📖 Livy, *History of Rome*; Ovid, *Fasti*

The only people who lived in the new city of Rome were the followers of Romulus, who were all men. One day, Romulus announced that he was going to hold a great festival dedicated to Neptune. He insisted that the Sabines – men and women from the nearby towns – be invited. But the festival was a charade, in reality a plot to rob the Sabines of their women, so the Romans could create a race of their own.

**At a given signal,** the young Romans overcame the fathers and brothers of the Sabine maidens.

**MASS ABDUCTION**
At the start of the festival, when the games were supposed to begin, the Roman men suddenly drew their hidden weapons. Threatening the Sabines with death, the Romans abducted every young Sabine woman present. In retaliation, the Sabines declared war on Rome and years of fighting ensued. The war ended only when the Sabine women – by now married to Roman husbands – intervened. Throwing themselves (and some say, their children) between the two warring sides, the women begged them to stop fighting.

# THE VIRTUE OF LUCRETIA

📖 Tragedy of lust
📑 Ancient Rome
🏛 Rome

📖 Livy, *History of Rome*; Ovid, *Fasti*

The generals of Rome were away at war, and in an idle moment during a long siege, they began to talk about their wives at home and wondered whose wife was the most virtuous. Deciding to ride back to Rome and find out what their wives were doing, they were shocked to find them drinking and having affairs with the men who had remained at home – all, that is, except one: Lucretia, wife of Collatinus.

Lucretia was at home, quietly spinning and weaving. On seeing this, one Roman soldier, Sextus Tarquinius,

was overcome with lust for Lucretia. He demanded to have sex with her, saying that if she did not give in to him, he would not only kill her but also shame her, by killing a slave and putting this humiliatingly lowly person in her bed.

Lucretia submitted to the rape, but sent word to her husband Collatinus and told him what had happened. He hurried home, but try as he might to convince her that she had done no wrong, she could live with herself no longer. Taking a knife from beneath her dress, she stabbed herself to death.

**Ancient Greek theatre**, myth, and history provided inspiration for the craftsmen of the Roman Empire. This tragic mask mosaic, dating from the 2nd century BCE, is from the House of the Faun in Pompeii. Another of its mosaics depicts the triumphs of Alexander the Great.

# VESTA AND HER PROTECTOR

📖 Virtue saved         ✍ Ovid, *Fasti*
📭 Ancient Rome
🏛 Mount Ida, near Troy (western Turkey)

One of the most popular Roman deities was Vesta, goddess of the fire in the hearth, and the Roman counterpart of the Greek goddess Hestia. The hearth was at the centre of Roman life, and Vesta was therefore one of the most important Roman deities. Unlike most Classical goddesses, she was a virgin and she guarded her virtue closely. One story tells how her famous chastity came close to being compromised by the god Priapus.

### KEY CHARACTERS

**CYBELE** • *mother of the gods*
**VESTA** • *goddess of the hearth*
**PRIAPUS** • *god of fertility*
**SILENUS** • *a satyr*

## PLOT SYNOPSIS

### CYBELE'S FEAST

The great goddess Cybele (*see p.94*) invited all the immortals to a feast. There was abundant food and everyone enjoyed themselves. Several of the guests got drunk, including the old satyr Silenus, who had not been invited but came in any case. As the night wore on, the celebrations got quieter and a number of the guests, exhausted by the festivities, fell asleep in the warm night air. Vesta was one of these.

### THE DESIRE OF PRIAPUS

Strolling away from the crowds, the god of fertility, Priapus, came across the sleeping Vesta. He was filled with desire and started toward her, intending to break her chastity. But just as he was about to touch her, Silenus's donkey, standing nearby, brayed loudly in Vesta's ear. She awoke, other gods and goddesses came running, and Priapus slunk away in shame. Vesta's virtue had been saved.

### THE VESTAL VIRGINS

Romans worshipped Vesta in their homes, but there was also a state temple of Vesta – a building in the heart of Rome that was circular, to remind people of the round huts of the earliest Roman settlement. Here both the goddess and Rome's eternal power were represented by a flame, kept continuously alight by chaste young priestesses known as the Vestals. These women lived in a house near the temple and served the temple for 30 years, after which time they returned to normal life. They were seen as sacred beings and if they failed to keep their chastity they were walled up in an underground chamber without food until they died.

**The Vestal virgins** were overseen by a high priest, the Pontifex Maximus. They were accorded extraordinary civic rights for Roman women, including being allowed to vote and own property.

# THE LARES AND THEIR HOUNDS

- 📖 Protectors of humanity
- 🏛 Ancient Rome
- 🏛 Rome

- ✍ Ovid, *Fasti*;
  Macrobius, *Saturnalia*

The Romans believed that every household was guarded by the Lares. These were twin protector gods, who watched over people's homes and also stood guard at crossroads.

The Lares were the sons of Mercury, messenger of the gods, and Mania, goddess of madness. They often borrowed the hounds of Diana, the goddess of hunting, and together the Lares and the dogs would chase away thieves and other wrongdoers. Most Romans worshipped the Lares by setting up an altar to them in their homes, hoping this would ensure their protection.

**A household shrine** to the two Lares, guardian gods, who were often shown holding horns and drinking cups.

# THE COMING OF THE PENATES

- 📖 Protectors of humanity
- 🏛 Ancient Rome
- 🏛 Rome

- ✍ Virgil, *Aeneid*;
  Cicero, *On the Nature of the Gods*

When the hero Aeneas, founder of Rome, arrived in Italy after the Trojan War (*see p.80*), he brought with him a pair of gods known as the Penates. These gods were first established in the city of Alba Longa, where Aeneas originally settled after the Trojan War, and from there they travelled with him to Rome. They were seen as the city's protectors from the earliest times.

In time, the Romans built a national temple to the Penates in the Forum. They also frequently installed altars to these gods in their own homes.

The Penates were traditionally represented in the temples and shrines in the form of two seated youths. They were sometimes associated with Vesta, goddess of the hearth (*see opposite*), as they were also seen as protectors of people's hearths and homes.

Because their name was also linked with the Latin word *penus* (meaning "food" or "provisions"), the Penates became gods of the table, and food was offered to the gods at the start of each meal to ensure that the larder would always be well stocked.

# THE SIBYL OF CUMAE

- Lust and revenge
- Ancient Greece and Rome
- Cumae, Italy
- Petronius, *Satyricon*;
  Virgil, *Aeneid*

The sibyls were female prophets based at various shrines in the Greek and Roman world. Working themselves into trances, they uttered all kinds of inarticulate sounds that the priests then "translated" into prophecies. For the Romans, the most famous of these prophets was the Sibyl at Cumae, who lived in a cave near Naples. Renowned for her guile, she met her match when she asked the god Apollo for long life, but forgot to ask for eternal youth to go with it.

### KEY CHARACTERS

**THE CUMAEAN SIBYL** •
*a prophetess*
**TARQUINIUS** • *last king of Rome*
**APOLLO** • *god of the sun and the arts*

## PLOT SYNOPSIS

### THE CLEVER SIBYL

The Cumaean Sibyl recorded her prophecies in nine books that she offered to sell to King Tarquinius of Rome. When he objected to the price, she burned three and offered him the last six for the original price. Refused again, she burned another three books but still held the price. Tarquinius ended up buying the last three volumes at the original price for all nine books. They were destroyed when the Roman capitol was burned in 83 BCE.

### THE DESIRE OF APOLLO

Apollo offered the beautiful Sibyl any gift she liked in exchange for a night with her. She asked for as many years' life as she could hold grains of sand. Apollo granted her wish, but she then refused to have sex with him. So he modified the wish by making her age rapidly, causing her to shrink within just a few years until she was as wizened as a cicada. Soon she was so small that she was placed in a jar – or in some versions of the myth, a cage – on the cave wall.

**The Sibyl's cave** was close to the crater of Avernus, believed to be an entrance to the Underworld.

# CASTOR AND POLLUX

📖 Heroic deeds
🏹 Ancient Greece and Rome
🏛 Messene; Rome

✍ Apollonius of Rhodes,
*Argonautica*

Castor and Pollux were the two sons of Zeus, king of the gods, and the mortal woman Leda (*see p.43*). They were widely known as the Dioscuri (from the Greek words *dios kouroi*, sons of Zeus) and were revered by the Romans. A pair of heroes, their most famous exploits occurred when they went with Jason on the voyage of the Argonauts. But for their Roman worshippers, they were more powerful in death than in life.

**KEY CHARACTERS**

**CASTOR AND POLLUX** • *the sons of Zeus and the mortal woman Leda (see p.43)*
**IDAS AND LYNCEUS** • *Argonaut twins, sons of Aphareus and Arena*

## PLOT SYNOPSIS

### THE QUARRELSOME TWINS
The twins Castor and Pollux were famous for getting into trouble. When they sailed with Jason on his voyage to find the Golden Fleece (*see pp.76–7*), they already had a long-running rivalry with another pair of twins among the Argonauts called Idas and Lynceus.

Because of this rivalry, they abducted two girls who were betrothed to Idas and Lynceus. These were the daughters of a man called Leucippus, ruler of Messene, and were known as the Leucippidae. As a result of the kidnapping, the two sets of twins fought

and Castor was killed. Zeus granted Pollux immortality, so he could go up to Olympus with the gods, but Pollux refused, wanting to die so that he could be with his beloved brother. The gods reached a compromise, whereby the pair spent alternate days in heaven and in the Underworld.

**The ruins of the temple** of Castor and Pollux – built around 484 BCE – can still be seen in the Valley of the Temples in Sicily.

### ST ELMO'S FIRE

The Romans held that one of the duties of the Dioscuri was to look after those who were lost at sea. They were said to send out their lights to guide sailors, and people thought that the flicker of St Elmo's Fire or the will o'the wisp (actually a result of electrical activity in the atmosphere) was the work of the twins. But the lights were not always entirely trustworthy – partly, it was said, because Helen, the sister of Castor and Pollux, sent rival lights to mislead and confuse mariners.

## THE ETRUSCANS AND THEIR MYTHS

The Etruscans were the indigenous people of central Italy, and their culture was the bedrock of Roman civilization. This is often overlooked because the Romans emphasized their Latin heritage, their legendary Trojan origins, and their Hellenic roots. After the Romans sacked the Etruscan city of Veii in 396 BCE, the Etruscans were assimilated into the Roman republic and their culture became almost invisible.

### A RULING TRIAD

The Etruscans believed in many gods. Their ruling triad consisted of Tinia, the ruler of the heavens; Uni, his wife, goddess of the cosmos; and Menrva, goddess of wisdom and war, who was born from Tinia's head. In Rome, this triad developed into the Capitoline gods Jupiter, Juno, and Minerva.

One of the few surviving Etruscan myths tells how a child with snakes for legs rose without warning from a ploughed furrow and began to chant sacred doctrines. His name was Tarchies, or Targes. Once his teachings had been recorded by the priest-kings, Tarchies fell dead. His teachings, the *Disciplina Etrusca*, instructed the Etruscans in the will of the gods. When the Romans appropriated Etruscan culture, they adopted these teachings, which included how to foretell the future from the entrails of a sacrificed animal, the meaning of thunder and lightning, and the rules for founding cities.

**Etruscan wind gods** battle a harpy on this bowl from the tombs in Caere (now the city of Cerveteri).

## PAINTED TOMBS

Etruscan tombs were lavishly furnished and decorated with mysterious iconography. The Tomb of the Bulls in Tarquinia, for example, depicts three levels – the world of the gods, the world of humans, and the world of the dead – together with a tree of life and a tree of death. Tombs often featured a doorway so that the soul of the deceased might pass through to the next world, guided by Turms, the messenger of the gods.

## THE AFTERLIFE

The Etruscans believed in eternal life in the world beyond, and hoped by means of making offerings and sacrifices to the gods to be allowed to enjoy it.

A narrative painting on the Tomb of the Baron, Tarquinia, Italy, centres on a couple walking toward a female figure, possibly a priestess,

### THE EARTH GOD

One god of supreme importance to the Etruscans was Voltumna, the Earth god. He was the patron of the Etruscan race, and therefore also a god of war and protection. His temple was the headquarters of the 12-city Etruscan confederacy, and site of the Etruscans' annual political assemblies. In Rome, Voltumna became Vertumnus, the god of the changing seasons.

Voltumna's cult centre was the ancient Etrurian city of Volsinii, which was in or near Orvieto, Italy.

Representations of the dead in tombs show them returned to the prime of life and health. However, tomb paintings also show horrific demons torturing the souls of the dead; one of these, Tuchulcha, has wings, the face of a vulture, and the ears of a donkey, and holds serpents in his hands. The rulers of the Etruscan Underworld were Aita and Persipnei (borrowed from the Greek Hades and Persephone), and its guardians were Mantus and Mania.

# THE ABDUCTION OF FLORA

📖 Loves of the gods    🖎 Ovid, *Fasti*
🏛 Ancient Rome
🏛 Fields and meadows

Flora, the Roman goddess of flowers and fertility (whom the Greeks called Chloris), was one of many Roman agricultural deities. She was originally a meadow-nymph, who was sublimely beautiful and lived in a place where everyone was happy and fulfilled. One day Favonius (the Greek Zephyrus), the impetuous god of the west wind, blew in her country and saw Flora. The god fell in love with her and, used to getting his own way, he chased and abducted her. But the incident ended well, because the nymph was smitten by the god and the pair married and stayed together quite happily. She reigned over the flowers, helping them to blossom and then to bear their fruit.

# THE WRONG PARTNER

📖 Loves of the gods    🖎 Ovid, *Fasti*
🖎 Ancient Rome
🏛 A cave in the countryside

The Roman fertility god Faunus began life as an early king who was promoted to the ranks of the immortals when he died. He was considered to be the protector of shepherds and their flocks.

One day Faunus was out in the countryside when he saw Hercules – or Heracles, in his Greek incarnation (*see pp.58–61*) – with his mistress Omphale. He fell in love with the beautiful Omphale and decided to follow Hercules and Omphale to a cave, where they fell into a bed and soon went to sleep.

### SURPRISED BY A TRICK
Faunus crept up on the pair and slid into bed beside the figure dressed in Omphale's clothes. But he had an unpleasant surprise. Beneath Omphale's garments he was astonished to find a hairy chest – the couple had swapped clothes for the night. Humiliated and appalled, Faunus crept away quietly. But he shunned the use of clothes from then on and was said to prefer his devotees also to be naked when worshipping him.

**The Roman god Faunus** took on many of the attributes of Pan, the Greek god of the countryside, including horns and hooves.

# POMONA AND VERTUMNUS

📖 Loves of the gods
📕 Ancient Rome
🏛 Northern Italy

✍ Ovid, *Metamorphoses*

Pomona was a nymph from Latium who was highly skilled in cultivating fruit trees. She became the goddess who watched over the fruit harvest. Carrying her pruning knife, she was often to be seen among her trees, which were always well tended and heavy with apples and pears. Many of the gods pursued her, but none more so than Vertumnus, god of the changing seasons.

Vertumnus adopted many disguises to woo Pomona: he came to her as a harvester, the keeper of a vineyard, a fisherman, and a soldier, but she did not want him. She would not even listen when he arrived disguised as an old woman describing the attractions of married love. Finally, Vertumnus appeared as himself, and when Pomona saw how handsome he really was, she fell in love with him.

**Pomona, the goddess of fruits,** with the god Vertumnus. Happily at last accepted as her lover, he is braiding her hair with corn.

# THE DEATH OF BONA DEA

📖 Transgression and punishment
📕 Ancient Rome
🏛 Rome

✍ Plutarch, *Life of Caesar*

The name of one Roman goddess was unknown – she was referred to simply as Bona Dea, meaning "the good goddess". Some said she was called Fauna and was the daughter of Faunus; others held that she was Faunus's wife. She drank too much wine one day and became very drunk – so much so that Faunus beat her mercilessly with sticks of myrtle and eventually killed her.

After her death she was revered as a goddess of the Roman people and a shrine was built to her in Rome. Her rites were celebrated by women only –

no man was allowed to attend. During the time of Julius Caesar, one man, called Clodius, attended the rites disguised as a woman, in order to have an assignation with Caesar's wife, Pompeia. He was discovered, and there was a major scandal when it became known that the secrecy of the rites of Bona Dea had been broken.

The hero Hercules was said to have drunk from the river at Bona Dea's temple site and completely drained it, before vowing to build his own single-sex temple, to be visited by men only.

# MYTHS OF THE GREAT MOTHER

📖 Fertility; revenge; divine intervention
🏴 Anatolia; Ancient Rome
🏛 Anatolia; Boeotia, Greece; Rome

✍ Ovid, *Fasti* and *Metamorphoses*; R. Turcan, *The Cults of the Roman Empire*; T. C. Worsfold, *History of the Vestal Virgins of Rome*

Cybele was an Anatolian goddess of fertility and mother of all living things, whose worship spread from Greece and then to Rome. The Romans called her *Magna Mater*, the Great Mother; Virgil and Ovid both call her the Mother of the Gods. In 204 BCE the sacred black stone that represented the goddess was brought to Rome, in accordance with a prophecy in the Sibylline books (*see p.88*), and a temple built for the goddess on the Palatine Hill.

### KEY CHARACTERS

**CYBELE** • *the Great Mother*
**ATTIS** • *Cybele's consort*
**SAGARITIS** • *a dryad*
**ATALANTA** • *a champion runner and famous huntress*
**HIPPOMENES** • *husband of Atalanta*

## PLOT SYNOPSIS

### A GODDESS BETRAYED

A beautiful Phrygian woodland boy named Attis had a heart so pure that he won Cybele's love. She wanted him to be the guardian of her shrine, and asked him to promise to remain a virgin. He agreed, but then seduced the dryad (wood-nymph) Sagaritis, breaking his promise. The furious goddess cut down the dryad's tree, killing her, and driving Attis mad. In a frenzy of guilt he cut off his own genitals – which is why Cybele's priests also castrated themselves. When Attis died he was reborn as a pine tree.

**After castrating himself** Attis returned to Cybele's service, and ancient artefacts often show him driving Cybele in her chariot, holding a shepherd's crook.

### INSULT TO THE GODS

The huntress Atalanta and her husband Hippomenes took refuge in a sacred cave by a temple of Cybele and made love, defiling the sanctuary. The temple images of the gods averted their eyes, and the enraged Cybele turned the lovers into lions, which she tamed and harnessed to her chariot.

### A VIRGIN SAVED

When Cybele's sacred stone was brought to Rome, the whole city, including the Vestal virgins, went to the mouth of the Tiber to greet the goddess. The boat grounded in the shallows and stuck there. One of the Vestals named Claudia Quinta, who had been accused of breaking her vows, stepped forward and prayed to Cybele to prove her innocence.

Claudia Quinta undid the flimsy sash around her waist, attached it to the tow rope, and gave a slight tug. Astonishingly, the boat lifted from the mud, and Claudia pulled the goddess into the city unaided, proving her innocence beyond doubt.

**RELATED MYTHS** ▶ The wooing of Inanna (*p.148*)

# THE BULL-SLAYER

📖 Fertility
🗺 Persia; Ancient Rome
🏛 The cosmos

✍ Robert Turcan, *The Cults of the Roman Empire*;
Franz Cumont, *The Mysteries of Mithras*;
David Ulansey, *The Origins of the Mithraic Mysteries*

Mithra was an ancient Persian god of light, the sun, and war. Adopted by the Romans as Mithras, this god became the focus of a male-only mystery cult that promised new life after death and was particularly followed by Roman soldiers. He was worshipped in underground temples called mithraea. As initiates were sworn to secrecy, we know only that Mithras slew a bull, in a symbolic act of death and renewal.

### KEY CHARACTERS

**MITHRAS** • *the Roman god known as the Unconquered Sun*
**A BULL**

## PLOT SYNOPSIS

### A STORY IN STONE
The following myth is reconstructed from pictorial carvings in mithraea. Creation was under threat from a drought caused by the forces of evil. A new god, Mithras, arose from a rock to take control of the cosmos. He shot an arrow and a spring gushed out to relieve the world's thirst. Then he caught a bull, which had been absorbing all the moisture from the moon, and sacrificed it. Various animals and plants were revivified by its blood.

### SACRIFICE IN THE STARS
In astrology, Mithras was the ruler of the cosmos. The constellation of Perseus/Mithras brandishes his sword above the Bull, and the bull-slaying re-enacts the moment when Taurus sets in the west for the last time before the spring equinox moves from the Bull to the Ram, revealing the existence of a god so powerful that he can shift the cosmos on its axis and start a new age.

### ELAGABAL – THE INVINCIBLE SUN

Elagabal ("god of the mountain") was a Syrian god. The high priest of his temple was a teenager named Bassianus, who was declared emperor of Rome in 218 BCE. He refused to leave the service of his god, so his helpers moved the black stone of Elagabal to Rome, where Bassianus decreed that the god, now renamed "Deus Sol Invictus" ("invincible sun god"), should be invoked before any other god. He also established a new triad, consisting of Elagabal and two unwilling spouses – Athena, and Tanit, the Carthaginian moon-goddess. The Romans, horrified at this attempt to usurp their other gods, took revenge by nicknaming their disliked emperor "the scoundrel of the sun".

**The 3rd-century** Roman emperor Bassianus was better known as Heliogabalus or Elagabalus.

**RELATED MYTHS** ▶ The wise lord (*p.154*)

# EUROPE

THE EARLIEST MYTHOLOGIES of Europe are almost completely lost to us; we have no names for the gods and goddesses, nor their stories. Nevertheless there is archaeological evidence that enables us to explore these mythologies: symbols carved on rocks; treasures buried in graves or offered to the gods at sacred sites; and paintings on the walls of caves deep underground.

## THE ICE AGE

The cave paintings of the Palaeolithic people of the Ice Age, from around 38,000 to 8000 BCE, typically show hunting scenes with animals such as bison, deer, and horses. Images of human figures, such as the famous "sorcerer" engraved on the wall at Trois-Frères in southern France, are often depicted with animal features such as horns and tails. These half-human, half-animal figures almost certainly represent Ice Age shamans, whose magical rites were relied on to ensure success in the hunt. Disguised as an animal such as a bull bison or a chamois stag, the shaman used dance and song to establish a magical link between himself and the animals that were to be hunted. The animals themselves are often shown being shot with magic arrows or brought down by magic spears.

Stone carvings of women with exaggerated curves are thought to be related to fertility magic, and may represent either pregnant women or a goddess of fertility and abundance. One such figure, dating from around 25,000 BCE, was found carved in stone in Laussel in the French Dordogne (*see top right*). She is called "Venus with the horn", because she is shown holding a bison horn which is possibly a primitive cornucopia or "horn of plenty".

## THE STONE AGE

From around 7000 BCE, after the end of the Ice Age, Neolithic Europeans added new elements to their myths and rituals to reflect the growing importance of agriculture alongside hunting and gathering. They carved stone images of gods and goddesses, but they also fashioned them from clay. Their figures often have animal or bird characteristics as well as human ones, and they sometimes wear masks. A clay statue found at Szegvár in Hungary, dating from around 5000 BCE, shows a seated man with a flat mask and

### THE CHARIOT OF THE SUN

The Chariot of the Sun dates from the 14th century BCE. It was found in a drained bog in Trundholm, Denmark, and is thought to represent the sun god crossing the sky in a wheeled chariot pulled by a bronze horse. Cult objects such as this seem to show a new veneration for the sun, perhaps because the sun represents fire, which is necessary for metalworking. One side of the sun disc is covered with gold foil, probably representing the sun by day; the other side is bronze, and probably represents the sun at night. The Greek sun god Helios traversed the sky in just such a chariot, drawn by four horses.

**The sun disc** carried by the Trundholm chariot measures around 25cm (10in) across.

a sickle in his right hand. This god may be an ancestor of the Greek god Cronos.

Many other figures show a female deity, sometimes with the characteristics of a bird or snake. This goddess, often decorated with spiral patterns that suggest rain, may be the goddess of water and air. She may also have been worshipped as the Great Mother, as there are terracotta figurines of her holding a baby. Another form of the Neolithic goddess is that of a bee, often associated with a bull. The Ancient Greeks believed that bees were born from the body of a slaughtered bull, and Stone-Age Europeans may have had a similar notion. Certainly the image of the bee-goddess seems to be associated with ideas of rebirth and regeneration.

**The Venus of Laussel** holds a horn with 13 stripes to represent the 13 lunar months of the year.

## THE BRONZE AGE

The Bronze Age saw a profound leap in human civilization, starting at around 2500 BCE. Bronze weapons and tools were invented, and there was a huge growth in culture, including writing and the invention of the wheel. This is the period of the great pre-Greek cultures of the Cyclades and Minoan Crete. The bird-goddess of the Stone Age and the hunting rituals of the Ice Age still had their place, but the worship of a powerful male sky god was growing in importance. This new god was to dominate the emerging mythologies of the Greeks, the Romans, the Scandinavians, and the Celts.

**A prehistoric bull-and-horse** cave painting found by four teenagers in Lascaux, France, in 1940 is one of around 600 paintings and 1,500 engravings made in the caves more than 16,000 years ago.

# THE MIGHTY DAGHDA

📖 Magical hero
📍 Ancient Ireland
🏛 Ireland

✍ Elizabeth A Gray, *Cath Maige Tuired, The Second Battle of Mag Tuired*; R. A. S. MacAlister & Eoin MacNeill, *Leabhar Gabhala: The Book of Conquests of Ireland*

Irish myths speak of a series of invasions of Ireland, each bringing new rulers to the country. The fifth of these invasions brought to Ireland the Tuatha Dé Danaan, a race of godlike people, skilled in magic. Their king was the Daghda, whose name means "the Good God". He was said to be very wise but was also a comic figure, whose tunic hardly covered his bottom and whose exploits brought smiles as well as success to his people.

### KEY CHARACTERS

**THE TUATHA DÉ DANAAN** • *a people skilled in magic and the occult arts*
**THE DAGHDA** • *the Good God, leader of the Tuatha Dé Danaan*
**THE MÓRRIGAN** • *goddess of war and fertility*

## PLOT SYNOPSIS

### CAULDRON AND CLUB

The Daghda was famous for his two most prized possessions, an enormous cauldron and a great club. The cauldron was so vast that it seemed bottomless – people said no-one went away hungry when a meal was served from it. The club was equally magical. One end killed anyone struck by it: on the battlefield, the enemy's bones fell like hailstones when the Daghda wielded his weapon. The other end of the club had the opposite effect – it could bring a dead person back to life.

**The Gundestrup cauldron,** from the 2nd century BCE, depicts several Celtic deities, including the Daghda.

### THE DAGHDA'S TRYST WITH THE MÓRRIGAN

At the feast of Samhain (Halloween), the Daghda was walking by the banks of the River Unius in Connaught when he came across a woman washing. It was the Mórrigan, the goddess of war, who could change into the shape of a raven and who was in the habit of haunting battlefields, changing the outcome of the fighting through her awesome presence. The Daghda and the Mórrigan made love by the river and she promised to give his people her backing in their next battle and her protection forever.

### THE MIGHTY MEAL

The Tuatha Dé Danaan were forced to fight their rivals the Fomhoire for power in Ireland. A date for battle had been agreed, but the Tuatha Dé Danaan realized that they would not be ready, so they sent the Daghda to the Fomhoire's camp to arrange a truce. The Fomhoire agreed, and to celebrate they prepared a meal for the Daghda. They knew he loved porridge, so to mock him they made enough to feed an army – filling a huge hole in the ground – and then threatened to kill him if he could not eat it all. The Daghda took up his ladle (which was "big enough for a man and a woman to lie in the middle of it"), and began to eat the porridge. When he had finished, he scraped the bottom of the bowl before falling asleep, with the Fomhoire laughing around him.

**RELATED MYTHS** ▸ King Arthur (p.110)

# ANGUS, THE DAGHDA'S SON

📖 Loves of the gods     ✍ Anon, *Yellow Book of Lecan*; *Book of Leinster*
🏴 Ancient Ireland
🏛 Ireland

The love god Angus was the son of the Daghda and Boann (spirit of the River Boyne). Because Boann was already married, the lovers wanted to conceal her pregnancy, so the Daghda made the sun stand still and their child was conceived and born on the same day. This may be why he was known as Angus mac Óc, "the young son". When he grew up he was famous for helping others who faced obstacles in their love-life.

### KEY CHARACTERS

**ANGUS** • *god of love, the Daghda's son*
**MIDHIR** • *a god*
**ETAÍN** • *Midhir's beloved*
**DIARMUD** • *lieutenant of the military leader Finn*
**GRÁINNE** • *fiancée of Finn*
**CAER** • *Angus's beloved*

## PLOT SYNOPSIS

### ANGUS AND THE LOVERS

The god Midhir had a wife called Fuamnach, but was in love with a woman called Etaín. When Fuamnach found out about this, she turned her rival into a butterfly. After long years Etaín was reborn as a girl, but forgot Midhir and was unwilling to rejoin him. Angus agreed to woo her on behalf of Midhir and the pair were reunited.

He also helped bring together Diarmud, lieutenant of the great leader Finn, and Gráinne, Finn's betrothed. Gráinne put Diarmud under a spell to make him love her, and the couple eloped. Angus, Diarmud's foster-father, helped by taking Diarmud's shape and challenging their pursuers, allowing the lovers to escape.

**Brug na Bóinne** is the Gaelic name for Newgrange in Ireland. This Neolithic complex was said to be Angus's home.

### ANGUS IN LOVE

Angus first saw his own beloved in a dream, discovering that her name was Caer Ibormeith and she could take the form of a swan. He found out that the only way to approach her was when she was in swan-form, so he waited until the Samhain feast on 1 November, and then transformed into a swan himself. She accepted him, flying with him three times around the lake, singing a magical song that sent everyone to sleep. The lovers then flew off to Angus's palace, Brug na Bóinne.

# THE VOYAGE OF BRAN

📖 Journey to the Otherworld
🚩 Ireland

🏛 Ireland; the Isle of Joy;
the Isle of Women
✍ Anon, *Book of Leinster*

The story of Bran tells of an Irishman who set off
to visit the Happy Otherworld, the dwelling-place
of immortals called the Sidhe. It consisted of two
places: the Isle of Joy, where the people were so
contented they laughed all the time, and the Isle of
Women, where people lived a life of pleasure. But
when they tried to return to Ireland, Bran and his
men realized the journey had been made at a
terrible cost: it was impossible to return home.

### KEY CHARACTERS

**BRAN** • *a hero*
**NECHTAN** • *one of Bran's followers*
**MANANNÁN MAC LIR** • *a sea god*
**THE SIDHE** • *goddesses or supernatural beings*

## PLOT SYNOPSIS

### THE FEAST OF BRAN
Bran held a great feast in
his hall. After a while he
decided he needed some
fresh air and sat down
outside. As he did so
he became aware of
beautiful music playing,
and the gentle tune lulled
him to sleep. When he
awoke he found a branch
from an apple tree,
covered in blossom, next
to him on the ground.

**The Ogham Stone** is carved with
a 5th-century Irish script used to
transcribe Celtic myths.

### SINGER OF THE SIDHE
Bran picked up the branch and took
it to show his companions. As they
began to admire it, a beautiful woman
appeared as if from nowhere. Her

strange clothes set her
apart from the women
of Bran's people and Bran
decided she must be one
of the Sidhe. As they
listened, she started to
sing, and the words of
her song described how
a group of strangers
would travel to the land
where the apple tree grew.
She sang on, saying that
if they made such a
journey they would know
neither illness nor death.

### JOURNEY TO THE ISLE OF JOY
Bran decided to make the journey,
gathering 30 men together and setting
sail. After two days and two nights they

met Manannán mac Lir, a sea god who rode the waves in a horse-drawn chariot. He told them that they would soon come to the Isle of Women. But first they arrived at the Isle of Joy, where a host of laughing people watched their boat from the shore. When the men shouted questions to the people, they laughed still more. One of Bran's men begged permission to stay with them. Once he had stepped on land he joined in their laughter and seemed not to want to come back to the boat, so Bran and his crew sailed on.

**An Irish goddess** lured Bran to the Otherworld promising a bountiful land where the sun always shone.

### THE ISLE OF WOMEN

After a further day and night at sea, they came to another island, the Isle of Women, where the inhabitants welcomed them ashore. They found peace and happiness here, and it seemed that they would never leave. But after they had been there a year, one of Bran's companions, a man called Nechtan, began to feel homesick and he persuaded the others to take him back to Ireland. When they told the women that they were going home, the women advised them to pick up their friend from the Isle of Joy, but then to stay on board ship and on no account to set foot on Irish soil again.

### BRAN'S RETURN

The men set sail and soon arrived at the Isle of Joy, where their former shipmate was ready to join them once more.

Another two days at sea brought them to the coast of Ireland. Soon people came out to look at Bran's ship. Bran called out to the people, saying that he was Bran, and had been travelling for a year. The people were astonished. They had heard stories of a man called Bran who had left Ireland hundreds of years ago. The travellers thought they had been away for a year, but they had actually been away for centuries.

### THE VOYAGE CONTINUES

As soon as he was within range of the shore, Nechtan jumped from the ship and started to run toward his waiting countrymen. But as he ran up the beach his body turned to dust. Bran and the others watched, horrified, and realized what the women had meant when they told them not to step on the soil of their homeland. They rowed back out into the deep ocean, and were never seen again.

**RELATED MYTHS** ▸ The Land of the Young (*p.107*)

# THE HOUND OF ULSTER

📖 Exploits of hero
📍 Ireland
🏛 Ulster, Ireland

✍ Joseph Dunn, *The Ancient Irish Epic:*
*Táin Bó Cuailnge (The Cattle Raid of Cooley)*

Cúchulain, originally called Setanta, was the son of Queen Deichtine of Connaught. His father was said to be either the sun god Lugh, or his own uncle, King Conchobar. Even when he was a young boy, Cúchulain had magical powers: light radiated from his head, animals submitted to him, and his strength was legendary. When he fought, he went berserk: his muscles bulged, his hair stood on end, and his howling voice chilled opponents.

**KEY CHARACTERS**

**CÚCHULAIN** • *hero of Ulster*
**CONCHOBAR** • *king of Ulster*
**MEDB** • *a queen of Connaught*
**CHULAIN** • *a smith*
**FERDIAD** • *Cúchulain's foster-brother*

## PLOT SYNOPSIS

### THE HERO ARRIVES
When he was still a boy, Setanta travelled to the court of King Conchobar of Ulster to join the king's band of 150 boy-warriors. But when he arrived, they challenged him and he ended up fighting them single-handed. As he began to knock them down, one after another, they capitulated and agreed to his leadership.

### A NEW NAME
Soon after Setanta had joined King Conchobar, the king and his followers paid a visit to Chulain, the smith. Chulain had a fearsome dog that guarded his flocks and would kill anyone who came near them. Unfortunately Setanta did not know about the hound, and strayed too near to the flocks. Immediately the dog attacked him, so Setanta hurled the creature against a rock and killed it. When Chulain saw what had happened he was in despair. With no dog to guard his flocks, the sheep would be stolen or killed. So Setanta agreed to guard the

**Cúchulain killed** his rival Ferdiad, but then mourned him, singing a lament over his slain body.

fields for a year until a new dog had been trained. From then on he was called Cúchulain, "the hound of Chulain".

### IRELAND'S CHAMPION
A famous story tells of how Cúchulain met a giant who challenged him and his two companions, Laoghaire and Conal, to a bizarre ordeal. Each man was offered the chance to behead the giant, provided that he would let the giant behead him afterwards. Laoghaire took up his sword and sliced off the giant's head, but then ran away. The giant merely picked up his head and put it back on his shoulders. Conal came forward, and everything happened just as it had with Laoghaire. Then it was Cúchulain's turn. The hero chopped off the giant's head, just as his two friends had done, but then did not run away; he offered his own neck in turn as promised. Impressed, the giant refused to behead Cúchulain, instead proclaiming that he was the bravest man in all Ireland.

## THE CATTLE RAID OF COOLEY

Under a later queen, Medb, the people of Connaught got into a serious dispute with Ulster over a bull. Queen Medb owned a great white-horned bull, which had strayed across the border and joined Conchobar's herds. Some said the animal, which was the father of many herds of fine cattle, was unwilling to be the property of a woman. Medb sought a replacement bull, and the best one was another Ulster beast: the Brown Bull of Cooley. Medb's men offered a good price for the creature, and boasted that they would take it by force if the owners would not agree to their ruler's terms. This boast was too much for the men of Ulster, and war was declared.

The torc was the symbol of the Celtic warrior. Of nearly 100 discovered in the British Isles, 31 came from the Connaught area.

## THE WAR BETWEEN ULSTER AND CONNAUGHT

The war began badly for Ulster when, because of an old curse, nearly all their warriors became ill. But Cúchulain was not an Ulsterman, so kept his health, and on his own fought off one hundred Connaught men. Queen Medb then agreed to let him fight her army in a series of single combats. Again Cúchulain prevailed until Medb sent her best fighter, Ferdiad, who happened to be Cúchulain's foster-brother. The pair fought for four days until Cúchulain slew Ferdiad. After more fighting, the rest of Medb's men were defeated, but Cúchulain, who would not attack a woman, let Medb herself escape to Connaught.

## THE DEATH OF CÚCHULAIN

Cúchulain was exhausted after the long battle. Realizing that he was near death, he strapped himself to an upright stone and prepared to meet his end unbowed. Even then no-one dared attack him. But when the war goddess the Mórrigan arrived in the shape of a crow and perched on his shoulder, it was clear that the great hero was dead.

# DEIRDRE OF THE SORROWS

📖 Tragedy of fate
🏴 Ireland
🏛 Ulster, Ireland

✍ Anon, *The Book of Leinster; The Yellow Book of Lecan*

Deirdre was the daughter of Fedlimid, the storyteller to King Conchobar of Ulster. Before the child was born, she was heard crying in her mother's womb and a druid called Cathbadh predicted that Deirdre would be very beautiful but would bring disaster to the people of Ulster. In spite of the king's attempts first to save her and then to control her, her tragic story unfolded as the result of this grim prophecy.

## KEY CHARACTERS

**CONCHOBAR** • *king of Ulster*
**FEDLIMID** • *the king's storyteller*
**DEIRDRE** • *Fedlimid's daughter*
**NAOISE** • *a warrior*
**EÓGHAN** • *a warrior*

## PLOT SYNOPSIS

### DEIRDRE AND NAOISE

When the druid Cathbadh prophesied that the girl-child Deirdre would bring ruin to Ulster, his followers wanted to put her to death. But King Conchobar sent her away to be brought up by foster-parents: taken by her beauty, he planned to marry the girl when she came of age. Deirdre, however, developed her own ideas. One day as she sat watching her foster-father skinning a slaughtered calf in the snow, she told her teacher Leabharcham that she would love a man with skin as white as snow, cheeks as red as the calf's blood, and hair as black as the raven who had flown down to drink the spilled blood. Her teacher then told her of a man called Naoise, one of the king's knights, who was just like this. The couple met, fell in love, and fled to Scotland.

### THE WARS OF ULSTER

The story of Deirdre is part of the Ulster Cycle – a group of around 100 tales about the kingdom of Ulster, which ruled northern Ireland from the 2nd to the 4th century CE. The Ulster Cycle was written in the 7th century, and includes one of the most important Irish myths: the book known as the *Táin Bó Cuailnge* (*The Cattle Raid of Cooley; see p.105*). Deirdre's story, also known as "The Exile of the Children of Usnach", is one of the introductory stories to the *Táin*, setting the scene for the wars between Ulster and Connaught. It is one of the most famous and best-loved stories from the Cycle.

**The theft of a magnificent bull,** here on the base of the Gundestrup cauldron, inspired one of the most famous stories in the Ulster Cycle.

### TRAGEDY UNFOLDS

When Conchobar heard what had happened, he enticed the couple back to Ireland, offering them safety and a pardon. But it was a trick, and on their return he ordered one of his men, Eóghan, to kill Naoise. After Naoise's death Conchobar asked Deirdre whom she most hated in the world, and she replied: "Conchobar and Eóghan". So as the ultimate punishment, Conchobar ordered her to live for six months of the year with him, and the remaining six months with Eóghan. Deirdre refused to do this and instead chose death, by throwing herself from a chariot.

# THE LAND OF THE YOUNG

📖 Journey to the Otherworld
🏴 Ireland
🏛 Ireland; the Land of the Young

✍ Michael Comyn, *Lay of Oísin in the Land of Youth*

In the 2nd century Ireland was defended by a group of warriors called the Fianna, who were led by the great warrior Finn MacCumhail. Finn's son Oísin fell in love with a woman called Niamh of the Golden Hair, who was the daughter of the king of Tir na n'Og (Land of the Young). Oísin and Niamh married, and travelled to the Land of the Young, where they would have lived forever, had Oísin not fatally failed to heed his wife's advice.

**KEY CHARACTERS**

**OÍSIN** • *son of Finn MacCumhail*
**NIAMH OF THE GOLDEN HAIR**
• *princess of Tir na n'Og*

## PLOT SYNOPSIS

### THE JOURNEY TO TIR NA N'OG

Oísin said a sad farewell to his father Finn and set off with his wife Niamh to take her back to her father's kingdom. They travelled far across the sea until they reached a place more beautiful than any Oísin had seen before: Tir na n'Og, Land of the Young. They lived happily there for years, and had three children. Everything seemed perfect.

### THE RETURN OF OÍSIN

But Oísin grew homesick and told his wife that he wanted to return to Ireland to visit his people. She told him to go, but on no account to dismount from his horse, or he would never return. So Oísin travelled to Ireland, and realized that he had been away for hundreds of years. Finn was long dead and his hall was in ruins. As Oísin was exploring, some men asked for his help in raising a slab of marble. He leaned over to lift

the stone and slipped from his horse. As soon as his body touched the ground he began to age: his body shrank, his legs crumpled, and he lost his sight. The Land of the Young was lost to him.

---

**RELATED MYTHS** ▸ The voyage of Bran (*p.102*) • The Odyssey (*p.72*) • Qayaq the wander-hawk (*p.206*)

**Niamh was riding** a white horse across the waves when Oísin first saw her and the couple fell in love.

# A GIRL MADE FROM FLOWERS

- 📖 Love triangle
- 📛 Wales
- 🏛 Gwynedd, North Wales
- ✍ Anon, The Fourth Branch of the *Mabinogi*

The story of Blodeuwedd tells of how a young woman was created by two magicians, Math and Gwydion, to be the wife of Lleu Llaw Gyffes, who had been condemned by his mother to have no human wife. But Blodeuwedd, the woman they made, is unfaithful to her husband, who then kills her lover. Blodeuwedd ends up being turned into an owl, condemned to fly only at night and to live ostracized by all the other birds of the air.

### KEY CHARACTERS

**MATH** • *lord of Gwynedd*
**GWYDION** • *Math's nephew*
**ARIANRHOD** • *Gwydion's sister*
**LLEU LLAW GYFFES** • *Arianrhod's son*
**BLODEUWEDD** • *the wife made for Lleu Llaw Gyffes*

## PLOT SYNOPSIS

### THE CHILDREN OF ARIANRHOD

Gwydion presented his sister Arianrhod to Math, lord of Gwynedd. Math made the young woman step over a magic wand to test her virginity, but as she stepped over the wand she dropped two small children. The first was called Dylan, but the second boy remained unnamed, as Arianrhod insisted that he would have a name only when she was ready to give him one. She then placed two more taboos on her son.

### THE TRICKS OF GWYDION

Gwydion dealt with the first taboo – not naming the boy – by tricking his sister into calling him Lleu Llaw Gyffes ("Bright One of the Skilful Hand").

#### THE MABINOGION

*The Mabinogion* is the most famous work of medieval Welsh literature. It is a collection of tales, first written down in the 12th century. It comprises four distinct sections, known as the Four Branches of the *Mabinogi*. They deal respectively with Pwyll, ruler of Dyfed, who visits the Otherworld; the children of the sea-god Llyr, including Brân (*see opposite*); Manawydan, son of Llyr; and Math, lord of Gwynedd. This last part contains many different stories, including Blodeuwedd's tale.

Her second taboo was that he would not bear arms until she was ready to arm him, but again Gwydion tricked her and she equipped her son. Finally she declared that her son would never have a human wife. This time Gwydion sought the help of Math, and together the pair used their magical powers to make Lleu a beautiful wife from the flowers of the broom, meadowsweet, and oak. The woman they created was called Blodeuwedd.

### THE TREACHERY OF BLODEUWEDD

Blodeuwedd proved faithless. She took a lover, Gronw Pebyr, and the pair plotted to kill Lleu. Blodeuwedd tricked Lleu into revealing the only circumstances under which he could be killed, and then she placed him in the perfect position, leaving Gronw to strike the final blow. But as the spear pierced him, Lleu turned into an eagle. He was restored to human form by Gwydion, then found Gronw and killed him. As punishment for her part, Gwydion turned Blodeuwedd into an owl.

# BRÂN'S HEAD

📖 Exploits of hero
🚩 Wales
🏛 Ireland and Britain

✍ Anon, The Second Branch
of the *Mabinogi*

Brân the Blessed, who was also known as Bendigeidfran, was a great British hero. His gigantic stature and huge strength made him a fearful opponent in battle, allowing him to prevail against the king of Ireland despite hopeless odds. He was fatally wounded in the fighting, but his magical power lived on because his companions carried his severed head back to London, where it protected Britain against invaders.

## KEY CHARACTERS

**BRÂN THE BLESSED** • *a giant*
**BRANWEN** • *Brân's sister*
**MATHOLWCH** • *king of Ireland and Branwen's husband*

## PLOT SYNOPSIS

### BRITAIN AT WAR

Brân allowed the king of Ireland, Matholwch, to marry his sister Branwen. But Matholwch abused and ill-treated his wife. When Brân heard of this, he set off to avenge her. The fighting between the British and Irish was bitter and the Irish had one great advantage: a cauldron that could revive dead men. In the end the British won the war, but by this time only Brân and seven of his men survived. Brân himself

**Brân's head** was buried on Gwynfryn (The White Mount) in London, where the Tower of London now stands.

had been fatally wounded. Knowing his time was short, Brân ordered his companions to cut off his head and take it back with them to London, where they should bury it, to protect Britain against future invasions. They did so and were amazed when it carried on speaking to them during the long trip home, right up until they reached London and buried it as Brân had ordered.

**Castell Dinas Bran,** Llangollen, Wales, now in ruins, was said to be home to the semi-human giant Brân.

# KING ARTHUR

⬜ Quest; love triangle
📖 Britain
🏛 Britain

✍ Geoffrey of Monmouth, *Historia Regum Britanniae*;
Thomas Malory, *Morte d'Arthur*

Some of the most enduring European myths are those of King Arthur and his Knights of the Round Table. Arthur was a mythical king, but his character may have been based on a British military leader of the Dark Ages. The stories tell how he ruled an ideal, chivalrous court at his castle of Camelot, of his knights' quest to find the Holy Grail, and of how the king's court finally broke up because of the treachery of Arthur's son Mordred.

### KEY CHARACTERS

**UTHER PENDRAGON** • *king of Britain*
**ARTHUR** • *Pendragon's son and later king of Britain*
**GUINEVERE** • *Arthur's queen*
**MORDRED** • *Arthur's son*
**MERLIN** • *a wizard*
**SIR LANCELOT** • *a knight*

## PLOT SYNOPSIS

### ARTHUR BECOMES KING

Arthur was the illegitimate son of Uther Pendragon, a British king, and Queen Ygern of Cornwall, and as a consequence was brought up in secret. Before he died, Uther embedded a sword in a block of stone in London and said that whoever could remove the sword would become king of the Britons. None of the knights who tried could even move

King Arthur with Lancelot, who betrayed him and ultimately caused the downfall of the legendary Camelot.

the sword in the stone, until Arthur pulled out the sword with ease, so becoming king. He later broke the sword in a duel with a giant, and the wizard Merlin took him to the watery home of the Lady of the Lake, from which a hand appeared holding another sword, called Excalibur, which Arthur took.

**The legend of Camelot** continues to fascinate with its themes of love, war, and betrayal, as shown in this 2004 film, *King Arthur*.

## THE ROUND TABLE

Arthur united all of Britain, married the beautiful princess Guinevere, and gathered around him the famous Knights of the Round Table – men such as the noble Sir Perceval and valiant Sir Lancelot. But one seat – the Siege Perilous, or Seat of Danger – was empty, because it was said that any knight who sat in it would die and the days of the Round Table would end. After many years a knight called Sir Galahad came to claim it. He was to go in search of the Holy Grail, the cup Jesus had used at the Last Supper.

Arthur's other knights decided to join Galahad in his quest. After many adventures, Galahad found the Grail and took it to Jerusalem – or, some say, died. Many of the other knights had also perished and, although some returned to Camelot, the peace and harmony of Arthur's court was gone forever.

**Glastonbury Tor** in the west of England may be the place that legend refers to when it speaks of Arthur and his knights merely sleeping under a hill, poised to be awakened when Britain's need is greatest.

## ARTHUR BETRAYED

Sir Lancelot was Arthur's closest friend, but he loved Guinevere, and they committed adultery. On being told this, Arthur was distraught, and banished the knight. At this weak point in Camelot's history, the king's own son, Mordred, seized the opportunity to fight his father for control of the throne.

There was a battle, and one by one the knights were killed until only Arthur and Mordred were left. The two fought bitterly, and Arthur killed the traitor. But he was so badly wounded that he knew he too was close to death. Arthur travelled to the land of Avalon to die. Avalon ("apple island") was a place where the apples of immortality grew and people said that it was here that the king's soul lived on.

### GEOFFREY OF MONMOUTH

*Historia Regum Britanniae* (The History of the Kings of Britain) was probably written by Geoffrey of Monmouth, a Benedictine monk, in around 1136. The book traces a line of British rulers from legendary figures such as Brutus (great-grandson of the Trojan hero Aeneas) to the kings of the 7th century CE, with special emphasis on King Arthur. Geoffrey's account mixes myth and history, but is well written and was very popular in the Middle Ages. It helped to make Arthur into one of the most charismatic of all British heroes.

# THE NORSE GODS

Just as the Titans fathered the Olympian gods, so the Norse gods were born from a race of giants (*see p.114*). On Loki the trickster's side are evil beings such as Hel, queen of the Underworld, and Fenrir the wolf; from Bor and Bestla are descended the Aesir, the principal clan of Norse gods, led by Odin – who, like the Greek Zeus, had several wives and consorts and a host of children.

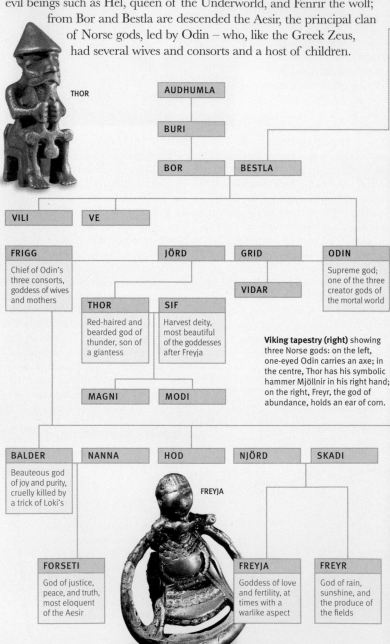

**THOR**

**AUDHUMLA**

**BURI**

**BOR** — **BESTLA**

**VILI**    **VE**

**FRIGG**
Chief of Odin's three consorts, goddess of wives and mothers

**JÖRD**

**GRID**

**ODIN**
Supreme god; one of the three creator gods of the mortal world

**VIDAR**

**THOR**
Red-haired and bearded god of thunder, son of a giantess

**SIF**
Harvest deity, most beautiful of the goddesses after Freyja

**Viking tapestry (right)** showing three Norse gods: on the left, one-eyed Odin carries an axe; in the centre, Thor has his symbolic hammer Mjöllnir in his right hand; on the right, Freyr, the god of abundance, holds an ear of corn.

**MAGNI**    **MODI**

**BALDER**
Beauteous god of joy and purity, cruelly killed by a trick of Loki's

**NANNA**

**HOD**

**NJÖRD**

**SKADI**

**FREYJA**

**FORSETI**
God of justice, peace, and truth, most eloquent of the Aesir

**FREYJA**
Goddess of love and fertility, at times with a warlike aspect

**FREYR**
God of rain, sunshine, and the produce of the fields

**Loki is bound** with a serpent above him dripping venom into his face for causing the death of Balder.

YMIR

GIANTS

SIGYN — LOKI — ANGRBODA

NARVI — VALI

HEL

FENRIR

Wolf predicted to kill and devour Odin at Ragnarok, the last battle

JORMUNGAND

HERMOD

BRAGI

God of poetry, possibly in charge of the mead of inspiration (p.123)

IDUN

Custodian of the apples that allowed the Aesir to remain young

TYR

One-handed god of single combat and heroic glory

# THE CREATION OF THE WORLD

📖 Creation
📑 Iceland
🏛 The cosmos

✍ Snorri Sturluson, *The Younger Edda*

The Norse creation story begins in the borderland between two cosmic regions, the frozen world of Niflheim and the hot realm of Muspell, a setting that recalls the icy terrain and bubbling geysers of Iceland, where the story has its origins. From the interaction of these two regions a primal being, the frost giant Ymir, is born. Eventually Ymir is killed and his body is transformed into the world by a trio of creator gods: Odin, Vili, and Ve.

**KEY CHARACTERS**

**YMIR** • *the first giant*
**AUDHUMLA** • *the primal cow*
**ODIN** • *god of war*
**VILI** • *Odin's brother*
**VE** • *Odin's brother*

## PLOT SYNOPSIS

### GIANTS AND GODS

As the heat of Muspell began to thaw the ice of Niflheim, the evil giant Ymir emerged. Then a cow called Audhumla formed out of the melting ice, and produced milk for Ymir to drink. As he drank and was further warmed by the air of Muspell, Ymir started to sweat, and two more giants were formed in the sweat under his left arm while another emerged from his legs. When Audhumla licked the ice, she freed yet another giant, called Buri, from inside the ice. These frost giants ruled the cosmos. Buri's son Bor married Bestla, daughter of the

**In this primitive Viking figurine** of Odin, the right eye is depicted as a single line: Odin was to give up one eye in exchange for knowledge.

giant Bölthorn, and had three children, the gods Odin, Vili, and Ve. Ymir was cruel to all around him, and the sons of Bor hated him. They fought the giant and killed him, and used his body as material from which to create the world. From his skull they made the sky; from his brains, the clouds. The gods made rocks from his bones and rivers and seas from his blood, which was so prolific that it drowned all the other frost giants except for two, Bergelmir and his wife.

# THE FIRST HUMANS

📖 Creation     ✍ Snorri Sturluson, *The Younger Edda*
📍 Iceland
🏛 The cosmos

The Norse creator gods Odin, Vili, and Ve had the power to breathe life into objects and to give living things new form. This allowed them to create new races in the cosmos. They transformed the dwarves, for example, who had been small maggot-like creatures born from the flesh of Ymir, the first giant, into intelligent humanoids. More notably still, they created the first man and woman, Ask and Embla, by giving life to a pair of logs.

**KEY CHARACTERS**

**ODIN** • *the god of war*
**VILI** • *Odin's brother*
**VE** • *Odin's brother*
**ASK** • *the first man*
**EMBLA** • *the first woman*

## PLOT SYNOPSIS

### UTGARD AND ASGARD
Once the creator gods Odin, Vili, and Ve had created the cosmos and the Earth, they gave the only giants that remained – the children of Bergelmir and his wife – a region in the east called Utgard in which to live. Then they built their own home at Asgard, and put up strong fortifications around it made from the eyebrows of Ymir, to protect themselves from the giants.

### THE FIRST MAN AND WOMAN
Odin, Vili, and Ve decided to explore their kingdom. As they were walking along the coast, they found a pair of tree trunks washed up on the shore. The trio decided to bring life back to the dead trees, but in a new form. They remodelled the logs into humanoid shapes, and brought them to life. Odin gave the logs breath and life. Vili gave them intelligence and emotion. Ve gave them the senses of sight and hearing (some versions of the myth say that he gave them expressive features and the power of speech).

### MIDGARD
The pair, who were named Ask and Embla, were the first man and woman. Ask and Embla needed somewhere to

**In Norse mythology** the first man and woman are created from the logs of dead trees, to be born as Ask (meaning "ash") and Embla ("elm").

live, so the creator gods built them their own realm, called Midgard (Middle Earth), midway between Asgard, where they themselves lived, and the cold realm of Niflheim. Asgard and Midgard were linked by a bridge, called Bifrost, which took the form of a rainbow. The gods told Ask and Embla that it was their responsibility to look after the plants and creatures and so they settled down to nurture their realm and to start the vast family that became the human race.

# THE WAR BETWEEN THE GODS

📖 War in heaven
🏳 Iceland

🏛 Asgard, home of the Aesir, and Vanaheim, home of the Vanir
✍ Snorri Sturluson, *The Younger Edda*

In Norse mythology there were at first two races of gods. The first group were the Aesir, the sky gods, who included the creator gods Odin, Vili, and Ve. The second group were the Vanir, who were gods and goddesses of fertility who presided over the sea and the Earth. Their leader was the sea god Njörd, together with his children Freyr and Freyja. One of the key episodes in the Norse tales of the gods concerns a long war between the Aesir and Vanir.

### KEY CHARACTERS

**NJÖRD** • *god of the sea*
**FREYJA** • *Njörd's daughter*
**FREYR** • *Njörd's son*
**ODIN** • *god of war*
**HONIR** • *Odin's companion*
**MIMIR** • *god of wisdom*

## PLOT SYNOPSIS

### BURNED AND REBORN
A Vanir visitor, who was either Freyja or someone disguised as her, arrived in Asgard. She began to talk obsessively about gold, and irritated the Aesir so much that they threw her on the fire three times, but each time she was reborn. Her treatment angered the Vanir, and they declared war.

The fighting raged on, with each side destroying the other's homeland, until finally a truce was agreed, guaranteed by a hostage arrangement: two of the Aesir, Honir and Mimir, would spend part of the year with the Vanir, while Freyr and Njörd would live with the Aesir.

### THE AESIR TRIUMPH
The two sides lived peacefully but remained suspicious, thinking that the hostages were acting as spies. The Vanir tried to make Mimir tell them the secrets of his wisdom, but he refused, so they chopped off his head and sent it back to the Aesir. But the head contained all the wisdom of the gods, so Odin took it, made it immortal, and kept it in Asgard. The Aesir now had all the wisdom in the world. The Vanir lived on, but had little power. Over time, these gods of health, wealth, and luck were assimilated into the tribe of their rivals, the Aesir.

**This prehistoric rock carving,** at Vitlycke, Sweden, shows gigantic warriors – possibly the Vanir and Aesir – fighting with hatchets.

**RELATED MYTHS** ▸ War of the gods and Titans (*p.38*)

# THE BUILDING OF ASGARD

📖 Trickery
🚩 Iceland
🏛 Asgard, home of the Aesir

✒ Snorri Sturluson, *The Younger Edda*

Asgard, the home of the Aesir, was at the top level of the cosmos, above Midgard, the human world, and Niflheim, the icy home of the dead. It was huge, with palaces, dense forests, lush pastures, and fields growing food for the gods. A wall surrounded it which was so strong that only immortals could break it down. But when the Vanir and Aesir went to war (*see opposite*), the wall was demolished. The ensuing peace presented a chance to rebuild it.

### KEY CHARACTERS

**THE AESIR** • *a race of Norse gods*
**A GIANT**
**SVADILFARI** • *the giant's horse*
**LOKI** • *the trickster god of fire*

## PLOT SYNOPSIS

### THE GIANT'S DEMAND
Rebuilding the huge wall of Asgard was an enormous task, so when a giant said that he could reconstruct Asgard's fortifications in a mere three seasons, the gods jumped at the chance. But the giant demanded a gigantic fee – the Sun, the Moon, and Freyja. Freyja was doubly desirable: she was a fertility goddess of great beauty and she had the power to grant immortality.

### THE TRICKSTER GOD NEGOTIATES
To avoid this extortionate payment, the trickster god Loki hatched a plan. The gods agreed to the giant's demands, but set a time schedule of a single season: too short a time for the giant to be able to finish the work.

This way, they would get their wall built, but would be able to reduce the giant's wages because he would be late in completing his task.

### MAGICAL SVADILFARI
But the giant had a magical horse called Svadilfari, who worked tirelessly with him, and it seemed the walls would be finished on time after all. Loki decided to save the day by distracting Svadilfari. He transformed himself into a mare and seduced the stallion, resulting in the birth of the eight-legged horse Sleipnir, who became Odin's steed. Working alone, the giant failed in his task, and flew into a rage, stopped only by a hammer-throw from Thor which killed him. The gods had their walls for free.

**The Viking settlement** at Trelleborg, Denmark, was built as a circular compound, perhaps reminiscent of the great wall that encircled Asgard.

**This Viking graveyard** is the largest ancient burial site in Scandinavia, with more than 600 graves dating back to the 8th century, the heyday of Norse mythology. Each boat-shaped arrangement of stones marks the resting place of a warrior of high rank in Viking society.

# ODIN AND THE RUNES

📖 Origin of language

🏳 Iceland

🏛 Yggdrasil, the World Tree at the heart of the cosmos

✍ Anon, "Hávámal", poem from *The Elder Edda*

The early Norse peoples used a script made up of letters called runes, characters formed mainly from vertical and diagonal strokes. They attributed great powers to the runes: communication and magic. People thought that the runic alphabet, which they called the "futhark" after its opening letters, must have been invented by the gods. The most popular myth explaining its origin tells how the god Odin gained knowledge of the runes.

## PLOT SYNOPSIS

### ODIN'S SACRIFICE

Odin wanted to know everything that there was to know. He decided that in order to become all-knowing he needed to give up something he already owned. First of all he gave up one of his eyes in return for one sip from the spring of wisdom. But this was not enough.

So Odin hung himself on the trunk of Yggdrasil, the World Tree, his body pierced by an arrow, offering up his body in exchange for knowledge. For nine days and nights he hung there, without food or

**This runic stone** is carved with a few letters from the pre-Viking, 24-character alphabet. The letters were split into three groups (*oettir*) of eight letters each.

water, until he finally fell from the tree, clutching the runes with their secret of knowledge in his hands.

### ULTIMATE WISDOM

With the runes in his possession, Odin became the wisest of all the gods. The runes gave him the ability to perform magic spells, and he put these to use in many different ways. On the battlefield, accompanied by his two wolves Geri and Freki, he was the most aggressive fighter and had the power to change shape, make his enemies blind or deaf, and blunt their weapons. In the arts of peace he was helped both by mastery of the runes and by a pair of ravens called Huginn (thought) and Munnin (memory). Each day they flew all over the world, seeing everything, before returning home to whisper all that they had seen and heard into Odin's ear.

# THE WORLD TREE

- 📖 Nature of the cosmos
- 🏴 Iceland
- 🏛 The cosmos

✍ Anon, "Völuspá" and "Grímnismál", poems from *The Elder Edda*

At the core of the Norse cosmos was an enormous ash tree called Yggdrasil. It was so vast that all the different realms of the Norse world, from Asgard, the home of the gods, to Midgard, the human world, were shaded by its branches or set among its roots. Its odd name means "Ygg's Horse" (Ygg being another name for Odin), and refers to the time that the god was suspended on the tree for nine days and nights in search of knowledge.

**KEY CHARACTERS**

**THE NORNS** • *three women, or fates*
**HRAESVELG** • *an eagle*
**NIDHOGG** • *the world serpent*
**RATATOSK** • *a squirrel*

## PLOT SYNOPSIS

### YGGDRASIL'S ROOTS
Yggdrasil rested on three enormous roots. One root spread to Asgard, home of the gods. A trio of women called the Norns, who controlled human destiny, lived close by. They nurtured the tree by watering it with water from their well of fate. The second root stretched to Jotunheim, home of the frost giants. Beneath this root lay the immortal, severed head of the sage Mimir *(see p.116)* and the well of Mimir, whose waters contained knowledge and wisdom. Yggdrasil's third root reached to the icy region of Niflheim and the boiling spring Hvergelmir. Here the serpent Nidhogg tormented Yggdrasil by gnawing continuously at its root.

### THE CREATURES OF YGGDRASIL
The branches of Yggdrasil were vast, spreading across the sky and covering the entire world. Among the branches lived the eagle Hraesvelg ("corpse-eater"), a bird that could see far and was very knowledgeable. The branches also held four stags that fed on the foliage. The most active of all the tree's creatures was the squirrel Ratatosk, whose main purpose was to carry messages of insult from the eagle Hraesvelg to the serpent Nidhogg.

**The four stags** that run in the branches of Yggdrasil and nibble at its leaves represent the four winds that blow between the worlds of the Norse cosmos.

# THE TREASURES OF THE GODS

- 📖 Weapons of the gods
- 🏴 Iceland
- 🏛 The cosmos
- ✍ Anon, "Thrymskvida", poem from *The Elder Edda*

Norse myths tell of precious objects belonging to the gods that had supernatural powers. There were magic rings, spears that could bring you success in battle, apples that kept the consumer youthful, and a ship with sails that always attracted a favourable wind. One of the greatest treasures was the hammer wielded by the sky god Thor, which was both a fearsome weapon and a powerful religious symbol, used to bless the bride at weddings.

**KEY CHARACTERS**

**THRYM** • *a giant*
**THOR** • *god of the sky*
**LOKI** • *the trickster god of fire*
**FREYJA** • *goddess of love*

## PLOT SYNOPSIS

### THOR'S HAMMER

Thor (meaning "Thunder") rode through the sky in a chariot. He had a mighty hammer, Mjöllnir, which had been forged for him by dwarves, and which he used to crush his enemies and bless those he wished well.

Many around him wished they could wield such a powerful weapon. The giant Thrym was so jealous that he stole Thor's hammer and buried it so that the god would not be able to find it. Thrym said that he would return the weapon only if he was allowed to marry the beautiful goddess Freyja.

Freyja refused to contemplate the idea, so Thor was forced to come up with a plan to rescue the hammer.

**Thor's hammer** was often used as a motif on jewellery, runic stones, and tomb carvings.

With the help of the trickster Loki, Thor disguised himself as Freyja and went – heavily veiled – to the wedding feast that Thrym had provided.

At first Thor nearly gave himself away by the amount he ate and drank, but then the hammer was brought out, as tradition demanded, to bless the bride. At this point Thor quickly grabbed the hammer, killed the giant Thrym and all his guests, laid waste to all around him, and returned to Asgard in glory.

# THE MEAD OF INSPIRATION

📖 Transformation;
   the origins of poetry
📍 Iceland

🏛 Jotunheim (realm of the giants);
   Asgard (home of the gods)
✍ Snorri Sturluson, *The Younger Edda*

Poetry was an important part of Norse culture, and one myth explains the origin of poetic inspiration as a magical fluid, "the mead of inspiration". It was made by dwarves after the war between the Aesir and the Vanir (*see p.116*). The mead was snatched by giants and then stolen by Odin for the use of the gods. In order to obtain the mead, Odin had to use his ability to change shape, taking on the forms of a snake, an eagle, and a human.

### KEY CHARACTERS

**ODIN** • *god of war*
**KVASIR** • *a giant*
**FJALAR AND GALAR** •
*two dwarves*
**SUTTUNG** • *a giant*
**BAUGI** • *Suttung's brother*
**GUNNLÖD** • *Suttung's daughter*

## PLOT SYNOPSIS

### MAKING THE MEAD

After the war between the Aesir and Vanir, the gods gathered around a cauldron and spat into it to seal their peace. Out of the spittle arose a giant called Kvasir, a poet full of wisdom. He saw his task as teaching those around him, but two malevolent dwarves, named Fjalar and Galar, tired of this and murdered him.

The dwarves took Kvasir's blood and distilled it in a magic cauldron. Then they mixed it with honey and produced a powerful mead that gave wisdom and poetic inspiration to any who drank it.

### ODIN STEALS THE MEAD

Shortly afterwards, the dwarves killed another giant and his wife, causing their son Suttung to pursue them, seeking revenge. They pacified him by offering him the mead in compensation. He took the mead and passed it to his daughter, Gunnlöd, to hide in her cave. Odin, meanwhile, was plotting to procure the mead for the gods. He disguised himself as a man called Bölverk and killed the nine servants of Suttung's brother Baugi. Then he offered himself as replacement servant, saying he would do the work of all nine men in return for a sip of mead in payment. Baugi agreed, but when he

**This Viking picture stone** shows Odin on his magical eight-legged horse Sleipnir (*see* The building of Asgard, *p.117*), holding a cup of mead.

asked Suttung to give his new servant some mead, Suttung refused. So Odin-Bölverk persuaded Baugi to help him steal the mead from Gunnlöd's cave. Baugi bored through the mountainside with a drill, whereupon Odin-Bölverk turned himself into a snake and slithered into the mountain. Once inside, he seduced Gunnlöd, who was still standing guard, and persuaded her to let him drink some of the mead. When she agreed, he downed every drop, changed himself into an eagle, and flew back to Asgard.

# THE TRICKS OF LOKI

📖 Trickery　　　　✍ Snorri Sturluson, *The Younger Edda*
🏴 Iceland
🏛 Asgard

The trickster god Loki was a shape-changer, a
frost giant brought up as Odin's foster-brother.
He often wreaked havoc amongst the gods, and
caused the death of Odin's hero-son Balder. Loki
was sexually rapacious, copulating with everyone
and everything, from giants to trees. Loki's wife
Angrboda bore him three monsters – Fenrir the
wolf, Jormungand the serpent of Midgard (the
realm of mortals), and Hel, the ruler of the dead.

### KEY CHARACTERS

**LOKI** • *the trickster god*
**THOR** • *god of the sky*
**SIF** • *harvest goddess,
Thor's wife*
**DVALIN** • *a dwarf*
**BALDER** • *god of light*
**FRIGG** • *goddess-queen,
Odin's wife*

## PLOT SYNOPSIS

### GIFTS FOR THE GODS

Loki once cut off all of the
harvest goddess Sif's hair.
The crops stopped ripening,
and Thor, her husband, said
he would kill Loki unless Sif's
hair was restored. So Loki
persuaded the dwarf Dvalin
to make her new hair, and also
some magical gifts for the gods.
These included a spear that
always hit its target, and a boat
that was big enough to hold all the
gods, but small enough to be folded
and carried itself. Loki told some
other dwarves that if they could do
better, they could cut off his head.
They did do better, but Loki survived
by reminding the dwarves that he had
never said they could damage his neck.

### BALDER'S NIGHTMARE

Balder, the son of Odin and Frigg,
often dreamed that he would die, so
Frigg made every living thing swear
not to harm him. But she forgot to
ask the mistletoe. As the gods hurled
things around one day, Loki took a
sharpened mistletoe twig and gave it to
the blind god Höd. When Höd, guided
by Loki, threw the twig, it flew straight
to Balder's heart and killed him.

**This Viking ship carving** shows
Loki's mischief-making. His
exploits could amuse the
gods, but often embarrassed
or even enraged them.

# TWILIGHT OF THE GODS

📖 Apocalypse
📕 Iceland
🏛 The cosmos

✍ "Völuspá", poem from *The Elder Edda*;
Snorri Sturluson, *The Younger Edda*

After Loki caused the death of Balder (*see opposite*), the gods punished him by chaining him up in a cave. A serpent dripped poison on his upturned face, but Loki's wife took pity on him and caught the venom in a dish. Even so, Loki was in agony, and when he writhed in pain, the earth quaked. According to the myths, Loki will remain in the cave until Ragnarok, a great battle at which almost all living things will be destroyed.

### KEY CHARACTERS

**LOKI** • *the trickster god*
**FENRIR** • *Loki's son, a wolf*
**JORMUNGAND** • *Loki's son, the world-serpent*
**HEL** • *Loki's son, ruler of the Underworld*
**LIF** • *a man*
**LIFTHRASIR** • *a woman*

## PLOT SYNOPSIS

### THE PROPHECY

After a long time in his chains, Loki will finally find the strength to break free and challenge the gods. At the same time a great force of evil beings will begin to fight the gods. Loki's monster-sons will be there: the wolf Fenrir will break his own chains and defeat the sun and moon; the world-serpent Jormungand will overwhelm the Earth, and Hel will bring ghost-fighters from the Underworld. Everyone will fight, and almost every living thing, both

**Fenrir was bound** with a magical chain made out of breath, footsteps, and occult elements.

evil and good, will be slaughtered. Towards the end of the battle, the giant Surt ("Soot") will hurl fire this way and that, killing most of those who have survived to this point.

Only a few living beings will remain: Yggdrasil, the World Tree and, hidden within it, a man called Lif ("Life") and a woman, Lifthrasir ("Longing for Life"). When the fires of destruction have finally died down, Lif and Lifthrasir will emerge to found a new human race in an idyllic world of goodness and happiness.

### THE VÖLUSPÁ PROPHECY

"Völuspá" ("The Prophecy of the Sibyl") is one of the most impressive poems among the many that make up the *Elder* (or *Poetic*) *Edda*. This is a body of anonymous verse from 800–1100 CE, which was mainly preserved in a 13th-century Icelandic manuscript called the *Codex Regius*. "Völuspá" is written in the form of a prophecy uttered by a prophetess to the god Odin, and tells of a final war before Earth's rebirth.

**Denmark returned** the precious *Codex Regius* to Iceland in 1971 after 300 years, to be stored within the University of Iceland.

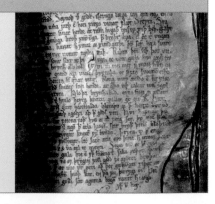

# SIGURD THE DRAGON-SLAYER

- 📖 Exploits of hero
- 🏴 Iceland
- 🏛 Asgard, home of the Aesir

- ✍ Anon, *Volsung Saga*

Soon after Sigurd was born, his father died, and the boy was brought up by a smith called Regin. Regin forged a powerful sword for Sigurd with which the young hero killed the dragon Fafnir. Sigurd's later adventures, though, were tragic. He fell in love with Brynhild, but then forgot his promise to marry her because he had been given a magic potion. Brynhild had Sigurd killed in revenge, but then killed herself in remorse.

**KEY CHARACTERS**

**SIGURD** • *Sigmund's son and Odin's descendant*
**REGIN** • *a smith*
**FAFNIR** • *dragon-brother of Regin*
**BRYNHILD** • *a shieldmaiden, or warrior-woman*

## PLOT SYNOPSIS

### MAGICAL GIFTS

When Sigurd killed the dragon Fafnir, he stole the creature's gold and acquired two priceless qualities. By eating its heart he learned how to understand animals, and by bathing in the dragon's blood he became invulnerable – except for one small spot on his shoulder. He learned from the birds that his foster-father Regin planned to murder him and take the gold, so to

Sigurd killed Fafnir with his mighty sword Gram, which was forged from the fragments of his true father's sword.

pre-empt this he killed Regin and, taking a gold ring from the treasure, he set off on his travels.

### DOOMED LOVE

The hero crossed the bridge of Bifrost and visited the Valkyries, a group of women who worked for Odin selecting warriors worthy of a place in Valhalla. He fell in love with a shieldmaiden named Brynhild, and to mark their betrothal he gave her the magic ring. Neither of them realized that it brought doom to all who wore it. Later on in his travels, at the court of king Gjuki, Sigurd drank a potion that made him forget his promise to Brynhild. He then fell in love with Gjuki's daughter, Gudrun. When Brynhild found out, she persuaded Gjuki's sons to kill Sigurd, which one of them, Guttorm, did by piercing Sigurd's one weak spot. But Brynhild repented and, overcome with guilt, she climbed onto Sigurd's funeral pyre.

### SIEGFRIED

The German myth of Siegfried, as told in the 13th-century *Nibelungenlied*, follows essentially the same story as here, but in the German version Sigurd is named Siegfried; Brynhild becomes Brünnhilde, and the hero is slain by another of Gjuki's sons. The 19th-century composer Richard Wagner read both myths when he wrote his cycle of four operas, *The Ring of the Niebelungs*.

**"Sigurd's helmet"** from the 7th-century Vendel boat grave in Sweden.

# BEOWULF

- 📖 Exploits of hero
- 🏴 England
- 🏛 Sweden, Denmark

✍ Anon, *Beowulf*

The epic poem *Beowulf,* written in Old English, tells the story of the hero of the same name, a warrior of a people called the Geats who lived in southern Sweden. Beowulf travels to the land of the Danes to rid their country of a monster called Grendel before returning to his own land and becoming its king. After a long and successful reign, Beowulf dies slaying another monster: a dragon that has been terrorizing his country.

### KEY CHARACTERS

**HROTHGAR** • *king of the Danes*
**BEOWULF** • *king of the Geats*
**GRENDEL** • *a monster*
**GRENDEL'S MOTHER**
**WIGLAF** • *Beowulf's comrade*

## PLOT SYNOPSIS

### SLAYING THE MONSTER

The Danish king Hrothgar's palace of Heorot and his people were under attack from a monster called Grendel for many years. Then a young Swede called Beowulf appeared, who offered to fight the monster, and killed it. The Danes rejoiced, and Beowulf was richly rewarded with gifts. But Grendel's fearsome mother then came to avenge her son's death. Beowulf went out to meet her at the lake by which she lived, fought her, and, when his own sword would not pierce her hide, slew her with a weapon from her own armoury.

**The legend of** Beowulf recounts the burial of the Danish king Scyld Scefing and his treasure under a mound like the one at Sutton Hoo in England.

Beowulf then returned to his own land, where he was made king. He ruled for 50 years, but when he was an old man, trouble came to his people, the Geats.

### AN OLD WARRIOR

A dragon guarding treasure grew angry when someone stole a piece of it, and turned on Beowulf's people in revenge. Beowulf, now an old man, attacked the dragon but could not penetrate the dragon's scaly skin. All his men fled in fear, except for brave and faithful Wiglaf. Together the pair attacked and killed the dragon, but not before it had poisoned Beowulf with its noxious breath. In his dying moments, Beowulf bequeathed his goods to Wiglaf.

*"...If you can forge the Sampo, brighten the bright-lid, you'll get the maid for your pay — for your work the lovely girl..."*

Elias Lönnrot, *Kalevala*

# THE KALEVALA

- 📖 National epic
- 📰 Finland
- 🏛 Finland
- ✍ Elias Lönnrot, *Kalevala*

## BEHIND THE MYTH

The Finnish scholar and folklorist Elias Lönnrot (1802–84) devoted much of his life to collecting the poetry, songs, and proverbs of the Finns, Lapps, and Estonians. Lönnrot travelled the country, listening to people singing and reciting, and wrote it all down. As well as writing various books of songs, proverbs, and traditional riddles, he combined much of the poetry into one continuous epic poem – Finland's national epic – which he called the *Kalevala*.

**Väinämöinen the hero** and musician famously played a harp-like instrument called a kantele, which he had fashioned from the jawbone of a giant pike. The kantele became the national instrument of Finland.

## A HEROIC EPIC

The *Kalevala* is a poem of more than 22,000 lines and tells many stories. It begins with a description of the creation of the world, and continues with accounts of the struggles between two countries: Kalevala, the land of the Finns, and Pohjola, in the Northland. The poem tells how the Maid of the North was wooed by three Finnish heroes: the seer Väinämöinen; the smith Ilmarinen, who forged the sky; and the adventurer Lemminkäinen. Central to the story is a mysterious object called the sampo, which is described as a mill that can produce flour, salt, and gold.

The *Kalevala* and its central character, the wise Väinämöinen, are enormously important to Finland. Lönnrot published the poem in 1835 when his country was forging its cultural identity as a nation. Like the Greek *Iliad* and *Odyssey*, and the Norse *Eddas*, the *Kalevala* gave the Finns a mythical, heroic history. It became a focus of national pride and an inspiration to Finnish artists, and helped establish Finnish as the national language.

### KEY CHARACTERS

**VÄINÄMÖINEN** • *a sage*
**ILMARINEN** • *a smith, Väinämöinen's brother*
**LEMMINKÄINEN** • *an adventurer*
**LOUHI** • *the queen of Pohjola*
**THE MAID OF THE NORTH** • *Louhi's daughter*

## PLOT SYNOPSIS

In the beginning there was no land, only sky and water. A duck, finding nowhere to settle, nested on the knee of Luonnotar, air-girl and water-mother. From her eggs Luonnotar made the land. Luonnotar was pregnant for 700 years without realizing it, until her son Väinämöinen climbed out of her body, already an old man. He defeated the frost giant Joukahainen in a musical contest, and was offered the giant's sister Aino as a prize. But she drowned herself rather than marry him, so Väinämöinen travelled to Pohjola, in the Northland, to find a bride.

On the way home he met Louhi's daughter, the Maid of the North, and asked her to marry him without the sampo. She agreed, provided that he performed a series of near-impossible tasks, including knotting an egg, peeling a stone, and splitting a hair using a blunt knife. But as he was making a boat from a weaving shuttle – the last task – he was distracted by spirits sent by Louhi and the task went unfinished. Undaunted, Väinämöinen continued his journey home where he asked his brother Ilmarinen, a great smith, to make the sampo for Louhi.

# "FAR AND WIDE THE NEWS IS HEARD... OF VÄINÄMÖINEN'S SINGING"

Elias Lönnrot, *Kalevala*

### VÄINÄMÖINEN IN THE NORTH

On his way to Pohjola, Väinämöinen had to swim for days, and was about to collapse with exhaustion when an eagle plucked him from the water and placed him on the shore. Soon afterwards he met Louhi, the ruler of Pohjola, who offered him her daughter in marriage if he could provide her with a sampo – a magic mill that could produce gold, flour, and salt. Agreeing to the challenge, Väinämöinen set off for home, where he intended to make the sampo.

Ilmarinen succeeded in making the sampo and then took it to Pohjola. Väinämöinen had forgotten that it was the maker of the sampo who would marry the Maid of the North, so his brother Ilmarinen and the Maid were married. Unfortunately they were not married for long because the Maid was trampled to death by her own cattle during a dispute with Kullervo (another of the *Kalevala*'s many characters). Ilmarinen returned to Finland as a widower and was reconciled with his brother Väinämöinen, who had resented the marriage. Ilmarinen told Väinämöinen that Louhi had refused to let him marry her other daughter, but

**Väinämöinen's mother** Luonnotar made the land, the sun, and the moon from the eggs of a wild duck that nested on her lap.

**Joukahainen's sister Aino** rejects Väinämöinen, thinking him too old. To escape marriage to him, she decides to join the water-maidens.

the people of Pohjola had kept the sampo. Thinking this unfair, the brothers decided to steal the device, so that prosperity would come to the people of Finland instead. Taking with them the adventurer Lemminkäinen, they boarded the shuttle-boat that Väinämöinen had finally completed.

### THE SAMPO DESTROYED

In the Northland, Väinämöinen made use of another of the *Kalevala*'s magical objects, a musical instrument similar to a harp, called a kantele. Its music had the power to enchant listeners and send them to sleep. When they arrived in Pohjola, Väinämöinen played his kantele, sending its ruler Louhi and all her people to sleep. The three adventurers stole the sampo and set sail for home, but Lemminkäinen sang a loud victory song as they sailed and woke Louhi, who sent storms to wreck their ship. As the ship was buffeted about, the sampo broke into pieces, which began to drift away.

### THE GIFTS OF VÄINÄMÖINEN

Väinämöinen rescued as many parts of the sampo as he could and took them back to Finland. Even the fragments would bring some prosperity to his country. By now a very old man, he prepared to die. He gave his country the magic of spring, to guard them against Louhi's attacks of cold weather, and he left them his kantele. Then he sailed away to a mysterious land between heaven and Earth, where – it is said – he still lives, ready to return if his people need him.

### ARTISTS' INSPIRATION

The *Kalevala* has inspired some of Finland's finest artists. The painter Akseli Gallen-Kallela often used its stories as subjects, as in the triptych above. The composer Sibelius (*right*) was inspired by the *Kalevala* to write a number of famous symphonic poems, such as *Luonnotar* (1913). Elias Lönnrot, who, during time spent as a district medical officer on the Finnish/Russian border, collected and wrote down the traditional poetry that would form the basis of his *Kalevala*, also found the time to write a practical medical book for Finnish peasants, and to master the kantele.

## THE SLAVIC GODS

The Slavic cultures of Eastern Europe had a thriving mythology before their conversion to Christianity, which occurred gradually between the 8th and 13th centuries. Sadly, very few of the Slavic myths were recorded in writing or in art, and much of what we know has been reconstructed from scraps of historical record and from the residue of pagan beliefs that survive in folklore.

### WHITE GOD, BLACK GOD

One of the most prominent features of Slavic mythology is its dualism. The world is seen as ruled by opposing deities of good and evil, a concept probably borrowed from the Zoroastrian and Manichaean mythology of ancient Persia. The Western Slavs called these deities the White God and the Black God – Byelobog and Chernobog – and believed in

**Thought by the ancient Slavs** to be the spent thunderbolts of the storm god Perun, these objects are in fact the fossils of belemnites – prehistoric relatives of squid.

an everlasting conflict between dark and light. Even after a thousand years of Christianity, Slavic creation stories often have God and the Devil creating the world together. For example, when God wanted to create the Earth, he sent the Devil to dive down into the primal ocean to

bring up the soil. The Devil obeyed, but as well as filling his hand, he also filled his mouth. The Devil watched as God sprinkled the soil he had carried up in his hand, making a perfectly flat Earth. When the Devil tried to speak, he choked on the soil he had hidden in his mouth. He fled in terror, coughing out earth that made the hills and mountains.

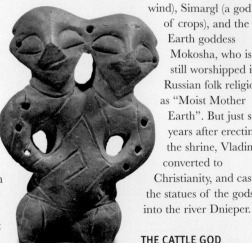

**A dual-headed** god is the subject of this ancient sculpture found near Novi Sad in Serbia.

### THE THUNDER GOD

The chief god of the pagan Slavs, known in Russia as Perun and in Lithuania as Perkun, was essentially a god of war, whose weapons were thunderbolts and lightning. Often described as the thunder god, Perun has been compared both to the Norse Thor and the Greek Zeus. It was by Perun that the Slavs swore their oaths of peace and war, believing that if they broke an oath to Perun they would die by their own weapons.

### CAST INTO THE RIVER

The six most important Slavic gods were depicted in a shrine built by Prince Vladimir of Kiev in 982. Alongside the statue of Perun were those of Khors (a sun god), Dazhbog (a god of fire and wealth, also said to be the sun), Stribog (god of the

**Elements of Perun survive** in the Russian mythical hero Ilya Muromets, shown here flanked by two fellow *bogatyrs*, or knights errant.

wind), Simargl (a god of crops), and the Earth goddess Mokosha, who is still worshipped in Russian folk religion as "Moist Mother Earth". But just six years after erecting the shrine, Vladimir converted to Christianity, and cast the statues of the gods into the river Dnieper.

### THE CATTLE GOD

The most important Slavic god not seen in Vladimir's shrine was Volos, the cattle god. The word for "cattle" also meant riches or money, and by extension Volos seems to have been the god of trading and wealth. In treaties, the names of Perun and Volos were invoked together to underpin promises of both peace and trade.

### GODS AND SAINTS IN RUSSIA

The period in which paganism and Christianity co-existed in Slavic culture has left a strong residue of pagan belief in Russian folklore. Volos the cattle god lived on in folk religion as St Vlasii, the patron saint of cattle. In the same vein Perun's function in sending thunder, lightning, and the rains was transferrred to the Prophet Ilya (Elijah). St George (Egorii) also inherited some aspects of Perun; he unlocked the Earth after the frosts of winter – a task formerly accomplished by Perun with the "golden key" of his lightning.

# THE GREAT FLOOD

📖 Creation and deluge
📕 Eastern Slovenia
🏛 Carniola, Slovenia

✍ A. H. Wratislaw, *Sixty Folk-tales from Exclusively Slavonic Sources*

This myth tells how the laziness of the first people caused a great flood that killed everyone except the watchman, Kranyatz. It is part of a cycle of myths that deal with the contests between Kranyatz and Kurent – the trickster – over who should rule the Earth. Kurent has been called the Slovenian Dionysus: the vine is his walking stick. Kurent uses the vine first to save Kranyatz, in the myth below, and then, in the myth opposite, to enslave him.

**KEY CHARACTERS**

**THE FIRST HUMANS** • *created from a drop of God's sweat*
**KURENT** • *the trickster, god of the vine; sometimes the predecessor of people on Earth*
**KRANYATZ** • *the watchman, sole survivor of the flood*

## PLOT SYNOPSIS

### FROM PARADISE TO DELUGE

The first humans enjoyed a life of paradisical ease in a valley where everything grew without the need for toil. The valley was irrigated by seven rivers that flowed from an egg, and was surrounded by high mountains. The people became very lazy and complacent: they could not even be bothered to pick the bread that grew on the trees, but instead set fire to the trees so that the bread fell into their hands. The people decided to break the egg and each take as much water as they wanted. The egg split with a roar like thunder and water poured from it, filling the valley, until there was nothing but an enormous lake.

### A SINGLE SURVIVOR

All the people died except Kranyatz, the watchman on guard on the highest mountain top. Kurent stretched down and held out his walking stick – a vine – to save Kranyatz, who clung to its tendrils for nine years until the flood waters receded, nourishing himself in the meantime on the vine's grapes.

# KURENT THE TRICKSTER

📖 Trickster
🏛 Eastern Slovenia
🏛 Carniola, Slovenia

✍ A. H. Wratislaw, *Sixty Folk-tales from Exclusively Slavonic Sources*

After he was saved from the flood by Kurent (*see opposite*), Kranyatz thanked the trickster as his preserver. This angered Kurent, who told him instead to thank the vine, and promise always to love its fruit above any other. This love of the fruit of the vine – which persists to this day – was to be the downfall of Kranyatz, and of humankind, for it enabled the trickster to overcome Kranyatz in a contest for rulership of the Earth.

**KEY CHARACTERS**

**KRANYATZ** • an early man, heroic in stature as all humans once were

**KURENT** • the trickster, god of the vine

**GOD** • the creator, whose every glance became a star

## PLOT SYNOPSIS

### A BATTLE FOR SUPREMACY

Kranyatz championed humanity to vie with Kurent over dominion over the Earth. Kurent devised a three-part contest to decide rulership. The first part of the contest – to decide who was to rule land and sea – was to leap over the ocean. While Kurent wet one foot in the water when he leapt on to dry land, mighty Kranyatz just stretched out his leg and stepped across. The second challenge – to decide dominion of the rock – was to split

**In Slovenian folk tradition,** masks depicting Kurent are still worn at festivals by the youngest and strongest of the men, who can bear the weight and heat of the sheepskin hoods.

the Earth: Kurent stamped his foot and broke through the Earth into a pit full of dragons, but Kranyatz again outdid the trickster, punching a hole that revealed underground rivers that ran with pure gold. The third trial, to decide dominion over the heavens, was also won by Kranyatz, who fired an arrow that flew for nine days – a whole day longer than Kurent's arrow.

### KURENT SUBMITS

"You are emperor of the world," conceded Kurent. Kranyatz, full of pride, climbed up the highest peak to sit at God's table, and began to eat meat that had been prepared for God. Kurent, declaring himself Kranyatz's servant, offered his master wine from his walking stick, the vine. The thirsty Kranyatz drank the wine and fell asleep. Finding a drunk Kranyatz at his table, God threw him down the mountain, where he lay for many years. When at last he revived, his strength had gone, and ever since then humans have been small and weak.

### A SLAVE TO WINE

Another form of this myth has Kranyatz fooled by Kurent's wine into ceding rulership. Kranyatz likes the wine so much that he tells Kurent, "Treat me with this wine, and rule both my body and soul, from henceforth forever".

# ASIA

T HE CONTINENT OF ASIA covers a vast area and is home to many peoples and cultures. Several of these cultures stand out because they have ancient roots, written traditions that go back many centuries, and particularly complex and fascinating mythologies. This chapter concentrates on four: the myths of China, Japan, India, and the ancient city-states of western Asia.

Although the civilizations of China, Japan, India, and western Asia are very different from one another, they are similar in that they all have huge numbers of gods and goddesses (so many that their numbers are sometimes described as infinite). From these a smaller number of major deities emerge as creators and powerful influences on humanity.

**A Thai depiction** of a monkey-warrior from the mythological Hindu epic the *Ramayana*.

## MESOPOTAMIA

The land around the Tigris and Euphrates rivers in what is now Iraq was the birthplace of one of the most distinctive early civilizations of the third millennium BCE. It was a culture of city-states, powerful kings, and huge temples known as ziggurats, which consisted of vast, stepped platforms of mud-brick. Ancient texts, written on clay tablets,

tell of the gods who were worshipped in these temples, and their stories make up one of the world's most ancient mythologies.

Different cities developed their own versions of the myths, often giving the deities slightly different names; for example, Inanna, goddess of sexual love, also appears as Ishtar. But there are also several common themes, such as creation from primal waters, divine laws that govern life, and the struggle of humans coping with their limitations as servants of the gods. Two of the problems they have to contend with – the Great Flood and the question of mortality – are dealt with in the area's most famous mythological text, the *Epic of Gilgamesh*.

## THE MYTHS OF INDIA

The complex body of belief that makes up Hinduism created an Indian mythology that seems one of the most complicated of all. There are said to be thousands of deities, and India's numerous languages and cultures date back thousands of years. But there is an underlying pattern that reveals a unity to this vast pantheon. All of creation, including the gods, are said to be aspects of one divine truth, known as Brahman, and three key gods – Brahma, Siva, and Vishnu – sit at the centre of the mythology. This core group of gods

**Gilgamesh, the hero** of a Mesopotamian epic and a precursor to the Greek Heracles, is shown here bearing a winged disc, perhaps a symbol of the sun.

is joined by one or two other deities such as the Great Goddess Devi, a figure with several names and forms.

Their stories have come down to us in a number of texts in the ancient Sanskrit language. The earliest are the *Vedas*, which were transmitted orally for centuries before being written down. Later collections such as the *Puranas* and the more ritual-based *Brahmanas*, plus the two vast epic poems, the *Ramayana* and *Mahabharata*, are also rich narrative sources for the Hindu gods.

## THE FAR EAST

The diversity of China's mythology comes from its ability to absorb stories from at least three different belief systems: the native Chinese traditions of Daoism and Confucianism, and the Buddhist faith, which came to China from India. The Chinese combined these influences to produce another vast collection of gods and goddesses. Their stories have come down to us in many texts, and also orally through the popular religion of Chinese communities around the world,

in which devotees pray or make offerings to gods and goddesses who control specific aspects of our lives.

The native religion of Japan, Shinto, also has many gods, or *kami*. These can be embodied in virtually any living thing, place, or phenomenon. Anything powerful or impressive – a tree, a mountain, an animal – can be a *kami*, and followers of Shinto speak of an infinite number of *kami*. Despite this, Japanese mythology concentrates on a handful of key deities, including a primal couple, Izanagi and Izanami, who create the world, or "invite it into being". Most important of all are their children: the sun goddess Amaterasu, whose descendants are said to have unified Japan, and her brother and rival, the storm god Susano.

**A Japanese** temple overlooking Mount Fuji, which was thought to be home to Kuni-toko-tachi, the Japanese Earth deity.

# THE SACRED DECREES

- 📖 Foundation
- ⚑ Sumer, southeastern Mesopotamia
- 🏛 The cities of Uruk and Eridu in Sumer

✍ Diane Wolkstein & Samuel Noah Kramer, *Inanna, Queen of Heaven and Earth*

Inanna, also known as Ishtar, is the most important goddess in Mesopotamian mythology. She is often referred to as "the goddess of love", but her name translates literally as "queen of heaven", and in fragments of poetry found on clay tablets dating to 4,000 years ago, she crowns herself queen of Earth. In this fragment she visits Enki, the god of wisdom, and wins from him the *me*, the sacred powers or laws that he used to establish order in the world.

### KEY CHARACTERS

**INANNA** • *goddess of love, queen of heaven and Earth*
**ENKI** • *god of the waters and of wisdom (in some fragments, Inanna's father)*
**ISIMUD** • *Enki's servant*
**NINSHUBUR** • *Inanna's servant*

## PLOT SYNOPSIS

### INANNA CLAIMS THE CROWN

Inanna, the goddess of love, picked up the crown of the Earth and placed it on her head. Then she lay back against an apple tree, and decided to go to Eridu to visit "…my father Enki, the god who knows the *me*, the sacred laws of heaven and Earth". When Inanna entered his holy shrine, Enki welcomed her with cakes, cold water to "refresh her heart", and beer, and they drank together at the table of heaven.

**Inanna valued** the gift of decision-making above all the other sacred powers.

### ENKI GIVES INANNA THE *ME*

Enki and Inanna toasted each other, and Enki, having drunk too much, offered his daughter Inanna the *me*. Fourteen times he raised his cup and ritually offered Inanna nearly 100 of his powers, including the high priesthood, the throne of kingship, the art of lovemaking, the mastery of power and truth, the giving of judgments, and the ability to descend to the Underworld and reascend to Earth. Inanna replied, "I take them!". Then she loaded the *me* into the Boat of Heaven and sailed with them towards her city of Uruk.

### ENKI SOBERS UP

When the effects of the beer wore off, Enki asked his servant Isimud to bring him the *me*, but Isimud told him: "You gave them to Inanna". Enki then sent Isimud after Inanna to fetch back the powers, and when Inanna refused to hand them over, he sent six terrifying demons after her. Inanna called on her servant Ninshubur to help her. Ninshubur sliced the air with her hand and sent the demons back to Eridu. With Ninshubur's help Inanna sailed the Boat of Heaven into Uruk, where there was rejoicing in the streets as Inanna placed the *me* in her holy shrine.

# SALT WATER AND SWEET WATER

- 📖 Creation; wars of the gods; city foundation
- ♙ Babylon
- 🏛 Babylon, Mesopotamia
- ✍ N. K. Sandars, *Poems of Heaven and Hell from Ancient Mesopotamia*; Stephanie Dalley, *Myths from Mesopotamia*

The creation epic of Babylon, the *Enûma Elish*, was recited at the New Year (spring equinox) festival in front of the statue of the god Marduk. It celebrates his victory over the god Tiamat, and his role in ordering and maintaining the universe. The rituals enacted at this time recreated Marduk's battle with Tiamat, and were supposed to ensure that the primeval forces of chaos would be kept in check, as the chant of creation puts it, "until time is old".

### KEY CHARACTERS

**APSU** • *the sweet ocean*
**TIAMAT** • *the salt ocean*
**MUMMU** • *the mist*
**ANU** • *god of the sky*
**EA** • *god of the Earth and water*
**MARDUK** • *son of Ea*
**KINGU** • *Tiamat's champion*

## PLOT SYNOPSIS

### THE TWO SEAS

At the beginning there were two seas, the sweet water and the salt, which were named Apsu and Tiamat. They were accompanied by a mysterious god named Mummu ("mist"). Apsu (the male) and Tiamat (the female) gave birth to two great gods: Anu, the god of the heavens, and Ea, the god of Earth and water.

A Mesopotamian priest prays before the symbols of Marduk, patron deity of the ancient city of Babylon.

and raised an army of monsters against Ea and Marduk. It was led by her champion Kingu, who fought with the Tablets of Destiny fastened to his breast.

### WAR AMONG THE GODS

Apsu and Tiamat were disturbed by the noise of the younger gods, and Apsu decided to destroy them. But Ea stepped in first, killing both Apsu and Mummu. He then created an underground chamber in which his son Marduk ("sun-child") was born. The enraged Tiamat turned into a dragon

### MARDUK VANQUISHES TIAMAT

Marduk agreed to fight Tiamat if the other gods accepted him as their king. He then attacked Tiamat and cut her into two halves, from which he formed the sky and the Earth. The rivers Tigris and Euphrates sprang from her eyes. Marduk then slew Kingu and used the Tablets of Destiny to establish the cosmos. He created mankind from Kingu's blood, and founded the city of Babylon to be the site of his temple.

**The Gate of Ishtar,** or Inanna, Sumerian goddess of fertility, was the eighth gate to the inner city of Babylon, which lay south of modern-day Baghdad in Iraq.

"*...He was wise, he saw mysteries and knew secret things, he brought us a tale of the days before the Flood...*"

The *Epic of Gilgamesh*

# THE EPIC OF GILGAMESH

📖 Culture hero; quest for immortality; flood
📍 Mesopotamia
🏛 Uruk, Mesopotamia
📜 The *Epic of Gilgamesh*

**Gilgamesh is the** tragic hero of the world's oldest surviving narrative poem. His fruitless quest for immortality assumed the status of legend in Mesopotamia.

## BEHIND THE MYTH

The Sumerian *Epic of Gilgamesh* dates back to around the 3rd millennium BCE, making it the oldest epic poem to survive. It has come down to us in fragmentary form on various clay tablets discovered by archaeologists in Mesopotamia (modern-day Iraq). The most complete set came from the library of the great Assyrian king Ashurbanipal, who ruled in the 7th century BCE and whose palace was at Nineveh – the oldest city of the ancient Assyrian empire. King Ashurbanipal sent his servants out to collect and translate texts from around the Mesopotamian world and the story of Gilgamesh was one of their greatest prizes. The Gilgamesh story became well known once more when British archaeologist Austen Henry Layard began excavations at Nineveh (now Mosul) in the 1840s, and found Ashurbanipal's tablets.

### THE WORLD'S FIRST TRAGIC HERO

In the poem, the hero Gilgamesh is king of Uruk (now called Warka), one of the greatest cities of Mesopotamia. Although there was a historical king called Gilgamesh, the hero of the poem is a mythical character who was part-god and part-man; he had the strength and beauty of a god, but he was doomed to die. The poem describes his adventures with his friend Enkidu, his encounter with the goddess Inanna, and his search for immortality.

The poem covers several of the great themes that were to inspire later writers: companionship in arms, the slaying of a monster, a great flood, the over-reaching hero, and the inevitability of death.

### KEY CHARACTERS

**GILGAMESH** • *king of Uruk*
**ARURU** • *goddess of creation*
**ENKIDU** • *Gilgamesh's friend and companion*
**HUMBABA** • *a monster*
**INANNA** • *goddess of love*
**ANU** • *god of heaven*
**SHAMASH** • *the sun god*
**SIDURI** • *goddess of wine and wisdom*
**UTNAPISHTIM** • *human survivor of the Great Flood*
**URSHANABI** • *the ferryman of the Underworld*

## PLOT SYNOPSIS

Gilgamesh was two-thirds god and one-third human. When he came to the throne of Uruk, he proved himself a tyrannical ruler, forcing the men of his kingdom into slavery and raping their women. The people prayed to the gods for help, and Aruru, the goddess of creation, responded. She made a wild man named Enkidu out of clay and sent him to fight and kill Gilgamesh. But when Gilgamesh heard about Enkidu, he merely decided to tame him. He started by sending a sacred prostitute of Inanna to seduce the wild man and show him the ways of civilization. The woman met Enkidu and persuaded him to leave the beasts of the countryside and go with her to Uruk. Enkidu, who was longing for

**Mesopotamia means** "the land between the rivers", and was often flooded by the Tigris and the Euphrates, making boats an essential part of life.

### A WINDOW ON THE UNDERWORLD

One of the Gilgamesh tablets describes an alternative version of the death of Enkidu. Inanna makes a ritual drum and drumstick from the wood of a tree. Gilgamesh drops them into the Underworld, but Enkidu offers to get them back. Gilgamesh warns him not to wear shoes or perfume, nor in any way to attract the ghouls, but Enkidu is too proud to do this, and is instantly captured. The god Ea makes a hole in the ground through which Enkidu's ghost appears and describes the sad souls of the dead.

male comradeship, agreed. When Enkidu arrived in Uruk and met Gilgamesh, the pair began to wrestle. As they fought they came to respect one another's strength, and saw there could be no winner. So they stopped fighting, embraced, and became friends.

### THE MONSTER HUMBABA

Unfortunately this meant that the city of Uruk was now troubled by both Gilgamesh and Enkidu. So the gods sent a monster called Humbaba to kill them both and free the people. Humbaba had a face of coiled intestines, breath of fire, and jaws like death itself, but was no match for Gilgamesh and Enkidu, helped by Shamash, the sun god. The monster suffered blow after blow, until he died.

## THE BULL OF HEAVEN

Angry that Gilgamesh had once more cheated death, the gods decided to defeat him through trickery. The goddess Inanna tried to seduce him, but he rejected her. She complained to the god Anu, who sent the bull of heaven to fight Gilgamesh and Enkidu, but they killed the bull and offered its heart to Shamash. Inanna then decided that she would defeat Gilgamesh and Enkidu herself. She began by killing Enkidu with a fever, sending him to join the bird-winged spirits in the house of dust, ruled over by the dread queen of the Underworld, Ereshkigal. The king was distraught: his friend had died, and he realized suddenly that he too would one day die. Gilgamesh began to ponder and desire the secret of immortality.

**Utnapishtim,** very like the Biblical Noah, survived a great flood with his family and with "the seed of all living creatures".

## THE STORY OF THE FLOOD

Gilgamesh asked Siduri, goddess of wine and wisdom, how to find Utnapishtim, the survivor of the Great Flood and the only human to be granted immortality. When he found him, Gilgamesh quizzed Utnapishtim about these events, and was told how the gods, angry at humankind's noisy and unruly behaviour, had decided to wipe out the mortals in a flood. But he himself had been saved because Ea, the god of water, had visited him in a dream and told him to build a boat. As he was still alive after the storm had subsided, the gods had granted him eternal life.

## THE PLANT OF ETERNAL LIFE

Utnapishtim told Gilgamesh to accept his fate, as nothing lasts forever. But he did reveal that there was a plant at the bottom of a lake in the Underworld which granted eternal youth. So Gilgamesh travelled to the lake, and, with the help of the boatman Urshanabi, dived in and found the plant. He then set off for Uruk, hoping to share the plant with his people and make them all immortal. But on the way he stopped at a lake to bathe, and a snake stole and ate the plant (which is why snakes can regenerate themselves by sloughing their skins). Gilgamesh returned to Uruk a desolate man, having lost both his friend and his only chance of immortality.

**RELATED MYTHS ▶** The Great Flood (*p.134*)

# THE WOOING OF INANNA

📖 Fertility
📍 Sumer, Mesopotamia
🏛 Sumer, Mesopotamia

✍ Diane Wolkstein & Samuel Noah Kramer, *Inanna, Queen of Heaven and Earth*; Samuel Noah Kramer, *Sumerian Mythology*

The myth of the marriage of Inanna, goddess of love, to the shepherd Dumuzi was central to Sumerian mythology. It describes how Inanna has to choose between the farmer and the shepherd for her husband, and the shepherd wins. Their sacred coupling was thought to ensure fertility, so it was re-enacted each new year by the king of Uruk and Inanna's high priestess. Another version of the myth uses the name Tammuz for Inanna's husband.

### KEY CHARACTERS

**UTU** • *the sun god*
**INANNA** • *Utu's sister, goddess of love and fertility*
**DUMUZI** • *the shepherd-god*
**ENKIMDU** • *the farmer-god*

## PLOT SYNOPSIS

### INANNA'S BRIDAL SHEET

The sun god Utu wove flax into a bridal sheet for his sister Inanna. "Who will be my husband?" asked Inanna. Utu replied that she was to marry Dumuzi, the shepherd. But Inanna was not happy with this choice. "The shepherd dresses in rough wool," she said. "I prefer the smooth flax that Enkimdu the farmer grows." Dumuzi and Enkimdu argued as to which of them was more fitted to be the husband of the goddess. Dumuzi provided the world with wool, milk, and cheese, while Enkimdu filled the granaries with grain, and provided flour, beer, and bread. Dumuzi was the most persuasive and won the day, but Inanna was not convinced until Dumuzi compared himself to her brother Utu, and filled her heart with longing.

### THE WEDDING

Inanna bedecked herself with jewels and anointed herself with oil, and the couple made passionate love in the bedchamber and in the garden. Inanna gave Dumuzi the kingship of Uruk and pledged the support of her strength and power. Then Dumuzi left her to take up the kingship, and Inanna was left alone with the sweet memories of their love.

# INANNA IN THE UNDERWORLD

- 📖 Death and resurrection; descent to the Underworld
- 🏛 Sumer, Mesopotamia
- 🏛 Sumer, Mesopotamia
- ✍ Diane Wolkstein & Samuel Noah Kramer, *Inanna, Queen of Heaven and Earth*

The descent of Inanna to the Underworld is one of the most powerful of all Mesopotamian myths. It has been interpreted as a rite of initiation into the mystery and power of womanhood. Inanna's reasons for descending to the Underworld are unclear; she feels impelled to go. Once there, she is brutally stripped of all she holds dear, and dies. Enki revives her, but she can return to the world of the living only if another takes her place.

> **KEY CHARACTERS**
>
> **INANNA** • *goddess of love and fertility*
> **ERESHKIGAL** • *Inanna's sister, Underworld queen*
> **NINSHUBUR** • *Inanna's servant*
> **DUMUZI** • *Inanna's husband*
> **ENKI** • *god of wisdom*

## PLOT SYNOPSIS

### INANNA FACES DEATH

Inanna, preparing to travel to the Underworld, told her servant Ninshubur: "I am afraid to enter that dark, parched land. I fear I will be buried in its dust." Nevertheless she descended. At each of seven doors she was progressively stripped of her clothes, her jewels, and the Tablets of Destiny which she carried, until she arrived naked and defenceless before the throne of Ereshkigal, her sister. The seven judges of hell sentenced her to death, and hung her corpse up on a spike.

**Astarte** was the Phoenician incarnation of Inanna, and was worshipped in Egypt, Ugarit, and Canaan.

### INANNA'S REBIRTH

Although Ninshubur pleaded with them, the gods refused to help Inanna, who had entered the Underworld of her own free will. Only Enki took pity on her. He made two creatures from the dirt under his fingernails, and sent them to Inanna with food and water to bring her back to life.

### INANNA SACRIFICES HER HUSBAND

The judges of hell refused to let Inanna return to the living world unless someone else took her place in the Underworld. Inanna would not let them take Ninshubur, nor her sons Shara and Lalal. "Take my husband, Dumuzi," she said. The Underworld demons set off in pursuit of Dumuzi, who was helpfully turned into a snake by the sun god Utu. But it was not enough. Inanna refused him protection and the demons caught him, beat him, bound him, and dragged him to the Underworld.

### THE FATE OF DUMUZI

Dumuzi (known to the Babylonians as Tammuz) was condemned to spend six months of each year in the Underworld. When he emerged, bringing the spring, his sister Geshtinanna took his place. His death and resurrection was marked by rituals which are mentioned in the Bible (*Ezekiel*, 8:14): "Then he brought me to the door of the gate of the Lord's house which was toward the north; and, behold, there sat women weeping for Tammuz."

**RELATED MYTHS** ▸ Demeter and Persephone (*p.54*)

# THE DEFEAT OF YAMM

📖 Wars of the gods      ✍ James B. Pritchard, *The Ancient Near East*;
📕 Ugarit                 S. H. Hooke, *Middle Eastern Mythology*
🏛 Canaan (northern Syria)

Ugaritic myth tells of the rivalry between Baal, god of fertility and of thunder and lightning, and Yamm (or Yam-Nahar), god of the seas and rivers. They were the two sons of the high god El (or Bull El) and his wife Ashtoreth. The myth is a symbolic tale of the contest between the destructive and creative powers of water.

### SIBLING RIVALRY

Yamm was jealous of his brother, and demanded that the gods make Baal his slave. The gods agreed, because they were frightened of Yamm's power. But the craftsman god Kothar (or Kothar-u-Khasis) gave Baal two weapons: Aymur ("driver") and Yagrush ("chaser"). Baal attacked Yamm with these weapons, and knocked him to the ground. He was going to kill him, but was restrained by their mother Ashtoreth, who said Yamm was now in the custody of the gods.

**The fertility god Baal** became king of the gods, and was also known as "Prince, Lord of the Earth".

# THE PALACE OF BAAL

📖 Wars of the gods      🏛 Mount Zaphon, Canaan (northern Syria)
📕 Ugarit                 ✍ James B. Pritchard, *The Ancient Near East*;
                              S. H. Hooke, *Middle Eastern Mythology*

After his victory over Yamm (*above*), Baal and his sister Anath asked the gods to allow them to build a palace on Mount Zaphon. The craftsman god Kothar designed a magnificent palace, but Baal objected to having any windows, as he feared that Yamm might spy on his concubines. Compromising, Kothar left just one window, so that Baal could still send down his rain, lightning, and thunder. His sister, the ferocious Anath, once held a great feast in the palace, to which she invited all of Baal's enemies. When they had assembled, she closed the door and slaughtered them all. It was said that she waded in blood up to her knees, and hung the heads of her victims around her neck.

**Baal's palace** lay to the north of the ancient city of Ugarit, now in Syria, where tablets describing these myths have been found.

# BAAL THE KING

📖 Wars of the gods
🏴 Ugarit

🏛 Mount Zaphon, Canaan (northern Syria)
✍ James B. Pritchard, *The Ancient Near East*;
S. H. Hooke, *Middle Eastern Mythology*

Having vanquished his brother and rival, the sea
god Yamm (*see opposite*), Baal proclaimed his enmity
for Mot, the god of death. Baal declared that he
would not send tribute to Mot, who was the new
favourite of the high god El. But the message that
Mot sent back (its content, sadly, unknown) was so
intimidating that Baal's resistance crumpled. Before
long, Baal himself was dead, and it took the courage
of his sister Anath to defeat Mot and revive Baal.

### KEY CHARACTERS

**BAAL** • *god of fertility*
**ANATH** • *Baal's sister,
goddess of love and war*
**MOT** • *god of death and
sterility*
**EL** • *the high god*
**SHAPASH** • *the sun goddess*

## PLOT SYNOPSIS

### BAAL'S DEFIANCE IS PUNISHED
"I will not pay tribute to Mot, however
much El loves him," said Baal. But Mot
thought, "I alone will rule both gods
and men". So Mot sent messengers to
Baal, with a message so terrifying that
Baal declared himself Mot's slave forever.

### DROUGHT AND FAMINE
When Baal at last came to die, the great
god El mourned him, and his sister
Anath carried his body to Mount
Zaphon for burial. For seven years
Baal lay dead. These were years of
drought and famine, for Mot was
the lord of the dry land of death.
Finally Anath, enraged, came
looking for her brother. When Mot
boasted that he had chewed Baal
up, Anath seized him, cut him with
her sword, winnowed him with
her fan, burned him with fire,
ground him in her hand-mill,
and sowed him in the ground.

### THE RETURN OF BAAL
Baal came back to life, but Mot was
also reborn, and soon they were fighting
again. They were eventually stopped by
Shapash, the sun goddess, who
persuaded them to take separate
kingships in the worlds above and below.

**When the great god El** learned that Baal was dead,
he left his throne to mourn him. He poured dust
on his head and cut his cheeks with a stone.

# THE VANISHING GOD

- 📖 Fertility
- 👤 Hittite culture, Anatolia
- 🏛 Anatolia, Middle East

- ✍ James B. Pritchard, *The Ancient Near East*;
  S. H. Hooke, *Middle Eastern Mythology*

Telepinu, the god of farming and fertility, had a terrible temper. One day he flew into an uncontrollable rage. "There must be no interference in my domain!" he shouted. He was so agitated that he put his right shoe on his left foot, and his left shoe on his right foot. Then he walked away and lost himself on the steppe. With Telepinu

gone, the logs in the hearth would not burn, the cows neglected their calves and the sheep their lambs, the grain would not grow, the springs dried up, and people ceased to procreate.

## STEALING HIS ANGER

The mother goddess Hannahanna sent her bee to find Telepinu and sting him on his hands and feet, to bring him back to himself. But he became angrier and more destructive than ever. The goddess of healing, Kamrusepa, was eventually able to leach the anger from him and redirect it to the netherworld, helped by humans performing a ritual with an eagle's wing. The doorkeeper of the netherworld opened its seven doors, and Telepinu's rage disappeared into the dark from which nothing returns. The fertility of the world was restored.

# DEFEATING THE DRAGON

- 📖 God versus monster; gods and mortals
- 👤 Hittite culture, Anatolia
- 🏛 Kiskilussa, Anatolia
- ✍ S. H. Hooke, *Middle Eastern Mythology*;
  Gary Beckman, *The Anatolian Myth of Illuyanka*

The storm god Teshub once fought a tremendous battle with the great dragon Illuyanka. Teshub was defeated by the dragon, and appealed to the other gods for help. Only his daughter Inara stepped forward, and she set about preparing a trap for the dragon. She asked a mortal man, Hupasiya, to help them, and he agreed on condition that she would sleep with him. She did so, and the three of them went together to the dragon's lair, where Inara filled some vessels with alcohol. She then used her beauty to entice

the dragon outside, where it drank the alcohol. Hupasiya tied up the dragon with rope, and then Teshub killed it.

## GODDESS AND MAN

Inara built a house in which to live with Hupasiya. She warned him never to look out, in case he saw his abandoned wife and children. But he did see them, and then begged Inara to let him return. It is unclear whether Inara let him go, but she did give her house to the king who established the Purulli festival, in which this myth features.

# THE TERRIBLE GODS

📖 Wars of the gods
🏛 Hurrian/Hittite cultures, Anatolia
🏛 Syro-Mesopotamia

✍ S. H. Hooke, *Middle Eastern Mythology*

One set of Hurrian and Hittite myths tells of a series of battles between fathers and sons. First the creator Alalu was displaced by his son Anu. He, in turn, was attacked by his son Kumarbi, who then spat out three gods, including the storm god Teshub. In order to counter Teshub, Kumarbi creates Ullikummi, the giant, who is ultimately defeated by the wisdom of the god Ea (showing the culture's debt to Babylonian mythology).

**KEY CHARACTERS**

**ANU** • *the sky god*
**KUMARBI** • *the son of Anu*
**ULLIKUMMI** • *a giant, son of Kumarbi*
**TESHUB** • *the storm god*
**UBELLURI** • *the god who holds up the world*
**EA** • *god of wisdom*

## PLOT SYNOPSIS

Kumarbi fathered a giant son called Ullikummi in the hope that he would be able to overcome the storm god Teshub. Kumarbi told the giant to sit on the right shoulder of Ubelluri, the god who holds up the Earth, and then to turn himself into a huge pillar of unbreakable rock. To the alarm of the gods, Ullikummi reached right up to heaven, and drove Teshub's wife Hebat from her temple. She complained to her husband, who sought help from Ea, the god of wisdom. Ea asked the gods why they

**Bulls lock horns,** symbolizing the conflict between the Hittite deities shown above them.

were allowing the world to be destroyed. Then he visited Ubelluri and told him to look over his shoulder so that he could see his monstrous new burden.

### THE GIANT TOPPLES

Ea used the copper knife with which they first severed Earth from heaven to cut loose Ullikummi's feet, and then Teshub gathered his thunder weapons and attacked him. Weakened, Ullikummi was still boasting that he would defeat Teshub to rule the world when the storm god finally killed him.

**RELATED MYTHS ▶** War of the gods and Titans (*p.38*)

### HITTITE CITIES

Little was known about the culture and history of the Hittites until 1906–7, when more than 10,000 clay tablets were found in the ruins of Hattasha (now Boghazköy), in Turkey, inscribed with Hittite and Hurrian mythology. Many of the tablets were broken, so the myths we have inherited are fragmentary. At the heart of Hattasha are the ruins of the vast main temple complex, where the Hittite king came to pay homage to the gods, in the hope that they would look favourably on his empire and people.

# THE WISE LORD

📖 Creation; good and evil; the end of the world
🏛 Persia

🏛 Persia
📚 Mary Boyce, *Textual Sources for the Study of Zoroastrianism*; R. C. Zaehner, *Zurvan*

Zoroastrianism was the ancient pre-Islamic religion of Persia, founded by the prophet Zoroaster in the 6th century BCE. The Persian language was close to that used in northern India, and Zoroastrian teachings are contained in the Indo-Iranian sacred texts of the *Avesta* and the *Gatha*. They contain the archetypal story of the struggle between good and evil, which will be resolved only by the appearance of the saviour, Saoshyant, and the end of time.

> **KEY CHARACTERS**
>
> **ZURVAN** • *the primal being*
> **AHURA MAZDA** • *the creator and wise lord*
> **AHRIMAN** • *the destructive spirit*
> **MASHYA AND MASHYOI** • *the parents of humanity*
> **SAOSHYANT** • *the saviour*

## PLOT SYNOPSIS

### THE PRIMAL VOID

In the beginning there was only the god Zurvan ("Time"), an androgynous deity who existed in the primal void. Zurvan longed for a son, and offered to sacrifice 1,000 years in order to create one. But as the time drew towards its end, he began to doubt his power of creation. Hence he conceived twins, one born of doubt, the other of optimism.

**Mithra was** the Persian god of light, who maintained cosmic order. Some said he was the son of Ahura Mazda, the world's creator.

### THE TWINS

Before the twins were born, Zurvan predicted that the first-born would rule the world. One of the unborn twins, Ahura Mazda, heard this, and told his wicked brother Ahriman, who then forced his way out first. He told Zurvan: "I am your first-born, Ahura Mazda."

But Zurvan was not fooled. "He is light and fragrant," he said, "but you are dark and stinking." Zurvan wept.

### THE CREATION

Ahura Mazda, the wise and all-knowing, made the sun, the moon, and the stars, and the Good Mind that works within man and all creation. Ahriman attacked him with demons, but Ahura Mazda banished him to the darkness. Then Ahura Mazda created the first man, Gayomart, and the world would have been perfect, but the malicious Ahriman broke through the sky in a blaze of fire, bringing with him starvation, disease, pain, lust, and death.

He defiled everything he touched, and rejoiced as he did so. "My victory is perfect," he crowed. "I have fouled the world with filth and darkness, and made it my stronghold. I have dried up the Earth, so that the plants will die, and poisoned Gayomart, so he will die."

### HELL ON EARTH
Gayomart did indeed die, but Ahura Mazda created the mother and father of humanity – Mashya and Mashyoi – from Gayomart's seed. All humans are descended from them, and are born good, but Ahura Mazda leaves them free to choose between good and evil. Ahura Mazda could not defeat Ahriman, so he set a limit to time, and trapped Ahriman inside creation. Ahriman was unable to escape, and will remain in the world doing evil until the end of time. Ahura Mazda does his best to counter this with the help of seven gods including Mithra, the sun god, said to be his son.

### THE COMING OF THE SAVIOUR
As the end of time draws near, the saviour Saoshyant will arise. He will prepare the world to be made anew, and help Ahura Mazda destroy Ahriman. People will become pure: they will stop eating and drinking, until at last they survive on air. Ahura Mazda will cast Ahriman from creation, time will come to an end, and the world will begin again, but this time it will be perfect. Saoshyant will raise the dead, and Ahura Mazda will marry body to soul.

# THE BIRTH OF BRAHMA

📖 Origin of the cosmos     📕 *Rig Veda*
📜 India
🏛 The cosmos

In ancient Hindu mythology there is a supreme god called Prajapati, Lord of the Universe, an eternal and uncreated deity who exists before all else. It is Prajapati who begins the process of creating the cosmos by bringing Brahma, the creator god, into existence. In later myths (*see opposite*), Prajapati merges with Brahma, who is one of the three most powerful Hindu deities, together with Vishnu (the preserver) and Siva (the destroyer).

## PLOT SYNOPSIS

### BORN FROM THE LOTUS
Prajapati, Lord of the Universe, meditated, and as he meditated a seed appeared in his navel. A lotus tree sprouted from the seed and as it grew, the tree was bathed in brilliant light. From this lotus and the light around it, Brahma was born. The light spread out through the cosmos and Brahma spread with it and mixed with it, so that Brahma became the essence of all things and the power contained within them. Brahma also became the essence of time – a single day of his life lasts 4,320 million human years. When these millions of years have passed, the cycle of creation will start again and a new age of the cosmos will begin.

### RIDING A SWAN
A divine swan serves as Brahma's vehicle. The swan has a magical ability to distinguish pure milk from water in a mixture of the two. Similarly, we must see that good and evil are intertwined in our universe, and learn to separate the two, keeping what is valuable and discarding that which is worthless.

### MOUNT MERU
The dwelling-place of the Hindu gods is said to be Mount Meru, a golden mountain at the centre of the world. Early accounts say Indra the sky god built his paradise at the top, while later versions place Brahma's palace at the summit, with those of Vishnu, Krishna, and other gods lower down. The mountain rested on seven lower worlds, all supported by the great serpent Vasuki.

**The soaring towers** of Hindu temples are said to represent the magnificent Mount Meru, whose foothills are the Himalayas.

# BRAHMA CREATES THE COSMOS

📖 Creation     ✍ *Rig Veda*
🚩 India
🏛 The cosmos

Hindu mythology, as one of the world's oldest and most diverse, has many different creation myths. In one, a divine carpenter constructs the universe and everything within it. In others, a primal god and goddess mate to produce the other deities. But the most persistent myth involves the creator god Brahma (also known as Prajapati), who uses both his meditative power and his sexuality to create everything, from the dawn to plants and people.

**KEY CHARACTERS**

**BRAHMA** • *the creator, first god of the Trimurti*
**THE DAWN** • *Brahma's daughter*
**THE NIGHT** • *Brahma's ignorance*

## PLOT SYNOPSIS

### BRAHMA MEDITATES

First of all Brahma contemplated the cosmos, which was nothing but swirling chaos without shape. As Brahma meditated, the cosmos began to take shape; order started to be revealed from chaos. But the creator realized that he still did not know what the universe would be like, and his very ignorance turned into a dark being, which Brahma then threw away in disappointment. This being turned into Night. Some say that as he continued to meditate, Brahma produced a succession of further beings, from the stars to the gods, before he produced a beautiful daughter, the Dawn.

### THE PROGENY OF BRAHMA

When Brahma saw his beautiful daughter the Dawn, he became sexually aroused. He made advances to her, but she turned herself into a deer. Brahma responded by transforming himself into a stag. According to one version of the story, Brahma's daughter would still not let him mate with her; he spilled his seed on the ground and this grew into the first man and the first woman. In the other version of the myth, the pair mated again and again, continuously changing their form, so that their

children became the first members of every animal species on the planet. When creation was complete, Brahma took up his dwelling on top of Mount Meru, although he is also said to be everywhere. He continues to meditate to give strength to the universe.

**Gods and other characters** of Hindu mythology depicted on the exterior of a temple in India. Most of the early Vedic gods represented natural forces.

# THE SOURCE OF SIVA'S STRENGTH

☐ Wars of the gods    ✍ *Mahabharata* (*see also pp.168–9*)
📖 India
🏛 The cosmos

Siva is the second god of the Hindu Trimurti, or triad of gods, and he is referred to as "the destroyer". His destructive power is balanced by his power to create, just as his savage dancing is complemented by a love of meditation and his quick judgment is tempered by mercy. Siva always had great strength and was powerfully armed, but he increased his strength by tricking the other gods when they were under attack from demons and needed his help.

**KEY CHARACTERS**

**BRAHMA** • *the creator, first god of the Trimurti*
**SIVA** • *the destroyer, second god of the Trimurti*
**A GROUP OF DEMONS**

## PLOT SYNOPSIS

### GODS VERSUS DEMONS
A group of demons, hungry for power, talked Brahma into giving them three of the strongest castles that had ever been built. They could be taken only by a god, using just one arrow. Once the demons were installed in their castles, the gods realized that none of them had an arrow that was powerful enough to destroy these strongholds. The demons were also aware of this, and soon began to attack the gods. Siva the destroyer was the strongest of the gods, so the other deities turned to him for help. He offered to lend them half his strength, but this did not work. To be an effective weapon, strength needs to be balanced by control, and none of the other gods had the ability to control even half of Siva's strength.

**Worshippers make** votive offerings during the Sivaratri festival – the most important celebration of Siva in the Hindu calendar.

### SIVA'S STRATAGEM
So Siva came up with a different plan. If the gods combined all their strength and then lent him half of it, he would be even stronger, and he would be able to control this enormous force. They would be able to defeat the demons. The gods agreed and Siva concentrated all of his new, combined strength into shooting a single arrow, which defeated the demons. When the war was over, the gods asked for their strength back, but Siva refused. He had become the most powerful of all the gods and he has kept it that way ever since.

# SIVA AND DAKSHA

📖 Loves and wars of the gods        📜 *Devibhagavata Purana*
🏴 India
🏛 The cosmos

One of the most famous myths featuring Siva concerns the god's feud with Brahma's family. It began when Siva cut off one of Brahma's heads and was banished from heaven. He then made trouble for Daksha, Brahma's son, and tricked his way into a marriage with Daksha's daughter. Far from bringing about reconciliation, the marriage enhanced the bad feeling between them. Only the intervention of Vishnu prevented a tragedy.

### KEY CHARACTERS

**BRAHMA** • *the creator, first god of the Trimurti*
**SIVA** • *the destroyer, second god of the Trimurti*
**VISHNU** • *the preserver, third god of the Trimurti*
**DAKSHA** • *Brahma's son*
**SATI** • *Daksha's daughter*

## PLOT SYNOPSIS

### SIVA'S TRICKERY

When Siva cut off one of the heads of Brahma, the other gods banished him from heaven. So when Daksha arranged a betrothal party for his daughter Sati, Siva was not invited. At the climax of the party, Daksha asked Sati to select her chosen husband from the assembled gods by throwing a garland. As Sati launched the garland into the air, Siva appeared and snatched it. So the two had to marry, much to the displeasure of Daksha, who continued to rail against Siva.

**Siva dances** toward cosmic destruction encircled by fire and stamping on a small man, symbolizing ignorance.

### DEATH AND DESTRUCTION

Sati hated the feud between Siva and Daksha and became more and more unhappy. Finally, as the pair continued to insult each other, she threw herself on to the sacrificial fire. Siva blamed Daksha, and attacked him in fury, chopping off his head. Then he sent demons to heaven to find Sati's body,

and when they brought it back, Siva danced the Tandav – the dance of death – with her corpse. The purpose of this dance was to bring about the end of the cosmos, and Siva, in his intense grief over the loss of his wife, was performing it before its time.

### SATI BECOMES PARVATI

The gods became very concerned, and when Vishnu (the preserver) observed what was happening, he intervened. He brought about the rebirth of Siva's wife as Parvati, a goddess even more beautiful than Sati had been, and the perfect wife.

With his wife restored to him, Siva decided to restore her father Daksha to life, but found that he could not give his father-in-law back his own head because the demons had stolen it. Instead he used the head of the nearest available creature, a goat. This did little to endear Siva to Daksha and they remained enemies.

# THE GENTLE GODDESS

📖 Loves of the gods    ✍ *Markandeya Purana*
📕 India
🏛 Mount Meru

Just as the many Hindu gods are all aspects of one ultimate truth, Brahman, so all the goddesses come together in one figure, the Great Goddess Devi. In her many roles she is also known as the peaceful mother goddess Uma, and the shining Jagadgauri ("light of the world"). But she is best known as Parvati, Siva's wife, the goddess who balances his destructive character with her sweet nature, bringing peace and harmony to the world.

> **KEY CHARACTERS**
>
> **SIVA** • *the destroyer*
> **PARVATI** • *the Great Goddess (also known as Devi, Sati, Uma, and Jagadgauri)*
> **SKANDA** • *Siva's son*
> **GANESHA** • *Parvati's son*

## PLOT SYNOPSIS

### SIVA'S CONSORT

When Siva's first wife, Sati, committed suicide (*see p.159*), she was reincarnated in the form of the gentle Parvati. The couple's relationship was not always an easy one, because of Siva's temper and Parvati's playfulness. On one occasion Parvati covered Siva's eyes with her hands, but this simple gesture brought darkness to the world and made her husband furious – he quickly made another eye appear in the middle of his forehead.

**Parvati and Siva** symbolize the power of marital bliss and its potential as a civilizing force.

Other myths tell how Parvati once exasperated Siva by falling asleep as Siva was explaining the scriptures to her, and how the couple fell out over a game of dice. But usually Siva's consort had a calming influence on him.

### SKANDA THE DEMON-SLAYER

The gods feared that the offspring of Siva and Parvati would be frighteningly powerful. So as the couple made love, the gods interrupted them, causing Siva's semen to spill into the Ganges, where it was fertilized. Skanda, god of war, was born, and he grew up to defeat a demon called Taraka, who was threatening to destroy the world. His bravery was rewarded by the gods, who made him their general, and by Parvati, who accepted him as her child.

### GANESHA THE ELEPHANT GOD

Parvati's other son, Ganesha, had an equally unusual birth. The goddess wanted a son to protect her, so she formed him from bath oil and the scrapings from her body when she was bathing. But when Ganesha prevented Siva from entering Parvati's room – acting as her protector – the god was angered, and knocked off Ganesha's head in fury. Parvati was distraught, so Siva replaced the head with the nearest one he could find: that of an elephant. Ganesha has had the head of an elephant ever since, and as a god is always invoked as "the remover of obstacles".

# DURGA THE WARRIOR

- Wars of the gods
- India
- The cosmos

✍ *Markandeya Purana*

In her role as warrior, the Great Goddess Devi is known as Durga ("the unapproachable"). In this form, she commands cosmic power, embodying all the warlike energy of the universe in a being more awesome than any other god. Most of the time she seems calm and serene, but Durga has the ability to change shape, to use any weapon, and even to turn herself into a mighty army in order to rid the world of the most threatening demons.

**KEY CHARACTERS**

**DURGA** • *the unapproachable (a form of the Great Goddess)*
**DURGA** • *a demon king*

## PLOT SYNOPSIS

### DURGA AND THE DEMONS

Durga defeated many demons. One of the most terrible was a demon king – also, curiously, named Durga – who had conquered the entire cosmos and thrown the gods from their palaces.

**Dancers align themselves** to re-enact one of Durga's many transformations, growing a multitude of arms with which to fight a demon.

**THE MANY FORMS OF DEVI**

The Great Goddess has a number of benevolent forms who are popular in India, especially among women devotees. As the goddess of the subcontinent's most sacred river, she is Ganga and blesses all who bathe in the Ganges. As the wife of Brahma, she is called Sarasvati, inventor of Sanskrit and goddess of the arts and language. Perhaps the most popular of all her forms is Lakshmi, goddess of good fortune, who is said to bring prosperity to all her worshippers.

In despair they asked Durga for her help, offering her all their strength and a choice of their weapons. She fought the demon alone, facing his armies of millions made up of horsemen, charioteers, elephant-riders, and infantrymen, by transforming herself into an army of millions and slaughtering the demon's men. She then faced the demon in single combat, growing a thousand arms so that she could force him to the ground and stab him to death.

## THE AVATARS OF VISHNU

Vishnu, the protector, is the third god of the Hindu triad. Some of the early myths describe him taking part in the creation. One describes how a lotus from his navel unfolds, holding Brahma, while another tells how his three strides defined the worlds of the humans and the gods. But the most famous myths describe his ten avatars, the forms in which he comes to Earth to protect it from danger or evil.

### PROTECTORS AND WARRIORS

The avatars are earthly forms of the god Vishnu. In his first three avatars, or forms, Vishnu visited Earth to protect the world from a series of natural disasters.

Vishnu surrounded by avatars in a lotus flower, an allusion to the birth of Brahma (*see p.156*).

As Matsya, the fish, he warned Manu, the first man, of the Great Flood, so that Manu could build a boat to survive. As Kurma, the tortoise, Vishnu took Mount Mandara on his back when the gods churned the ocean to produce the elixir of life. As Varaha, the boar, he raised the Earth out of the water, so that it could survive another inundation. The next three avatars – Narasimha the man-lion, Vamana the dwarf, and Parashurama the brahmin – saved the world by defeating various enemies, including demons and warriors.

Vishnu, the supreme god and preserver of the Earth, is here revelling in music played by one of the royal musicians.

## THE MYSTICAL AVATARS

The final two avatars of Vishnu have a more spiritual aspect. The first is the Buddha, the great religious leader and teacher who left behind a life of riches and privilege to find spiritual fulfilment. He shows people the path to enlightenment and cunningly misleads evil-doers so that they will be punished.

The final avatar has not yet appeared. His name is Kalkin. It is said that he will appear riding a white horse, banish evil, and begin a new golden age.

## RAMA AND KRISHNA

The seventh avatar, Lord Rama, is one of the greatest heroes in Hindu mythology. a warrior who destroys the evil king of Lanka. His story is told in the great Hindu epic, the *Ramayana* (*see pp.164–7*). Next Vishnu came to Earth as Krishna, destined to defeat evil demons and worshipped as a god in his own right. Krishna is also famous for his lovers, especially the faithful Radha, whose adoration of him is seen as a perfect example of how a worshipper should love a god.

When the world was created, a huge serpent called Shesha came out of the water, and became a favourite resting-place for Vishnu.

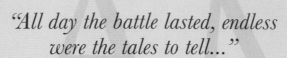

"All day the battle lasted, endless were the tales to tell..."

The *Ramayana* (19th-century translation)

# THE RAMAYANA

- Hero's adventures
- India
- India, Sri Lanka
- The *Ramayana*

**The adventures of Rama,** the seventh incarnation of Vishnu, are the subject of the *Ramayana* epic. Pictured opposite is the monkey-warrior Hanuman, an important ally of Rama in his quest to rescue his wife from the clutches of the evil giant Ravana.

## BEHIND THE MYTH

One of the two great Hindu epics, the *Ramayana* is a poem of some 50,000 lines, which was written in the language of Sanskrit and assembled around 200 BCE. It is said to be the work of the poet Valmiki, who gathered together many different myths and characters – some from the oral tradition, and some from earlier writings, such as the *Vedas* – and moulded them into a whole.

The *Ramayana* centres on the earthly life of Rama, the seventh avatar of the god Vishnu (*see pp.162–3*). Each of the poem's seven books concentrates on one aspect of Rama's life, but the core story concerns his love for the beautiful and virtuous princess Sita. It includes her abduction by the demon Ravana, and her rescue, as Rama defeats the demon.

### A GOD WITH HUMAN FLAWS

The key characters of this narrative are all shining examples of virtue. But like all the most interesting heroes, Rama is flawed. His unfounded jealousy and suspicion of Sita brings about some of the key events in the story. He is inclined to be pompous; he sometimes cares more about appearances than he does for his own or Sita's happiness. Only at the end of the poem, when he is reunited with Sita in heaven, does he completely understand his status as a god, and the true value of his relationship with his wife.

As befits a work that is both a gripping adventure story and a work of moral seriousness, the *Ramayana* has immense significance in Hinduism. Rama is widely revered as a husband who, unlike many other Hindu gods, remains faithful to a single wife.

### KEY CHARACTERS

**RAMA** • *seventh avatar of Vishnu*
**SITA** • *Rama's wife*
**LAKSHMAN** • *Rama's brother*
**SURPA-NAKHA** • *a demon*
**RAVANA** • *Surpa-nakha's brother, a demon*
**SUGRIVA** • *king of the monkeys*
**HANUMAN** • *monkey-hero*

**PLOT SYNOPSIS**

Rama was the eldest son of King Dasharatha of Ayodhya. He grew up happily at his father's court, but as a young man he travelled to the court of King Janaka, where he met the king's daughter Sita, and fell in love with her. King Janaka held an archery contest to help Sita choose a husband, and Rama won. He was the only person there who could draw the heavy bow, a weapon that had once belonged to the god Siva. Rama claimed his bride, and at first their marriage was an ocean of calm and happiness.

### RAMA'S WIFE IS ABDUCTED

After a while Rama unreasonably suspected Sita of being unfaithful, and the couple argued. As a result they found themselves banished to the forest, where they were joined by Rama's faithful brother Lakshman. While

> ### HANUMAN, THE MONKEY-GENERAL
>
> The monkey Hanuman, a mixture of hero and trickster, is one of the best-loved characters in the *Ramayana*, partly because of his devotion to Rama. He finds healing herbs when Rama is injured, and at one point opens his skin to reveal Rama and Sita sitting in his heart. Hanuman is also admired because he can turn the tables on his enemies. When his tail is set on fire by the demon Ravana, he waves his burning tail around, setting alight Ravana's fortress and the city of Lanka.

to Sita's aid, fighting off the demon and injuring her. Raising the stakes, Surpa-nakha complained to her brother Ravana, mightiest of all the demons, and Ravana hatched a plan to kidnap Sita and defeat Rama for good. Ravana knew of Rama's passion for hunting, so he disguised one of his

## "TRUTHFUL STILL IN DEED AND WORD, SITA IN HER SILENT SUFFERING SORROWS FOR HER ABSENT LORD."

The *Ramayana* (19th-century translation)

they were living in the forest, a female demon called Surpa-nakha saw Rama and fell in love with him. Rama rejected the demon's advances, so in a fit of rage, she attacked Sita. Lakshman came

demons as a deer, and while Rama was out hunting the demon-animal, Ravana pounced on Sita and carried her off to his palace in Lanka. When Rama returned from the hunt to find his wife abducted, he was distraught, but a spirit whom he had helped advised him to go to the monkey-king Sugriva for assistance. Sugriva was looking for an ally to win back his kingdom, which had been taken by Balin, his half-brother. Rama helped King Sugriva fight

**Rama was helped** in his fight against the demons by his favourite brother, Lakshman.

**Rama and his brother** Lakshman receive envoys in a scene from the *Ramayana* reflecting their debt to the monkey-army in winning back Sita from Ravana.

Balin and take back his throne. In return Sugriva offered Rama the services of his general, Hanuman, to accompany him to Lanka and rescue Sita. Hanuman was a monkey whose magical powers included the ability to fly, enabling him to find the imprisoned woman quickly. Hanuman's army of monkeys then built a bridge across the sea to Lanka and attacked the palace. Rama killed Ravana, Sita was rescued, and the couple returned home.

## SITA'S EXILE AND DEATH

After Rama and Sita returned to the kingdom of Ayodhya, there were unfounded rumours that Sita had been unfaithful to her husband while in captivity. Rama became suspicious, and finally decided to send her into exile. In exile Sita met the sage Valmiki (reputedly the author of the *Ramayana*) and gave birth to her twin sons in his hermitage.

Rama did not meet the boys until they were adults, when he immediately recognized them as his own sons, and summoned his wife back to the palace. Sita returned but, still unhappy, called to Mother Earth to take her to her bosom as proof of her faithfulness. As she spoke the earth opened in front of her, and she fell into the ground. Rama, saddened that his jealousy had brought about her loss, threw himself after her. The pair were reunited in heaven, where they lived in peace.

# THE MAHABHARATA

📖 Wars of the ancestors    ✍ *Mahabharata*
𝐏𝐔 India
🏛 Bharata (Upper India)

The *Mahabharata* is the second of the two great
Indian epic poems. It was compiled by a number
of anonymous writers, despite being attributed
both to the sage Vyasa and the god Ganesha. It
includes dozens of stories, but its main plot deals
with the rivalry between two ruling families. The
epic is especially precious because it includes a poem
called the *Bhagavad Gita* ("Song of the Lord"),
containing the teachings of Krishna.

### KEY CHARACTERS

**THE PANDAVAS** • *sons of
King Pandu*
**THE KAURAVAS** • *sons of
King Dhritarashtra*
**KRISHNA** • *avatar of Vishnu
(see pp.162–3)*
**YUDHISTHIRA** • *leader of
the Pandavas*

## PLOT SYNOPSIS

### RIVALS FOR THE KINGDOM

When King Pandu of Bharata
died, he left his kingdom to
the eldest of his five sons,
Yudhisthira. But this boy
and his brothers (together
known as the Pandavas)
had rivals for power in
their 100 cousins, the
Kauravas, who were sons
of a blind king called
Dhritarashtra. They were
also the incarnations of
demons who were enemies
of the gods.

**Ganesha,** the god of prosperity,
is traditionally named as the
author of the *Mahabharata*.

The Kauravas first tried
to get hold of the throne
by trickery, cheating Yudhisthira out of
his kingdom in a game of dice and
banishing the Pandavas. The Pandavas
eventually returned, but the Kauravas
would not yield the kingdom to them.

they could either have the
backing of his vast army
or his help in person.

Duryodhana chose
to have Krishna's army,
while Arjuna asked for
the support of Krishna
himself. As a result
Krishna decided to be
Arjuna's charioteer.
Arjuna, a gentle prince,
did not really want to go
to war. To spur him on
Krishna recited the
*Bhagavad Gita* to him.
The poem explained that
everything is the result of
immutable fate. The soldier must fight
and his victim must die: this is their
destiny. Krishna's words reconciled
Arjuna to the fighting.

### KRISHNA AND ARJUNA

The two sides prepared to fight for
the kingdom. At this point Krishna,
the eighth avatar of the god Vishnu,
intervened. He was related to both
families, and met with the two sides'
military leaders: Yudhisthira's brother
Arjuna, and Duryodhana, leader of the
Kauravas. He offered them a choice:

## THE CONCEPT OF MAYA

The Hindu concept of *maya* means "illusion". For the gods, things that do not last are *maya*: only the eternal is real. Savitri, one of the characters in the *Mahabharata*, loses her husband, Satyavan, to Death. When Death offers her a favour, she asks for life for herself. But life for her is complete only with Satyavan, so he must be revived. Savitri concludes that, to a truly wise person, Death himself is *maya*, and the living spirit is real.

**The myth of Savitri** (*right*) is one of the multiple narratives embedded within the *Mahabharata* and illustrates true devotion.

### THE GREAT BATTLE

The Pandavas fought a long and bloody battle with the Kauravas. The fighting lasted for 18 days and many people on both sides were killed. The Pandavas were victorious because they had Krishna himself on their side, but they lost many members of their own family. The surviving Kauravas, including Dhritarashtra, went into exile.

### LEAVING THIS WORLD

Feeling remorseful for all the killing, Yudhisthira decided to make a pilgrimage to the palace of the gods on Mount Meru. His brothers and their "collective wife" Draupadi went with him. With Krishna's blessing they installed Parikshit, Arjuna's grandson, as ruler of Bharata, and set off. The journey nearly defeated them. Only Yudhisthira reached the gate of heaven unscathed, and he refused to enter until he was sure that his brothers and Draupadi could enter too.

**The *Mahabharata*,** written between the fourth and fifth centuries ce, is still performed worldwide, as here in a Thai production.

# LORDS OF THE EARTH

📖 Creation
🪕 Baiga, central India
🏛 The Mandla hills, Madhya Pradesh, India

🖋 Verrier Elwin, *The Baiga*;
*Myths of Middle India*

Verrier Elwin, the great authority on the Baiga people of the Mandla hills in India, writes: "Of all the tribes I know, they are the most possessed by their mythology". That mythology places the Baiga at the very heart of Earth's creation, and makes them lords of the animals. Nanga Baiga and his sister Nanga Baigin help the Earth's creator to stabilize the Earth; in return their people are given power over the Earth and animals forever.

## KEY CHARACTERS

**BHAGAVAN** • *the creator*
**KARICAG** • *the crow, daughter of Bhagavan*
**NANGA BAIGA** • *Earth's stabilizer, later lord of the Earth*
**NANGA BAIGIN** • *Nanga Baiga's sister and helper*

## PLOT SYNOPSIS

### BHAGAVAN MAKES THE WORLD
In the beginning there was nothing but water. There was no choice of god, no wind, no land, no jungle. Bhagavan floated on the water on a great lotus leaf, alone. One day he rubbed his arm, and with the dirt that came off it he made a crow, his daughter Karicag.

He told her: "Go and find some Earth for me. I am lonely. I want to make a world."

Karicag flew and flew until she dropped onto the back of the great tortoise, Kekramal Chattri. Together, they persuaded the twelve brothers who first smelted iron to make them an iron cage, in which they were lowered to the bottom of the sea. There they found the worm, Gichnaraja, who had swallowed the Earth. Karicag and Kekramal Chattri frightened the worm into vomiting up the Earth.

### TRADITIONAL FARMING

Nanga Baiga was instructed never to tear the body of Mother Earth with a plough, so the Baiga practise a sacred form of slash-and-burn agriculture, known as the *bewar*. This was the source of serious conflict with forestry officials in the mid-19th century, who forced them to abandon their axes and hoes to take up the plough. Their forest rights were restricted, and they were allowed to practise *bewar* only in the Baiga Chak reservation, where many Baigas now live.

## STRETCHING OUT THE EARTH

Karicag took the Earth to Bhagavan, who rolled it out like an enormous chapatti, and spread it on the surface of the water. But it was not stable: the Earth tipped up if someone stood on it. Even the giant Bhimsen couldn't help Bhagavan fix the Earth securely.

## THE BIRTH OF THE BAIGA

Meanwhile, in the forest, under a clump of bamboo trees, two children had been born from the womb of Dharti Mata (Mother Earth), called Nanga Baiga and Nanga Baigin. One day, when they were grown, Nanga Baiga went to watch Nanga Baigin bathing, and they mated among the trees on the bank of the pond.

## BHAGAVAN ASKS FOR HELP

Bhagavan sent a series of messengers to ask the two Baiga to help secure the Earth. At first they refused, but then they announced that they would take on the task together with the Gond people, because one member of the Gond tribe had been the only person willing to sit with them and share their food. Seeing that the Baiga had no clothes, the Gond sent to Bhagavan, who tore his own garment in half and sent it to them.

*Baiga magicians* or medicine men – *gunia* – are still highly respected, especially for their ability to control tigers, which they inherited from Nanga Baiga.

## SECURING THE EARTH

Nanga Baiga and Nanga Baigin dressed and began to travel the world. They sacrificed a sow to Dharti Mata, Mother Earth, and when the first drop of blood fell on her, she stopped rocking to and fro. Then they got four great nails and drove them into the four corners of the world to hold it steady.

Bhagavan called all the tribes together to select a king. Everyone came dressed in fine clothes, except Nanga Baiga, who was dressed in leaves. Bhagavan wanted to make him king of the world, but Nanga Baiga refused. "Make the Gond king," he said, "for he is my brother."

Then Bhagavan said: "Kings may lose their kingdoms, but you will never lose the jungle. You are made of the Earth and are lords of the Earth, and shall never forsake it. You must guard the Earth, and keep its nails in place. You must never tear the breast of your mother with a plough."

**RELATED MYTHS ▸** Izanagi and Izanami (*pp.180–1*)
• Turtle Island (*pp.194–7*)

# PAN GU AND NÜ WA'S CREATION

📖 Creation
📍 China
🏛 The cosmos; the Earth

✍ Hsu Chung (attrib.), *Sanwu liji* (*Historical Records of the Three Sovereign Deities and the Five Gods*); Xujung (attrib.), *Wuyun linianji* (*Chronicle of the Five Cycles of Time*)

The most widespread Chinese creation myth tells of the primal creator Pan Gu, who wakes from a long sleep and begins the process of creation by smiting the chaotic elements with his hand. He then holds the Earth and sky apart before falling back to sleep, and his body becomes the rest of the cosmos. The goddess Nü Wa appreciates the glories of Pan Gu's creation, but feels there is something missing, and supplies this want by creating humanity.

## PLOT SYNOPSIS

### PAN GU WAKES

For thousands of years, Pan Gu the creator slept, gathering his strength for the work of creation. When he awoke he looked all about and was angry at the chaos and disorder of the elements around him. In his anger he lashed out, and his vast hand hit the swirling elements with an almighty boom.

Pan Gu's blow sent the elements of the universe moving in new directions.

**The goddess Nü Wa** is portrayed as a hybrid figure, with the body of a serpent and the head of a young woman.

Gradually they started to become more ordered – the heavy elements sinking downwards to form the rocks of the Earth, the lighter things floating upwards to make the sky. The Earth and sky grew, and Pan Gu stood beneath them, keeping them apart. As the Earth and sky expanded, so did Pan Gu, and as the creator got taller, the Earth and the sky were pushed farther and farther away from each other. For long years Pan Gu held the Earth and sky apart, until he was certain that if he

moved they would not collapse back into chaos. When he was sure they had found their final positions, he lay down exhausted and slept deeply.

### PAN GU'S REST

As Pan Gu slept his body turned into the rest of the universe. His eyes became the sun and moon and the hairs of his beard split into thousands of fragments and became the stars. Parts of his body turned into the Earth's mountain ranges and the rest of his flesh turned into the soil. The hairs of his head took root in the soil and became plants and trees. They were nourished by the blood from his veins, which became the rivers, and the sweat from his brow, which became the refreshing morning dew.

### A LONELY GODDESS

Nü Wa's sharp eyes saw far across the Earth. She enjoyed the sight of the mountains and plains, flowers and trees that Pan Gu had created and she liked to visit Earth and marvel at the beautiful landscape. But she found she was lonely on her visits, and decided something should be done about this.

## NÜ WA FORMS THE FIRST PEOPLE

Nü Wa noticed that on some parts of the Earth's surface, the ground was made of soft, yellowish clay. She picked up some of this clay and began to mould it into a shape. Soon she had made a figure, and when she placed him on the ground he came to life. Nü Wa had made the first man. The goddess was pleased with her creation, especially when he began to run around and dance, so she made more and more of the little figures. Before long the world was populated with an entire race of men and women made by Nü Wa.

## THE NEXT GENERATION

The humans travelled far and wide across the Earth and found places to live. They were happy, and Nü Wa was pleased with their happiness and enjoyed visiting them when she came to Earth. But she noticed that after a while her creations showed signs that they were getting old, and the goddess knew that they would begin to die. So she gave them the power to have children and showed them how to use this power to make love and to multiply.

## DEATH IS OVERCOME

The people treasured their children, knowing that through them, the human race as a whole would overcome the death of the individual. Both Nü Wa and the people rejoiced that there would always be humans living on Earth.

# YI SHOOTS THE SUNS

📖 Natural disaster     ✍ Liu An, *Huainanzi* (*The Masters of Huainan*)
📕 China
🏛 The Earth

China has several myths about natural disasters, in which immortals help the human race through an environmental crisis. The story of Yi is about a drought caused by ten suns that shine together in the sky. Yi, the heavenly archer, comes to Earth to shoot nine of the suns, but is so efficient that it seems he might bring down all ten. Catastrophe is averted by the emperor Yao, who takes away one of Yi's arrows, so that life on Earth can continue.

**KEY CHARACTERS**

**THE EMPEROR OF HEAVEN** •
*creator of the ten suns*
**YAO** • *emperor of China*
**YI** • *a skilful archer*

## PLOT SYNOPSIS

### THE TEN SUNS

Long ago there was not just one sun in the sky, but ten different suns. These ten suns took it in turns to shine in the sky. As long as only one sun shone on any one day, the Earth was warmed, crops grew, and everyone on Earth was contented. But one day the ten suns grew bored of this routine and decided all to shine at once. In the scorching heat the crops perished and the

**Yi earned the title** of Heavenly Archer for shooting down nine of the Earth's ten suns, and was granted immortality.

rivers and lakes dried up – even the rocks themselves began to melt, and people began to starve. It seemed as though the Earth was dying. In desperation, Yao, the emperor of China and one of the Three August Ones, decided to pray for help to the Emperor of Heaven, the father of the ten suns.

### THE COMING OF YI

The Emperor of Heaven heard Yao's prayers and sent Yi, his finest archer, to Earth to shoot down nine of the suns. When Yi arrived it was night.

Emperor Yao looked at Yi's fine bow, but doubted whether it was enough to defeat the mighty suns. The pair waited until dawn to see if the ten suns would emerge. They did so, and once more the Earth began to crack and scorch. Yi raised his bow, took aim, and shot at the first sun. It disappeared and its spirit, in the form of a huge crow, fell to the ground.

### THE DROUGHT IS DEFEATED

One by one, Yi brought down the suns with his mighty bow. When six were shot, Yao saw that the archer still had four arrows left. Yi was so good at his task that the emperor feared he would shoot down all ten suns and plunge the Earth into eternal darkness. So, while Yi was next taking aim, Yao quietly removed one of the arrows from Yi's quiver. Yi hit every one of his targets, shooting down nine of the suns, and the planet began to recover from its terrible drought.

# YU TAMES THE FLOODS

📖 Natural disaster    ✍ *Chuci (Songs of Ch'u)*
🏳 China
🏛 China

Since the beginning of Chinese civilization, China has relied on its rivers for transportation and food. The rivers often flood, and one Chinese myth tells of a mighty flood brought about by the Emperor of Heaven as a punishment for humanity's wicked ways. It is the job of the dragon Yu, miraculously born from the corpse of the emperor's grandson, to persuade the emperor to allow him to repair the flood damage so that life on Earth can continue.

## KEY CHARACTERS

**THE EMPEROR OF HEAVEN**
**GUN** • *grandson of the Emperor of Heaven*
**YU** • *a dragon*

## PLOT SYNOPSIS

### THE GREAT FLOOD

Long ago, the Emperor of Heaven grew angry with humanity because of its sinful ways, so he sent a terrible flood as punishment. The rivers burst their banks, houses were destroyed, and many people were drowned.

Gun, the grandson of the Emperor of Heaven, took pity on the people and went down to Earth to mend the river banks. He took with him soil from heaven to absorb the water. But he did not tell his grandfather what he was doing, and when the Emperor of Heaven found out, he was angry again, and had Gun killed.

### THE ARRIVAL OF YU

Gun's body did not decay like a human body. Instead a new life-form, the dragon Yu, grew inside his corpse and emerged from Gun's body. When Yu saw the flood damage

he flew off to heaven to plead with the emperor to have mercy on humanity. The emperor relented and allowed Yu to repair the damage.

Yu worked hard, raising new hills and mountains, mending the river banks, and building new channels to take away the water. After 30 years the floods were banished and the planet was safe once again.

**RELATED MYTHS** ▶ Daughter of the Sun (*p.198*)

**The rivers** of China were formed by Yu's thrashing tail, according to some versions of this myth. His taming of the floods allowed farming to resume.

# CHINESE GODS AND THE CHINESE COURT

The stories of China's enormous pantheon of gods were written down in many different texts, some as early as the 5th century BCE. By the time of the Song dynasty (960–1279 CE), these diverse myths were seen to mirror the court of the Chinese emperor. Heaven had its own emperor and he was attended by a vast celestial civil service of deities, just like the imperial bureaucracy on Earth.

## THE HEAVENLY COURT

The emperor of heaven was known as Yuhuang, the Jade Emperor. Like his earthly counterpart, he was said to live in a huge palace surrounded by servants. Court notables included his wife Wang Mu and his chief minister Dongyue Dadi, a deity presiding over 75 different parts of the heavenly civil service. Each of these divisions was run by its own god.

**Yuhuang, the Jade Emperor,** was the ruler of heaven and patron of the imperial family.

## MANY FAITHS, MANY GODS

This multitude of gods had diverse origins. Some began in the Daoist religion and were said to have been mortals who, by study, insight, or following the instructions of a sage, had found immortality through their faith. Others came from the Confucian tradition and were great scholars or followers of Confucius before becoming immortal. Still others were the revered figures of Buddhism who had attained enlightenment and whose aid was widely invoked by Chinese people. Foremost among these Buddhist immortals were the Buddha himself and Guan Yin, the goddess of mercy, who heard all who called for her help.

The mythologies of these three belief systems – Daoism, Confucianism, and Buddhism – began to merge, and as a result Chinese mythology contains important elements from all three.

## LINKS BETWEEN HEAVEN AND EARTH

After the Song dynasty, earthly emperors began to claim that they were in direct contact with Yuhuang, but said that other mortals would have to communicate with heaven by praying to one of the minor gods. People also spoke to heaven via the messenger of the gods, Zao Jun the kitchen god, who reported on people's behaviour. Every year Chinese families would burn the picture of him that had been displayed on their wall for the past year; the smoke would take Zao Jun's annual report up to heaven.

**The Temple of Heaven** was the holiest of China's temples, used by the emperor himself during harvest ceremonies.

## ROLES OF THE GODS

Many immortals had specific roles, and people would pray to them because of their particular influence. The dragon-king Longwang, for example, was the guardian of rivers and seas and he also controlled the rains. Farmers would pray to him when crops needed water.

Some gods presided over specific phases of people's lives. Yue Lao, the old man of the moon, was said to use a cord to join together couples who were to marry. Other gods protected humanity, like Zhong Kui, whose image was said to keep away evil spirits. When Zhong was a mortal, he did well in the civil service tests, but was stripped of his title because of his untidy appearance. He committed suicide and was made immortal, becoming the god of examinations.

**The Forbidden City** in Beijing was the Chinese imperial palace and seat of power from 1420 until the Chinese Revolution of 1911–12.

**Depictions of the** auspicious Chinese dragon date back to Neolithic times. The first emperor, Shi Huangdi (r. 221–209 BCE), was said to have been immortalized as a dragon to ascend to heaven. The dragon then became the symbol of imperial power, and flew on the Chinese flag.

# IZANAGI AND IZANAMI

📖 Creation
📍 Japan
🏛 Japan; the Underworld

✍ *Kojiki* ("Record of Ancient Matters");
*Nihonshoki* ("Chronicles of Japan");
Juliet Pigott, *Japanese Mythology*

Izanagi and Izanami were the first couple, who descended from heaven on a rainbow. They stirred the primal ocean with a spear and created the islands of Japan, then procreated to give birth to the other gods. Their story ends unhappily, when Izanami dies giving birth to the god of fire. Although Izanagi follows her down to the Underworld, as in the Greek myth of Orpheus, the experience of death has turned Izanami against him.

### KEY CHARACTERS

**IZANAGI** • *He Who Invites, a creator god*
**IZANAMI** • *She Who Invites, a creator goddess*
**KAGUTSUCHI** • *god of fire*
**HIRUKO** • *a leech-child*

## PLOT SYNOPSIS

### THE FIRST GODS
At the beginning of heaven and Earth, three invisible gods came into being: the Heavenly Centre Lord, the High Generative Force, and the Divine Generative Force. They were the first of the *kami*, or gods. From the primal ooze sprouted reed-shoots, which became two more gods: the god of Excellent Reed-Shoots and the god of Heavenly Standing. These first gods are the five Separate Heavenly Deities.

### MALE AND FEMALE
Izanagi and Izanami were the seventh generation of gods. They represent the yin and the yang, the male and female principles, and they are the ancestors of all creation.

**The "wedded rocks"** at Ise, Japan, are named after Izanami and Izanagi, the primal couple of Japanese mythology.

## CREATING THE LAND

Izanagi and Izanami descended the Rainbow Bridge, and created Onogoro, the first island. Observing the lovemaking of a pair of wagtails, Izanagi and Izanami felt desire for each other. They walked around a pillar, one from the right and one from the left, and when they met they had intercourse. This was their first wedding, but it was flawed, because Izanami spoke first.

## THE CHILDREN OF IZANAGI AND IZANAMI

Their first child was Hiruko, the Leech-Child, whom they floated away on reeds. The gods advised them to repeat their wedding,

**Izanami and Izanagi** stand on the Rainbow Bridge and create an island using the Heavenly Jewelled Spear.

but with Izanagi speaking first. They did this, and Izanami then gave birth to all the islands of Japan, and to the gods of the seas, rivers, winds, trees, mountains, and plains. Lastly she gave birth to the god of fire, Kagutsuchi, who burned her, making her vomit up and excrete yet more gods.

## DEATH BY FIRE

Izanami was so badly injured that she died, and descended to Yōmi, the Underworld. Izanagi cut off Kagutsuchi's head in rage, and yet more gods were born from his blood. Grieving, Izanagi descended to Yōmi, and begged Izanami to return, but she told him: "You are too late. I have already eaten at the hearth of Yōmi." She promised to plead with the gods of Yōmi to let her return, but warned Izanagi not to follow her. But Izanagi did

follow her into the darkness; he broke off a tooth from his comb and lit it to use as a torch. When the light fell on Izanami, he saw that her body was already a putrefying mass of squirming maggots, which turned into thunder gods.

## THE FLIGHT OF IZANAGI

Izanagi turned and fled up the long tunnel, with the warriors of Yōmi at his heels. He managed to delay them by throwing down items that magically changed into food. But Izanami was also following, and could not be tricked so easily. She was right at the top of the tunnel when Izanagi jumped out and sealed the tunnel entrance with a great rock. Trapped in the Underworld, Izanami shouted through the rock that she would take revenge for her humiliation by killing 1,000 people every day; Izanagi countered by promising to create 1,500 new babies every day.

**RELATED MYTHS** ▶ Orpheus in the Underworld (*p.57*) • Daughter of the Sun (*p.198*)

### NATURE AND ANCESTOR WORSHIP

The mythology of gods such as Izanagi and Izanami belongs to the Shinto religion, which is known as *Kami No Michi*, "the way of the *kami*". The word *kami*, variously translated as soul, spirit, and deity, is the key to the Shinto religion. The major *kami* are the gods, such as Izanagi, Izanami, and Amaterasu (*see p.182*). But every living thing has a *kami*, including human beings, whose *kami* live on after death. In this way Shintoism combines worship of the sacred powers of nature and of human ancestors.

# STORM VERSUS SUN

📖 Wars of the gods
📍 Japan
🏛 Japan

✍ *Kojiki* ("Record of Ancient Matters");
*Nihonshoki* ("Chronicles of Japan");
Juliet Pigott, *Japanese Mythology*

Three of the most important Japanese gods –
Tsuki-yomi the moon god, Susano the god of
storms, and Amaterasu the sun goddess – were
produced when Izanagi the creator god cleansed
himself after abandoning his wife and co-creator
Izanami in the Underword (*see pp.180–1*). The
rivalry between two of these gods threatened to
plunge the world into darkness and destroy it.
The other gods' resourcefulness saved the day.

## PLOT SYNOPSIS

### RITUAL PURIFICATION
Izanagi emerged from the Underworld
filthy and polluted, so he cleansed
himself in a river, creating more gods.
When he washed his left eye, the sun
goddess Amaterasu came into being.
When he washed his right eye, the
moon god Tsuki-yomi came into being.
And when he washed his nose he
created Susano, the storm god.

### A CRYING CHILD
Susano would not stop weeping for his
dead "mother", Izanami, who remained
in the Underworld. He howled with
grief until his beard was eight hands
long. He longed to join Izanami.
"In that case," said Izanagi, "you
cannot stay here." Susano replied:

"Before I go, I will take leave of my
sister Amaterasu." He set off in a
storming rage.

### DEFILING THE SACRED HALLS
Susano broke down the rice paddies
of Amaterasu, defecated in the Hall
of the First Fruits, and defiled the
Weaving Hall, where his sister and her
maidens made the divine garments, by
dropping a flayed pony through a hole
in the roof. Amaterasu was so shocked
that she struck her genitals against a
weaving shuttle and injured herself.

### THE SUN GOES OUT
Amaterasu fled in terror and hid inside
a cave, closing the entrance with a great
stone. The world fell into darkness;
nothing grew, and evil
spirits ran riot. The
gods tried to lure her
from the cave with
various stratagems,
such as having cockerels
crow a false dawn. But
nothing worked, until
Omohi-kane, the wise

**Many Shinto shrines** contain a
sacred mirror, in memory of the
moment at which Amaterasu is
blinded by her own reflection.

## JAPAN AND THE SUN

Amaterasu, the sun goddess, was regarded as the original ancestor of the imperial family. The first emperor, Jimmu-tenno, was said to be her great-great-great-grandson. As a result she became the most important deity. Her shrine at Ise has been renewed every two decades for the last 2,000 years; every Japanese person tries to visit it at least once in their life. The word "Nippon" (Japan) means "sun-origin".

**During WWII**, the Japanese flag featured the rays of the sun.

thought-combining god, came up with a plan. Omohi-kane asked the dawn goddess Ama-no-uzume to perform a striptease on an upturned sake tub. In a state of divine possession, the goddess exposed her breasts and her genitals to the gods, who fell about with roars of laughter. Intrigued, Amaterasu opened the cave door a chink to see what was so funny. "What's all this racket about?' she asked.

## GREATER THAN THE SUN

"We are celebrating because there is a goddess who shines even more brightly than you", Ama-no-uzume replied. When Amaterasu opened the door further, the gods held up a mirror and dazzled her with her own reflection. The god Ta-jikawa-wo ("Hand-strength-male-deity") seized the door and pulled it open. He grabbed

Amaterasu's hand and led her, still dazzled, out of the cave. Then the gods fastened a sacred rope across the cave entrance, so she could never go back in.

## THE EXPULSION OF SUSANO

To punish Susano, the gods fined him, cut off his beard and nails, exorcised him, and expelled him from heaven to wander the world as an outcast. There he found the Rice Paddy Princess, Kusa-nada-pime, being threatened by an eight-headed dragon. Susano turned Kusa-nada-pime into a comb, and stuck her safely into his hair. Then he made the dragon drunk on sake and hacked it to pieces with his sword. Inside the dragon's tail he found the sword known as Kusa-nagi, the Grass-cutter, which he presented to his sister Amaterasu as a token of apology. He then turned the Rice Paddy Princess back into a girl, and married her.

---

**RELATED MYTHS ▸** Demeter and Persephone (p.54) • The vanishing god (p.152) • Daughter of the Sun (p.198)

# AN UNWELCOME FEAST

📖 Fertility
🗺 Japan
🏛 Japan

✍ *Kojiki* ("Record of Ancient Matters");
*Nihonshoki* ("Chronicles of Japan");
Juliet Pigott, *Japanese Mythology*

In this myth about Ogetsu, the goddess of food, Tsuki-yomi, the moon god, is as violent as his brother Susano, the storm god (*see pp.182–3*). In fact the *Kojiki* text actually ascribes Tsuki-yomi's actions to Susano. In the myth the death of the goddess is necessary for the production of the staple food crops of Japan. It also explains why the sun and the moon, although brother and sister, are generally so reluctant to be seen together in the sky.

> ### KEY CHARACTERS
>
> **TSUKI-YOMI** • *the moon god*
> **OGETSU (OR UKE-MOCHI)** •
> *goddess of food*
> **AMATERASU** • *the sun goddess*

## PLOT SYNOPSIS

### A HUNGRY GOD
Amaterasu, the sun goddess, hearing that the food goddess Ogetsu was in the Central Land of the Reed Plains, sent Tsuki-yomi, the moon god, to see what she was doing. Tsuki-yomi did so, but he was hungry, and rudely demanded a meal from Ogetsu. Affronted, the goddess vomited and excreted a feast

**One myth says** that Ogetsu, Japanese goddess of food, was married to the god of rice, Inari, before she died (*see* God of the Rice Fields, *opposite*).

for him. While she faced the fields, boiled rice streamed from her mouth; while she faced the sea, she vomited up fish and edible seaweed; while she faced the hills, she produced game animals.

### FOOD FROM A CORPSE
Tsuki-yomi was in turn so angry at this insult that he drew his sword and killed Ogetsu. From the corpse of Ogetsu sprang all the staple crops of Japan. Rice grew from her eyes, millet from her ears, red beans from her nose, wheat from her genitals, and soy beans from her rectum. Cows and horses emerged from her forehead, and silkworms from her eyebrows.

### THE SUN AND THE MOON
When Tsuki-yomi told his sister Amaterasu what he had done, she was so appalled that she vowed never to set eyes on him again, which is why the sun and full moon are never seen together. Amaterasu then sent a messenger to collect all the useful things that had come from Ogetsu's body, so that she could distribute them to humankind.

# GOD OF THE RICE FIELDS

📖 Fertility  
🏵 Japan  
🏛 Japan

✍ Juliet Pigott, *Japanese Mythology*;  
J. W. Robertson Scott, *The Foundations of Japan*

Rice is the staple food of Japan, and so there is a special god of rice, named Inari. This god appears as a bearded man, a woman, and even a fox.

Inari comes down from his home in the mountains in the spring, and returns in the autumn, like the water from the mountains that feeds the paddy fields. Because rice is a symbol of wealth, Inari is also the god of merchants.

The rice to be served at the coronation of the emperor was planted with special rites to call down the blessing of the gods on the crop and on his reign. A small Shinto shrine was built overlooking the rice fields,

and all the implements used – in preparing the fields, and in cultivating, harvesting, and threshing the crop – were new. The men and women who planted the crop first ceremonially purified themselves in a specially built bathhouse, then sang a prayer to Inari.

# MARRIED TO A FOX

📖 Loves of the gods  
🏵 Japan  
🏛 Japan

✍ Juliet Pigott, *Japanese Mythology*; Yanagita Kunio, *Guide to the Japanese Folktale*; Carmen Blacker, *The Catalpa Bow*

Although foxes are generally mistrusted in Japan, one Japanese folktale tells of a fox-woman who may be the rice god Inari in human form.

A farmer took a wife from another district, and was very happy with her until one night he saw a fox's brush hanging below the edge of the quilt. His wife was a fox in human form! (In another version, the fox-wife is betrayed by her son, who

tells his father that his mother is brushing the yard with her tail.) Many a man might have been dismayed at this, but the farmer loved his wife, and she had no evil intentions. In fact she helped him outwit the taxman, by showing him how to sow his rice field so that the rice grew upside-down, hiding the crop from prying eyes.

**Foxes are** associated with Inari, the rice god, in Japanese mythology and their likeness appears at many sacred sites.

## MYTHS OF THE AINU

The Ainu are the indigenous people of Japan, who now live largely on the island of Hokkaido. Culturally, they have affinities with other hunter-gatherers of the North Pacific, such as the Inuit of Alaska and the Chukchi of Siberia, especially in their reverence for the spirits of the natural world. Ainu mythology is contained in a vast oral literature of sung epics, known as *kamuy yukar* – the songs of the gods.

### SONGS OF THE GODS

The *kamuy yukar* tell of the interaction between gods and people. The gods are thought of as human in form, but often appear as animals, such as the bear and killer whale, in myth.

By singing the songs of the gods, humans (*ainu*) can communicate with non-humans (*kamuy*), with whom they share the physical world. The *kamuy yukar* are sung in the first person, as if by the gods themselves – a form of story-telling unique to the Ainu. The gods can also speak directly through the mouths of female shamans when they are in a state of divine possession.

**The Ainu** believe their souls will ascend to *kamuy mosir* (Land of the Gods).

### APPEASING THE GODS

In the animistic beliefs of the Ainu, Killer Whale (Repun Kamuy) controls fish, and Bear (Kimun Kamuy) controls game birds and animals. The gods visit the human world, often in animal form, to trade with people, exchanging the gift of animal disguise for wine, food, and sacred willow-stick carvings that are prized in their own world. Not surprisingly, rituals to appease these gods are central to Ainu culture.

**Bears are a traditional** quarry of Ainu huntsmen. Every aspect of hunting, killing, and eating an animal has deep spiritual meaning for the Ainu.

**Ainu men** wear full beards and the women have moustache-like tattoos above their mouths.

## SENDING OF SPIRITS

One of the *kamuy yukar*, "Song of a Bear", tells how the mountain god Kimun Kamuy follows his wife down to the human world, with their baby on his back. His bear body is killed by a hunter's arrow tipped with aconite poison, but the god himself jumps on a hunter's back, hitching a ride to the village, where he is welcomed and given gifts. His cub is kept to be raised for the *iyomante* ceremony – a ritual in which the spirit of a visiting god is sent back to heaven. In the *iyomante*, bear cubs are ritually raised to be killed and eaten at a ceremonial winter feast, at the end of which the god is sent home laden with gifts, including sake, dried salmon, and dumplings. The god takes pleasure from the feast as he watches the Ainu dance and listens to them sing the *kamuy yukar*. The villagers cut short the final song so that the god will return to hear how the story ends.

## THE SACRED FIRE

Fuchi, the goddess of fire, is important in Ainu ritual because it is believed that she carries prayers to the gods – which she does when a fire is ritually sprinkled with wine. One myth tells of how Fuchi engages in a magic contest with the goddess of water, who had stolen away her husband. Fuchi wins, and her husband returns, sheepish and cowed, to sit meekly at her hearth.

# FIRE FOR RICE

- 📖 Culture heroes
- 🏴 The Ifugao culture, Philippines
- 🏛 Central Cordillera, Luzon island

✍ Roy Franklin Barton, *The Mythology of the Ifugaos; The Religion of the Ifugaos* (as told by Ngidulu)

The Ifugao are a mountain people of the Philippines. Their culture centres around rice-growing, and their huge rice terraces have been called the eighth wonder of the world. According to the Ifugao, they were taught how to build the terraces by hero ancestors known as the Field-Makers. The following myth tells how the Field-Makers won rice from the gods of the Skyworld, in exchange for the gift of fire.

### KEY CHARACTERS

**WIGAN** • *a hunter and the first Field-Maker*
**KABIGAT** • *a hunter*
**BUGAN** • *Wigan's wife*
**LIDUM** • *a Skyworld god*
**HINUMBÍAN** • *a Skyworld god*
**DINIPAAN** • *a smithy god*

## PLOT SYNOPSIS

### HUNTING A PIG

Two hunters from Kayang, Wigan and his brother Kabigat, once sacrificed a chicken to see if they would have any luck hunting that day. They invoked the gods for help, such as the Tired-Ones of the Upstream Region, and the Alabat gods who live in the mountains and own all the game.

The omens were good, so the hunters set off with their spears and their dogs in search of wild

**The Ifugao** use bamboo sticks for many things, including water-carrying, making musical instruments, and fire-lighting.

pigs. They roused a pig, and pursued it through the forest, and then up the mountainside. The pig climbed higher and higher, until it reached right up into the Skyworld, where the two hunters caught up with it and killed it.

### ARRIVAL OF ANGRY GODS

The gods Lidum and Hinumbían arrived on the scene, and accused the men of killing one of the Skyworld pigs. "It is no pig of yours," protested Wigan. "Our dogs trailed it all the way from

Kayang." After counting their pigs, the gods accepted the truth of this. Then Wigan cut up the pig to share the meat with the gods. The gods cut off small pieces of meat from the larger ones, mixed them with rice, and offered the morsels to Wigan to eat.

But Wigan told them, "I will not eat with you, for the meat is uncooked".

### TRADING FIRE

Wigan took a piece of bamboo and set about making it into a fire-saw. First he cut the bamboo in half. Then he cut a hole into the side of one of the pieces of bamboo, and placed a small pile of crushed dry leaves inside. As he started to rub the second piece of bamboo across the hole, sparks appeared and set light to the dry leaves within the bamboo. Wigan carefully moved the smouldering leaves to a larger pile, and built it into a fire to cook the meat and rice for the gods. The gods were amazed. They were so

**The Ifugao terraces** of the Philippines are now a World Heritage Site. They reach up to 1,500m (5,000 ft) high, and have been used for producing rice and wheat for more than 2,000 years.

impressed that they offered Wigan anything he wanted in exchange for the gift of fire. He refused their jewels, and asked instead for the delicious rice that grew in the Skyworld, and so the gods taught Wigan how to make terraced rice fields. All he had to do was stab a digging stick into the ground of the harsh mountainsides, and it would become a field. The process could be repeated for as long as his wife was able to stay completely still.

## MAKING THE RICE FIELDS

Back in the Earthworld, Wigan began to make the rice fields. His wife Bugan moved slightly after Wigan had made eight fields, and after that nothing happened when he stabbed his digging stick into the Earth.

"Never mind," said Bugan. "We have enough."

So Wigan stabbed his stick into the bank above the fields, and water gushed out to irrigate the rice, carrying with it the water-lilies that flower on the surface of the fields.

## THE FIRST HARVEST

When the rice was ripe, the people needed tools with which to harvest it. Dinipaan, the blacksmith god, set up his bellows and forged iron into knives. He went to Kayang and offered the people the knives in exchange for

baskets of chickens. The next day Wigan supervised the first harvest and the storage of the rice in the granary, with all the necessary rituals and sacrifices to the gods of the Skyworld, the Underworld, the Upstream Region, and the granary-gods. And finally he recited this very story and invoked the gods again, so that in his home of Kayang the rice would always increase and flourish.

### THE RICE GODS

In their complex yearly cycle of rituals and ceremonies, the Ifugao invoke around 1,500 separate gods and their wives. These gods are often highly specialized, such as the Bulols (or Bululs), the rice-granary deities. The Bululs are represented by wooden effigies which are activated by a ritualistic feast, during which priests are "possessed" by the Bulol gods and run on all fours around the house, dancing with the effigy and yelping and whining. The effigies are served rice wine and rice cakes to call the gods back into the image; in return the Bulols are believed to help with the rice crop. There are 25 Bulol gods, including Balulung, "the Yoked Bulol", who is yoked like a pig to stop him running away. The effigy of Bulol the Mute recalls the myth of the first Bulol, son of the Underworld god Tinukud, who became mute, but was later miraculously cured.

**Bulol effigies** such as this are carved from narra wood from the Downstream Region, in the shape of either a man or a pig.

# THE AMERICAS

T HE MYTHOLOGIES OF THE AMERICAS are as varied as the cultures to be found there, but some themes resonate across the continent. From the Inuit in the Arctic to the Yamana of Tierra del Fuego there is reverence for the animal-human beings of the creation-time, for the force that connects all living things, and for the mythic lore pervading the natural world.

The mythologies of the Americas are highly varied and also highly fluid. Within an essentially oral tradition, different versions of a myth can evolve from teller to teller or from time to time. Myths can also react to new circumstances, and absorb new information. For example, between two well-sourced accounts of Hopi mythology, the god Taiowa, regarded by the first as a minor god of the sun, has become "the Creator". Another point of variance is between the versions of myths known to all in a particular culture, and the versions known only to initiates in a particular society, or to shamans or priests. So to an ordinary Lakota Indian, the Great Spirit is a single entity, Wakan Tanka. But to

**Drumming** is a powerful spiritual tool in North American ritual, often used to induce a shamanic trance.

the Lakota holy men, Wakan Tanka is not one spirit but 16, the "Four-times-four".

## THE FAR NORTH

The Inuit of the Arctic Circle believe that every living thing has a soul, or *inua*, which is the life-force. The whole world is therefore infused with a sense of mythic potentiality. Myths express the truth of life; life expresses the truth of myth.

The cultural identity of the Tikigaq people of Alaska is encoded in the myth of Raven and the whale. Tikigaq was the name of the very first whale, which was harpooned by Raven and turned into their land. The Tikigaq igloo, with its whalebone entrance passage, represents the whale. When the men hunt whales, they enact the part of Raven, in raven-skin capes; meanwhile the women stay in the igloo, playing the part of the whale's *inua*.

## NORTH AMERICA

The first words of the creation myth of the Maricopa tribe of Arizona are: "The Earth was the mother, and the Sky the father." With this, many of the Indian nations would agree. The whole world is sacred in Native American belief, and united by a mysterious unseen power, the living spirit of the Great Mystery. Myths show the workings of this power through gods, animals, and men. Many myths are concerned with the creation-time, and

**Taos indians** perform the sacred eagle dance in New Mexico. The eagle is considered a link between heaven and Earth in many American mythologies.

the doings of the animal-people who are the ancestors and teachers of humankind; others relate to the staples of life, such as corn, buffalo, or salmon.

## MEXICO AND CENTRAL AMERICA

The mythologies of Mexico and Central America are dominated by the Aztec and Maya cultures, whose elaborate myths reflect the blood debt humankind was believed to owe to the gods. The Hero Twins of the Maya are reflected in North American mythologies, especially in the southwest. Maya myths, and the complex Mayan calendar, also persist among the highland Maya today, such as the Tzotzil-speaking Zinacantecs, who believe this world is a cube, resting on the shoulders of the Four-corner gods; the navel of the world is a low mound of earth in the ceremonial centre of Zinacantán, where offerings are made.

## SOUTH AMERICA

The myths of the Inca and their subjects are just one aspect of South American mythology, which stretches from the Warao in the Orinoco Delta to the now culturally-extinct Yamana at the tip of Tierra del Fuego. Each tribe has its own complex mythology, often closely related to the environment in which they live. Once again, the focus of many myths is the animal-people of the creation-time.

**Known previously** to only a few local farmers, the Inca city of Machu Picchu was discovered almost by accident in 1911. It remains a mysterious place, and its true purpose has never been revealed.

"It was determined that soil from the bottom of the primal sea should be brought up and placed on the broad, firm carapace of the Turtle..."

Jeremiah Curtin & J. N. B. Hewitt, *Seneca Fiction, Legends, and Myths*

# TURTLE ISLAND

📖 Creation
📍 Northeastern USA
🏛 Northeastern USA

✍ J. N. B. Hewitt, *Iroquoian Cosmology*; Jeremiah Curtin and J. N. B. Hewitt, *Seneca Fiction, Legends, and Myths*

**The face of Hadu'i** the Iroquoian Whirlwind – a primal being of disease and death – carved into the living wood of a tree trunk. Hadu'i was vanquished by Sky Holder, grandson of Old Woman. With his nose broken, Hadu'i promised to make amends for poisoning the Earth by helping humanity.

## BEHIND THE MYTH

The myths of the Iroquois and Algonquin peoples of the northeastern USA share many themes and story patterns. Notable among these is the creation myth that has given North America the name by which many Native Americans know it – Turtle Island. In the words of Cath Johnson, one of the Wyandot nation of Kansas, "We are all living on the top of the Turtle's shell now. When she moves, it causes the earthquakes."

## THE FIRST MOTHER

Most tribes have their own version of this myth, in which Old Woman is expelled from the sky world, and becomes the First Mother. One of the best recorded is that of the Seneca – the "People of the Great Hill" who traditionally lived in what is now New York. An account collected from their chief John Arthur Gibson fills no less than 138 tightly packed pages. The Seneca call First Mother Eagentci, which means "old woman" and she is, essentially, the Earth herself, the source of all food. The Penobscot of Maine tell that First Mother sacrifices herself to save the first humans from starvation. She dies so that "her power would be felt all over the world and that all men should love her".

It is Old Woman's grandsons who complete the creation. To the Seneca these rival creators are known as Sky Holder and Flint, or Good Mind and Evil Mind. As these names suggest, Good Mind is benevolent, and arranges the Earth to be pleasant for man, while Evil Mind is malevolent and attempts to spoil the work of creation.

### KEY CHARACTERS

**ANCIENT ONE/EARTH HOLDER**
• *the chief of the sky world*

**OLD WOMAN/FIRST MOTHER**
• *Ancient One's wife*

**OLD WOMAN'S DAUGHTER**

**SKY HOLDER/GOOD MIND AND FLINT/EVIL MIND** • *sons of Old Woman's daughter and the Wind*

## PLOT SYNOPSIS

### ANCIENT ONE AND OLD WOMAN

Earth Holder, the Ancient One, lived in the sky world. In the centre of this world grew a great tree that bore flowers and fruit, and sustained all those who lived there. Earth Holder took Old Woman to be his wife, and she became pregnant by inhaling her husband's breath. But Earth Holder became jealous and suspicious, and began to waste away.

He dreamed that the answer to his problems was to uproot the great tree, so he pulled it out, leaving a gaping hole in the floor of the sky world. Earth Holder called Old Woman to look through the hole, and when she came he pushed her through it. As she fell, she grasped seeds from the tree with one hand, and a tobacco-scented root with the other. Old Woman fell towards the water which then covered the Earth. The ducks saw her fall, and wove their wings together to catch her, and then the Great Turtle rose from the underworld and, with the curve of his shell, made a resting-place for her above the water.

**The muskrat** made Old Woman more comfortable by bringing mud for her to rest upon.

### A NEW WORLD

A muskrat dove under the water and brought up mud, which he smeared on to the Turtle's shell. As the surface began to expand, Old Woman released the seeds and the root that she was holding. The Earth was soon covered with plants, and a new tree grew from the root.

Old Woman built herself a lodge beneath the tree, and there she gave birth to a daughter, who in turn became pregnant by the Wind. The daughter heard two voices inside her, arguing about which should be born first; one voice was gentle, the other harsh and rough.

## TURTLE DRUMS AND RATTLES

The turtle shell, with its associations with creation, plays a prominent role in the rituals of Native American peoples. The Iroquois fashion rattles from the whole shell, with the handle representing the head and neck of the turtle. Such rattles are used by healers to exorcise illness. The Mandan of the Great Plains used four drums – representing turtles – in their central ceremony, the Okeepa, or buffalo-calling dance.

**The Chumash people** used turtle rattles filled with pebbles for music-making when curing illness and for teaching children.

"If you won't let me out first," said the second voice, "I shall force my way out." And the child with the rough voice burst out of his mother's armpit.

### THE BIRTH OF SKY HOLDER

Old Woman's daughter had just enough strength to give birth to the other child before she died. She was the first to die, and to make a path from this world back to the sky world. The boy born

**From the grave of** Old Woman's daughter grew the Three Sisters – corn, beans, and squash – as well as tobacco, whose smoke rises as incense to the sky.

from her armpit was called Flint, and his heart was cold and hard. The other boy, Sky Holder, was warm and loving.

### THE FIRST PEOPLE

When the boys were grown they decided to enlarge Turtle Island. Flint created the mountains and hills in the west, while Sky Holder made the valleys and meadows in the east. "You're making it too comfortable," said Flint, and he did everything he could to spoil the new land. He even stole the sun and hid it in the southwest; although Sky Holder won it back, Flint had created winter. Sky Holder saw his own reflection in a pool of water. Taking some clay, he made six pairs of humans in his own image – the first man and woman of the six nations of the Iroquois.

### THE BROTHERS IN CONFLICT

Sky Holder taught the people how to live, but every good gift from Sky Holder was matched by a bad gift from Flint, and so disease and evil came into the world. Whenever Sky Holder made a healing plant, for example, Flint made a poisonous one. Eventually Sky Holder challenged and beat Flint, imprisoning his brother in a cave. Sky Holder also vanquished other enemies of humanity, such as the Whirlwind, the Wind, and the Fire Beast. He made the stars, the sun, and the moon and when his work was done, Sky Holder followed his mother's path up to the world in the sky.

# DAUGHTER OF THE SUN

📖 The origin of death
🏛 Cherokee (Aniyunwiya), Southeastern USA
🏛 Cherokee territory in Georgia, North and South Carolina, and Tennessee
✍ James Mooney, *Myths of the Cherokee*, as told by Swimmer

In Cherokee legend, the heat of the Sun once grew so intense that the people decided to kill her, but unfortunately they mistakenly killed her daughter. The Sun was so devastated by her loss that she locked herself away, and the world grew dark and cold. Fearing the Earth might die, the people resolved to rescue the daughter, and went to bring her back from the dead. They nearly succeeded, but at the last moment she escaped from them.

### KEY CHARACTERS

**THE SUN**
**THE MOON** • *her brother and lover*
**THE DAUGHTER OF THE SUN**
**SPREADING ADDER, COPPERHEAD, RATTLESNAKE, AND UKTENA** • *four men turned into snakes*

## PLOT SYNOPSIS

### THE SUN AND HER DAUGHTER

When the Sun was young, she had a lover who visited her only at night and refused to let her see his face. One night she rubbed ashes on her lover's face, to see if she could later identify him. On the following night, as her brother the Moon rose in the sky, the Sun noticed, with horror, that his face was covered in spots. The Moon was so ashamed that from then on he stayed as far away from the Sun as possible.

The Sun shone so intensely that the people could never look at her without screwing up their faces, but they smiled at the Moon. Jealous and angry, the Sun began to burn more and more fiercely, until people began to die from the heat. The people became desperate and decided to kill the Sun.

The Sun lived on the eastern side of the sky vault, and her daughter lived in the centre. Every day as the Sun climbed the sky-arch towards the west,

she stopped at her beloved daughter's house for her midday meal. The people knew this, and decided to use this routine as part of their plot to kill her. Two men were turned into snakes – the Spreading Adder and the Copperhead – and sent to lie in wait for the Sun at the door of her daughter's house. But when she arrived the following day, her light was so blinding that the Spreading Adder could only spit out yellow slime when he tried to bite, and the Copperhead just crawled away.

### A DAUGHTER'S DEATH

The people did not give up. A third man turned into a Rattlesnake and a fourth into a huge Uktena snake. The Uktena's blood was poisonous and his look alone could kill, so he seemed the perfect candidate to kill the Sun.

The two snakes went to the daughter's house to lie in wait. But when the door opened, the Rattlesnake rushed forward blindly and struck the person standing there. It was the Sun's daughter, and she died instantly.

### THE PLEAS OF A GHOST

The Sun was filled with grief for her daughter. She locked herself away, and the world lost all light and heat. So the

**The Cherokee** believe that the Sun still sometimes cries for her daughter and her tears fall as rain.

people vowed to bring the daughter back from the Darkening Land. They travelled there and found her dancing with ghosts. They captured her and put her in a box, but were told on no account to open it. All the way home the girl begged them to let her out. First she said she needed to eat, then that she was desperate to drink. Finally, she said that she couldn't breathe. So the people opened the lid of the box, just a little. There was a fluttering sound, and the cry of a redbird: "Kwish! Kwish!" and something flew from the box. The daughter of the Sun had turned into a redbird and flown away.

### THE HEALING POWER OF LAUGHTER

When the men returned without her daughter, the Sun's grief was overwhelming. She wept so hard that she flooded the Earth. People tried to cheer her up, but it wasn't until an expert drummer began to play with a humorous rhythm that she started to smile, and the world was again filled with light. Since then, the Sun's heat has never changed, but people still cannot look at her without squinting.

**RELATED MYTHS ▶** Demeter and Persephone (p.54)
• Yi shoots the suns (p.174)

**A Kiowa boy** participates in a corn-dance ceremony in New Mexico. Dancing propitiated the spirits of the hunters' prey, such as buffalo, and also of the "three sisters": corn, beans, and squash. For the celebrated Kiowa Gourd Dance, rattles are traditionally made from dried squash.

# THINKING WOMAN

📖 Creation
📕 Keres
🏛 Southwestern USA

✍ Franz Boas, *Keresan Texts*; Matilda Coxe Stevenson,
*The Sia*; Matthew W. Stirling, *Origin Myth of Acoma*;
Ruth Benedict, *Tales of the Cochiti Indians*

The work of creation among a number of the
Pueblo peoples is largely a female affair. Among
the Keres, the original creator is sometimes said
to be female, sometimes (perhaps under Christian
influence) male. This first creator may make the
world from a discarded clot of blood, or simply
use the power of imagination. Thinking Woman,
the spider, is said to have created the universe from
the web of her own thoughts.

### KEY CHARACTERS

**SUS'SISTINAKO** • *Thinking
Woman, the creator*
**IATIKU** • *the Corn Mother*
**IATIKU** • *Iatiku's daughter,
mother of the Indian peoples*
**NAUTSITI** • *Iatiku's
daughter, mother of the
white peoples*

## PLOT SYNOPSIS

### THE CREATION

At first there was only one being, a
spider called Sus'sistinako, meaning
"Thinking Woman". Sus'sistinako sent
her thoughts outward into space, and
used them to weave the fabric of the
universe. Beneath the Earth she placed
Iatiku, the Corn Mother, also known as
"the breath of life". It was Iatiku who
created all the elements that make up
the world – even fun, in the shape of
the clown Koshare, whom she shaped
from rubbings of her skin in order to
make people laugh.

Iatiku had two aspects: one who
remained underground, and to whom
the dead returned; and another who
travelled up to the world, bringing the
gift of life. She had two daughters, to
whom she gave baskets filled with seeds
and images. They were to use these to
bring life into the world.

### THE EMERGENCE

The first daughter was named Iatiku,
after her mother, because they so closely
resembled one another. The second
daughter was not given a name.

## WOVEN INTO SOUTHWEST MYTHOLOGIES

Spider Woman has a central, often a creator role in the mythologies of other peoples of the American Southwest. The Hopi believe that Spider Woman wove the moon out of white cotton, and made the first people out of clay. For the Diné (Navajo), Spider Woman span the rope ladder by which the people climbed up into this world; her gift to them was weaving. The Diné never kill spiders, which help human beings by catching insects, flies, and mosquitoes.

**Diné girls** are encouraged to rub spiders' webs on their arms to make them tireless weavers.

The two daughters travelled up to the Earth, and when they emerged, the world was still dark, so they decided to create light. Singing a creation song, they created the sun from shells and red stone, then they travelled east, carried the sun up a high mountain, and dropped it over the other side. The next morning the sun rose for the first time.

## BASKETS OF LIFE

Iatiku and her sister continued to scatter the seeds and images from their baskets, and each thing came alive as it fell. They made the moon, and then the stars, which were all in perfect groups

**The Pueblo peoples** of Arizona and New Mexico take their name from the word the Spanish used to describe their ancient settlements.

until a little girl peeped into the bundle of stars and let them out, scattering them randomly across the sky.

## A CONTEST BETWEEN SISTERS

Iatiku noticed that her sister's basket was more richly filled than her own, so she decided to name her sister "Nautsiti", meaning "more of everything in her basket". The two sisters then held a contest to see which of them should have precedence in the world. Iatiku won because Thinking Woman sat on her shoulder in spider form and whispered to her, telling her what to do. As the victor, Iatiku stayed to become the mother of the Indians, while Nautsiti went away, to become the mother of the whites.

# RAVEN STEALS THE SUN

📖 Culture hero
📜 Tsimshian, Canada
🏛 British Columbia

✍ Franz Boas, *Tsimshian Texts* and *Tsimshian Mythology*
(as recorded by Henry W. Tate); Marius Barbeau,
*Tsimsyan Myths*; Barbeau and Beynon, *Tsimshian Narratives*

At one time the world was completely dark, and
people could take human or animal form. A chief's
son died, but came back as a shining youth who
refused to eat until he was fed a scab and became
voraciously hungry. He was sent away in the form
of a raven, and seeded the land and rivers from
the air. Then he flew to heaven
and stole daylight from the
Chief-of-the-Skies.

### KEY CHARACTERS

**THE CHIEF OF KUNGALAS AND
HIS WIFE**

**RAVEN** • *their son*

**THE CHIEF-OF-THE-SKIES** •
*the creator*

**THE DAUGHTER OF THE
CHIEF-OF-THE-SKIES** •
*Raven's second mother*

## PLOT SYNOPSIS

### A BELOVED SON

The chief of Kungalas and his
wife had a son whom they adored.
When he died, they and their tribe
wailed by his corpse every morning.
One morning the mother went to the
site and discovered a youth as bright as
fire in place of the corpse. She went
back to the chief and told him:
"Our son has come back to life."

The chief went to where the youth
quietly waited, and cried, "Is it you, my
beloved son, is it you?"

The shining youth replied, "It is I."

**Raven** is a well-known
trickster god among several
tribes of the American Northwest.

### THE SHINING YOUTH

The chief and his wife loved their
reborn son more than ever. Their only
worry was that they could not persuade
him to eat. Then one day the slave
Mouth-at-Each-End offered the boy a
piece of whale meat wrapped around
a scab from his shin-bone. Once the
boy had swallowed it he became
ravenous, and could not stop eating.

He ate everything in sight, until
finally the chief decided he must send
the boy away. He gave his son a raven
blanket, and berries and fish roe to
scatter on the land and water, so that
he would never want for food.

### STEALING THE LIGHT

The boy put on his raven skin and
flew up to the sky world, which was
light. He waited by a spring until the
daughter of the Chief-of-the-Skies

## TOTEM POLES

The Native Americans of the northwest coast have a complex structure of kinship, visually codified in the carvings on totem poles. These are not religious artefacts but expressions of family pride, tracing a lineage back to an animal-people of the creation-time. Carvings of these animal ancestors often depict myths. Raven, for example, may be shown with the moon in his beak. Someone travelling to a strange village had only to look at the house totem poles to see which families shared his clan's totem, and would therefore offer him a welcome. Totem poles also have a mythological significance as representations of the World Tree, "the pole that holds up the sky".

came by, then transformed himself into a cedar leaf floating on the stream. The girl drank in the leaf with some water, and in due course gave birth to a baby boy. Everyone in the sky world loved him, but he never stopped crying, and they did not know why. Eventually they realized he was crying for the ball in which the daylight was kept. So they gave him the bladder of light to play with and he played with it happily for a long time, until one day he placed it onto his shoulder and ran to the hole in the sky. Putting his raven skin back on, he flew with the light back to Earth.

## THE WORLD TURNS BRIGHT

The world was still dark when Raven came down near the Nass River. The people were gathered there, eating olachen (candle-fish). Raven was as hungry as ever, so he called out: "Throw me one of those things you are catching." But they refused and shouted abuse at him.

"I have brought you light in a ball," Raven said, "and if you don't give me a fish, I shall break it." They just laughed, so Raven burst the bladder, and so it was that the daylight spilled out all over the world.

# QAYAQ THE WANDER-HAWK

- Culture hero
- Inuit
- Alaska

Knud Rasmussen, *The Eagle's Gift: Alaska Eskimo Tales*, as told by Nasuk; Lela Kiana Oman, *The Epic of Qayaq: The Longest Story Ever Told By My People*

Qayaq is the hero of an epic cycle of Alaskan Inuit tales, in which he wanders across the landscape in the creation-time. As he travels, he transforms himself into all kinds of animals, birds, and fish. Qayaq's journey is one of discovery and mastery of the secrets of the natural world: a process of learning by being. In its sad ending, he returns home to find his parents long dead, before undergoing his final transformation, into a wander-hawk.

### KEY CHARACTERS

**QAYAQ (WANDER-HAWK)** •
*transformer hero of the Alaskan Inuit*

**THE WOODMAN** • *Qayaq's father*

## PLOT SYNOPSIS

### THE WOODMAN

One day a young man came walking down to the coast at Selawik. No-one knew from where exactly; only that he had been born right in the heart of the country. He was a great hunter and trapper, and they named him the Woodman. He married, and with his wife had four sons, but one after another these sons went hunting and never came back. The grieving parents went down to the beach and there the Woodman took a piece of flint and struck sparks while he chanted magic words. Then he said, "Now we

**Inuit mythology** has no gods; instead there are spirit masters of the creatures they hunt.

shall have a son." When the child – a son – was born, the Woodman washed the baby's body with the skin of a falcon, and this skin became the baby's first amulet.

### WANDER-HAWK

They called the baby Wander-Hawk, although he was also called Qajartuarungnertoq, which means "He who shall always long to go roaming in his qayaq", so the people called him simply Qayaq. The Woodman brought Qayaq up to be a great hunter, and so that he would not suffer the fate of his brothers, he made

him more magic amulets to protect him. Every day he tested the magic. When Qayaq took his first steps, the Woodman threw a knife at him, but Qayaq dodged it. While Qayaq slept, the Woodman fired an arrow at him, but Qayaq dodged that too. So Qayaq grew into the greatest hunter of all time, and when he was old enough, he set out to avenge his brothers.

## QAYAQ'S ADVENTURES

As he wandered the land, Qayaq met many people who were really animals. He even married a girl who was a night-owl, but once she was expecting a son who could hunt for her, Qayaq continued on his quest.

He overcame all kinds of enemies, and also met many of the "friends of humankind", such as the man who stands by the river splitting chips from spruce trees to turn into salmon. Qayaq turned himself into a trout, an ermine, a maggot, and other creatures. Sometimes he was caught and eaten, but by the magic of his amulets he came alive again.

## QAYAQ'S HOMECOMING

When he had travelled round the whole world, along the Selawak, the Kobuk, the Noatak, and the Yukon, and

> ### SEDNA THE SEA-BEAST
>
> Sedna, the mistress of the sea-beasts, lives at the bottom of the sea. She was an orphan girl who was thrown into the sea because no-one cared about her. She tried to cling on to the qayaq, but the people chopped off her fingers, which became the first seals. Because she has no fingers, Sedna cannot brush her hair, and shamans must swim down past the dog that guards her to untangle and braid her hair for her.

avenged the deaths of his brothers by killing the monsters that preyed on humans, he came back to the place of his birth. But his father and mother were not there: they were long dead. Even the great tree that had grown from the ruins of their home was no more than a stump. Qayaq turned himself into a wander-hawk, and sat on the stump and wept. Then he spread his wings, rose into the air, and disappeared into the woods from which his father had emerged so many years before.

"*...and when the ball was dropped again, it was the head of Hunahpu that rolled over the court...*"

Denis Tedlock, *The Popol Vuh*

# THE HERO TWINS

📖 Culture heroes
🏹 Maya
🏛 Quiché kingdom, Guatemala

✍ Dennis Tedlock, *The Popol Vuh*; Schele & Miller, *The Blood of the Kings*; Karl Taube, *Aztec and Maya Myths*

**Hun Hunahpu,** father of the Hero Twins, was killed and beheaded by the lords of Xibalba. His sons tried to put him back together, but he could not name all his body parts, and so had to remain in the Underworld. The Mayans regarded him as the god of maize, and he is often depicted with corn cobs.

## BEHIND THE MYTH

The *Popol Vuh* is the sacred book of the Quiché Maya, transcribed in the mid-16th century as a retelling of an ancient hieroglyphic original. It contains both their creation and foundation myths and their history.

As in several other mythologies, there are in the Mayan beginning several botched attempts to create the human race, by the sea creator-god Gucumatz and the sky creator-god Heart of Sky. Their first beings are unable to speak the names of the gods; they squawk, howl, and chatter, and become the animals. A second race made of clay cannot talk sensibly either, and dissolves in water. The creators consult the diviners Xpiyacoc and Xmucane, two beings older than the gods, and on their advice create a new race, fashioning the men from wood and the women from reeds. But these proto-humans have no souls and refuse to worship the gods, so Heart of Sky sends a flood to destroy them.

## JOURNEY TO THE UNDERWORLD

In the end it is the grandsons of the two diviners who clear the way for the successful creation of humanity, by overcoming death. These two boys, the Hero Twins, venture into the Underworld to avenge the humiliation and murder of their father and uncle at the hands of the vicious lords of Xibalba. These are some of the most action-packed sections of the *Popol Vuh*. The way the clever Twins come to life again after their bones have been ground to powder inspires their grandmother, Xmucane, to fashion the first four humans, ancestors of the four Quiché patrilineages, from a flour-and-water dough.

### KEY CHARACTERS

**XPIYACOC AND XMUCANE** • *diviners, the matchmaker and the midwife of humanity*

**HUN HUNAHPU AND VUCUB HUNAHPU** • *sons of Xpiyacoc and Xmucane*

**XQUIC** • *a maiden of the Underworld*

**XBALANQUE AND HUNAHPU** • *Hero Twins, sons of Hun Hunahpu and Xquic*

**HUN CAME AND VUCUB CAME** • *lords of Xibalba, the Underworld*

## PLOT SYNOPSIS

### THE BALL-PLAYERS

Xpiyacoc and Xmucane had two sons, Hun Hunahpu and Vucub Hunahpu. These boys did nothing all day but throw dice and play ball. The noise they made disturbed Hun Came and Vucub Came, the lords of Xibalba, the Underworld. So the lords of death sent their owl-messengers to challenge the boys to come down to play them at ball.

### THE BOYS ARE MOCKED AND KILLED

When Hun Hunahpu and Vucub Hunahpu arrived in Xibalba, Hun Came and Vucub Came asked the boys to sit down; but they soon jumped up again, because the bench was boiling hot. The lords of Xibalba roared with laughter. Then they led them to the House of Darkness, with only a torch and two cigars for light. They were told to keep these burning. The next day, Hun Came and Vucub Came asked them, "Where is our torch? Where are our cigars?" When the boys could not produce them, for they were burned up, they were told, "For that you will be killed." The boys were sacrificed and buried at the Place of Ballgame Sacrifice. Hun Hunahpu's head was cut off and stuck in a tree. The tree bore fruit, which were the first calabashes.

The Mayan Underworld mirrored their civilization above ground, with an elite class – the lords of Xibalba – and temple and ballcourt complexes similar to Mayan centres such as Chichén Itzá.

The sacred ballgame of the Mayans had its origins in the story of the heroic brothers. The circular ring above is a goal used in this game.

### THE ARRIVAL OF THE HERO TWINS

Xquic, a maiden of Xibalba, went to see the calabash tree. When she reached up for a fruit, Hun Hunahpu's head spat in her palm. She became pregnant, and gave birth to the Hero Twins, Hunahpu and Xbalanque. The twins were just as keen on playing ball as their father and uncle. Once more, their shouts disturbed the lords of Xibalba, and so a fresh challenge was issued.

Hunahpu and Xbalanque crossed the river of Pus and the river of Blood and entered Xibalba. Each night they were made to stay in one of the terrible houses of Xibalba: the Dark House, the Razor House, the Cold House, the

Jaguar House, and the House of Fire. Each time they survived the tests to play the ballgame against the lords of Xibalba the next day; in the House of Darkness, for example, they prevented the cigars from burning up by sticking fireflies on the tips instead of lighting them. Finally, in the House of Bats, the Twins slept inside their blowguns for safety; but when Hunahpu put his head out to see if dawn had come, a bat snatched his head off, and sent it rolling onto the ball court.

Xbalanque carved a new head for Hunahpu from a squash, so when dawn did come, both Twins emerged. The ballgame started with Hunahpu's head as the ball; Xbalanque hit it clear out of the court, to where a rabbit was waiting to secretly bring it back to him. While the lords of Xibalba searched for the ball, Xbalanque replaced Hunahpu's head. And then the Twins thrashed the lords of Xibalba at the ballgame.

## A TERRIBLE DEATH

The lords of Xibalba could not bear this defeat. They burned the Twins in an oven, ground their bones like flour, and sprinkled them into the river. But six days

> ### MAYAN CALENDRICAL NAMES
>
> The prefixes "Hun" and "Vucub" mean "one" and "seven": Hun Hunahpu translates as "One Blowgunner", and Vucub Came as "Seven Death". Many Mayan mythological characters have names containing numbers that relate to the complex cycles of the Mayan calendar, which observed the solar year, the lunar year, and the Venus cycle in a series of interlocking timelines. Underpinning it all was a 260-day almanac, approximating to the human gestation period of nine months.
>
> **MAYAN CALENDAR STONE**

later the Twins returned to Xibalba, handsome as ever. The Twins boasted that they could bring the dead back to life. The lords of Xibalba challenged them to prove it. So Xbalanque spreadeagled Hunahpu and cut out his heart. Then he said, "Get up!" and Hunahpu came back to life. Hun Came and Vucub Came were so excited, they screamed, "Do it to us! Do it to us!" So Hunahpu and Xbalanque cut out the hearts of the lords of death, but they did not bring them back to life again. The power of death was now broken and diminished. Their work done, the Twins ascended to the sky, where they became the sun and moon.

# THE PLUMED SERPENT

📖 Creation
📜 Aztec
🏛 Mexico

✍ John Bierhorst, *History and Mythology of the Aztecs*; Díaz & Rodgers, *The Codex Borgia*; Bernadino de Sahagún, *Florentine Codex*; Karl Taube, *Aztec and Maya Myths*

The Aztecs believed that our world was the fifth sun, or creation, the others having been destroyed in turn by jaguars, wind, a rain of fire, and a great flood. The world was then recreated by the brothers Quetzalcoatl and Tezcatlipoca, who turned themselves into serpents to tear apart the Earth goddess Tlaltecuhtli, and create the Earth and the heavens. Quetzalcoatl then rescued the bones of the previous race to create new humans.

## KEY CHARACTERS

**QUETZALCOATL** • *god of the wind*

**TEZCATLIPOCA** • *trickster god, Quetzalcoatl's brother*

**MICTLANTECUHTLI** • *ruler of Mictlan, the Underworld*

**CIHUACOATL** • *a fertility goddess*

## PLOT SYNOPSIS

### DESCENT TO THE UNDERWORLD

Quetzalcoatl went to Mictlantecuhtli, ruler of the Underworld, to ask for the bones of the last race of humans, with which to people the Earth. The chief agreed, if Quetzalcoatl could ride four times round the dead land, blowing his conch horn. But the conch had no holes, so Quetzalcoatl called for worms to bore holes in the shell, and for bees to swarm into it and amplify the sound.

**Quetzalcoatl has a ruff** or fan of feathers from the Resplendent Quetzal, a spectacular bird with iridescent red and green plumage.

### A PROPHECY FULFILLED

In the months before the Spanish arrived in Mexico in 1519 under Cortés, the Aztec kingdom was full of dire prophecies.

Hunters brought Montezuma, the king, a bird with a mirror in its head, in which the heavens could be seen. The king looked into the mirror and saw a host of armed men. When Cortés first landed, Montezuma thought Quetzalcoatl had returned.

**HERNÁN CORTÉS**

### MICTLANTECUHTLI CHANGES HIS MIND

Quetzalcoatl was duly given the two precious piles of bones from men and women. He had to lie to the ghosts that he was leaving the bones behind, but they realized and tripped him as he fled, causing him to scatter the bones, which were gnawed by a quail.

Quetzalcoatl took the bones to the goddess Cihuacoatl, who ground them up so that Quetzalcoatl and the other gods could drip their blood onto them, resulting in the rebirth of humanity. But because the quail had nibbled the bones, people are all different sizes and doomed to die again.

# THE SMOKING MIRROR

📖 Culture hero     ✍ John Bierhorst, *History and Mythology of the Aztecs:*
📕 Aztec              *The Codex Chimalpopoca*; Bernadino de Sahagún,
🏛 Mexico         *Florentine Codex: General History of the Things of New Spain*

Post-Conquest accounts of Aztec mythology speak of Quetzalcoatl both as a god and as the human king of Tollan, Topiltzin Ce Acatl Quetzalcoatl (817–95 CE), a model for all the Aztec kings. In this human incarnation, Quetzalcoatl is credited with having introduced the Aztec calendar and many rituals. He refused to practise human sacrifice, so his evil brother Tezcatlipoca tricked him into disgracing himself, and resigning the kingship.

> **KEY CHARACTERS**
>
> **TOPILTZIN CE ACATL QUETZALCOATL** • *king of Tollan, human form of the god Quetzalcoatl*
> **TEZCATLIPOCA** • *a trickster, Quetzalcoatl's brother*
> **QUETZALPETLATL** • *Quetzalcoatl's sister*

## PLOT SYNOPSIS

### A LIFE OF PRAYER

Tezcatlipoca, Topiltzin's brother, was a sorceror and, jealous of his brother, he schemed against him. He carried a magic mirror that emitted smoke and killed his enemies. He was also a supporter of human sacrifice, and it was over this issue that he argued with his brother. Topiltzin refused to make payment to the gods with human hearts. Instead he shut himself in his house of prayer, confining himself to autosacrifice (giving up his own blood), prayer, and the sacrifice of snakes, birds, and butterflies. Because Topiltzin did nothing but pray, he wasted away, until he became horrible to look at. His eye sockets sank back into his skull, and his eyeballs bulged.

Tezcatlipoca announced: "I shall give him his body." He sent his brother a mirror, and Topiltzin was horrified at the sight of himself. So he asked the featherworker Coyotlinahual to make him a mask of turquoise set with serpent fangs, and a head fan and fringe

**An embellished skull** sculpture representing the fearsome Tezcatlipoca, god of the "smoking mirror".

of feathers from the quetzal and spoonbill birds. When Topiltzin looked in the mirror and saw himself so finely arrayed, he left the house of prayer a relieved and happier man.

### INCEST AND EXILE

His happy state led Topiltzin to drink pulque, and he became inebriated. He called for Quetzalpetlatl, his sister, who then also became drunk, and the brother and sister slept together. When they awoke, they were filled with sadness and shame. Mortified, Topiltzin sailed away to the east on a raft of serpents, vowing to return one day.

In another version of the myth, he casts himself on a funeral pyre in remorse, only to rise again as the Lord of the Dawn – the morning star, or Tlahuizcalpantecuhtli. Both versions of the myth promise his eventual return.

---

**RELATED MYTHS ▸** Inanna in the Underworld (*p.149*)
• The Hero Twins (*pp.208–11*)

# AZTEC SACRIFICE

The Aztecs thought humans owed the gods a blood debt, because the gods had given their own blood to recreate humanity, and had offered their hearts in order to make the new sun move across the sky. So sacrifice lay at the heart of their culture, from blood-letting rituals by priests and individuals to the full-scale sacrifice of human captives, from whom the still-beating hearts were cut out to offer to the gods.

## THE DEBT TO THE GODS

At the start of the fifth sun (cycle of creation) Quetzalcoatl, god of the wind, and Tezcatlipoca, the trickster god, dripped their own blood onto the bones of the previous human race to restore them to life (*see p.212*). As a result they were hungry for the sustenance offered by the beating hearts of the sacrificed. So, too,

**Victims** were flung down temple steps, re-enacting the Aztec fire god's slaying of an evil goddess.

was the goddess Tlaltecuhtli, whom the two gods tore in half to make the Earth and the heavens, causing her terrible pain. From her body grew all the plants that sustain humanity – but the gift came at a cost, for in the night, Tlaltecuhtli cried out for the hearts of men to eat.

## TEMPLE SACRIFICE

Hearts cut from human victims with sacrificial blades of obsidian were offered to the gods in a vessel called a *cuauhxicalli*, an "eagle gourd". After the heart had been removed, the victims were flayed and decapitated, and their skulls displayed on a skull rack.

## CALENDAR RITES

The Aztec ritual year was marked by sacrifices to other gods and goddesses at fixed points in the various interlocking cycles of the Aztec calendar. For instance, every 260 days a man representing Mictlantecuhtli, the god of the Underworld, was sacrificed at night in the temple of Tlalxicco, "the navel

of the world". It is thought that the victim was then eaten by the priests. Less high-ranking celebrants ate figures made of dough into which blood was mixed, known as *tzoalli*. To break apart *tzoalli* and consume them was to commune with the gods.

## FINDING VICTIMS

To ensure a constant supply of sacrificial victims, the Aztecs practised a kind of warfare known as "Flowery War", in which the object was to capture the enemy, not kill them. Ideally suited to Aztec culture, this method of fighting was hopelessly inadequate against the Spanish conquistadors under Cortés. Within 80 years of their arrival in 1519, defeat and European diseases had reduced the Aztec population from 20–25 million to one million.

## AUTOSACRIFICE

Not all ritual offerings involved the slaughter of enemies. The gods could also be propitiated with the smoke from incense and tobacco, and by foodstuffs and precious objects. The plumed god Quetzalcoatl appreciated

### XIPE TOTEC, THE FLAYED GOD

For the festival of Tlacaxipehualiztli, men impersonating the god Xipe Totec wore the flayed skin of a sacrificial victim. As the skin rotted, the wearer emerged from beneath it like a fresh sprout from a seed. This is how Xipe Totec is represented, as one man inside the skin of another. A fertility deity, he was also patron of goldsmiths.

**A gold mask** of Xipe Totec, the Flayed One, whose statues were covered in real human skin.

sacrifices of butterflies and hummingbirds. The Aztecs also let their own blood, from the tongue, the earlobe, or the penis, using either an obsidian blade or the thorn-like spine of a maguey, or agave plant. This bloodletting – or autosacrifice – not only nourished the gods in general, but specifically honoured the god Nanahuitzin, who won the contest between the gods to become the sun of the fifth age with an offering of maguey spines spotted with his own blood. This was deemed a more precious tribute than any of the priceless jewels offered by other gods.

**Many Aztec temples** are ornamented with stone representations of the *tzompantli*, the rack used to display the skulls of sacrificial victims.

# CHILDREN OF THE SUN

📖 Creation
👥 Inca
🏛 Lake Titicaca & Cusco, Peru

✍ Bernabé Cobo, *Inca Religion and Customs*;
Juan de Betanzos, *Narrative of the Incas*;
Gary Urton, *Inca Myths*

The Inca empire of Tawantinsuyu was founded in the city of Cusco around 1200, and by 1532 Inca rule extended across Peru, Ecuador, Chile, and parts of Bolivia and Argentina. The Incas believed that they were the children of the sun. Inti, the sun god, was worshipped in the Temple of the Sun; his image was a gold face surrounded by sunrays. But the creator was Viracocha, who moulded humans from stone still malleable from the creation.

### KEY CHARACTERS

**VIRACOCHA** • *the creator god*
**INTI** • *the sun god*
**ATAHUALLPA** • *the last Inca emperor*

## PLOT SYNOPSIS

### EMERGENCE FROM A LAKE

Viracocha emerged into the primal dark from the sacred waters of Lake Titicaca. He created a race of giants, but they angered him, so he drowned them and turned them to stone. Next he called the sun, the moon, and the stars out of the Island of the Sun in the centre of the lake. He picked up stones by the lakeside and shaped these into the first men and women, painting them with clothes, and giving each nation its own language, songs, and foods. Viracocha and his sons travelled among the peoples, teaching them how to live, before walking away across the Pacific Ocean.

### A FALSE RETURN

The Incas, believing that in their age the sun and the stars were at war, tried to tie them together by rituals at the Hitching-Post of the Sun at Machu Picchu. They pleaded with Viracocha: "May the world not turn over", and eagerly anticipated his promised return. Atahuallpa, the last Inca emperor, thought that the Spanish invader Pizarro was Viracocha come again; by the time he realized his mistake, he was Pizarro's prisoner and the Inca empire was being stripped of its wonderful treasures.

**Inti Raymi,** the Festival of the Sun, marks the start of a new year. It is still a huge festival in Cusco.

# THE BEGGAR CREATOR

📖 Creation; culture hero
🏹 Yauyos
🏛 Huarochirí, Peru

✍ Frank Salomon & George L. Urioste, *The Huarochirí Manuscript*; Gary Urton, *Inca Myths*

Among the Yauyos Indians of the Andean highlands, the foundation myths of the ruling Inca state were less relevant than their indigenous local myths. The remote Incan creator god Viracocha (*see opposite*) was for them an altogether earthier deity named Coniraya Viracocha. More trickster than creator, he had power over the animal kingdom, and frequently visited Earth disguised in the ragged clothes of a poor Indian.

### KEY CHARACTERS

**CONIRAYA VIRACOCHA** • *trickster culture-hero*
**CAVILLACA** • *a goddess*
**CAVILLACA'S SON**
**PACHACAMAC** • *maker of Earth and time*

## PLOT SYNOPSIS

Coniraya Viracocha wandered the land as a beggar. Spurned by the beautiful Cavillaca, he spilled his semen into a fruit, which she ate. One year after her baby's mysterious birth, she summoned all the male gods, who arrived in their finery except for Coniraya, who was in rags. When Cavillaca put her son on the ground, he identified his father by climbing onto the beggar's lap. Appalled, Cavillaca seized the baby and fled to the coast, home of the maker of Earth and time, Pachacamac.

**The ruins of Pachacamac**, built for the god of that name, the father of two beautiful daughters.

Coniraya set off in pursuit. On his way he encountered all the animals, and rewarded them with good or bad characteristics depending on how they answered his enquiries. The condor was encouraging, so Coniraya granted him long life; the skunk was not, so Coniraya gave him a vile smell. When he arrived at the coast, Coniraya found Cavillaca and her son turned to stone – so he made love to Pachacamac's elder daughter instead.

## MYTHS OF THE COMMON PEOPLE

The Hatunruna (common peoples) of the Inca empire, such as the Yauyos, believed that the landscape was alive with spirits of the "huacas", or sacred places. In addition to venerating these personifications of the sacred landscape, they worshipped the mummified bodies of their ancestors. Some of these mummies still survive, and the Quechua people of today believe them to be the first beings, or ancient ones.

**A huaca was a** sacred site, often a temple, bridge, or mountain. But a mummy, especially of a high-ranking Inca, might also become one.

**Rituals celebrating** the lives of ancestors can be traced back to many ancient American cultures, including the Aztecs. One of the most boisterous of these festivals is Mexico's Day of the Dead, where orange marigolds, called *cempaxochitl* in the Aztec language, are used to decorate graves.

# MOTHER OF THE FOREST

📖 Culture hero
📕 The Warao culture
🏛 Orinoco Delta, Venezuela

✍ Johannes Wilbert, *Folk Literature of the Warao Indians*; *Mystic Endowment: Religious Ethnography of the Warao Indians*

The story of Dauarani, the Mother of the Forest, arises from the myth of Haburi and his escape from the frog-woman. Haburi's father, a hunter named the Roaster, was married to two sisters. One day an evil spirit killed the Roaster and chased the sisters and baby Haburi to the house of an old frog-woman named Wauta. In a bid to escape, Haburi invented the dugout canoe and the paddle, which transformed themselves into Dauarani and her lover.

## KEY CHARACTERS

**THE ROASTER** • *a hunter*
**TWO SISTERS** • *Otter-women, wives of the Roaster*
**HABURI** • *son of the younger sister*
**WAUTA** • *a frog-woman*
**DAUARANI** • *Mother of the Forest*

## PLOT SYNOPSIS

### A CANOE AND PADDLE TRANSFORMED

When the women and baby Haburi arrived at Wauta the frog-woman's house, Wauta turned the baby into a man, who committed incest with the women. Haburi then invented the dugout canoe and the paddle, so the three of them could escape from Wauta. They canoed to the northern world mountain, where the water god Nabarima lived.

Redundant, the cachicamo-wood canoe turned into a giant snake-woman, and the paddle turned into a man, her lover. They returned to the centre of

the Earth, where the snake-woman became Dauarani, the Mother of the Forest. The Warao people, looking down from a hole in the sky world where they lived, saw the world with all its food, and slid down to Earth on a rope. Dauarani became the first of the Warao priest-shamans, whose name, Wishiratu, means "Masters of Pain".

### DUGOUT CANOES

The name Warao means "boat people". The Warao virtually live in their dugout canoes, and when they die they are buried in them. The canoes are made from the wood of the cachicamo tree, like the canoe that turned into Dauarani. Each boat is a recreation of the original, and boat-building is seen not as a craft but as a spiritual exercise, in which the craftsman becomes the lover of Dauarani herself.

**Boat-building is** a spiritual and sexual process to the Warao, who see the canoe as symbolic of the great goddess Dauarani's vulva.

# THE COMING OF THE NIGHT

📖 Creation
📏 The Yekuana (Makiritare) culture
🏛 Upper Orinoco River, Venezuela

✍ Marc de Civrieux, *Watunna: An Orinoco Creation Cycle*; David M. Guss, *To Weave and to Sing*

Wanadi the creator sent his spirit messenger, also called Wanadi, down to Earth, which at the time basked in constant daylight. The Earth-Wanadi created the first people and buried his own placenta, which sprang up from the Earth as Odosha, an evil man. Odosha persuaded the people to kill Wanadi, and they were turned into animals as punishment. A second and third Wanadi were then sent to Earth, but only the fourth will finally destroy Odosha.

**KEY CHARACTERS**

**WANADI** • *the creator and his incarnations*
**ODOSHA** • *the spirit of evil*
**KUMARIAWA** • *Wanadi's mother*
**IARAKARU** • *Wanadi's nephew*
**KUDEWA** • *a parrot*

## PLOT SYNOPSIS

### WANADI PLAYS WITH DEATH

The second incarnation of Wanadi was determined to prove to people that death was an illusion. He sat in silence, smoking and dreaming, and dreamed his own mother into being as a grown woman, named Kumariawa. When Wanadi thought "Life", she was born; when he thought "Death", she died. He did this to show his power to Odosha.

Wanadi buried Kumariawa in the ground, and left Kudewa the parrot watching the grave, saying, "She'll come back soon. Don't let Odosha near her." He also left his chakara (his shaman's medicine pouch) with his nephew Iarakaru, and told him on no account to open it, or the night would escape. Then Wanadi went hunting.

**Capuchin monkeys** are called iarakarus in the Orinoco region of Venezuela, after Wanadi's nephew, who turned into a monkey after letting out the night.

### THE NIGHT IS BORN

Kumariawa's arm suddenly reached out of the ground. Kudewa screeched a warning, and Wanadi came running back. As he ran, the dark of night fell all around him for the first time. Odosha had whispered in Iarakaru's ear, and he had opened the chakara, letting out the night. Iarakaru was so frightened he turned into a white monkey (the first of all the capuchin monkeys). As Wanadi's mother continued to rise from the earth, Odosha threw his urine over her. A fiery poison, it scorched the flesh from her body, leaving only bones. Kudewa screamed, but when Wanadi arrived there was nothing he could do. All was darkness, ash, and bones.

"There is no light. The world is not mine anymore," Wanadi said. "The people will all die now." He went back to the sky world, taking his mother's bones with him, and brought her back to life in heaven. He left the Earth to Odosha. But Odosha will not live forever; he will die when evil disappears, and then a new race of good, wise people will be born on the Earth.

# AFRICA

T HE MYTHS OF AFRICA, passed on orally in more than 1,000 languages, are not very widely known. They contain the essence of what Africa is, has been, and can be. Gods, spirits, and ancestors congregate here in a supernatural dimension that overlaps the visible world. Twins have special significance, representing the balance between opposing forces that exists in the natural world.

Belief systems in sub-Saharan Africa tend not to be very rigidly organized, and attempts to categorize deities into pantheons are not especially helpful. Even in Benin, where the royal family made a deliberate effort to organize the traditional Fon religion, no-one has ever managed to list all the gods and cults. In Mali, Dogon mythology infuses every aspect of life with spiritual meaning, and is so complex it would take a lifetime to fully understand.

**A bushman** of the Kalahari examines rock paintings of the early San people, depicting animals and deities.

This complexity and richness is reflected also in the one written mythology of Africa, that of Ancient Egypt. Yet even in Egypt, where the myths were recorded, they have often survived only in fragmentary form.

## THE GODS OF EGYPT

Egyptian texts speak of so many gods they could not be numbered. These gods were aspects of the limitless creator, the "Hidden One whose eternal form is unknown". Each existed first as a kind of abstract power, a state of being that encompassed many potentialities. These potentialities could take individual forms, the nature of which was often represented by an animal.

The state of flux in which the gods existed can be seen both by the variety of animal forms they could assume

(Anubis, for example, could be jackal, snake, or falcon) and by the way in which two or more gods could join forces to form a combined divinity, such as Ra-Horakhty (Ra and Horus), or Isermithis (Isis and Renenutet).

The Egyptians did not worship animals in themselves, but revered the animal forms in which their gods manifested themselves. Animals linked to particular gods – such as the crocodile of the god Sobek, the cat of the goddess Bastet, the falcon of the god Horus, or the sacred ibis of the god Thoth – were bred in their temple sanctuaries. Worshippers would pay for the embalming and burial of a temple animal as an act of piety, and the animals were mummified so that they might come to life again in the next world and act as intermediaries between the gods and humankind.

## SUB-SAHARAN MYTHS

Storytelling remains one of the endless natural resources of sub-Saharan Africa. As one San shaman put it: "A story is like the wind: it comes from a distant place, and we feel it." One famous myth from the Ashanti of Ghana tells how the stories themselves – the myths that describe cosmology and creation, and defined

**Egyptian sphinxes** are mythical hybrids with the body of a lion but the head of a human or ram.

the social order – were won from the demanding sky god Onyankopon by the trickster spider, Anansi. At first the sky god refused to give Anansi the stories; when the spider insisted that the god name his price, Onyankopon asked Anansi to bring him Onini the python, Osebo the leopard, Mmoboro the hornet swarm, and Mmoatia the spirit – an impossible task. But with the help of his wife, Anansi trapped all the creatures, and even added his own mother to the haul for good measure.

Onyankopon was both amused and impressed, and gave Anansi the stories. Anansi stories are now commonly told in the Caribbean as well as in Ghana, having travelled out with African slaves, who brought their myths and their gods with them to the New World.

**The Dogon tribe** of Mali believe that dancing creates a bridge into the supernatural world.

# THE CREATION

📖 Creation
📍 Ancient Egypt
🏛 The Nile Valley, Egypt

✍ E. A. Wallis Budge, *The Gods of the Egyptians*; Miriam Lichtheim, *Ancient Egyptian Literature*; D. Meeks and C. Favard-Meeks, *The Daily Life of the Egyptian Gods*

The highly complex mythology of Ancient Egypt has several creation stories, all with the same main themes of order versus chaos, and creation versus destruction. In the primal ocean before time began, the creator rested in the form of a cosmic serpent, an ouroboros, symbol of eternity and the endless renewal of time. The creator manifested himself as Ra, the sun god, who was also known as Atum, "the all", and Nebertcher, "the lord without limit".

### KEY CHARACTERS

**RA** • *the sun and creator god*
**SHU** • *god of dry air*
**TEFNUT** • *goddess of moist air*
**GEB** • *the Earth god*
**NUT** • *the sky goddess*
**THOTH** • *the moon god*

## PLOT SYNOPSIS

### THE DAWN OF AWARENESS
In the great ocean of Nun, "non-being", the creator became aware of himself. He was Ra, the sun god. Ra created the other gods from within himself, by an act of masturbation or auto-fellation. From his nostrils he sneezed out Shu, the god of dry air; from his mouth he spat out Tefnut, the goddess of moist air.

### THE ELEMENTS OF CREATION
Ra used three innate forces to bring the world into being – forces that would later become gods themselves, and accompany Ra in his solar barque (his sky-ship). These forces were Heka,

creative power or magic; Sia, perception; and Hu, pronouncement. Using these forces he called out all the elements of creation, creating them as he spoke their names. He then created a fourth power, Ma'at, the goddess of truth and cosmic harmony, to regulate his creation.

### MAKING THE WORLD
Ra sent Shu and Tefnut out across the water. He caused the primal ocean of Nun to recede so that he had an island on which to stand (this primal mound was called the Benben Stone, and would become the model for the pyramids). Ra "thought in his heart" about how

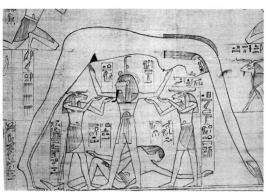

**Nut, the sky goddess** and vault of the heavens, is held up by her father Shu, the god of dry air.

things should be, and then called forth from Nun all the plants, birds, and animals of the Earth. He spoke their names and they came into being.

## THE EYE OF RA

Ra sent his eye, the goddess Hathor, to look for Shu and Tefnut. When she returned with them, she was angry, for another eye had grown on Ra's face in her place. She wept bitterly, and her tears became the first human beings. Then Ra placed her on his brow in the form of an enraged cobra, to be with him ruling over the world until, at the end of time, all creation will pass away and the world will once more be covered by the infinite flood of Nun.

## EARTH AND SKY

The children of Shu and Tefnut were Geb, the dry Earth, and Nut, the moist sky. Nut lay on top of Geb, and the sky mated with the Earth, giving birth to the

**The sacred lake** at Karnak, Egypt, symbolized Nun, the primeval waters of chaos, from which Ra rose to create the world and all its inhabitants.

stars. Consumed with jealousy, their father Shu wrenched the pair apart, holding the sky aloft with his hands and pinning down the Earth with his feet.

## THE ENNEAD

After the birth of the stars, Shu cursed his daughter so that she would never again give birth in any month of the year. But Nut gambled with Thoth, the moon god and time-reckoner, and won five extra days from him, to be added to the 12 lunar months of 30 days each. On these days she gave birth to her five children: Blind Horus, Osiris, Seth, Isis, and Nephthys (*see p.232*). The last four of these joined Ra, Shu, Tefnut, Geb, and Nut to form the Ennead – Egypt's nine greatest gods.

# THE NIGHT BARQUE OF RA

📖 World renewal
🏺 Ancient Egypt
🏛 The Nile Valley, Egypt

📜 E. A. Wallis Budge, *The Gods of the Egyptians*; Miriam Lichtheim, *Ancient Egyptian Literature*

"Hail to you Ra, perfect each day!" opens an Egyptian hymn to the sun god, the uncreated creator who "traverses eternity", and to whom each day is but a moment. Every night Ra sails through the Underworld in his night barque. He is attacked each night by the chaos serpent Apophis; if Apophis were ever to vanquish Ra, the sun would fail to rise. To help prevent this, the Egyptians performed elaborate rituals against Apophis.

### KEY CHARACTERS

**RA** • *the sun god*
**NUT** • *the sky goddess*
**APOPHIS** • *the chaos serpent*
**SETH** • *the god of chaos and confusion*
**MEHEN** • *a serpent-god*

## PLOT SYNOPSIS

### THE FORMS OF THE SUN
The sun god Ra took three main forms: Khepri, the scarab beetle, who was the rising sun; Aten, the sun's disc, who was the midday sun; and Atum, the setting sun, often depicted as an old man leaning wearily on a stick.

### SWALLOWED BY THE SKY
Each evening, as the sun reached the westernmost peak of Mount Manu, the sky goddess Nut swallowed it. Each morning, she gave birth to it once more in the East. This daily cycle of death and rebirth came to symbolize the life-cycle of mankind, who hoped after death to find a new birth, "the birth of Ra in the West".

**The Egyptian god** Ra's nightly voyage represents the classic and eternal battles between light and darkness, good and evil, and life and death.

### THE CHAOS SERPENT
During the day Ra travelled across the sky in his solar barque. At night he sailed in a different ship, accompanied by Seth, the god of chaos (*see p.232*), and Mehen, a serpent-god who coiled his body around the vessel. As they sailed through the Underworld, Ra and his companions were assailed by demons led by the monstrous serpent Apophis. In the darkest hour before dawn, Apophis would make his most desperate attack. Each night Seth would spear the serpent, and Ra, in the form of a cat, would cut off its head. And each day the sun would rise again.

### RA AND TUTANKHAMUN

The fanatical New Kingdom pharaoh Akhenaten tried to establish Aten, the disc of the midday sun, as the only god. He abandoned the old capital of Thebes, where Ra was worshipped as Amun, the hidden god, and built a new city at el-Amarna in honour of the Aten. He even named his son Tutankhaten, "Living image of the Aten". But with the abandonment of Akhenaten's city and reforms, the boy took the name by which history now knows him, Tutankhamun, "Living image of Amun".

# THE SECRET NAME OF RA

📖 Rivalries of the gods
📜 Ancient Egypt
🏛 The Nile Valley, Egypt

✍ E. A. Wallis Budge, *The Gods of the Egyptians*; Miriam Lichtheim, *Ancient Egyptian Literature*

Ra had so many names that even the gods did not know them all. The full names of the gods were so long that some could take years just to pronounce. The Egyptians considered someone's name to be an essential part of the person; to destroy someone's name by defacing their monuments after death was literally to rub them out, and so destroy them in the Underworld. Hence the importance of Isis's quest to discover Ra's secret name.

**KEY CHARACTERS**

**RA** • the sun god
**ISIS** • goddess of motherhood
**HORUS** • god of kingship, son of Isis and her husband Osiris

## PLOT SYNOPSIS

### BITTEN BY A SNAKE

Each evening, Ra became old. His mouth grew slack, and his spittle dribbled to the ground. The goddess Isis, the mistress of magic, collected the spittle, shaped it into a snake, and left it lying in Ra's path. The snake bit him, and Ra, king of the gods, fell down with a terrible cry. His limbs trembled as the poison surged through him like the Nile in flood.

"I have been wounded by some deadly thing – some thing that I did not make," said Ra. "I have never tasted such pain. My secret name has been hidden in my body since before I was born, to protect me from the spells of others. Yet something has stung me. My heart is burning and my body is trembling like the waves."

### ISIS STEALS RA'S NAME

Isis, radiant with power, said she would drive out the poison if Ra would tell her his secret name. The poison burned in Ra's veins, so he allowed his name to pass from his body into hers.

Then she chanted: "Flow out, poison, and spill to the ground! I, Isis, command you, by the name which has passed from Ra's heart to mine. Flow out, and spill to the ground! By the power of his name, Ra shall live and the poison shall die. Flow out, and spill to the ground!" Ra was cured, but Isis knew his name.

**Isis inherited power** from Ra when she learned his name, and she in turn passed this power to her son Horus, as shown on the Temple of Isis at Philae.

**The Great Pyramid of Khufu** at Giza, near Cairo, is the only one of the ancient Seven Wonders of the World still standing. The first step-pyramid tomb was designed for the 3rd Dynasty pharoah Djoser by the architect Imhotep, later revered as a god of wisdom, writing, and medicine.

# SIBLING RIVALRY

📖 Rivalry of the gods
🏳 Ancient Egypt
🏛 The Nile Valley

✍ Plutarch, *Of Isis and Osiris*; E. A. Wallis Budge,
*The Gods of the Egyptians*; Miriam Lichtheim,
*Ancient Egyptian Literature*

The sibling rivalry between the brothers Osiris,
Seth, and Blind Horus reflects the struggle between
order and chaos in Egyptian creation myth. Both
Osiris and Seth took one of their sisters as their
wife, as did the Egyptian kings, and each lusted
after the other's wife. The only possible outcome
of their jealous rivalry was murder. Seth first killed
Blind Horus and then Osiris, but Isis bore a child
who would avenge them.

### KEY CHARACTERS

**OSIRIS** • *first king of Egypt*
**SETH** • *Osiris's brother, god
of chaos and confusion*
**BLIND HORUS** • *Osiris's
brother*
**ISIS** • *Osiris's sister-wife*
**NEPHTHYS** • *Osiris's sister,
Seth's sister-wife*

## PLOT SYNOPSIS

### THE FIRST KING

Osiris was the first king of the
upper world. He earned the name
Wennefer, "eternally good", and
his sister-wife Isis was equally
well liked for the life-skills she
taught the women. But Osiris
had a violent brother named
Seth, who had already killed
one brother – Blind Horus –
and now decided to murder
another. He tricked Osiris
into a wooden chest, which
he sealed with molten lead
and floated down the Nile.
Osiris's wife Isis rescued
his body, but Seth found it,
cut it up, and scattered the
pieces all over Egypt. "It is not possible
to destroy the body of a god," he said,
"but I have done so."

**Osiris is usually** depicted
carrying the crook and flail
that signify divine authority.

### THE FIRST MUMMY

Isis and her sister Nephthys
gathered all the fragments.
With the help of Anubis (the
jackal-god of the dead) and
Thoth (the moon god), the
sisters pieced them together
to make the first mummy.
Then Isis transformed herself
into a kite and hovered over
Osiris's body, fanning breath
into it just long enough to
become pregnant. She fled
from Seth, accompanied by
seven scorpions. When a rich
woman refused her shelter,
the scorpions stung the
woman's son, but Isis took
pity on him and saved him. Later, when
her infant son Horus was bitten by a
scorpion, Isis was unable to save him,

## THE MYSTERIES OF OSIRIS

The story of the death, mummification, and resurrection of Osiris was the myth that offered the Egyptians the hope of life after death, in Osiris's kingdom. The cult centre of Osiris was at Abydos, where for more than 2,000 years the mysteries of the god were celebrated every year. The public festival involved the re-enactment of the story of Osiris's murder by Seth, but the secret rituals were never revealed.

**When Anubis mummified** his father Osiris, he set a precedent for a long funerary tradition. Prayers were often written on the linen bindings.

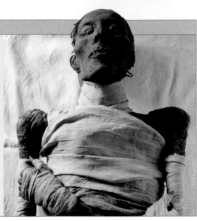

because she had used up her power. But her anguish was so great it halted Ra, the sun god, causing the whole world to falter. Ra saved the day – and the world – by sending Thoth to cure Horus.

## EIGHTY YEARS OF ARGUMENT

Horus grew up and claimed that he should inherit the throne. For 80 years Seth and Horus contested the throne, in a series of ferocious and darkly comic battles. Once Seth surprised Horus lying asleep in an oasis, and tore out his eyes. Isis found Horus blind and weeping in the desert, and restored his sight.

## RAPE AND REVENGE

Seth invited Horus to a feast, and that night inserted his penis between Horus's thighs. Horus caught Seth's semen in his hand. When he showed it to Isis, she cut off his hand, threw it into the Nile, and made a new hand for him. Then she collected semen from Horus, and spread it on a lettuce in Seth's garden, so that Seth ate it.

## THE COURT OF THE GODS

Seth told the gods that Horus was not worthy, because Seth had lain with him. Horus denied it, and counter-charged. The court asked the semen of Seth to speak out, and it spoke from the river; then they asked the semen of Horus to speak out, and it spoke from within Seth. It came out from the top of Seth's forehead as a golden sun-disc, which Thoth seized and put on his own head.

## SHIPS OF STONE

Seth then challenged Horus to a race in ships made of stone. But Horus plastered over a ship made of pine, while Seth made his from a mountain peak, and it sank. He was so furious that he turned into a hippopotamus and wrecked Horus's ship. After this, Horus was finally awarded the kingship, while Seth was exiled to the desert.

**RELATED MYTHS ▸** Demeter and Persephone (*p.54*) • The vanishing god (*p.152*) • Storm versus sun (*p.182*) • Daughter of the Sun (*p.198*)

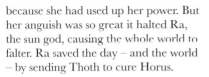

# THE EGYPTIAN AFTERLIFE

The Egyptians were not obsessed with death, but with life. All their rituals of death – mummification, entombment, and ritual remembrance – were to ensure a new life after death. They wanted to live as perfect beings in the Field of Reeds, Osiris's domain, where the blessed dead gather in rich crops of barley and wheat.

**Canopic jars** carrying the deceased's name held organs removed during mummification, to be reunited with their owner in the afterlife.

### PRESERVING THE WHOLE PERSON

The Egyptians believed that in order to ensure this new life, all the elements that went to make up a person had to be cared for: the physical body, the name, and the shadow. The body had to be preserved because it was to the body that the *ka* – the body's vital force – would return for sustenance. If the body decayed, the *ka* would starve, and be unable to unite with the *ba*, the soul or personality, to create the *akh*, the perfected spirit that could enjoy life in the Field of Reeds.

Mummification allowed the deceased to be identified with Osiris, through a ceremony that re-enacted the god's death and resurrection and brought the gift of eternal life. The chief embalmer and overseer of the mysteries enacted the role of the jackal-god Anubis, the protective god of the dead.

**The winged being,** or *ba* bird, represents a component of the departed soul, which had to be reunited with the mummified body every night.

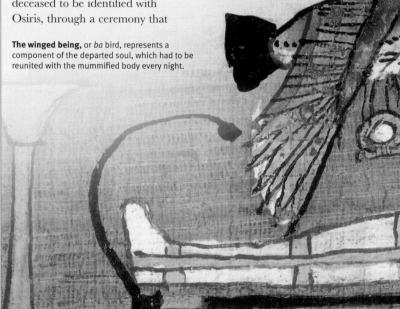

The process of mummification took 70 days. It began with the Opening of the Mouth ceremony, a series of 75 ritual acts that transformed the corpse into a vessel for the dead person's *ka*. All the parts of the body that might be needed in a new life, starting with the mouth, were touched with special instruments to restore their function.

## THE TWO TRUTHS

The deceased then negotiated the path from this world to the next, avoiding perils such as the god with a dog's head who swallowed shadows and tore out hearts. They were then led by Anubis into the Hall of the Two Truths. There the dead person's heart was weighed in balance against the feather of Ma'at, or Truth. If the heart, heavy with shame and sin, outweighed the feather, it would be gobbled up by Ammut, the she-monster devourer of the dead. If the feather outweighed the heart, Horus led the deceased into the presence of Osiris and the 42 gods who sat as judges in the Underworld.

**The jackal god** Anubis, god of the dead, was said to have invented the art of embalming.

## THE FINAL JUDGMENT

The Underworld was a narrow valley with a river running through it. It was separated from the living world by a mountain range, from which the sun rose and set. In the Underworld the wicked suffered a second death from which there was no return; ordinary mortals entered the service of Osiris; while the good enjoyed happy, eternal life. An Ancient Egyptian song tells us: "Earthly life is just a fleeting dream. When you reach the land of the dead, you are welcomed safely home."

# /KAGGEN'S ELAND

📖 Creation
🗿 San, southern Africa
🏛 Kalahari Desert

✍ D. F. Bleek, *The Mantis and His Friends*;
J. D. Lewis-Williams, *Stories that Float from Afar*

The culture of the San Bushmen – the indigenous people of the Kalahari Desert in southern Africa – stretches back at least 30,000 years, making the San one of the oldest peoples in the world. The "clicks" in their language, represented here by a forward slash (/), are traces of the earliest human speech. The San creator /Kaggen is a trickster, who features in many of their myths in diverse guises – foolish, wise, helpful, or playful.

**KEY CHARACTERS**

**/KAGGEN** • *the San creator, who can take on the form of a human, or one of many animal forms, such as a mantis, eland, or hare*
**KWAMMANG-A** • *the Rainbow*
**/NI-OPWA** • *the Ichneumon*

## PLOT SYNOPSIS

### MAKING AN ELAND
Kwammang-a, the Rainbow, lost a piece of his shoe. His father-in-law /Kaggen, the Mantis, found it and soaked it in a pool of water. It turned into the first eland, although it was only small. /Kaggen tracked the eland, and trilled to it to come to him, calling it "Kwammang-a's shoe-piece".

Whenever he called, the eland came to him. /Kaggen rubbed the eland with honeycomb to make it shine, and fed it on honey until it was full-sized. When he saw how beautiful it was, /Kaggen sang for joy.

**For San bushmen,** intricately detailed rock paintings were more than just depictions of life; when shamans painted an eland, they harnessed its essence.

### THE DEATH OF THE ELAND
Kwammang-a and his son /Ni-opwa, the Ichneumon, wondered what /Kaggen was doing with all the honey, so /Ni-opwa spied on his grandfather and saw the eland. Kwammang-a lay in wait for it and killed it while it drank from the pool. When /Kaggen arrived, and saw Kwammang-a cutting up the eland, he wept.

### THE COMING OF THE NIGHT
/Kaggen took the eland's gall-bladder and pierced it with a stick. Darkness poured out, covering the world. So that there might be some light, /Kaggen tossed his own shoe into the sky, and it became the moon.

### THE MYTH'S LEGACY
To this day the eland is the most spiritually charged of animals, appearing in four key rituals of the Bushmen – a boy's first kill, a girl's puberty, marriage, and the trance dance, in which San shamans (*see box, opposite*) attempt to take on the potency of the eland.

# THE ORIGIN OF DEATH

- 📖 Origin of death
- 📍 San, southern Africa
- 🏛 Kalahari Desert

✍ W. H. I. Bleek and L. C. Lloyd, *Specimens of Bushman Folklore*; Janette Deacon and Thomas A. Dowson, *Voices from the Past*

In San mythology, the moon walks across the night sky like the shoe he once was (*see opposite*); when the moon is full, the sun pierces him with his knife, so that he decays, leaving only his backbone. Then, following the promise of the creator /Kaggen, the moon is slowly reborn, until once again he feels truly alive. Until he was annoyed by the hare, the moon wanted the animal-people of the San creation-time to enjoy the same privilege.

## KEY CHARACTERS

**/KAGGEN** • *the San creator, who dreamed the world into being*

**THE MOON** • *formed from the shoe of /Kaggen*

**THE HARE** • *a human in hare form*

## PLOT SYNOPSIS

### THE TIME BEFORE DEATH
Just as the moon always rose again after his death, so the moon intended for people to return after their deaths. The moon wished for people to do as he did, for allowing them to be reborn would bring them joy.

### THE DANGER OF DESPAIR
A human in the form of a hare was grieving for his dead mother. "My mother is dead, and will never come back," he lamented. The moon said, "Don't cry: she will come back." "No," said the hare, "she is dead and will never return." Because the hare would not agree with him, the moon flew into a rage. He struck the hare, leaving a scar on his lip, and cursed him. The angry moon declared: "As for men, now they shall die and never return," and with his words began death.

### SAN SHAMANISM

For the San, the natural and supernatural worlds are inextricably entwined, and San rock paintings, found all across southern Africa, testify to the central importance of shamanism in San culture. The San say that /Kaggen dreamed the world into being and San shamans can enter a similar creative dream-state to exercise their powers, such as rain-making, healing, and hunting magic. When in this state a shaman is said to have died; his or her heart has become a star. One of the main sources of San mythology was the /Xam shaman /Kabbo, whose name translates as "Dream", and who is said to have derived his powers directly from /Kaggen. San shamans are said to be able, like /Kaggen, to shape-shift, particularly into the form of a lion.

**In Yoruba voodoo,** male dancers at the Gelede festival wear carved masks as a "second face". They see themselves as representatives of a spirit, the "Great Ancestral Mother". Initiates into Gelede society are regarded as guardians of its morality and order.

# THE RAINBOW SERPENT

📖 Creation; the end of the world

🏴 The Fon culture of Dahomey, Benin

🏛 Benin, West Africa

✍ Melville J. Herskovits and Frances S. Herskovits, *Dahomean Narrative*; Melville J. Herskovits, *Dahomey*

Mawu-Lisa is a god with two faces. The first is that of a woman, Mawu, whose eyes are the moon; the second is that of a man, Lisa, whose eyes are the sun. Mawu rules the night and Lisa rules the day. Mawu has a servant, the serpent Aido-Hwedo, who helped her to create the world. Like Mawu-Lisa, Aido-Hwedo is a twinned male-female form; one half lives in the sky and the other in the sea. On the latter half depends the safety of the world.

**KEY CHARACTERS**

**MAWU-LISA** • *the male-female creator god*

**AIDO-HWEDO** • *the rainbow serpent*

**ADANHU** • *the first man*

**YEWA** • *the first woman*

## PLOT SYNOPSIS

### CREATING THE WORLD

When Mawu was making the world, Aido-Hwedo, the rainbow serpent, was her servant. It is said that he came into existence with the first man and woman, Adanhu and Yewa. Aido-Hwedo carried Mawu in his mouth wherever she wanted to go, which is why the Earth curves and winds: it was carved from the sinuous movements of the serpent. Wherever they rested there are now mountains, which are the excrement of Aido-Hwedo. It is for this reason that great riches (metals) can be found within the mountains today.

### TOO MANY THINGS

When Mawu had finished her work of creation, she saw that she had made too many things: too many trees, too many mountains, too much of everything. The Earth could not bear the weight. So she told Aido-Hwedo to coil himself into a circle

beneath the Earth, to support it. Aido-Hwedo does not like heat, so Mawu made the cold sea as a home for him. When the Earth chafes him, Aido-Hwedo shifts, and causes earthquakes. He eats iron bars, forged for him by red monkeys that live beneath the sea, and when the iron runs out, Aido-Hwedo will begin to starve. In desperation he will gnaw through his own tail. He will convulse, and the Earth and all its burdens will tip into the sea.

**RELATED MYTHS** ▸ African gods in the New World (*p.242*) • The Rainbow snake (*p.249*)

**Fon tribespeople** make yearly offerings to the gods to ensure the gods' protection and benevolence.

# MONKEY NEARLY BECOMES A MAN

📖 Creating the animals
🚩 The Fon culture of Dahomey, Benin
🏛 Benin, West Africa

✍ Melville J. Herskovits and Frances
S. Herskovits, *Dahomean Narrative*

Mawu-Lisa, the male-female creator god, became pregnant and gave birth to seven children, including Da Zodji, god of the Earth; So, god of thunder; Agbé, god of the sea; and Gu, god of iron and war. The god's female half, Mawu, then populated the Earth and sent her male half, Lisa, with Gu, down to Earth to teach people how to live. Mawu then made the animals – and found that one of them also needed a lesson in good behaviour.

> **KEY CHARACTERS**
>
> **MAWU-LISA** • *the male-female creator god*
> **GU** • *god of iron and war*
> **MONKEY** • *one of the animals created by Mawu*

## PLOT SYNOPSIS

### MAWU MAKES THE ANIMALS

After Mawu had created people, she started to create all the animals. She told them she would name them when she had completed her task, but first they must help her work the clay from which she was moulding more creatures.

The animals all began to knead the clay, softening it in readiness for Mawu's creative hands. Mawu happened to notice the monkey she had made, and said: "As you have five fingers on each hand, if you work well I will put you among men, not among the animals."

Monkey was thrilled at the prospect. He went around to all the other animals in turn – the lion, the elephant, the hyena, and all the rest – boasting that

**According to some** versions of the myth, the monkey fell foul of Mawu by saying he could bestow the gift of life, so she killed him by poisoning his porridge.

he was so much better than they were. "Tomorrow I won't be among you animals; I'll be a man," said Monkey, utterly pleased with himself.

### PRIDE GOES BEFORE A FALL

Monkey was so busy showing off to the other animals that he didn't do any work at all. When Mawu came back, she saw Monkey clapping his hands and singing: "Tomorrow I will be a man, tomorrow I will be a man." Mawu was so angry she kicked him, and said to the foolish creature: "You will always be Monkey, and you will never walk erect."

### FA DIVINATION

Fon mythology features a trickster god called Legba, who is also the god of divination (or Fa). Legba has a dual-sexed sister named Gbadu who has 16 eyes and lives at the top of a palm tree, watching over the whole world. It is Legba's job to climb the palm each morning and open Gbadu's eyes; he asks her which eyes she wants opened, and she communicates by putting palm kernels in his hand. An earthly Fa diviner also learns Mawu's will by throwing palm kernels to open Gbadu's eyes.

# AFRICAN GODS IN THE NEW WORLD

Between the 16th and 19th centuries, more than 12 million people – many from the Fon, Yoruba, and Ewe tribes of West Africa's notorious "slave coast" – were transported to the Caribbean and North America. In the crucible of slavery, their myths and rituals fused into new religions – candomblé in Brazil, santería in Cuba, obeah in Jamaica, and, in North America and Haiti, voodoo.

## PRESERVING THEIR ROOTS

The new hybrid religions helped the slaves to celebrate their West African identity and served as a focus for resistance and rebellion. Not surprisingly, the slavemasters tried to stamp out these beliefs, so voodoo devotees often adopted the cover of Christianity. Each of the voodoo gods, the *lwa*, was identified with a Catholic saint: for example, the rainbow snake Dambalah Wèdo,

the *lwa* of luck and happiness, was associated with St Patrick; Ezili, the *lwa* of love, with the Virgin Mary; and Legba, keeper of the crossroads between the human and supernatural worlds, with St Peter and St Andrew.

Voodoo in its various forms is a religion without any formal structure that relies on a belief in divine

**A voodoo ceremony** in progress on the sidewalks of Port-Au-Prince, Haiti. The word "voodoo" comes from the West African word *vodun*, meaning spirit.

## GÉDÉ

In Haiti, Gédé is a *lwa*, master of both life and death. Some regard the Gédé as a family of spirits of the dead, with Baron Samedi at their head, rather than as a single *lwa* with many aspects. Gédé is recognizable by his dark glasses, top hat or bowler, undertaker's clothes, nasal voice, and his obscene, greedy, and lascivious speech and behaviour.

**Baron Samedi's** make-up emphasizes his dual nature. With his left eye he surveys the universe; with his right he keeps an eye on his food.

possession. Ecstatic believers dance in a circle around a post that links Earth and heaven, while "ridden" by the spirits of the *lwa*. The relationship between the devotee and the *lwa* is highly personal; some initiates even enter into a "marriage" with their chosen *lwa*.

### VOODOO REVOLT

In Haiti, the voodoo *lwa* are embedded in culture and politics – especially emancipation. On 14 August 1791, a voodoo ceremony marked the start of the first successful slave revolt. Led by the voodoo priest Boukman Dutty, worshippers swore to die rather than live as slaves. And

**A candomblé celebrant** in Brazil dresses as Obalouaye – a deity equated with St Lazarus.

as Boukman called on Dambalah Wèdo, the rainbow snake, for aid, a priestess sacrificed a black pig, and anointed the rebels with its blood.

Boukman was killed in the revolt, but his place as its leader was taken by the brilliant strategist Toussaint Louverture, who declared Haiti's independence, and the end of slavery, in 1801. Voodoo remained a political tool through the 20th century: Haiti's dictator François "Papa Doc" Duvalier adopted the dark glasses and black hat of the *lwa* Gédé and named his secret police the Tonton Macoutes after a mythical Haitian bogeyman.

# OCEANIA

T HE MYTHS OF OCEANIA are some of the richest in the world. The elaborate creation chants of Polynesia, such as the Hawaiian *Kumulipo*, which describes how the night gave birth to all creation, are masterpieces of world literature. Australia, home for more than 40,000 years to the Aborigines, has its past, present, and future simultaneously encoded in the myths of the Dreaming.

The cultures of the South Sea islands that make up Polynesia, Micronesia, and Melanesia are alive with myth. Micronesia, an area including more than 600 islands in the North Pacific, uses playful myths to embody the culture of its peoples. Melanesia is another vast collection of islands lying south of Micronesia, and it is home to the oldest people in the region – the Papuans – who have lived there for more than 40,000 years. The Melanesians skilfully interweave the concepts of sexuality and social organization in a way that shapes, defines, and expresses cultural identity.

**Aboriginal rock art** includes intricate patterns that are visual codes for retellings of myths.

## ANCIENT AUSTRALIA

The Aboriginal Dreaming of Australia tells of a world with a beginning but no end; of eternal mythical beings who may die only to be transformed into parts of the landscape. The Dreaming

exists, and is kept alive, through storytelling, song, dance, ritual, and paintings – on the sand, on the human body, and more recently, on canvas.

## LIVING DREAMS

Dreamings are intimately connected to the land, so that what to a stranger might seem a featureless desert is really a kind of living myth, in which every hill, rock, creek, or waterhole reveals the tracks of the ancestral beings of the Dreaming. Landscape features are regarded as the actual bodies of these ancestors. These features are invested with a spiritual potency known as *djang*; the most *djang* place of all is Uluru (also known as Ayers Rock), which sits at the heart of a web of interconnecting Dreaming tracks that weave across the entire continent.

## MELANESIAN BELIEFS

In Melanesia, the myths of New Guinea and the Torres Straits have clear similarities with those of Aboriginal Australia. Myths of peoples such as the Marind-Anim of Irian Jaya also validate every aspect of their clan system: their customs, religious beliefs and rituals, and their sexuality. A key Marind-Anim myth tells of the origin of fire (*rapa*). Uaba and Ualiwamb became trapped in copulation; when Aramemb, the god of medicine men, pulled them apart, the first fire shot out from Ualiwamb's genitals.

**Aboriginal Australians** believe that through ritual they can communicate with the spirits of the Dreaming, and release their power and knowledge.

The whole of Marind-Anim ritual life depends upon an unceasing round of burdensome Otiv-Bombari ceremonies, which are rites of multiple copulation.

Another feature of Melanesian myth is the rise of cargo cults following the islands' first contact with Europeans. These cults believe an ancestor or god will appear bearing with them "cargo" or wealth similar to that of the Europeans. On Tanna Island in Vanuatu, Prince Philip of the British royal family is the subject of a cargo cult.

## MICRONESIAN MYTHS

The coral atolls of Micronesia are home to some of the most attractively balanced, peaceful, and cooperative of all human societies. The myths of Ifaluk Atoll are poetic and full of praise for the kindly gods,

**Melanesian island** societies recognize ancestral ghosts and magic as part of daily life, maintaining calm seas and sleeping volcanoes.

**Polynesian statues** often show the gods with disproportionately large heads, as the head was regarded as highly sacred.

who have provided the people with all the knowledge they need to navigate the seas and provide for themselves.

## POLYNESIAN LEGENDS

In Polynesia, priestly castes and hereditary rulers gave myths shape and structure, particularly in Hawaii and New Zealand. As a result, a vast oral literature has been collected, much of it related to an accepted pantheon of gods with Rangi and Papa, the sky and the Earth, at its head. There are many variations – Tangaroa, for example, is the Tahitian creator, but he is the Maori's god of the sea. But there is also a remarkable degree of cohesion. Tangaroa appears even in the remotest Polynesian outpost, Rapa Nui (Easter Island), as a king who becomes a seal. He lands on Rapa Nui, only to be killed and cooked by disbelieving islanders.

# LUMALUMA

📖 Culture hero
🪃 Gunwinggu (Kunwinjku), Australia
🏛 Arnhem Land, Australia

✍ Ronald M. Berndt & Catherine H. Berndt,
*This Speaking Land*; Berndt & Berndt,
*Man, Land & Myth in Northern Australia*

Lumaluma, the sacred ancestor of the Gunwinggu people, brought them their religious and cultural knowledge. He was a whale who came out of the sea in the form of a man to teach the sacred rites. But he was greedy, and whenever he saw something he wanted to eat he placed a taboo on it, in order to keep it for himself. Eventually the starving people killed him, but even as he lay dying he tried to continue teaching them the sacred rites.

### KEY CHARACTERS

**LUMALUMA** • *a whale who became a man*
**LUMALUMA'S TWO WIVES**
**MEN AND WOMEN OF THE GUNWINGGU PEOPLE**

## PLOT SYNOPSIS

### BRINGING THE RITUALS

Lumaluma the whale emerged from the sea in the form of a man, and stole two wives while their husbands were out fishing. He journeyed west, bringing with him the sacred rituals. When he saw people collecting delicious honey or yams, or hunting kangaroo, he would declare the food *mareiin*, so that it became sacred and only he could eat it.

Whenever he found a place to stop, Lumaluma taught the *mareiin* rituals to the people. He taught the men how to transform themselves, and his wives taught the women their rites.

**The mythological beings** of the Dreaming are regarded more as being "at rest" than dead; they live on in the landscape, in songs, and in pictures.

The people hid their food from Lumaluma, but he was still hungry, so he began to eat the bodies of their dead children. The people feared that he would eat them too, so they trapped him on the beach and attacked him.

### LUMALUMA RETURNS TO THE SEA

"Spear me slowly," he said, "I still have more to teach you." As he was dying he asked, "Did you get it all, that sacred information I gave you? Tell me!"

And the people answered him, "Yes, we have it all." Then Lumaluma died. They did not bury him, or he would have died forever; they left his body by the sea, and it slipped beneath the waves, transformed back into a whale.

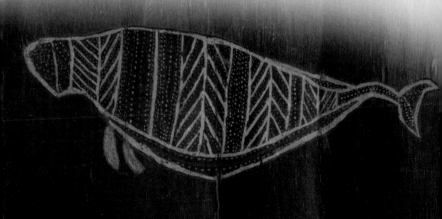

# THE RAINBOW SNAKE

📖 Hero versus monster
📍 Ngulugwongga (Nanggiomeri), Australia
🏛 Arnhem Land, Australia
✍ Ronald M. Berndt & Catherine H. Berndt, *This Speaking Land*

Rainbow snakes are powerful figures in Aboriginal mythology. Both male and female, mammal and reptile, they are creative powers of the Dreaming. As they travelled the country, their movements created the hills, valleys, and waterways of the ancestral landscape. Rainbow snakes are dangerous creatures if irritated – as here, where one grows angry with a crying baby. In this myth Gabad is lucky to kill the rainbow snake with a single blow.

**KEY CHARACTERS**

**BULALOYI (RAINBOW)** • *a rainbow snake*
**GABAD** • *a mother*
**ANOTHER WOMAN**
**WULGUL** • *a sorcerer-owl*

## PLOT SYNOPSIS

### A CRYING BABY
Bulaloyi, a rainbow snake, lived at Anson Bay. One day he heard a baby crying at deg-Dilg in Ngulugwongga territory. He thought, "I'll go and eat that child." As Bulaloyi travelled, his huge body formed mountains, rivers, creeks, and billabongs, while with his tail he made rainbows.

At deg-Dilg, two women were making dilly bags for collecting bush tucker. One woman was named Gabad, and it was her baby who was crying. As the women knelt plaiting their dilly bags from bush string, Gabad watched her baby while Wulgul the owl copulated with the other woman from behind.

**Today the rainbow snake** is associated with fertility and abundance, community and peace. It has life-giving powers but punishes law-breakers.

### THE SNAKE STRIKES
Bulaloyi used his body to break a road through the hill at deg-Dilg, and slithered along it to where the two women sat making their bags. Then he raised his head to swallow the crying baby.

"Ah! Rainbow is here!" said Gabad.

As the snake stretched his neck forward, Gabad pulled out her dilly-bag stick and clubbed Bulaloyi with it, breaking his neck. The rainbow snake, Gabad, her child, the other woman, and Wulgul are all still there, as rocks, at deg-Dilg in Ngulugwongga.

#### SHAMANIC POWERS

The shamanic powers of Aboriginal "clever men" are obtained from the rainbow snake. Shamanic candidates are said to be swallowed by the snake, reduced to the size of a baby, then taken to the sky world and killed, before being brought back to life with healing powers and the ability to visit the sky and the dead.

**Aboriginal shamans** use a fly-whisk as part of their rituals of death and rebirth.

**RELATED MYTHS ▶** The rainbow serpent (*p.240*) • African gods in the New World (*p.242*)

# THE DÉMA SUN GOD

📖 Creation
📌 Marind-Anim, New Guinea
🏛 Irian Jaya, western New Guinea

✍ J. Van Baal, *Déma*

The spirit-beings known as déma are the clan ancestors of the Marind-Anim tribe of western New Guinea. Their invisible world is in many ways more important to the Marind-Anim than the visible world in which they live. At first there were just two déma: Nubog, the female Earth, and Dinadin, the male sky. They had two children named Geb and Sami; even when the people rose up against Geb, he continued to provide for them.

## PLOT SYNOPSIS

### THE PUNISHMENT OF GEB

Geb lived in an anthill, which radiated unbearable heat. He could find no wife, but had to make do with a piece of bamboo stem, which nevertheless bore him several children. Geb also kidnapped human children, especially red-skinned boys, and took them back to his fiery lair, where he cut off their heads. The people decided something must be done about him. The men were reluctant to approach the anthill, but the women urged them on, and brought water to quench the heat. They poured water onto the anthill, and when Geb emerged they cut off his head.

### THE SUN AND THE LAND

Geb's head fled eastward underground, and emerged at Kondo, the place of the sunrise. There, it climbed up a yam tendril into the sky, to become the sun. It travelled westward across the sky, before dipping back down to Earth and returning to Kondo underground. It has made this trip every day since then. Geb's body was divided up among the different clans, and became the land.

**RELATED MYTHS** ▸ The night barque of Ra (*p.228*) • The origin of death (*p.237*)

# THE ORIGIN OF HUMANKIND

📖 Creation            ✍ J. Van Baal, *Déma*
🏴 Marind-Anim, New Guinea
🏛 Irian Jaya, western New Guinea

The déma of the Marind-Anim tribe of western
New Guinea are spirit-beings of the creation-time;
they were creators of the world and ancestors of
the clans. The déma can take human or animal
form. This Marind-Anim myth of the origin of
humankind tells how the first human beings
emerged from a water-hole in fish form, and were
given their human shape by a déma in the form of
Aramemb, the déma of medicine men.

### KEY CHARACTERS

**GIRUI** • *a déma-dog*
**A DÉMA-STORK**
**ARAMEMB** • *déma of
medicine men*
**GEB AND SAMI** • *the
Marind-Anim forefathers*
**BRAGAI** • *déma-ancestor
of the Bragai-zé clans*

## PLOT SYNOPSIS

### AN UNDERGROUND FEAST
The déma once held a great feast
underground, in the far west of the
Marind territory. As they feasted, they
travelled eastward under the ground.
Meanwhile, up on the surface of the
Earth, a déma-dog named Girui heard
the commotion and wondered what was
happening. Girui started to track the
déma as they moved beneath the Earth.

### FISH-LIKE BEINGS
Girui followed the noise until he
reached Kondo, where the sun rises.
There the noise became very loud and
Girui could sense that whatever was
causing the noise was close to this spot.
He scratched away at the bank of a
creek and as he dug, water poured out
of the bank, bringing with it a number
of strange fish-like beings, which looked
like catfish. They were in fact human
beings, but their facial features were
flat, and their arms, legs, fingers, and
toes were not separated from their
torsos. A déma-stork began to peck
away at them, but they were too hard,
and the stork's beak bent, as it is today.

Aramemb, the déma of medicine
men, chased away the dog and the
stork, and made a fire of bamboo on
which to dry out the fish-people.

**The myth of the** catfish-people may have been
inspired by air-breathing species of this fish that
can "walk", or wriggle between water sources.

### DIVIDING UP THE CLANS
Each time the bamboo stems cracked,
the people's ears, eyes, noses, and
mouths exploded outward from their
faces with a "pop!". Then Aramemb
took his bamboo knife and cut their
arms, legs, fingers, and toes free from
their torsos. He threw away the
trimmings, which became leeches.

Geb and Sami arrived in their canoes
to take the new humans aboard. They
were first divided into two groups:
Geb and Aramemb took the people
who made up the Geb-zé and
Aramemb clans; while Sami and
another déma, Bragai, took charge of
the Mahu-zé and Bragai-zé people.

# THE BIRTH OF THE GODS

📖 Creation         ✍ Antony Alpers, *Legends of the South Seas*
🅿 Polynesia
🏛 Tahiti

In New Zealand, Tangaroa is the god of the sea, but on a number of Polynesian islands Tangaroa is said to be the maker of all things. This version of the myth comes from Tahiti, and similar myths, with variations on Tangaroa's name, have been collected from the islands of Samoa, Tonga, Tuvalu, Tubuai, and elsewhere. In these myths Tangaroa emerges from the primal egg to create the world, and to give birth to the other gods.

### KEY CHARACTERS

**TANGAROA (TANGALOA, TA'AROA, A'A)** • *the creator god*
**TU (KU)** • *the war god and master craftsman*

## PLOT SYNOPSIS

### CREATING THE WORLD
For a long time Tangaroa remained in the darkness of a shell, named Rumia, which was shaped like an egg. Nothing else existed; just the shell, and the void. This was the period of continuous, impenetrable darkness.

At last Tangaroa broke through the shell. "Is there anyone there?" he called, but there was no answer from the emptiness.

Tangaroa made the dome of the sky from the broken shell. From his backbone he made a mountain range, and

**According to Maori** tradition, Tangaroa was the son of Ranginui (the sky father) and Papatuanuku (the Earth mother).

from his entrails he made the clouds. He made the Earth from his flesh. In fact Tangaroa made everything that exists from his body and the eggshell. He even used his fingernails and toenails to make the scales and shells of the fish of the sea. From within himself Tangaroa called forth the other gods. With the help of Tu, the great craftsman god, he created men and women and persuaded them to approach one another.

### POLYNESIAN CREATION MYTHS

There are many different Polynesian creation myths, some very long and complex. Many record in detail a series of copulations by which all things are created, starting with the union of light and dark. Hieroglyphs yet to be fully deciphered on the wooden *rongorongo* boards of Rapa Nui (Easter Island) seem to record lists of such couplings and the resulting offspring. One Easter Island chant tells us that: "Small Thing by lying with Imperceptible Thing made the Fine Dust in the Air."

### EVERYTHING HAS A SHELL
Just as Tangaroa had a shell, so does everything else. The sky is a shell, containing the sun, the moon, and the stars. The Earth is a shell that contains the rocks and the water, the earth and the plants. A woman's womb is a shell, from which new life is born. The shells of the world are so vast in number that it would be impossible to name them all.

**RELATED MYTHS ▸** The primal egg (*p.36*) • Pan Gu and Nü Wa's creation (*pp.172–3*)

# THE ORIGIN OF DEATH

📖 Origin of death
🏳 Maori
🏛 New Zealand

✍ Katharine Luomala, *Voices on the Wind*; Roslyn Poignant, *Oceanic Mythology*

The name Tane means "man", and of all the Polynesian gods, Tane is perhaps the closest to humankind. He was the Maori's forest god, and by creating trees he gave humans the gift of wood and plant fibre. This allowed people to make many things, including fishing equipment, which earned Tane the enmity of his brother, the god of the sea. Unfortunately, despite being a friend to humans, it was Tane who brought death into the world.

## PLOT SYNOPSIS

### A LONELY GOD

Tane, god of the forest, was lonely, and wanted a sexual partner. His mother rejected him, and his other partners produced only inadequate things such as streams, grass, and stones. So finally he went to the beach at Hawaiki, mixed together some mud and sand, and shaped it into a woman. He breathed life into her, and called her Hine-hau-one, the Earth-formed Maiden.

### FATHER AND DAUGHTER

Hine-hau-one gave birth to a daughter, Hine-titama, the Dawn Maiden. Not knowing that Tane was her father, Hine-titama also became his wife. One day Hine-titama went down to the village and idly asked who her father was. When she heard the answer, she fled to the darkness of the Underworld.

### THE COMING OF DEATH

When Tane realized Hine-titama had disappeared, he went looking for her. He could hear her singing her sad song, "Are you Tane, my father?" and called to her, but he could not enter Po, the Underworld.

She called to him, saying: "Stay in the world of light, and foster our offspring. Let me stay in the world of darkness, and drag our offspring down."

Her name was changed from the Dawn Maiden to Hine-nui-te-po, the Great Goddess of Darkness. Before this happened, death did not exist, but now all living things must die, sucked down to the Underworld by Hine-nui-te-po.

**A high-status Maori warrior,** recognizable by his tattoos, would ritually thank Tane for providing the wood to make his staff-weapon, the *taiaha*.

# MAUI OF A THOUSAND TRICKS

📖 Creation; trickster god
📫 Polynesia
🏛 Polynesia

✍ Katharine Luomala,
*Maui-of-a-Thousand-Tricks*

Maui is the great trickster hero of Polynesian mythology. In one important myth he fished up the islands of Polynesia using a great fishing-hook. Some say the hook had belonged to Kuula, the god of fishing, and some that it came from the jawbone of his great-grandmother, Muri-ranga-whenua. Maui pushed up the heavens, stole fire from the Underworld, and even snared the sun to slow it down. He could do anything except conquer death.

### KEY CHARACTERS

**MAUI** • *the trickster*
**HINA** • *Maui's mother*
**MURI-RANGA-WHENUA** •
*Maui's great-grandmother*
**KUULA** • *the god of fishing*
**HINA-NUI-TE-PO** • *the
goddess of death*

## PLOT SYNOPSIS

### PULLING UP THE ISLANDS

Maui was given a magic fishhook by his mother Hina. He cast the line, and the "fish" he caught was so huge that he could not pull it clear of the sea. It was the land mass of Polynesia, which has remained forever slightly submerged, appearing as a series of islands.

### SNARING THE SUN

Maui thought that the sun moved across the sky too quickly, and wanted to slow it down. He lassoed it with a rope made of coconut fibre, but the sun burned through it. So he made another from his sister's hair, and caught the sun at dawn. He refused to release it until it agreed to shine for long days in summer and restrict the short days to winter.

### HALF IN LOVE WITH DEATH

Maui decided to conquer death. He descended to the Underworld and tried to rape the goddess of death, Hine-nui-te-po, as she slept. He crawled right up inside her, meaning to travel through her and emerge from her mouth. When only his little legs were waving outside, the birds in the trees found the sight so funny they burst out laughing and woke the goddess, who squeezed her thighs and crushed Maui to death.

**In some versions** of the myth, Maui snares the sun over the volcano of Haleakala ("House of the Sun") on the island of Maui, and gives the island his name.

# GODDESS OF THE VOLCANO

📖 Love and revenge
📿 Polynesia
🏛 Hawaii, USA

✍ Martha Beckwith, *Hawaiian Mythology*; Nathaniel B. Emerson, *Unwritten Literature of the Hula*

Pele is a Polynesian goddess who presides over a family of fire gods in the volcano at Kilauea, Hawaii. She is the daughter of the mother goddess Haumea, and her tempestuous character makes her the perfect goddess for a volcano. Only she can control its lava flow. Pele travelled from Tahiti looking for a new home, finally choosing Hawaii. She fell in love with a young chief from another island, and her jealous love led to murder.

## KEY CHARACTERS

**PELE** • *fire goddess*
**HI'IAKA** • *her younger sister*
**HOPOE** • *Hi'iaka's friend*
**LOHIAU** • *a chief*
**HAUMEA** • *a mother goddess, Pele's mother*
**KANE** • *protector-father god of living creatures*

## PLOT SYNOPSIS

### AT THE DANCE

Pele first saw the handsome young chief Lohiau at a hula dance on a nearby island, and decided she must have him. She asked her sister Hi'iaka to fetch him, and Hi'iaka agreed, on condition that Pele made sure that no harm came to her forests or her friend Hopoe while she was away.

### BROUGHT BACK TO LIFE

When Hi'iaka eventually tracked down Lohiau, she found he had died of a broken heart. But she caught his spirit and used her magical powers to bring him back to life. Meanwhile, Pele's suspicion at the length of time Hi'iaka was taking turned to fiery jealousy.

**Kilauea volcano** in Hawaii is supposed to be the dwelling-place of the passionate goddess Pele, who would cause eruptions with her *pa'oe*, or magic stick.

### THE CURSE OF LONO

Lono is the Hawaiian god of rain, fertility, music, and peace. He descended to Earth on a rainbow to marry a mortal woman. Wrongly convinced that she was unfaithful, he beat her to death and left the island in sorrow, promising to return one day. This myth was celebrated on Hawaii every year, and coincidentally Captain Cook first visited the island on that very day, so he was treated as if he were the god returned. He later returned to Hawaii at a time dedicated to Ku, the god of war, and was killed.

### THE WORLD ERUPTS

Pele belched forth fire, devastating Hi'iaka's forests and killing Hi'iaka's friend, the beautiful Hopoe. When Hi'iaka returned home and saw what Pele had done, she turned to Lohiau, whom she had come to love. Pele saw them embrace and was furious. She erupted, spewing lava, turning Lohiau to stone and convulsing the Earth and sea. Only the intervention of the god Kane saved the world from utter ruin.

The extraordinary moai of Rapa Nui (Easter Island) are huge stone memorials to past chiefs. One moai, taken from the sacred site of Orongo, is now in the British Museum in London. The islanders call it Hoa Hakananai'a ("stolen friend"), and still hope for its return one day.

# MAKEMAKE AND HAUA

📖 Foundation; culture hero
🏛 Rapa Nui (Easter Island), Polynesia
🗺 Rapa Nui (Easter Island), Polynesia
✍ Alfred Métraux, *Easter Island*

Rapa Nui – Easter Island – is the most remote of all the Polynesian settlements; its name translates both as "the navel of the world" and as "the end of the Earth". Its mythological founder was the Great Parent, Hoto Matu'a, who sailed there after his tattooer Haumaka had dreamed of a land that lay eastward across the ocean. Rapa Nui's creator god was Makemake, who is virtually identical to the Polynesian god Tane (or Kane in Hawaii).

### KEY CHARACTERS

**MAKEMAKE** • *the creator and the god of seabirds*
**HAUA** • *goddess wife of Makemake*
**A PRIESTESS**
**HOTO MATU'A** • *the great parent*
**HAUMAKA** • *the tattooer*

## PLOT SYNOPSIS

### THE PRIESTESS AND THE SKULL
A priestess used to stand on the beach of the bay of Tonga-riki, keeping watch over a skull that sat on a rock there. One day a huge wave crashed on to the beach and swept away the skull. The priestess dived into the sea and swam after it, but she was unable to catch it. After three days she came ashore on an island. The goddess Haua appeared and asked her what she was doing there.

"I am looking for my skull," she replied. "The sea washed it away."

"That is not a skull, it is the god Makemake," Haua told her.

### THE MOVE TO RAPA NUI
One day Makemake, the creator god and god of the seabirds, said, "Let's drive all the seabirds to Rapa Nui."

Haua agreed, and added, "The priestess shall come with us. She must reveal our names to the inhabitants, and teach them the rites with which they must worship us."

So Makemake and Haua drove the birds across the sea to Rapa Nui, and settled them on the rocky islets off the coast at Orongo.

### WORSHIPPING THE GODS
The priestess taught the people of Rapa Nui how to worship the gods. When they planted crops, they were to place a skull in the ground and say: "*Ka to ma Haua, ma Makemake*" ("Plant for Haua, for Makemake"). When they sat down to eat their crop, they were to set aside a portion, with the words, "Makemake and Haua, this is for you!"

**The oval eyes of the moai,** the Easter-Island statues, show that they represent human beings, not gods. They are memorials to the great chiefs, the *matato'a*.

# THE CULT OF THE BIRDMAN

📖 Foundation; culture hero
🏹 Rapa Nui (Easter Island), Polynesia
🏛 Rapa Nui (Easter Island), Polynesia

✍ Alfred Métraux, *Easter Island*;
John Flenley and Paul Bahn,
*The Enigmas of Easter Island*

Carved on rocks at the sacred site of Orongo on Rapa Nui are images of a man with the head and beak of a bird, clutching an egg. This is the Birdman, the living representative of the god Makemake. A new Birdman was appointed each year, after a daring competition to gather the first egg of the season. The Birdman's egg, blown and hung in his hut, was believed to generate food, and was revered by a people always close to starvation.

## PLOT SYNOPSIS

### GATHERING OF THE CLANS
Every July the clans gathered at Orongo to await the nesting seabirds. The *matato'a* (chiefs) would compete for the title by appointing *hopu* (servants) to swim for them across the shark-infested sea to the islet of Moto Nui to watch for birds. Regardless of their skill or daring, the swimmers would find a bird's egg only if the *matato'a* they represented found favour with Makemake. Otherwise a *hopu* would not notice the first egg even if he touched it with his foot.

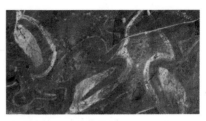

**The Birdman** was the living representative of the god Makemake on Earth, and his devotion ensured the island's supply of potatoes, chickens, and fish.

### THE EGG IS FOUND
When the first egg was found, the *hopu* shouted to his chief: "Shave your head!" This chief then became the Birdman. Carrying the sacred egg in the palm of his hand, the Birdman retreated to the seclusion of a special hut for a year, where he shaved his head, prayed, and protected the sacred egg of Makemake.

### SECRETS OF THE MOAI

When Captain Cook visited Rapa Nui in 1774, many of the moai had been damaged in the "wars of the throwing-down of the statues". The people, demoralized by war and famine, traded their four most sacred objects – statues of Makemake, Haua, Vie-kana, and a wooden hand (representing the Birdman) – to Cook's interpreter, Mahine.

# THE WORK OF THE GODS IN TIKOPIA

Tikopia, one of the Solomon Islands in the southwest Pacific, has one of the most intensely studied cultures in the world, and was the subject of many books by Raymond Firth, a New Zealander anthropologist writing in the 1930s. One complex ritual cycle, the Work of the Gods, was central to Tikopian society. This Polynesian ritual is comparable to rites such as the Makahiki of Hawaii or the Inasi of Tonga.

The institutions and values of Tikopian society were shaped and sanctioned by its ritual life. The most important cycle of rites, the Work of the Gods, was aimed at pleasing the *atua* – powerful spirits or gods who would ensure plentiful harvests. Twice-yearly, for six weeks, the whole of Tikopian society devoted themselves to performing the rites, divided into the Work of the Trade-wind and the Work of the Monsoon.

**Kava, a mildly** narcotic drink prepared from plant material, was offered up in ritual vessels.

## TRADING WITH THE GODS

The Work of the Gods was regarded not so much as worship as a logical system of trade between human and spirit beings. Many of the activities involved, such as repairing canoes or plaiting mats, were economically valuable; and as the *atua* consumed only a small portion of the food and kava offered to them, the remainder was available for human consumption.

## APPEASING MAPUSIA

The rites were said to have been instituted by Mapusia, the most powerful and feared *atua*, who was also the principal spirit of the Kafika clan. Their chief – the Ariki Kafika – therefore acted as the high priest of the rites. It was he who decided when to "throw the firestick" to set the ritual sequence in motion.

Turmeric, a spice that was used as a sacred dye and as ritual body paint, was said to be the perfume of Mapusia, and its ceremonial extraction took place over several days in the trade-wind season.

## THE LIVING GOD

The question of whether to translate *atua* as spirit or god is complicated by the fact that Mapusia was originally a man, named Saku. This name was

**Tikopia was home** to the fearful Mapusia, also known as Te Atua I Kafika (the god of Kafika) and Te Ariki Fakamataku (the fear-causing chief).

sacred and never uttered; even the name Mapusia was rarely used. In his life as a man, Saku was a culture hero. He gave the people clothing, and by doing so awoke their human consciousness, giving them "minds". He made the sacred adzes (carving tools), and established the Work of the Gods. In those days everything had a voice, even trees and rocks, but Saku ordered them all to be silent. He told the stones to rise up and form a pile, and the earth to cover it, to make the very platform where the temple of Kafika was raised.

## SAKU BECOMES IMMORTAL

When Saku died in a dispute over territory, he flew to the gods. As he had allowed himself to die, rather than rising up to kill his opponent, he was "pure" and could demand that each of the *atua* give him their *mana* (sacred powers). Renamed Mapusia, he then became the most ferocious *atua*. If offended, he could destroy whole villages with drought, pestilence, or tropical cyclones.

**When Firth photographed** the Taomatangi (the dance to quell the winds), the Tikopians were surprised not to see the gods in his pictures.

# CHARTING THE SEA

📖 Culture hero
𐦀 Ifaluk, Micronesia
🏛 Caroline Islands, Micronesia

✍ Edwin G. Burrows & Melford
E. Spiro, *An Atoll Culture*

Ifaluk is a coral atoll in the Caroline Islands, with a peaceful and creative culture typical of Micronesia. The art of seamanship is essential to Ifaluk life and canoe-makers and navigators are highly esteemed. The arts they learn were established by the god Aluluei and other gods of the sea and shipbuilding. Although Aluluei was a master navigator, at first he did not know all the secrets of the sea. This myth tells how he acquired the first chart of the ocean.

**KEY CHARACTERS**

**ALULUEI** • *god of seamanship*
**ALULUEI'S DAUGHTER**
**VALUR** • *god of fish*
**WERIENG** • *god of seabirds*
**SEGUR** • *god of navigators*

## PLOT SYNOPSIS

### AN ISLAND PARADISE
Aluluei settled on the island of Bwennap and became its chief. It was a small island of sand with one tree but many people. Aluluei married a woman there, and had two sons and a daughter.

### A CANOE FULL OF GODS
One day a canoe arrived on the shores of Bwennap, carrying three of Aluluei's sons from an earlier coupling: Valur, Werieng, and Segur. Aluluei's daughter was bathing in the sea, and hailed them. They just kept on paddling, but

**The extraordinary sea journeys** of Micronesian peoples dominate their mythology. Aluluei and his father, Palulop, are the patron gods of navigation.

she waded out to them with a little coconut, no bigger than her fist, calling: "Aren't you thirsty?" The gods scoffed at the tiny coconut. "That's not enough for us," they said. But all three drank their fill, and still the nut was full of milk. They laughed to think that one little coconut could hold so much, and were so grateful that they gave the girl the first sea chart, which they had been compiling.

The girl took it back to her father, who was overjoyed to see how it showed the positions of all the islands, and all the birds and fish of the sea. He passed on all of this knowledge to his sons, and they taught it to the people.

# WOLFAT BRINGS TATTOOING

📖 Culture hero, trickster god
📌 Ifaluk, Micronesia
🏛 Ifaluk, Micronesia

✍ Edwin Grant Burrows, *Flower in My Ear: Arts and Ethos of Ifaluk Atoll*

When anthropologist Edwin Grant Burrows studied the people of the Ifaluk atoll in the late 1940s, the total population was only 250. Yet Burrows collected from them a large volume of beautiful poems. In many of these poems, Ifaluk women admire the tattooing sported by their sons and lovers. This myth tells of how tattooing was brought to the Ifaluk by the god Wolfat, who discovered that it made him intensely desirable.

### KEY CHARACTERS

**WOLFAT** • the trickster god
**LUGWEILANG** • *Wolfat's father*
**ALUELAP** • *the ruler of the sky, Wolfat's grandfather*
**ILOUMULIGERIOU** • *a human woman*

## PLOT SYNOPSIS

### THE SKY OF FLOWERS
Wolfat the trickster god lived in the sky of flowers with the other gods, the *alusiang*. His father Lugweilang visited the islands every day to report to his own father, Aluelap, the god of the sky, on what the people were doing. Wolfat was the first god to "put on" tattooing; being a god, he could put it on and take it off again.

### WOLFAT TEACHES THE MORTALS
One day Wolfat looked down to the Earth and saw a beautiful woman, Iloumuligeriou, who took his fancy. He decided to visit her. The woman awoke to find a strange man in her house, and kindled a fire so she could see who it was. When she saw the black designs on his body, she was filled with desire.

**South-Sea islanders** have traditionally covered their whole bodies with tattoos. Each of the many shapes they use has a symbolic meaning.

### AN IFALUK WOMAN'S LOVE SONG

The composers of the poems and songs of the Ifaluk regarded themselves as "canoes of the gods". Here, a wife awaiting her husband's return from a sea journey sings of her feelings:
"My heart longs for you,
With your fine tattooing,
The lines down your sides
And the curves about your hips.
I do not forget."

In the morning Wolfat returned to the sky. But he wanted the woman again, so the next night he returned, but with his skin undecorated. The woman rejected him; so he went out, put on his tattooing, and she happily welcomed him back into her bed.

The next morning Wolfat showed the other men how to make themselves more attractive by tattooing their bodies, using black soot and a needle made from a man-of-war bird's wing.

# WHO'S WHO
# IN MYTHOLOGY

T HE WORLD'S MYTHS CONTAIN thousands of gods and goddesses who fulfil hundreds of different functions. Different parts of the globe have different deities to preside over objects and phenomena, from rocks to whirlwinds. In many cultures every tree, stream, hill, and valley has its deity. And the gods control every major event, from the creation to the end of the world.

How can we make sense of this vast range of gods and goddesses? One way is to classify the most important deities by their function: the role they play in the mythology, the job they actually do, and the importance they have for their devotees.

This section describes many of the most important and well-known deities of the world's mythologies. It begins with the creators and the high gods who stand at the head of their people's hierarchy of deities. Some of these figures are vast and unknowable, coming into being at the beginning of time, shrouded in mystery. Others, equally powerful, are the supreme gods, deities who stand at the heart of their culture's mythology, such as the Greek god Zeus and the Egyptian Ra. Most of these are male, and their female equivalents are the mother goddesses and Earth deities, figures such as the Hindu Devi.

**A culture's deities** can be so numerous that later artists occasionally provide a key, as with these Olympians.

childbirth, and warfare. Although many of these figures are less powerful in cosmic terms than the high gods, they were still very important to the daily lives of those who worshipped them. To hunter-gatherer peoples in the frozen wastes of Arctic North America, or on a Pacific Island, paying respect to the gods was a way to ensure a successful hunt, and therefore guarantee human survival. The same was true of the worship of agricultural deities in societies that produced their food by farming. The final part of this section covers the gods of the Underworld. These often frightening gods were important because they helped people to make sense of what happened when they died, often through offering some kind of moral assessment system – a final judgment – that held out the promise of a comfortable afterlife for those who had lived a good life or for those who had worshipped the gods correctly.

## A GOD FOR EVERY FUNCTION

The categories within this section cover the majority of those gods and goddesses whose prime function is to preside over a specific part of the universe or a particular area of human activity. They range from the gods of sea, sky, and cosmos to deities who are responsible for hunting, farming,

## TEMPLES AND WORSHIP

What emerges from these accounts of the gods is the deities' reality for their worshippers. Their lives were not simply good, interesting stories. For their original followers, they were also figures to be respected, worshipped, and prayed to. They were as vital a part of life as trees, cattle, or human flesh and blood. Evidence of worship survives in the remains of temples, shrines, and cult centres, and in texts that tell us about rituals and ceremonies. Throughout this section there are text boxes giving additional information about how and where the deities were worshipped.

## THE PANTHEON

There is huge variety amongst the world's deities, but there are also striking similarities across

**Many figurines** that clearly represent deities or spirit-beings have become unidentifiable.

cultures: sun gods that cross the heavens, sky gods that produce thunder, deities that rule over the changing seasons. So in spite of the fact that the pantheons of the world's cultures are

very diverse, there are also strong parallels. There are unities within some pantheons, too. Although cultures may have hundreds or thousands of deities, sometimes these gods are seen as aspects of one greater god. This amalgamation of deities may be conceptual, as in Hinduism, in which all gods are said to be aspects of the absolute truth, Brahman. Sometimes it is more literal, as in the case of the Polynesian sea god Tangaroa, who in some versions of his myth is said to house all the other gods in his belly. Tangaroa's stomach both protects and is nourished by all the gods, just as today their stories continue to provide spiritual and intellectual nourishment.

**The use of symbols** displayed on or around representations of gods and other mythical figures allows them to be readily identified.

# CREATORS AND HIGH GODS

Every mythology reserves a special place for the creator, the deity who brings himself or herself into being and shapes the features of the universe. But due respect is also paid to the rulers of the pantheon, figures who do not themselves create the cosmos, but play a leading role in the affairs of both supernatural and mortal beings.

The creators themselves are often rather shadowy figures. The Chinese and the Greeks, who produced many statues and paintings of their gods, made very few images of certain deities, such as the Chinese creator Pan Gu or the Greek primal goddess Eurynome. The work of these deities is so vast and mysterious that it is difficult to picture.

But with the high gods it is a different matter. They have distinct personalities, such as the lustful Greek Zeus or the wise Ahura Mazda of Persia.

**The Hindu god Vishnu** as Kurma, the tortoise-avatar; the second of the ten avatars that he created from himself.

### SACRED COURTS

Deities like these proved easy for worshippers to relate to because in some ways they resembled their own kings and queens. They, too, played an important part in human affairs, and inspired major cults and large temples.

These gods often embodied powerful forces that affect the human world: sun gods like the Egyptian Ra and Aten, for example, or thunder gods, like Zeus.

The high gods even operated as rulers at the centre of a court, like a mortal king. This could either be a literal court complete with celestial civil servants, like that of the Chinese Jade Emperor, or a less structured one, at which the high god was surrounded by lesser deities. In both cases the myths describe a palatial dwelling-place where the court assembled around the ruling deity.

The link between mortal king and heavenly ruler worked both ways. Many historical rulers, keen to increase their power, portrayed themselves as gods or as people who, like Chinese emperors and Egyptian pharaohs, expected to join the immortals when they died.

# Zeus

🏛 Greece    ♃ Jupiter (Rome)

The sky god Zeus was the greatest deity of the Ancient Greeks. On Mount Olympus he ruled supreme. On Earth, he was said to cause phenomena such as thunder and rain, and to intervene in the lives of men and women.

Zeus was the son of the Titans Cronos and Rhea, and had to fight the Titans for his power (*see pp.38–9*). When the gods divided up the universe at the end of this war, Zeus became lord of the heavens, and was also given overall control of the universe. He became famous not only for his great power, but also for his sexual appetite and his many loves (*see pp.42–3*). Zeus sired many of the heroes and heroines of Greek mythology.

## ZEUS AND THE MORTALS

It was said that Zeus shaped the characters of men and women by controlling whether they were predominantly good or evil. At the gates of his palace there were two jars, one containing good and the other containing evil. When a mortal was born, Zeus usually gave them a little from each jar, but occasionally he handed out only one of these attributes, which would result in a person being entirely good or completely evil.

Like the other Olympians over whom he presided, Zeus influenced the adult lives of mortals. During the Trojan War, for example, several heroes enjoyed the backing of different gods and goddesses, but Zeus presided over key turning-points in the war. It was Zeus who weighed the fate of the Greek leader Achilles against that of the Trojan hero Hector. When he found for Achilles, he also prevented Apollo from intervening on Hector's behalf.

### WORSHIP

*The most famous shrine to Zeus was the oracle at Dodona in Epirus, in northwestern Greece. The oracle's prophesies were usually interpreted from the sound of a spring that rose from the roots of a sacred oak tree, or sometimes from the rustling of its leaves.*

# Jupiter

📖 Ancient Rome　　🜨 Zeus (Greece)

The supreme Roman deity, Jupiter was the god of the sky and daylight, the leader of the council of the gods, and the source of all power.

Jupiter was a god of the city of Rome and was worshipped there for centuries before the Romans established their empire. When they conquered Greece, Jupiter acquired many of the main characteristics of Zeus (*see p.269*). He was worshipped in temples all over the empire, especially by generals, consuls, and emperors, who regarded him as their protector.

**Statues of Jupiter** (usually flanked by the other two major Roman deities, Juno and Minerva) were placed in the main temples in most provincial cities.

### WORSHIP

*Jupiter's most famous temple was built on the Capitoline Hill, Rome. • Festivals of Jupiter were held on March 15, May 15, and October 15, on which date the annual Capitoline Games in his honour also took place.*

# Eurynome

📖 Ancient Greece

The most ancient of the Greek creation myths, which survives only in part, concerns the Goddess of All Things, known as Eurynome ("wide-wandering"). This primal goddess brought the universe into being and gave the ancient race of the Titans their power over the various parts of the cosmos.

Eurynome emerged naked from Chaos, divided the sea from the sky, and then danced upon the water. Her movements created the north wind, which she rubbed between her hands to produce a serpent, Ophion. Eurynome mated with Ophion, while the warm north wind blew on the goddess and made her fertile. She took the form of a dove and laid an egg, from which hatched the elements of the cosmos: the stars, the planets, the sun, the moon, and the Earth. Eurynome arranged the power structure of the cosmos by appointing a Titan and a Titaness to rule over each planet. The final part of the myth tells how the human race began. Eurynome made the soil of Arcadia especially fertile, and from this soil sprang the first man, Pelasgus, and his fellow humans. Pelasgus taught the people how to build huts, make clothes, and find food.

# Odin

**Norse**    Woden (Anglo-Saxon); Wodan, Wotan (Germanic)

The Norse god of magic, war, wisdom, and poetry, Odin was powerful and complex. He was a shape-changer, the ruler of all the gods, and the deity who welcomed the souls of dead heroes to his hall, Valhalla.

Odin used his ability to transform to turn into an extraordinary range of beings and phenomena, from fish to fire and serpents to smoke, in order to achieve whatever he wanted. After sacrificing one of his eyes, he drank from the well of Mimir in order to gain knowledge of everything in the past, present, and future, and he then won the mead of inspiration for the gods *(see pp.120, 123)*. The resulting combination of immense knowledge, inspiration, and experience of life in all its forms gave Odin universal wisdom, and this underpinned his enormous power. He was renowned for using this power capriciously, and his titles included Svipall (Capricious One) and Glapsvidir (Swift Trickster).

The prowess of Odin in battle was legendary. He was known to instigate wars and would influence battles to produce whatever outcome he desired.

He was helped not only by his own supernatural powers, but also by two of his magic attributes: his spear and his horse. Odin's spear was called Gungnir. Made for him by dwarves, it never missed its target, was unstoppable in flight, and symbolized Odin's rule over the "point of no return", the moment when the spear leaves the thrower's hand. Odin's horse, Sleipnir, was the offspring of the god Loki and the horse Svadilfari. Its eight legs made it the fastest mount in the world and its enormous power enabled it to leap the walls of Niflheim, realm of the giants.

**In this 19th-century** painting, Odin watches the world burning during the battle of Ragnarok, the final war, signalling the end of the world.

## WORSHIP

*The great gilded temple in Gamla Uppsala, Sweden, held images of Odin, Thor, and Freyr. • Humans and animals were ritually sacrificed and hung from trees, imitating Odin's search for knowledge (see p.120).*

## Luonnotar

📕 Finland   ♀ Ilmatar

Also known as the "air girl", Luonnotar is the primal goddess in the Finnish epic, the *Kalevala* (*see pp.128–31*). As she lay on the sea, a duck laid its eggs on her knee and when Luonnotar moved, the eggs fell and broke. The pieces made the cosmos – the shells became the Earth and sky, the yolks became the sun, and the whites the moon.

### WORSHIP

*On cliffs at Rauma in southern Finland are five large stone tables, thought to have been used to make offerings to the pagan gods.*
*• As Ilmatar, Luonnotar's name or feast day is celebrated in Finland on 26 August.*

## Väinämöinen

📕 Finland

The son of Luonnotar and the sea, Väinämöinen was the Finnish god of song and poetry. Because he spent more than 700 years in his mother's womb, he was already old when he was born and was instantly recognized as a sage. Skilled in magic, Väinämöinen travelled to Tuonela, the Underworld, to gain knowledge of the most powerful spells. He possessed a magical singing voice with which he could enchant and transform almost anything; he could even control the elements and command the land with his songs. Finland's national epic, the *Kalevala*, tells of his many adventures (*see pp.128–31*).

## The Daghda

📕 Ireland

Leader of the Tuatha Dé Danaan, the last race of magical people to inhabit Ireland, the Daghda was known as "the Good God" because of his many powers and skills, ranging from warfare to music. One of his roles was as god of plenty. He possessed a huge cauldron (*see p.100*), which would fill with milk and meat to provide food for all of his followers. He also kept an orchard with trees perpetually laden with fruit, and a pair of pigs that renewed themselves after each slaughtering. As god of war, the Daghda's weapon was a club so huge that it had to be pulled along on wheels. One end of the club had the power to kill, the other to bring the dead back to life.

## Sucellus

📕 Celtic

King of the gods of Celtic Gaul and Britain, Sucellus ("the Good Striker") was a strong, bearded figure who carried a long-handled hammer. He could use his hammer in various ways. He could strike the ground, making the plants grow in spring; he could hit his enemies with it, quickly dispatching them to the Underworld; or he could carry it as a symbol of his great strength and importance. In addition, it may have been a craft tool, suggesting the god's skill in creating things. Sucellus is usually depicted with his consort, Nantosuelta, goddess of fertility, hearth, and home.

**Sucellus was** a magical leader; he was the Gaulish equivalent of the Daghda.

## Teutates

🏛 Celtic   ⚱ Toutates

The god Teutates was a major deity of Celtic Britain and Gaul. He was commemorated in many inscriptions, and was probably a protector god of several Celtic tribes, but little is known about him for certain. The Roman writer Lucan said that devotees of Teutates made human sacrifices to the god, and a later writer said that Teutates preferred sacrificial victims to be drowned. This has led to the theory that some of the Iron-Age bodies that have been found preserved in European swampland were the victims of sacrifice to this god.

**Sacrificial victims** of Teutates were tipped headfirst into a vat of liquid, probably ale.

## Raven and Tangen

🏛 Chukchi, Siberia

The Chukchi creator Raven excreted the world. Taking the form of an old man, and with the help of his son Tangen, Raven made the first people from handfuls of earth, using grass for hair, and blew on them to bring them to life. Tangen tried to give them speech by writing, but his efforts failed. So Raven turned himself into a bird and cawed at the people, "Krya, Krya". The people cawed back, and then they found they could speak. Raven stole the sun from heaven, hiding it in his mouth, but Tangen tickled Raven so thoroughly he had to laugh, and spat the sun up into the sky to light the world.

## Byelobog & Chernobog

🏛 Slavic   ⚱ Belebog and Crnobog

The Slavs believed in the eternal conflict between good and evil, and this manifested itself in their mythology in the shape of twin creator gods known by the western Slavs as Byelobog and Chernobog. Byelobog was the "white god", the god of sun, happiness, and good fortune, while Chernobog was the "black god", the god of darkness and evil-doing. This duality has been compared to that of Zoroastrianism, with its opposing gods Ahura Mazda and Ahriman, and indeed the Slavs were enthusiastic followers of the teachings of the Bogomils or Cathars, a heretical medieval religious sect that emphasized the duality of good and evil and has links to Zoroastrianism.

## Perun

🏛 Russia   ⚱ Perkun, Perkuna, Perkunas

Only scraps of myth survive regarding the warlike Perun, the most important of the pagan Slavic gods. In one Lithuanian fragment, as Perkun, he cuts the (male) moon with his sword as punishment for courting the morning star and betraying his wife, the sun. Perun is usually identified as the thunder god; his sacred tree was the oak, perhaps because oaks are so often struck by lightning.

### WORSHIP

*Priests of Perun maintained eternal flames at his shrines. • The cult statue of Perun in Kiev, Ukraine, had a silver head and a gold moustache. • Cocks, domestic animals, and even humans were sacrificed to Perun.*

## Enlil

📜 Mesopotamia    🔔 Ellil (Akkadian)

The air god Enlil was one of the most important deities in the mythologies of the Sumerians, Babylonians, and Hittites. The god who separated heaven and Earth, he was the father of many other gods and goddesses.

Enlil's city of Nippur was thought to have existed before the creation of man; it was called "the bond of heaven and Earth". Enlil himself was regarded as the ultimate source of civilization and agriculture. One long poem describes his invention of the pickaxe; another tells of how he created the cattle god Lahar and the goddess of grain, Ashnan, to provide food and clothes for the gods. The gods then created humankind in order to make full use of the gifts of Lahar and Ashnan. Enlil was married to Ninlil (sometimes called Sud or Mullissu), a mother goddess. The poem "Enlil and Ninlil" tells of how Enlil rapes Ninlil and is banished to the Underworld, but she follows him there and he couples with her three more times in disguise.

### WORSHIP

*The cult centre of Enlil was the temple of E-kur ("Mountain House") at Nippur, near the Zagros mountains in modern Iraq. Enlil is sometimes called "the Great Mountain".*
*• It was said that new cities would rise only with the blessing of Enlil.*

## Marduk

📜 Babylon

The son of the god of Earth and water, Marduk was the chief god of Babylon. He was worshipped in the temple of Esagil, with his wife Sarpanitu, the goddess of childbirth. His power grew as the city of Babylon became capital of an empire. The *Enûma Elish* or "Epic of Creation" hails him as the king of the gods. Marduk slew the dragon Tiamat and created the Earth and sky from her body; by seizing the Tablets of Destiny from her champion Kingu, he became the ruler of the cosmos.

## El

📜 Canaan

El, often called the Bull El, was the father of the gods in Canaanite (Ugaritic) mythology, and was married to the goddess Ashtoreth. El was also titled El Elyon, "God Most High". He is traditionally depicted as an old man (sometimes with wings or bull's horns), seated, and with his arms raised. The Greeks identified El with their god Cronos, king of the Titans.

Many of the Canaanite myths tell of strife between the gods, in particular between two of El's sons, Baal, the storm god, and Yamm (Yam-Nahar), the god of seas and rivers. The ruler El favours Yamm over the rebellious Baal, but despite this it is Baal who ultimately triumphs. El himself was a remote high god, approached through gods such as Baal rather than directly. El had no temple in Ugarit, whereas Baal had a magnificent one (*see pp.150–51*).

# Ahura Mazda

**⚑** Persia    **☉** Ohrmazd

Ahura Mazda is the all-knowing creator, whose plans for a perfect universe are thwarted by his evil twin Ahriman. Ahura Mazda represents goodness and light, while his brother Ahriman lurks in darkness in the House of Lies.

Ahura Mazda is a wise and tolerant god who allows humans the freedom to choose between good and evil, although it is said that the Earth is happiest where one of the faithful is standing. The history of the world is the story of the struggle between the Holy Thought (Spenta Mainyu) of Ahura Mazda and the Evil Thought of Ahriman. Ahura Mazda will eventually win with the help of the saviour Saoshyant (or Soshans), who will be born to a virgin impregnated by the miraculously preserved sperm of the

**Ahura Mazda,** the supreme being of ancient Persia, struggles to divide the forces of good and evil which keep the world he created in constant turmoil.

### WORSHIP

*On the tomb of Darius I (see p.155), the winged disc of Ahura Mazda floats above the king.*
• *Zoroastrians expose their dead to be eaten by vultures. The dead cannot be buried, as they are polluted by Ahriman; but as the creation of Ahura Mazda, they cannot be burned.*

prophet Zoroaster (Zarathustra). The teachings of Ahura Mazda were given directly to Zoroaster, and enshrined in the 17 hymns known as the *Gathas*. Zoroaster is said to have been the only baby to have laughed when he was born, instead of crying.

# Elagabal

**⚑** Syria; Italy    **☉** El Gabal, Ilaha Gabal

Elagabal was worshipped at Emesa (now Homs in Syria) in the form of a black meteorite. His Aramaic name is Ilaha Gabal, meaning "god of the mountain". A freak occurrence made Elagabal briefly the supreme god of Rome, called "the unconquered sun", when his high priest became the Emperor Bassianus. Elagabal was one of several Levantine deities to find favour in the Roman Empire, including the Baal of Baalbek (now in Lebanon) and the Palmyrenian triad of Bêl, Iarhibôl, and Aglibôl.

# Zurvan

**⚑** Persia

Zurvan ("Time") is the dual-gendered cosmic god of Persia who existed in the primal void. The androgynous Zurvan gave birth to the opposing principles of good and evil, Ahura Mazda (*above*) and Ahriman. Barsom twigs, the sacred symbol of Zoroastrian priesthood, were then given to Ahura Mazda by Zurvan as a sign that he was Zurvan's true son. Worship of the unified god Zurvan became a heresy of the Zoroastrian faith, which regards Ahura Mazda and Ahriman as having existed in duality from the beginning of time.

# Brahma, Vishnu, and Siva

**♊** India

Three closely related gods stand at the centre of
Hindu mythology: Brahma, who created
the cosmos; Vishnu, who protects it;
and Siva, who will finally destroy it.

Brahma is said to exist on a different
plane and in a different timescale
from mortal life. One day in
Brahma's life lasts the equivalent of
4,320 million human years. This
cosmic scale makes Brahma rather
remote; the other two gods of the
triad have more contact with the
mortal world and are worshipped
far more. Siva is the embodiment
of strength and knowledge, and
represents the coming-together
of opposites. Vishnu comes to the
aid of Earth when it is in danger by
adopting one of ten avatars (*see p.162*).

> **WORSHIP**
>
> *There are many temples to Siva and Vishnu
> in India, but only one to Brahma, at Pushkar
> in Rajasthan. • A brahmin (priest) acts as the
> intermediary between the worshippers and
> the god in Hindu temples.*

**The four heads** of Brahma
symbolize the four *Vedas* and
face the four compass points.

# Bhagavan

**♊** Baiga, central India

The creator Bhagavan instituted almost
every aspect of Baiga spiritual, social,
and economic life. He lives "far away"
in a palace on an island guarded by two
rivers of fire, where he welcomes the
souls of the dead before returning them
to Earth for rebirth. He is not entirely
benevolent: he sent a snake to poison
the first man – and so brought death to
the world – out of pure jealousy, and he
cheated Nanga Baiga's descendants out
of his magic. This ambivalence is
reflected in his palace, half of which
blazes with light while the rest is rotting.

# Phan-Ningsang

**♊** Singpho, northeastern India

Phan-Ningsang is the greatest of all
the Singpho gods, and the sky god
Mathum-Matta is his minister. After
the world was made, Phan-Ningsang
and Mathum-Matta decided to explore
it. They found a gourd in the shape of
a man, and when they broke it open
many little people spilled out. Phan-
Ningsang carved breasts on the women
with his axe and Mathum-Matta
carved male organs on the men. They
played a charm to them with a golden
pipe, which made the people scatter
across the world and love each other.

# Pan Gu

📕 China     ♂ Pan Ku

The creator of the world according to Chinese mythology, Pan Gu came into being when the two primal forces, Yin and Yang, combined at the beginning of time. He lay inactive for 18,000 years while chaos swirled around him, and then took a further 18,000 years to grow, finally forcing apart the two halves of the primal egg until they became the Earth and the sky (*see p.172*). Some versions of the myth say that Pan Gu was helped in the creation of the cosmos by a group of mythical animals (ever since seen as powerful or auspicious in Chinese mythology): a dragon, a phoenix, a unicorn, a tortoise, and, sometimes, a tiger.

# Fu Xi

📕 China     ♂ Fu Hsi, Pao Hsi, Mi Hsi

In Chinese mythology the god Fu Xi is seen as a kind of primal emperor and founder of China. He married the goddess Nü Wa, who created human beings by moulding them from clay, and showed humanity the skills of civilization, from hunting and fishing to metalworking and farming. Fu Xi established the idea of rule by king or emperor, showed people how to calculate the time, and invented a series of symbols called the Ba Gua ("eight trigrams"). These symbols had magical powers and were used to tell the future.

**Fu Xi created** the Ba Gua, later used in the *I Ching*. Here he holds a medallion decorated with trigrams.

# The Jade Emperor

📕 China     ♂ The Emperor of Heaven, the Supreme Ruler

In ancient China the Emperor of Heaven or Jade Emperor (*see pp.176–7*) was a being of awesome power. He stood at the head of a court of gods and goddesses that mirrored the earthly court of the emperor of China.

As the supreme deity in Chinese mythology, and one who had reached enlightenment through cultivating the Dao ("the Way"), the Jade Emperor was the final arbiter in any disputes between the other gods and goddesses. This was often thought to be his main business, and some said that he was thus so exalted and remote that, unlike other gods, he could be neither worshipped directly nor even represented. But when he was depicted, he was dressed like a mortal emperor, wearing the imperial crown or *mien*, a flat-topped crown decorated with 13 dangling cords, each threaded with beads. He exercised his vast power through spirits who were capable of destroying anyone who offended him. His usual way of controlling human life, however, was more subtle. Helped by messengers who reported on earthly events, he kept detailed records of every person's life, ready for the day when they would die and have to go to the courts of the Underworld for their final judgment.

## Izanagi and Izanami

🇯🇵 Japan

The primal couple of Japanese folklore, Izanagi and Izanami created the islands of Japan, celebrated the first marriage, and procreated the gods, or *kami*. Their names can be translated as Noble Male and Noble Female.

Their myth is recorded in *Kojiki* ("Record of Ancient Matters"), completed in 712 CE, and *Nihonshoki* ("Chronicles of Japan"), a later text completed in 720 CE. The myth tells of how the Separate Heavenly Deities asked Izanagi and Izanami to make the Earth by stirring the sea with a magical spear. Singly and as a couple the pair then gave birth to many gods and goddesses, including the wind god Fujin, who completed their creation of Japan by blowing away the mist to reveal the islands.

Izanami later died while giving birth to the god of fire. After her death, Izanagi followed her down to the Underworld and tried to rescue her, but he was no more successful than Orpheus in Greek mythology (*see p.57*). Izanagi looked at Izanami despite specific instructions to resist, and

Izanami – who, like Persephone, had eaten food in the Underworld – was trapped there forever.

Izanagi, horrified after witnessing the decaying body of Izanami, purified himself by washing in a river. For this reason some people regard Izanagi as the founder of the practice of *harae*, the Shinto purification ceremonies. In these the body is cleansed and prayers are said for the removal of sin and misfortune. The purification can be focused on an individual, a town, or a whole nation.

### WORSHIP

*In the sea near Ise on Honshū (site of the temple of Amaterasu) are the "wedded rocks" that house the spirits of Izanami and Izanagi (see p.180). A rope that ties the rocks together is renewed every year. The larger rock holds a sacred gateway to a Shinto temple.*

## Kotan-kor-kamui

🇯🇵 Japan

The Ainu people of Hokkaido say that the world was created by Kotan-kor-kamui, "the land-making deity". The Earth was originally a lifeless swamp, with six heavens above and six worlds below. Kotan-kor-kamui sent a wagtail down to make land, which it did by beating the water with its tail, as the bird still does today. Gradually the land appeared, and Kotan-kor-kamui made the first Ainu to live on it. These early people had earthen bodies, chickweed hair, and willow sticks for spines, which explains why people bend with age.

## Tohan

🇲🇾 Chewong, Malaysia    ☪ Allah Ta' Allah

Tohan, the God Most High who gave the breath of life to the first humans, is respected as a superhuman being rather than worshipped as a god. Tohan lives on this world, which is known as Earth Seven in Chewong cosmology. He gave Nabi, his servant, breath for the humans, but Nabi let some escape, and the breath turned into evil spirits (*bas*). When the world becomes polluted by too much death, blood, and faeces, Tohan turns it over and starts again on the flat underside, creating new plants, animals, mountains, and humans.

# Raven

📖 Northwest Native American 🖤 Crow

Raven is the most important character in the mythologies of the northwestern USA and the sub-Arctic and Arctic regions of North America. He appears in many myths, in roles that include creator, transformer, hero, and trickster.

On the northwest coast of the USA, the first creator is generally a remote figure, such as the Tsimshian people's Walks-all-over-the-sky, who made the stars when sparks flew from his mouth as he slept. Raven is a much more practical creator. His name among the Haida means "the one who is going to order things", and his main task was to organize the world. He did this by transforming the first things that existed and then by establishing the laws of nature.

The Tsimshian myths of Raven tell of how he stole the sun from the sky world, and also of how he married Bright-cloud-woman, a salmon-woman who had only to dip her fingers into water to create more salmon.

## BORN FROM A PEA-POD

In Alaska, the Unalit Inuit myths say that after Raven made the Earth there were still no people. But the first man was there, coiled up in the pod of a beach-pea. One day he burst out and stood up, a grown man. Raven landed near him, pushed his beak up to his forehead (like a present-day dancer pushing up a Raven mask) and turned into a man. When the man told Raven he had come from the pea-pod, Raven said, "I made that plant, but I never thought something like you would come from it."

**In some versions** of the myth, Raven finds many people emerging from a clam shell on the beach.

## A CURE FOR LONELINESS

When the man became hungry, Raven turned back into a bird and went to fetch berries for him to eat. Then he turned back into a man, moulded some sheep and reindeer from clay, and brought them to life. He told the man: "You will be lonely, all by yourself," before taking more clay to fashion a woman with fine watergrass for hair. When he flapped his wings, she came to life, to become a beautiful companion for the man from the pea-pod.

> **WORSHIP**
>
> *The ceremonial house of the Kwa-kwa-ka'wakw people in British Columbia, Canada, had Raven's beak as its entrance. The lower part swung open, then with the weight of a footfall inside, clapped shut to "swallow" the entrant.*

## Wakan Tanka

🏴 Lakota, North America (Plains)

Wakan Tanka is often referred to as an all-seeing deity, and his name translates as the Great Mystery. The Lakota (Sioux) refer to everything that is sacred or mysterious as "wakan". A typical Lakota prayer might be simply, "Wakan Tanka, pity me." Wakan Tanka is also a group of 16 spirits, the Four-times-Four. These benevolent powers include Sun, Rock, Thunder, and Earth, who together control the world. Among the Omaha, Wakan Tanka is defined as Wakon'da, who is viewed as an all-pervading life-force rather than a god.

## Awonawilona

🏴 Zuni, southwestern USA

Early accounts of Zuni mythology speak of an androgynous creator, Awonawilona, but it is now understood that the term covers a group of powerful "raw people": animal-human beings of the creation-time who can transform into any shape they like. This group includes Sun Father (Yatokka Taccu) and Moonlight-Giving Mother (Yaonakka Citta). The Sun Father has two houses, one in the east and one in the west. Moonlight-Giving Mother is his wife, but she is always separated from him. His sister is Old Lady Salt.

## Quetzalcoatl

🏴 Aztec, Mexico    🗝 Ehécatl, Ce Acatl Topiltzin, Kukulcan, Gucumatz

The name Quetzalcoatl means "plumed serpent". This benevolent Mesoamerican god takes the hybrid form of a quetzal bird and a rattlesnake.

Quetzalcoatl was one of the most important Aztec gods, dating back to *c*.1000 BCE. As co-creator of the present age with his brother and rival Tezcatlipoca, it was he who descended to the Underworld to rescue the bones of a former race and recreate humanity for this era. Quetzalcoatl is known to have had other guises too, notably Ehécatl, god of the wind. In this form he was also the culture hero who taught mankind how to live. The god Quetzalcoatl has become closely identified with Topiltzin

**This stone head of Quetzalcoatl** as the feathered serpent hangs on a wall at the temple dedicated to him at Teotihuacán, the City of the Gods, Mexico.

### WORSHIP

*The Pyramid of Quetzalcoatl, part of the complex of Teotihuacán, which lies north of Mexico City, has the earliest representations of Quetzalcoatl as the Plumed Serpent. His devotees made pilgrimages to Cholula, which was a temple devoted to him.*

Ce Acatl Quetzalcoatl, human king of the legendary city of Tollan. This king was said to have sailed to the east on a raft of serpents, ashamed at having been tricked by Tezcatlipoca into sleeping with his own sister. Some people believe that Quetzalcoatl was reincarnated as the planet Venus.

# Viracocha

📍 Inca, Peru   ⚬ Con Ticci Viracocha, Coniraya Viracocha

Viracocha, creator and culture hero of the Andes, was the pre-eminent deity of ancient Peru. An Inca prayer refers to the deity as "Lord of the Universe", and suggests that this god could be viewed as either male or female.

Viracocha called forth the sun, moon, and stars from the Island of the Sun in Lake Titicaca, and then created the first humans. Although the Incas venerated Viracocha, they also considered themselves "children of the sun" or the sun god, Inti. The eighth name in the Inca king lists is Viracocha Inca; this human king was so-named because he said that the creator appeared to him one night. Stories about the god Viracocha and the king Viracocha Inca have become inextricably entwined.

For the peoples of the high Andes, a version of this god called Coniraya Viracocha was a trickster-creator, who travelled as a beggar. In this guise (*see p.217*), he searched for his lover, the goddess Cavillaca, and their child. Coniraya travelled all the way to the coast and the home of the creator deity Pachacamac ("he who animates the Earth"). There he seduced one of the daughters of Pachacamac and Urpay Huachac, and incidentally seeded the ocean with fish from Urpay Huachac's fishpond, so she became known as mother of the sea-fishes.

### WORSHIP

*The statue of Viracocha in his shrine at Cusco was made of gold, and showed him as a bearded white man in a long tunic. In this form – Con Ticci Viracocha – he travelled the highlands of Peru healing the sick and restoring sight to the blind.*

# Sky Holder

📍 Iroquois, North America   ⚬ Teharonhyawágon, Good Mind, Sapling, Little Sprout

For the Iroquois nations of northeastern North America, Sky Holder is the creator, a figure who merges with the culture hero and Master of Life, Hawenniyo. He has an evil twin brother called Flint, who forced his way into the world through their mother's armpit, killing her in the process.

Sky Holder and Flint are twins born to the daughter of Old Woman, who fell from the sky to rest on the back of the Great Turtle (*see pp.194–7*). The daughter was made pregnant by the wind; in one version the personified wind simply lays two arrows beside her – one plain and one flint-tipped. Flint ("evil mind") mars every good thing that Sky Holder ("good mind") creates, while Sky Holder tries to temper every one of Flint's evil acts. For instance, Sky Holder made the rivers flow both ways so that it was easy to paddle a canoe in either direction, but Flint changed them to flow in just one direction. Flint made the mosquito so big that it could uproot a sapling, so Sky Holder compressed it to minimize the harm it could do.

### WORSHIP

*The Iroquois prophet Handsome Lake founded the Longhouse religion in 1799. In visions, the Master of Life had told him that the Seneca people must continue their rituals or the world would be consumed by fire.*

## Olodumare

🏳 Yoruba, Nigeria    ♛ Olorun

The name Olodumare means "great everlasting majesty". This god is also called Olorun, "the owner of heaven". He created Earth from the primeval swamp, and breathed life into the beings shaped from earth by the god Obatala to create the first humans. (Some humans are flawed because the trickster Eshu gave Obatala too much palm wine as he worked.) Olodumare hears and sees everything that happens on Earth, albeit from a distance – originally, heaven was so close that the gods could travel up and down on a spider's web, but humankind annoyed Olodumare by wiping their dirty hands on the sky, so it was lifted higher.

## Mawu-Lisa

🏳 Fon, Benin    ♛ Segbo

Mawu-Lisa, the dual-sexed creator, is a sky deity combining the female moon (Mawu) and the male sun (Lisa). Mawu Lisa rode in the mouth of the cosmic serpent Aido-Hwedo as he-she shaped the world; then Mawu-Lisa mixed clay and water, in the same way as building materials are prepared for a house, to create the first people. The first man and woman, sometimes called Adanhu and Yewa, established the worship of Mawu-Lisa and of the lesser gods he-she gave birth to. In the mythology of the Fon sky-cult, the world was first created by another androgynous deity, Nana-Buluku, but this creator is rarely remembered today.

## Amma

🏳 Dogon, Mali

In the complex cosmology of the Dogon, Amma is the creator, who first existed in the form of a cosmic egg containing all the seeds of the physical and spiritual universe. These were quickened to life by internal vibrations and unfolded in a helix, breaking through the egg to be flung into space, creating the cosmos. A race of divine twin-beings, the Nommo, were also in the egg. One of these, Yurugu, broke free and tried to create a rival universe, but failed without his female aspect. The Earth was made from his placenta. Another Nommo sowed the seeds that engendered humans, animals, and plants, and brought the Earth to fruition with rain.

**This Dogon sculpture** of a Nommo shows him adopting the position for "hooking in" the rain-bearing clouds needed by crops.

## Juok

🏳 Shilluk, Sudan    ♛ Jok, Jwok, Joagh

The name Juok is used in all the Nilotic languages to signify the divine. The concept of Juok embraces the entire supernatural world, and both good and evil. This fact led to some missionaries translating the word as "god", while others interpreted it as "devil". Among the Shilluk, an ethnic group of southern Sudan, Juok is conceived as a universal, formless, invisible spirit. As the creator of the world, he is present in everything, and controls the destinies of all humans, plants, and animals. Juok can be approached only through Nyikang, an intermediary, the mythic ancestor of the Shilluk, who is reincarnated in the Shilluk kings. Sacrifices are made to Nyikang asking him to influence Juok to send rain, heal sickness, or send good fortune.

# Ra

🏴 Egypt   ⚱ Re, Khepri, Aten, Atum, Nebertcher, Amun-Ra, Ptah

Ra, the sun god, was the visible form of the creator.
He was also called Nebertcher ("the lord without limit")
and Atum ("the all"). However, he also had a secret name,
the knowledge of which could bring great power (*see p.229*).

Ra could take different forms: as
Khepri, the scarab beetle, he was
the rising sun; as Aten, the sun's disc,
the midday sun; and as Atum, an old
man leaning on a stick, the setting sun.
Each evening the sun was swallowed
by the sky goddess Nut, and Ra sailed
through the netherworld in his night
barque. There, he was assailed by the
chaos serpent Apophis. After the god
Seth speared the serpent, Ra would
take the form of a cat to cut off its
head. Ra could then continue on his
passage to be born again at sunrise. Ra
also had different aspects. Another
hymn tells us: "God is three gods above
all – Amun, Ra, and Ptah. His nature as
Amun is hidden, he cannot be known.
He is Ra in his features, and Ptah in his
body." All three were combined in the
same creator god, "the great god who
listens to prayers, who comes at the
voice of the poor and distressed, who
gives breath to the wretched".

**The sun god Ra** is depicted with outstretched wings
and a ram's head in this wall painting of the solar
cycle from the tomb of Queen Tausert (*c.*1190 BCE).

### WORSHIP

*Ra's most significant temple was at Heliopolis
("sun city" in Greek) on the Nile Delta. • Ra
was also worshipped at the great temple
complex of Karnak at Thebes (modern-day
Luxor) as Amun, or Amun-Ra, the hidden god.*

# Aten

**Ancient Egypt**   **Aton, Yati**

Originally, Aten was simply a name for the sun god Ra, represented in art as the disc of the sun, or a winged sun. During the New Kingdom (1550–1069 BCE), however, Aten increasingly became the focus of separate worship.

The Egyptian pharaoh Amenhotep IV (1352–1336 BCE) took the worship of Aten to extremes, denying other gods and effectively making the worship of Aten the state religion. Even before his reign, Aten had become a distinct form of the sun god. However Amenhotep, who changed his name to Akhenaten ("servant of Aten"), made Aten the supreme solar god. The names of the other gods were hacked from temple walls, in an attempt to destroy them by denying their existence. The pharaoh built a new capital of Akhetaten ("the horizon of the Aten") at El-Amarna, on the east bank of the Nile, where Aten was worshipped as the sole god. A "Hymn to the Aten", supposedly written by Akhenaten himself, has a number of parallels with the Biblical Psalm 104. The hymn addresses Aten as "the sole god", saying: "You alone made the Earth, according to your will."

### WORSHIP

*Akhetaten was home to a Great Aten temple.*
*• There is evidence of a priesthood to Aten at Heliopolis (the centre of worship for Ra).*
*• There appear to have been temples to him at Memphis, Egypt, and Sesebi in Nubia.*

# Hapy

**Ancient Egypt**   **Hapi, Hep, Hap**

The Nile itself was simply *iterw*, "the river". But the Nile inundation was a god, Hapy, who was also known as "Lord of the fishes and birds of the marshes". The whole of Egypt's civilization depended on the flooding, and its deposit of new, fertile silt for planting crops along the banks of the Nile.

Hapy lived in a cavern at the Nile's first cataract at Aswan, from whence the flood swelled each year. He was depicted as a pot-bellied man with large female breasts (possibly to signify fertility). The flood poured forth from his cavern in unstoppable bounty, "making the meadows laugh". No temples were raised to Hapy, though he did have cult centres at Gebel el-Silsila and Aswan. In the "Hymn to Hapy" the sun god Ra is said to be the son of Hapy, equating Hapy with Nun, the primal waters from which Ra emerged. Hapy also took the form of a cosmic serpent, the symbol of the endless renewal of time.

**As god of Upper** and Lower Egypt, Hapy was often shown as twin gods, one crowned with papyrus from the north (*left*), the other (*right*) with southern lotus.

# Tangaroa

**Polynesia** ♦ Kanaloa, Tangaloa, Ta'aroa, A'a

Tangaroa is the Maori name for the Polynesian god of the ocean, whose breath creates the tides. In western Polynesia, under the names A'a, Tangaloa, and Ta'aroa, Tangaroa was the pre-existing creator, who lived alone in the primal void and made all things.

In Tahiti, as Tangaloa, he first came to consciousness inside a shell "like an egg revolving in endless space", and broke out of this shell to create the world. A Samoan myth tells how Tangaloa created the Samoan island of Manu'a by dropping a rock into the ocean, and then made the rest of the islands, including Tonga and Fiji. He created the Peopling Vine as shade for his bird, Tuli, and this vine spread over the land. When the vine withered, Tangaloa made the first humans from the maggots that squirmed in the rotting vegetation, giving each a heart and a soul.

### WORSHIP

*A cult statue of Tangaroa as A'a which is in the British Museum in London shows other gods crawling over his shell-body; inside is a hollow cavity that originally held wooden figures of yet more gods.*

**In Maori myth** Tangaroa, god of the seas, is the brother of Tane, god of the forests. In Hawaiian mythology Tangaroa was known as Kanaloa.

# Baiame

**Australia** ♦ Bunjil, Nooralie

Baiame, the all-father creator god, is possibly the most important in southeastern Australia. His mythology has to some extent been influenced by Christianity. Baiame lives in the sky, and created the animals and humans; he took all the discontents from the animals (who were self-aware in the Dreaming) and gave them all to the humans. Birrahgnooloo, the all-mother, is his wife, and their son is Daramulun. Baiame sent Daramulun down to Earth to teach the people the laws by which life should be lived.

# Rainbow Snake

**Australia**

An important figure in Aboriginal mythology and religion, the rainbow snake emerged from a waterhole during the Dreaming, or creation-time. As the snake travelled around the country, its movements created the hills, mountains, valleys, and waterways of the ancestral landscape. Many of the myths speak of the dangers of irritating a rainbow snake or damaging its eggs; to do so causes the snake to send a flood. The snake now arches above the land as a rainbow in the sky, and can be seen in the scintillation of light on water.

# MOTHER GODDESSES AND EARTH DEITIES

In many mythologies there is a supreme goddess, a generally benevolent but occasionally destructive figure who looks after the Earth and is seen as a kind of cosmic mother. Her role embraces the conception and birth of the Earth itself, so figures such as the Ancient Greek Gaia and the Maori goddess Rangi represent "Mother Earth".

**M**other Earth was a figure who helped to explain the creation of the world and the existence of humanity. In many cases she was made fertile by her partner (usually a sky god), and then created, sometimes out of her own body, a place where humanity could live. So the birth of the Earth and human childbirth were seen in a similar way.

**Hera was an Olympian,** and the most senior of the female Greek deities. Her jealousy over Zeus's infidelities was well known.

simply means "goddess") is a kind of essence of all Hindu goddesses, who can embrace all moods, from nurturing to destructive.

## SECRET RITES
Like the process of childbirth itself, the worship of the mother goddess or Earth goddess was frequently a female preserve. Women devotees often kept their rites secret from their menfolk, who were excluded from the temple or shrine. In the case of the Roman goddess Bona Dea, even her personal name was unknown to outsiders, a fact that enhanced the mystery and importance both of the goddess herself and of the matters of fertility and abundance over which she presided.

## PERSONAL GODS
Although some of the mother goddesses were distant figures, many were also involved in the daily lives of their worshippers as goddesses of childbirth or marriage. Their importance often places them at the very top of the sacred hierarchy. The Roman goddess Juno was one of the three principal deities of Rome. In the Hindu pantheon, Devi (the name

# Bona Dea

**Ancient Rome**

One important Roman Earth goddess was Bona Dea, the "good goddess". She is a mysterious figure, whose personal name was never publicly revealed. She was worshipped by women in unrecorded secret rites.

There has been much speculation about the identity of Bona Dea, and it is likely that she was one of the nature goddesses who were known to Romans under another name. One candidate is Maia (May), a goddess associated with Vulcan, to whom the month of May was sacred. Another is Ops, the Sabine goddess of plenty. She was the wife of Saturn and controlled the harvest, so was linked closely to the Earth and its bounty. But most likely is the goddess Fauna, who was popular with women and was the sister and wife of Faunus (god of the shepherds and mythical early ruler of Latium).

## WORSHIP FOR WOMEN

Bona Dea was said by her admirers to have the gift of prophecy. She was also held to be chaste, and her rites were

**Bona Dea's festival** was attended by women only, until it was notoriously infiltrated by a disguised man, thought to be one Clodius Pulcher, in 62 BCE.

directed by Vestal virgins in women-only ceremonies. Worshipped regularly in a temple in Rome, she also enjoyed a special festival held in her honour each year. Bona Dea was invoked to promote good health, chasteness, and fertility. She was popular with freed slaves and those who hoped to be free one day.

The women who attended the rites of Bona Dea were said to offer flowers, wine, and a hog to the goddess – the wine drunk in her honour was referred to as milk. Music was played during the ceremony, and one account alleged that this music would drive all the women present into a frenzy.

### WORSHIP

Bona Dea's main temple was on the Aventine Hill in Rome, and admitted only women.
• The main festival of Bona Dea took place in December. The words "wine" and "myrtle" were banned because Bona Dea had once been made drunk and beaten with myrtle.

## Cybele

[𝄞] Ancient Greece and Rome    [♁] Kybele

The goddess Cybele came originally from Phrygia (in modern Turkey) and the Greeks are believed to have brought her cult back with them after the Trojan War. She became widely revered as the "Great Mother", and was worshipped all over the Greek, then the Roman world. Cybele's priests, the Galli, castrated themselves to serve her.

**Worshippers of Cybele,** who danced themselves into an ecstatic frenzy, were known as Corybantes.

## Gaia

[𝄞] Ancient Greece    [♁] Ge

The Ancient Greek goddess of the Earth was called Gaia. She emerged from the primal chaos of the universe and played a pivotal part in creation by giving birth to the first race of beings, the Titans (see p.36). She was also the mother of several other mythical races, including the one-eyed Cyclopes, the Hecatoncheires (or hundred-handed giants), and the Eumenides, fearsome female deities who punished those who betrayed their own family.

## Hera

[𝄞] Ancient Greece    [♁] Juno (Rome)

Hera was the sister and wife of Zeus and therefore the most senior of the goddesses of Mount Olympus. Her children included the gods Ares and Hephaestus, and the goddess Hebe.

Revered by women, Hera was a protector of wives and had the power of prophecy. Festivals commemorating her marriage to Zeus were held regularly in Greece. But there was a darker side to her character. When Zeus, Poseidon, and Hades divided up the universe, Hera was left out, and this, together with Zeus's many love affairs (see pp.42–3), made her resentful. Her jealousy, unleashed against her rivals and Zeus's children with other partners, became her dominant trait. It contributed to some of the most dramatic episodes in Greek mythology. She took part in a rebellion against her husband, and because of her resentment when she lost a divine beauty contest (see p.70), she provoked the conflict that became the Trojan War.

## Juno

[𝄞] Ancient Rome    [♁] Hera (Greece)

The protector of women, Juno had various other titles that emphasized different aspects of her character. As Juno Lucina she was the goddess of childbirth. As Juno Moneta she alerted people to danger: on one occasion, the geese in her sanctuary made a noise as the Gauls were about to invade, so the army was alerted and Rome was saved.

**Jupiter tried to immortalize** his half-mortal son Hercules by holding him to Juno's breast. Some of her milk shot upwards and formed the stars.

# Nerthus

🏳 Germanic

The Roman historian Tacitus describes the goddess Nerthus as Mother Earth. He said that she was goddess to tribes on a Baltic island, and would appear among the people in a chariot drawn by cows, which no-one but her priest was allowed to touch. While she was among the people, they all lay down their weapons and peace prevailed. Then she returned to her grove, where slaves washed her chariot and were then put to death to preserve her secrets.

# Mokosha

🏳 Slavic    ♂ Mokosz

The pagan Earth goddess Mokosha survived in Russian folk religion as *mat' syraia zemlia* –"Moist Mother Earth". She was a goddess of fertility and bounty, and was owed the respect of a mother: the custom of asking forgiveness of the Earth before death lasted into recent times. She is also associated with weaving and spinning, and is represented in Russian folk embroidery as a female figure with arms raised, flanked by two horsemen.

# Frigg

🏳 Norse    ♂ Frea, Friia

As both the daughter and consort of Odin, Frigg was one of the most powerful of all the Norse gods. She was a sky goddess, described as being clothed in clouds that turned dark when she was angry.

Frigg was associated with marriage and also linked to love, fertility, birth, and domesticity. She sat alongside Odin and, like him, intervened in human affairs, although she usually took the opposite side to her husband. This was just one source of conflict between the couple. Although a goddess of marriage, she had affairs with both of Odin's brothers, the creator gods Vili and Ve, and according to one account she also had sex with a slave. Frigg's relationship with her son, Balder, was also troubled. She unwittingly played a part in his tragic death (*see p.124*) and sent Balder's brother, Hermod, to the Underworld to beg for his reprieve.

### WORSHIP

*In Asgard, Frigg's home of Fensalir ("Marsh halls") suggests that she may have been worshipped at springs and ponds. • Frigg was identified with the Roman goddess Venus, whose Latin day became Friday, Frigg's day.*

# Devi

📍 India    ♀ Uma, Sati, Parvati, Lakshmi, Durga, Kali, Gauri

The word Devi means "goddess" and it is the name of the principal female deity in Hinduism. She embodies all goddesses: creative and destructive, peaceful and warlike. Most importantly, she is the consort of the god Siva.

Just as all goddesses come together in the figure of Devi, so all divine powers, both masculine and feminine, are united in the marriage of Siva and his wife. Kali and Durga, renowned as slayers of demons, represent the destructive side of Siva's consort, while loving and gentle Parvati is her benign counterpart. Devi can also be seen in the consort of Vishnu, when she is called Lakshmi and rules as the goddess of wealth and bringer of good luck.

**Devi is the mother of all,** and the goddess of nature and life. In her right hand she holds joy and pain, while her left hand dispenses life and death.

# Kwannon

📍 Japan    ♀ Guan Yin (China)

Kwannon is the goddess of mercy, a fount of compassion. Originally she was a male bodhisattva (in Buddhism, an enlightened one), Avalokitesvara, "the lord who looks down in pity". Poised on the brink of nirvana, Avalokitesvara was unable to pass beyond the temporal world while there was still suffering to be relieved, and so transformed into a goddess who redeems and sustains. Consequently Kwannon is sometimes shown in masculine guise; as a goddess she is often depicted with many arms, as Kwannon of the Thousand Hands.

**Kwannon is often** shown looking downward to signify that she watches over the world.

# Pachamama

📍 Inca, Peru    ♀ Pacha Mama

Pachamama is the Andean Earth goddess whose cult was long established by the time of the Inca empire. Farmers would set up long altar-stones in the middle of their fields to the Earth mother, praying to her to make the soil fertile and to provide a good harvest. Modern Quechua people in the Cusco area still venerate Pachamama as the goddess of agriculture, who lives inside the Earth. She is particularly regarded as a goddess of women, who pray to her as their "companion". For the Andean peoples, the whole landscape is alive with supernatural power, accessible at sacred spots known as *huacas*.

# Dauarani

📍 Warao, Venezuela

The Mother of the Forest (*see p.220*) in the mythology of the Warao people of the Orinoco Delta, Dauarani originated from the first canoe, made by the god Haburi. Warao carpenters shape canoes in a likeness of Dauarani's vulva. Apprentice canoe-makers must journey through the body of the great sky-snake to reach Dauarani's home on her world-mountain in the southeast. There, in dazzling light, the apprentice receives the secrets of canoe-making in an ecstatic experience that is recreated in the building of each new canoe.

# Changing Woman

📍 Diné (Navajo), southwestern USA

Changing Woman is the most important goddess of the Diné nation. The daughter of Long Life Boy and Happiness Girl, she was brought to life by Talking God from a turquoise image, and reared by First Man and First Woman. Changing Woman represents the essence of life: she grows old and is then rejuvenated in the endless cycle of the seasons. She gave birth to the hero twins Monster Slayer and Born for Water. She moved further west, but became lonely, so created the Diné from skin rubbed off her body.

# Geb

📍 Ancient Egypt

Geb (shown left with the falcon god Horus) was the god of the Earth. He is often depicted reclining on his back with an erect penis, having been forcibly separated from Nut, the sky; sometimes he is coloured the green of vegetation.

Geb, praised as "the lord of millions of years", was the son of Shu, the god of the dry air, and Tefnut, the goddess of the moist air. Geb, the dry land, and his sister Nut, the watery expanse of the sky, gave birth to the most important Egyptian gods: Osiris, Blind Horus, Seth, Isis, and Nephthys. Geb's other main role in myth is to act as judge over the rival claims of Seth and Horus to the throne; he favours Horus.

A myth inscribed on a stele from the Ptolemaic period tells how Geb's father Shu, having ruled Egypt for many years, became weak and ill, and ascended to heaven. For nine days the world fell dark, and wind howled across the land. Geb, who lusted for his mother Tefnut, seized his chance. He went to Shu's palace in Memphis, seized Tefnut, and raped her. Far from being punished for this act, at the end of the nine days

of darkness Geb ascended to the throne of Egypt, while Shu remained with Ra, the sun god.

Geb is unusual in world mythology in being a male Earth god, rather than a female Earth mother. He was said to have laid the Great Egg at the dawn of time, from which the Benu bird hatched (*see p.304*). One of Geb's names was the Great Cackler, because of the cackle he gave when he laid this egg. Geb's cult animal was the goose, and he was usually depicted either as a goose or with a goose's head.

## WORSHIP

*At his shrine in Iunu (near Cairo), Geb was worshipped as a bisexual god.* • *The House of Life at Abydos, Egypt, was a sacred replica of the universe and its floor was Geb.* • *In funerary texts Geb is seen as a threat because he seeks to imprison the dead within his body.*

# GODS OF THE SEA, SKY, AND COSMOS

To ancient peoples, the land seemed to be surrounded by forces – such as the sea, sky, and stars – of stupendous size and power. The motion of the sun and the ebb and flow of the tides seemed to speak of powers beyond human understanding, and these were usually explained as the movements of the most powerful of the gods.

Some deities embody the vastness of the heavens, and these sky gods, such as the Mesopotamian An, can be rather remote and aloof. But they also represent the sky's huge potential for creation. The Maori god Rangi is just such a deity: a vast figure who fathers the first gods. The Ancient Egyptian sky goddess, Nut, also provides an image of the vast expanse of the heavens. Her body, which curves in a great arc across the sky, forms an arch over which the sun god Ra travels in his sky-ship daily.

**The Tritons** were the merman sons of Poseidon, who blew into twisted seashells to calm or stir up the waves.

## COSMIC FORCES

The cosmic forces of the sea and sky are full of contradictions. The sea can bring life-threatening storms, but also nourishing supplies of fish. The sun warms the Earth, but can also dry up rivers and turn the soil to dust. Some ancient sea and sky gods embodied this unpredictability. The Greek Poseidon summoned storms with his trident; the Norse Thor drummed up thunder with his hammer; the Hindu god Indra, Lord of Water, brought thunder and rain.

## GOOD AND EVIL

All of these deities embodied real human anxieties about the cosmos, and in some ways worshipping them helped to appease those terrifying forces. The gods of the cosmos are not always destructive; their power also gives them creative strength. These two opposing forces are sometimes represented by a pair of gods, who are often siblings. In Japanese mythology, for example, the boisterous sea and storm god Susano is complemented by his more gentle sister Amaterasu, goddess of the sun.

# Cronos

Ancient Greece    Kronos, Cronus; Saturn (Rome)

Cronos the sky god was the son of Gaia and Uranus, and a member of the first race of beings to inhabit the cosmos, the Titans. His difficult relationship with his children, the gods of Olympus, led to war (*see pp.38–9*).

The Olympians won their war against the Titans. In the most familiar myth, the defeated Titans were banished to a shady region of the universe called Tartarus. But the Orphic tradition tells the story differently. In this version of the myth, Cronos made peace with Zeus and became the first king to rule over both heaven and Earth in a happy period known as the Golden Age. Zeus gave Cronos and his consort Rhea a beautiful home called the Isles of the Blessed. This was said to be in the far west, beyond the stars, and the pair ruled there in peace and contentment.

**Cronos devoured five** of his children in his attempt to defy an oracle's prediction that he would be overthrown by one of his own offspring.

### WORSHIP

*The Omphalos Stone at Delphi was said to be the very one that Cronos was tricked into swallowing, believing that it was his infant son Zeus. • The Omphalos Stone was ritually anointed with oil and then offered wool.*

# Poseidon

Ancient Greece

God of the sea, Poseidon (*see also p.50*) also presided over springs and lakes. When he appeared in his chariot, surrounded by sea-creatures and sea-nymphs, his storms and the earthquakes he also had power over were much feared. He helped the Trojans build their city walls, but when they argued about his payment, he sent a sea-monster to terrorize them, and later backed Greece against Troy in the Trojan War.

# Uranus

Ancient Greece    Ouranos, Uranos

Uranus was the son of Gaia (or, some say, Aether, the upper sky). He was the Greek personification of the sky and the father of the Titans (*see p.36*). It is said that he was killed by his son, Cronos, at Gaia's behest. As a sky deity he was noted as an astronomer. One tradition says that he was a real, human king who taught his people astronomy and the arts of civilization before dying and ascending to the heavens.

# Thor

 Norse     Thunor (Anglo-Saxon); Donar (German)

With his piercing eyes, red beard, and fearsome hammer, Thor was the strongest of the Norse gods. He made thunder as he crossed the sky in his chariot, and he came to the aid of the gods when giants threatened them.

Several accounts of Thor list the many giants he killed. He was helped in this not only by his powerful hammer, Mjöllnir, which always struck a true blow and would return to Thor each time he threw it, but also by iron gloves and a belt that doubled the god's strength when he wore it. The dreadful Midgard Serpent was one of the few enemies he could not dispatch (although it was prophesied that Thor will finally kill it in the last battle of Ragnarok).

Although he had notoriously large appetites and a fierce demeanour, Thor was the most popular god among the people of northern Europe. Many memorial stones survive in Denmark and Sweden with inscriptions to Thor and carvings of his hammer. Hammer-shaped amulets, as shown above, were worn and buried in people's graves.

Norse poetry provides descriptions of different temples to Thor in which there would always be a bowl to catch the blood of sacrificial animals. At the centre of these temples would stand a large gilded statue of the god, seated in a chariot pulled by a pair of goats.

**Thor was best known** as a giant-slayer, dispatching his enemies with a single blow of his hammer.

### WORSHIP

*In many temples in Dublin (Ireland), Uppsala (Sweden), and Thrandheim (Norway), Thor took pride of place. In Dublin his image was black; in Uppsala he always stood holding his hammer; and in Thrandheim he was adorned with gold and silver, and seated in a chariot.*

# Manannan mac Lir

Irish/Celtic    Manannan, Manandan, Monanaun; Manawydan (Welsh)

The Irish sea god Manannan mac Lir ("son of the sea") was said to live on Emain Ablach, an island off the coast of Scotland. From his home he rode across the waves in his horse-drawn chariot, travelling to support the other gods in their battles, and meeting Irish heroes on their journeys.

Manannan was an impressive figure, good-looking and powerful in his magical cloak, which changed colour from one moment to the next like the sea and had the power to change people's destinies when the wearer swept it through the air. He carried with him his magical bag, which contained all his possessions, and his sword, which could penetrate any armour. If Manannan needed extra powers, he could call on a wide repertoire of spells, which he also taught to the Druids. One further trick that he could call into being was a dense mist in which he could hide from attackers or take opponents by surprise.

**Manannan mac Lir** is usually said to travel the waves in a chariot or on horseback, but sometimes he uses a magical boat with neither sails nor oars.

# Nanna

Mesopotamian    Sîn (Akkadian)

The moon god Nanna was fathered on the maiden Ninlil by the air god Enlil. His wife was the goddess Ningal, and their children were the sun god Utu (Shamash) and the Great Goddess Inanna (see p.315). Nanna's chief temples were at Ur and at Harran in northern Syria. His name could be written simply as the number 30, the number of days in a lunar month.

**Crescent moons** flank the lunar god Nanna on this Assyrian stone relief.

# Enki

Mesopotamian    Ea (Akkadian)

Enki was the god of the freshwater ocean beneath the Earth, called *abzu*; his cult centre at Eridu was E-abzu ("Abzu House"). He was also the god of wisdom and magic, and in the myth of Inanna and Enki (see p.140) he is the owner of the *me*, the sacred powers that control the world order; he loses these to Inanna while drunk. In the myth of the Great Flood, it is Enki who takes the part of humanity against the gods. His wife was the goddess Damgalnuna.

## An

 Mesopotamia     Anu, Anus

The name An means "heaven" in
Sumerian, and An was the supreme
god of heaven, the offspring of Ansar
and Kisar, heaven and Earth. After
heaven and Earth were divided, An
occupied the topmost heaven. He was
an important but remote deity, and as
such was almost never represented in
the art of Mesopotamia. Known as
Anu or Anus in Hittite myth, he usurps
his father, the creator Alalu, and is in
turn usurped by his own son Kumarbi,
who kills Anu by biting off his genitals.

## Utu

 Mesopotamia     Shamash

Utu, the Sumerian sun god, was the son
of Nanna, the moon, and brother of
Inanna, the goddess of love and war.
In one myth about Inanna it was Utu
who arranged her marriage, and his
relationship with her was spiced on
both sides with sexual desire. Utu's own
wife was Sherida (Aya), a goddess of
light associated with love and sexuality.
They were worshipped together at
temples at Sippar and Larsa. Bearded
Utu emerged each morning from the
doors of heaven to traverse the sky.

## Indra

 India

Armed with his thunderbolt and bow,
the ancient Hindu sky god Indra
brought refreshing rains to India,
banishing Vritra, the god of drought
and death. This life-giving quality
endeared him to the ancient people of
India and he is the main subject of the
hymns of the *Rig Veda*, the earliest
Indian religious texts, which praise his
power and helpfulness to humans.
Indra's thunderbolt heralded the rain
and was also a weapon
that he hurled through
the air to defeat his
enemies. With his
thousand eyes Indra
could see the entire
cosmos, and with his
elongated arms he
could span the heavens.
He lived in his heaven,
Svarga, with his wife
Indrani. Periodically he
left his throne to battle
with demons.

**This carving** from Hoysalesvara
Temple shows Indra killing the
serpent-demon Vitra.

## Susano

 Japan     Susano'o, Susanowo

Susano, the god of storms, is an
ambivalent god. In his anger he defiled
heaven, and drove his sister, the sun
goddess Amaterasu, to hide away in
a cave, plunging the world into darkness
(*see pp.182–3*). But once expelled from
heaven, his anger blown out, Susano
became a largely beneficent figure.
He saved the Rice Paddy Princess from
a terrible dragon, killed the dragon by
trickery, and discovered in its tail one
of the three great
treasures of the
Japanese imperial
regalia: the sword
Kusa-nagi ("Grass-
cutter"), which is now
kept at the Atsuta
shrine, near Nagoya.
Susano's tendency
to turn violent and
destructive when he
lost his temper reflects
the nature of storms;
in psychological terms,
it is his internalization
of the loss of his
"mother" Izanami.

## Amaterasu

Japan

Amaterasu, the sun goddess, is the protective deity of Japan, and the first ancestor of the imperial family. At her shrine at Ise on Honshū, a simple thatched structure that is renewed every 20 years, she has been worshipped from earliest times as the Great Heaven Shining Deity. A harvest prayer to Amaterasu reads, "As you have blessed the ruler's reign, making it long and enduring, so I bow down my neck as a cormorant in search of fish to worship you and give you praise..."

**Amaterasu** is enticed out of her cave by the gods. She had retreated there, depriving the world of light, when she was cross with Susano (*facing page*).

## Di Jun

China  Dijun, Ti Chün

The Chinese deity Di Jun was the god of the eastern sky. His wife Xi He was a sun goddess. In some accounts of their story, Xi He crosses the sky in her chariot, spreading daylight as she travels; in another version Xi He is a male sun god who performs a similar light-bearing role. According to one version of this myth, the children of Di Jun and Xi He were ten suns that shone in turn in the sky. But on one occasion all ten suns shone together, causing unbearable heat and drought. The Emperor Yao asked Di Jun for divine intervention. Di Jun provided the heroic archer Yi with a powerful bow so that he could shoot down nine of the suns and restore the climate to normality (*see p.174*). Di Jun was also famous for his family: several of them became culture heroes, travelling around the world, founding different countries and spreading the arts of civilization.

## Inti

Inca, Peru

The sun god Inti was the mythical progenitor of the Inca royal dynasty. His temple at Cusco held a massive gold sun-disc conceived as a human face surrounded by rays. Inti was served by priests and "Virgins of the Sun", who were sworn to chastity. Their high priestess was considered the wife of the sun, although in the realm of the gods Inti was said to be married to Mamaquilla (Mama Kilya), the moon goddess.

## Coyolxauhqui

Aztec, Mexico

When the mother goddess Coatlicue became pregnant with Huitzilopochtli, her jealous daughter Coyolxauhqui and her 400 sons (the stars) slew her. Huitzilopochtli avenged her by dismembering his sister and tossing her head into the sky, where it became the moon, which is "killed" by the sun each month.

**Aztec sacrificial** practices echoed Coyolxauhqui's dismemberment.

# Horus

Ancient Egypt     Horemakhet, Ra-Horakhty

There were two gods named Horus. The first, Blind Horus, was killed by Seth, the god of chaos. Reborn as Horus to Isis and Osiris, he became identified with the ruling pharaoh and was worshipped in numerous forms.

The sky – and Horus – was thought to be a falcon with outstretched wings, whose eyes were the sun and moon. His first incarnation, Horus the Elder, or Blind Horus, earned his name because on a moonless night, he could not see. Blind Horus was a warrior god, armed with a sword, and he was particularly dangerous during these periods of blindness. He was the first victim of the jealousy of the chaos god Seth, who was his brother. Seth attacked and killed him, aided by the seven stars that make up the constellation of the Great Bear.

## A GOD REBORN

Horus was reborn as the son of Isis and Osiris, and most of the myths about him concern his long struggle with Seth for the throne after Seth murdered Osiris. At one point Seth tore out Horus's eye – the moon – but it was healed by the goddess Hathor (who appears in myths as both his bride and his mother). This restored *wedjat*-eye became the most common Egyptian amulet (*above*), a symbol of wholeness, protection, strength, and perfection. In Ancient Egypt the pharaoh was thought to have divine power to rule, being the living incarnation of Horus the god.

> **WORSHIP**
>
> *The Temple of Horus at Edfu is one of several devoted to this god.* • *Priests dressed up as Horus to ritually purify the path of a coffin.* • *The pharaoh's name was written in a shape – the* serekh *– depicting a falcon.*

**The white part** of Horus's crown represents Upper Egypt, and the red part is the crown of Lower Egypt.

## Thoth

📖 Ancient Egypt    🜚 Djehuty

Thoth, god of writing, knowledge, time, and the phases of the moon, was depicted as a baboon or as an ibis, the curve of the ibis's beak being thought to resemble both the crescent moon and a reed pen. At the temple of Thoth at Saqqara an estimated four million sacred ibises – and several million more at Tuna al-Gebel – were ritually killed, mummified, and stacked in pottery jars.

The Ancient Egyptians believed that when they died, Thoth would read out a list of their deeds in the Underworld's Hall of Two Truths, so that the 45 gods who judged a person's purity could determine the deceased's eternal fate.

**Thoth (right)** and his consort Nehmetaway were worshipped in the city of Khmun, Egypt.

## Nut

📖 Ancient Egypt

Nut was the Egyptian sky goddess. She was one of the Ennead, the nine great gods. Her body was the vault of the sky, and her hands and feet were the four cardinal points of Ancient Egyptian classical astrology: the eastern horizon where the sun rises, the western horizon where it sets, and the highest and lowest points of the sky. Every night Nut swallowed the sun god Ra, giving birth to him again the following morning.

Nut was the daughter of Shu, god of dry air, and Tefnut, goddess of moist air, and she mated with her brother Geb, the Earth, to give birth to the stars. Shu raised Nut into the air to separate her from Geb's body in the defining act of creation, separating the "waters" of the sky from the Earth. Nut was also the mother of Osiris, Blind Horus, Seth, Isis, and Nephthys. The pharaohs believed that when they died they entered Nut's body, from which they would later be resurrected. The sycamore of Nut (a mythological tree) stood at Heliopolis.

## Mujaji

📖 Lovedu, South Africa    🜚 Modjadji

Mujaji is the title of the Rain Queen of the Lovedu, who is the living incarnation of the rain goddess and transformer of the clouds, Khifidola-maru-a-Daja. The Rain Queen, the leader of a 400-year-old matriarchal dynasty, regulates rainfall and the cycle of the seasons. When she dies, drought is sure to follow, so she is meant to carefully choose her moment for death through suicide. Mujaji V, however, refused to commit suicide and died a natural death, setting a new precedent.

## Rangi

📖 Polynesia    🜚 Langi, Langit, Lagi, Atea

In Maori mythology, Rangi the sky god was one of the primal couple, locked in eternal copulation with Papa, the Earth goddess. The pair were separated by the upward growth of their son Tane, the forest god, which pushed them apart and allowed light into the world. The loving tears of the separated couple still mingle in the mist and the dew. In eastern Polynesia, Rangi was known as Atea, "limitless space". A longer Maori name, Hanui-o-Rangi, means "father of the winds".

# DEITIES OF ANIMALS AND HUNTING

Deities often take animal form, adopting shapes that range from birds that soar through the air and powerful creatures that roam the forests to enormous serpents that dwell underground. The mythologies of every continent contain both animal gods and deities who bring success to hunters, showing how human societies depended on the natural world.

A nimal gods often have their origins in animist religions. These sets of beliefs, held by traditional societies as far apart as Africa and America, assume that every object and being, from a boulder to a beetle, is a vital link in the chain of life, and that one thing can turn into another. Every beast contains a spirit, and animal gods abound, especially in Africa, Oceania, and America.

## SPECIAL RELATIONSHIPS

The gods themselves often have a special relationship with animal deities and magical creatures. Many of the Norse and Hindu gods had powerful steeds that carried them around the cosmos, and one of the most popular characters in Hindu mythology is the monkey Hanuman, whose powers and wit come to the aid of Rama and Sita in the *Ramayana*.

**Artemis, the Greek** goddess of the hunt, was also the divine protector of all young animals.

## ANIMAL POWERS

Animals form a close link to many natural forces. The ancient Egyptian god of the River Nile, Sobek, took the form of a crocodile. In many Native American myths, lightning, thunder, fire, and rain are controlled by birds, while the creator god of some North American peoples is a raven. Stories about such deities could explain unpredictable phenomena and their worship could protect people from danger.

## ANIMAL LINKS

People often came closest to animal gods through hunting, when the quarry could command a deep reverence. Or, an animal might have a profound link with a people's ancestors, forging a relationship central to their mythology. In nearly all systems of myths, people have close links with the animal world.

# Artemis

🏛 Ancient Greece    ⚱ Diana (Rome)

Artemis, daughter of Zeus and Leto and twin sister of Apollo, was the Greek goddess of hunting. She was a virgin, always portrayed as a young woman carrying a bow. As well as putting her weapon to use in the chase, she used it against her enemies, who were many, because she had a vengeful nature. For example, when Niobe, who had many children, insulted Leto, who had only two, Apollo and Artemis avenged their mother Leto by slaughtering Niobe's offspring. Artemis also killed the huntsman Orion, who, according to some accounts, attempted to rape either her or one of her attendants. The unruly Artemis was worshipped mostly in the remote and mountainous parts of Greece. But she was not always vengeful and violent; she was also the protector of vulnerable children.

# Diana

🏛 Ancient Rome    ⚱ Artemis (Greece)

Diana was a virginal goddess of hunting and of light, her name being related to *dies*, meaning "day". In ancient Italy she was associated with woodlands, and had a sacred forest in Aricia in Latium. She became a more significant deity for the Romans, and eventually prominent shrines were built for her throughout the Empire, including in Rome itself. Men were excluded from many of her festivals, and people said that her hunting dogs would tear to pieces any man who tried to enter her shrine while the rites were taking place. Her main quarry were deer, and at one of her shrines, at Capua, there was a hind dedicated to the goddess. It lived there for many years, and people said that the city would be safe for as long as the animal survived.

**Diana was also** the patron goddess of slaves, who could ask for asylum in her temple.

# Cernunnos

🏛 Celtic

The god Cernunnos, literally the "horned one", had the body of a man and the horns of a stag, and he was one of the central gods of Celtic Europe. Cernunnos was the god of animals, fruit, and corn, and this range of responsibilities suggests that he was probably worshipped as a source of fertility as well as a provider of food. His striking image has been found in many locations in Europe.

# Lahar

🏛 Sumer, Mesopotamia

Before the Sumerian god Enlil created Lahar in the creation chamber of heaven, the gods had no clothes, so Lahar was created as the god of cattle and sheep to provide the gods with hides and milk. His sister, Ashnan, was created as grain goddess. At first the two siblings worked in harmony, but then they got drunk and quarrelled so fiercely that the gods intervened; the ending of their story is unknown.

# Prajapati

📍 India     ♂ Brahmarishi, Brahmaputra

Prajapati, the "Lord of the Beasts" or "Lord of Creation", is the term often used for the Hindu creator god. It is a title rather than the name of a specific deity, and has also been applied to Indra, Brahma, and his mind-born sons.

Prajapati is one of the most ancient of the Hindu gods, and in later Hinduism he becomes identified with the god Brahma. One account of Prajapati tells how he created himself by sheer will from the waters of the primal sea. When he looked around he became sad because the cosmos was so empty. He wept, and some of his tears fell into the sea and became islands; others he flicked from his face and they became the stars. Over time, the process of creation continued as Prajapati made demons, gods, humans, and all the animals from parts of his own body.

## THE CREATIVE IMPULSE

Prajapati gave both form and name to all the gods and to all living creatures. But to later Hindus he represented just one half of the creative impulse; the god Visvakarman provided the other half. Visvakarman was seen as a more practical divine architect, who formed weapons and chariots for the gods on his lathe using shavings from the sun. He was the craftsman, while Prajapati represented a more deep-seated need to create, demonstrating a power that was so strong he could bring gods and other creatures into being simply by focused meditation.

**In the rare depictions** of Prajapati, he has three faces and sits in the yogic lotus position; sometimes he has horns (*see picture top left*).

### WORSHIP

*Prajapati created the fire god Agni, who would have devoured him had Prajapati not quickly produced some sacrificial butter, offering it with the word "Svaha" (meaning "greatness has spoken"), which is still said reverently with each fire-offering to the gods.*

# Sedna

📖 Inuit, North America    🏺 Nuliayuk; Samn

Sedna is the Inuit mistress of the sea-beasts. She was cast out by her village either because she married a mysterious lover – who turned out to be a dog or a seabird – or, in the Netsilik version, simply because she was unwanted. From Greenland to the Canadian Arctic, Sedna was the highest spirit-being.

The origin of the sea-beasts is described in an Inuit myth in which Sedna's father throws her from a kayak. In some versions Sedna is an innocent victim; in others, she deserves her punishment. The girl clings desperately to the boat, but her father chops off her fingers, which transform into sea mammals as they float down to the ocean floor. Sedna herself becomes a sea-spirit and mistress of the seas, responsible for driving the whales and walruses towards the hunting Inuit. If the humans break taboos,

Sedna retaliates by trapping the sea-mammals, so the people starve. If food becomes very scarce, a shaman swims down to Sedna's ocean home to untangle and brush her hair, as she cannot do this with her fingerless hands. Happy again, she releases the sea-beasts.

**The Inuit** depend upon the goodwill of Sedna for a steady supply of animals to hunt.

## Master of the Animals

📖 Native American

All across the Americas hunters believe in a Master or Mistress of the Animals who has the power to release or hide game. Hunters must propitiate this Master with offerings, and treat the game they catch with respect, before and after death. In 1762 Neolin, a Delaware holy man, made a visit to the Master of Life, who had power over the souls of humans and animals. The Master told Neolin that the Indians were becoming corrupted by the white man's ways, so he had withdrawn the game animals. This vision united many tribes who rose up against the British under Chief Pontiac in 1763–66.

## Buffalo & Corn Woman

📖 Native American

Buffalo Woman and Corn Woman are regarded as the key providers of food to the Arikara and other Plains nations of North America, such as the Pawnee. Buffalo Woman never eats meat, only corn; while Corn Woman never eats corn, only meat. Buffalo Woman travels all around the world to summon the buffalo, but she does this within the miniature world of the Medicine Lodge, walking from post to post, each time changing her moccasins, which become quite worn-out from all her travelling. The Hidatsa people call Corn Woman the "Old Woman Who Never Dies", so significant is the crop to their lives.

## The Benu bird

🏳 Ancient Egypt

The Benu bird is depicted in Egyptian art as a gigantic heron. Later, the Greeks called it the phoenix, in recognition of its role as an aspect of the sun god. The Benu bird was said to have flown across the dark waters of Nun before the first dawn and landed on a rocky pyramid called the Benben Stone. Here it let out a harsh cry that shattered the eternal silence and ushered light and life into the world. At the great temple of Amun at Karnak (now in Luxor), a duck was released across the waters of the sacred lake each morning in imitation of the Benu bird.

## Sobek

🏳 Ancient Egypt

Sobek was the Egyptian crocodile-god. His chief shrine at Medinet el-Fayum was known as Crocodilopolis. All his temples, which were built throughout Egypt, had pools containing sacred crocodiles. Sobek was the son of the war goddess Neith, and as Sobek-Ra he was worshipped as a manifestation of the sun god. Several myths tell of his insatiable appetite; he was so greedy that he even gobbled down part of the dismembered body of the god Osiris, for which he was punished by having his tongue cut out.

**Sobek was also** called "Lord of Faiyum". He was worshipped as controller of the Nile waters.

## Bastet

🏳 Ancient Egypt   👁 Bast, Ubasti, Ailuros

Bastet was the Egyptian cat-headed goddess of love and laughter. She was a gentler form of the rampaging lioness Sekhmet, herself a form of the goddess Hathor. Bastet's cult centre was at Bubastis on the Nile.

Bastet was the goddess of domesticated cats, and cats were sacred to her. When a pet cat died, the whole household would shave off their eyebrows as a sign of mourning. The name Bastet means "She-of-Bast"; and the goddess's temple at Bast was named Per-Bastet (House of Bastet). The Greeks corrupted this into their name for the town, Bubastis (now known as Tell Basta).

    Worshippers sailed to Bast in barges for the festival of Bastet. The women on board would lift their skirts and expose themselves, reflecting the behaviour of Hathor, who once hitched up her own skirts to cheer up Ra.

# Makemake and Haua

🏴 Rapa Nui (Easter Island)

Makemake is the supreme god of Rapa Nui (Easter Island) who created the people and provided food for them every year by driving the seabirds to nest there. Each year one of the chiefs became Makemake's living representative.

The shortage of food was a problem on Rapa Nui from its first settlement under the Polynesian king Hoto Matu'a. The settlers are supposed to have brought breadfruit, yams, coconuts, and other things to plant with them, but when they arrived on the island after a long ocean journey, they were dismayed to discover the lack of fresh water. The desperate shortage of food and drink soon became a constant nightmare for the people, who sought to assuage it by the introduction of the Birdman cult, under the guidance of the creator god Makemake. During an elaborate ceremony, an island chief became Makemake's representative on Earth – the Birdman – for one year. He would then hang the sacred egg in his hut, shave his head, and say prayers, in order to worship Makemake and encourage the egg to generate food.

At the sacred site of Orongo, carvings all over the rocks of the caves feature the skull-mask of Makemake, his wife Haua's vulva (a fertility symbol), the frigate-bird god, Vie-kana, and the sacred Birdman.

### WORSHIP

*The clans gathered at Orongo to await the seabirds that nested every year on the islets. Daring swimmers vied to collect the first egg of the season for their chief, while others chanted the great creation myths, saying that they were simply "boats" of the gods.*

# Tinirau

🏴 Polynesia   ♂ Sinilau, Kinilau, Timirau, Tinilau

Tinirau, said to be the son of the sea god Tangaroa, continuously restocks the sea with fish from the saltwater fish-ponds on his island in the centre of the sea. In the sea he has the form of a shark or whale; in the air that of a man-of-war bird; on land that of a handsome man.

Tinirau is called the Engulfer, because his waves can swallow a canoe full of men. Many accounts of the love of Tinirau and his wife Hina have been recorded; in some of them she is a moon goddess, while in others they are both high-born humans. In all of them Hina finds the handsome Tinirau irresistible, unaware as she is of his ambivalent nature (the Tahitians used to call him "Two-Faced Tinirau"). One myth from Mangaia in the Cook Islands tells how Hina plunged into the sea in search of him and was carried to his island by Tekea, the king of the sharks. This myth ends happily, but in others Tinirau is cruel to Hina, and she has to be rescued by her pigeon-brother Rupe.

### WORSHIP

*Before important ceremonies, Tahitian priests spend all night reciting the names of the many gods invited to attend the ritual. At dawn they call upon the dawn clouds to rise from the ocean, where they have spent the night with Tinirau, the Lord of the Ocean.*

# DEITIES OF FERTILITY AND AGRICULTURE

When peoples began to settle in permanent towns and villages, and to produce their food by farming, they soon started to acquire gods and goddesses of agriculture: figures whose responsibility was to ensure plentiful crops and wholesome livestock. The very survival of each agricultural community depended on these vital deities.

E nsuring an adequate food supply is one of the most basic human needs, and it is likely that some of the earliest prehistoric goddesses, represented by stone figures found all over Europe (*see pp.98–9*), were deities of abundance and fertility. By the time the earliest civilizations were writing down their myths, food and fertility deities were prominent, from the Mesopotamian Ashnan to Demeter and Persephone, two of the Ancient Greeks' most popular goddesses.

The ample figure of the Venus of Willendorf (*c.24,000* BCE) makes her a potent fertility symbol.

## FERTILITY AIDS

Often the first task of this class of gods was to show people how to grow food. Techniques for planting corn and irrigating fields were thought to be gifts from the gods. These deities also controlled fertility generally, helping animals and humans to reproduce.

## DUAL PROTECTION

In some cultures there were many agricultural gods, with different deities protecting individual crops or aspects of farming. The Romans had an abundance of such deities – partly because they had a large empire with many local gods, and partly because a constant food supply was important both for cities and for armies on the march. Faunus was the protector of shepherds, as were Pan, Pales, and Aristaios. Flora, goddess of the spring, helped the trees to bear fruit, as did Pomona. Ops was the goddess of grain, a crop that was also protected by Robigo. Vertumnus, god of the changing seasons, helped the flowers transform themselves into fruit. For the Romans, as for many peoples, the life-giving processes of agriculture were, literally, miraculous.

# Demeter

Ancient Greece　　Ceres (Rome)

The Greek goddess of agriculture was worshipped alongside her daughter Persephone, who, abducted to the Underworld (*see p.54*), was then allowed back to Earth in the spring and summer months to help the crops grow.

Demeter was one of the most important goddesses of Ancient Greece. Daughter of Cronos and Rhea, the Titan king and queen, she was responsible for agriculture, one of the cornerstones of Greek life. This bond was forged when Demeter visited various places in Greece in search of her abducted daughter Persephone: each time the local people offered her hospitality, she taught them about growing crops in return.

There were a number of festivals devoted to the goddess at various shrines throughout the year. As well as the famous Mysteries established by Demeter at Eleusis (*see* The Temple of Eleusis, *p.54*), she was celebrated at Thesmophoria, an autumnal festival largely for married women that took place when the grain was sown; its rites were believed to help the crops grow.

### WORSHIP

*The Greeks of Eleusis (modern Elefsina, a suburb of Athens) continued to worship their goddess Demeter as St Demetra after they had converted to Christianity. In 1801, Edward Clarke caused a riot when he stole a statue of St Demetra and carried it off to England.*

**Demeter, distraught,** grew tired of making the Earth fruitful while her daughter was in the Underworld.

# Liber

**ᛈ** Ancient Rome    **⚲** Liber Pater

An ancient Italian god, Liber became the Roman god of fertility and wine. His good looks and his influence over agriculture and the food supply made him widely popular.

Liber was especially celebrated on his feast day, 17 March, when there was a combined festival – the Liberalia – of the god and his female counterpart, Libera. Liber's symbol, a large phallus, was carried ceremoniously through the fields and into Rome. As the procession moved along, explicit songs were sung, to remind bystanders of the god's power over the fertility of crops, farm animals, and humans. Roman boys who had reached the age of 14 traditionally wore their first adult togas on this day, perhaps indicating that Liber presided over their transition into adulthood.

## Ceres

**ᛈ** Ancient Rome    **⚲** Demeter (Greece)

The goddess of the Earth and growth, Ceres was an early Italian deity adopted by the Romans. She and her daughter Proserpina became identified with the Greek Demeter and Persephone. Ceres was said to have introduced humans to agriculture, making the sun warm the earth so that crops would grow, and encouraging oxen to bow down their heads so that men could yoke them to pull the plough. A festival to the goddess held at harvest-time was attended by women only, who made offerings of corn.

**Ceres was identified** with corn and a good harvest – vital ingredients for a happy nation.

## Persephone

**ᛈ** Ancient Greece    **⚲** Proserpina (Rome)

The beautiful Persephone became the goddess of the Underworld. After being abducted by Hades, she was forced to spend part of the year in his dark kingdom, emerging annually on Earth to herald the spring and summer months (*see p.54*). She is often portrayed holding a sheaf of corn, to symbolize her importance for the harvest, or bearing a torch, representing the time that she spent kidnapped in the gloomy Underworld. Persephone was worshipped at many cult centres, most famously with her mother Demeter at the Mysteries of Eleusis (*see box, p.54*).

# Freyr and Freyja

**ᛈ** Norse    ♉ Frey and Freya

Freyr was the most important of the Norse fertility gods, being also the god of sun and rain. Freyja, his sister, was the goddess of love, birth, and the harvest. The son and daughter of the sea god Njörd, they were part of the Vanir tribe of gods.

At first Freyr and Freyja were lovers. They both rode around on pigs: Freyr on the golden boar Gullinborsti, his sister on a pig called Hildisvini ("battle-boar"). After the war between the two clans of Norse gods (*see p.116*), the pair split up. Freyr became the husband of the giantess Gerd, while Freyja married Od, god of the sun. But Od disappeared and Freyja wept tears of gold, which turned into fertile corn seeds that took root in Asgard. Both Freyr and Freyja were said to encourage sexual desire in others, and Freyja's

**Freyr's long chin** was a phallic symbol, representing fertility.

power was increased further by a magical necklace, the Brisingamen, which was made for her by a group of four dwarves with whom she had slept, and a cloak of feathers that allowed her to turn into a falcon. She also presided over magic, protected women in childbirth, and led the Valkyries – the women who bore the dead to Odin's hall, Valhalla. Freyr was a god of prosperity and peace, and was known for his help and counsel. Freyr and Freyja's wide sphere of influence ensured that they were worshipped throughout Scandinavia.

## WORSHIP

*In winter, an image of Freyr was taken in a cart from cities to outlying settlements. • Sacred horses from Freyr's sanctuary at Thrandheim were sacrificed "for Freyr to eat". • Bronze-Age rock carvings at Östergötland, Sweden, appear to feature Freyr.*

## Volos

**ᛈ** Slavic    ♉ Veles

Volos was the Slavic god of cattle and trade; with the coming of Christianity, many characteristics of Volos were taken over by St Vlasii, the patron saint of cattle. In folklore Volos survived as the protector of grain, and the custom of "plaiting Volos's beard" – weaving unreaped stalks of corn in a field to give it supernatural protection – survived into the 1900s. In one 12th-century text, the famous bard Boyan the Wise is called the "grandson of Volos", so Volos may also have been the god of music and musicians.

## The Matres

**ᛈ** Celtic    ♉ Triple Mother, Matrones

Sculptors all over the Celtic world produced numerous images of a trio of goddesses. The figures wear long dresses – often revealing one naked breast – and carry items such as cornucopias, baskets full of fruit, or babies. These are the Triple Mothers or Matres, three goddesses associated with fertility. They were worshipped in various forms: as deities of the house and home, as healing goddesses, and as figures who promoted both the fertility of the fields and the fecundity of human mothers.

# Ashnan

◫ Sumer, Mesopotamia

The grain goddess Ashnan was created alongside her brother Lahar, the god of cattle and sheep, in order to provide food and clothing for the gods. Both were the children of Enlil, the supreme Mesopotamian god. A Sumerian poem about them reads: "In the assembly they brought abundance; in the land they brought the breath of life; the decrees of the god they direct; the contents of the warehouses they multiply; the storehouses they fill full." It goes on to describe the gods Enki and Enlil stepping in to stop the couple fighting. The end of the poem is missing, leaving the myth incomplete.

# Telepinu

◫ Hittite    ♂ Telepinus

The myth of Telepinu, god of farming and fertility, tells of a catastrophic blight that falls on the world when the god storms off in a rage. Lost on the steppe, Telepinu falls asleep, and the world becomes infertile and barren. His father, the god Teshub, searches for him unsuccessfully, and finally the goddess Hannahannah sends a bee to find him and sting him awake. Unfortunately, this just enrages Telepinu further. Eventually the goddess of healing, Kamrusepa, calms Telepinu with the help of some humans, who perform an obscure ritual with an eagle's wing. Telepinu is at last coaxed out of his sulk.

# Shen Nong

◫ China    ♂ Shen Nung

Shen Nong is one of the culture heroes of China, an emperor who was said to have taught the Chinese the secrets of agriculture and traditional Chinese medicine. One of the myths tells of how he tested healing herbs on himself, finally dying of poison and becoming one of the immortals. As a farmer and fertility god he was credited with introducing into China basic crops such as rice and wheat, and herbs that could be used both in cooking and in healing. There are also myths that attribute important agricultural inventions such as the plough, the axe, and crop-rotation to Shen Nong.

**Shen Nong** (on the right) was said to have spoken just three days after he was born.

# Ogetsu

◫ Japan    ♂ Uke-Mochi

Many cultures explain the origin of their staple foodstuffs from the body of a goddess (see the myths of Turtle Island, *pp.194–7* and Pan Gu, *p.172*, for Native American and Chinese variants). The Japanese food goddess Ogetsu initially provides food by vomiting it up, but then she is slain, either by the moon god Tsuki-yomi or the storm god Susano, according to different versions of the myth. As she dies, food pours out of her body: an ox and a horse spring out of her head; millet comes from her forehead; rice from her belly, and wheat and beans from her genitals. Once she was dead, her role as goddess of rice was taken by the rice god Inari.

# Tane

🗺 Polynesia     ♂ Kane

The forest god Tane (known as Kane in Hawaii) is also the god of artistic beauty and of light, because he let light into the world by separating Rangi (sky-father) and Papa (Earth-mother). Of all the gods only Tane could do this, because his is the undeniable force of the growth of living things. The main myth of Tane tells of how he makes a wife for himself, called Hine-hau-one (Earth-formed Maiden) out of mud and sand. Their daughter, Hine-titama, became goddess of the night.

### WORSHIP

*Tane is the patron of all woodworkers. On the Society Islands, canoe-builders prayed to Tane as they put their axes to "sleep" at night in the temple and "woke" them in the sea the following morning.*

# Wigan

🗺 Ifugao, Philippines

Wigan is one of the class of Ifugao deities known as the Matungulan, "the Paybackables". The god of the Upstream village of Kaiyang, Wigan is the ancestral culture hero who won rice from the gods of the Skyworld in exchange for fire. The culture of the Ifugao centres around rice-growing, so he was a hugely important god. Wigan and his sister Bugan, both children of the Skyworld deities Kabigat and Bugan (the wives of all 1,500 Ifugao gods are named Bugan), were washed down to Earth by heavy rain. In order to procreate, they broke kinship rules and married; their four daughters married four of their sons, but the fifth son married a pig, and procreated various demons that plague mankind, such as Childlessness and Sleeplessness.

# Rongo

🗺 Polynesia     ♂ Lono, Ono, Lo'o

Rongo is the Polynesian god of agriculture and cultivated foods, particularly associated with kumara (sweet potatoes). Rongo is his Maori name; in Hawaii he is known as Lono, in the Marquesas as Ono, and in Samoa as Lo'o.

Rongo was one of the great gods born from the primal couple, Rangi (sky-father) and Papa (Earth-mother). When the people of the South Island, New Zealand, brought kumara back from Hawaiki (the creation place), it would not grow, because of the extreme cold. So Rongo set off from Hawaiki with new forms of the vegetable that would flourish. However, his canoe overturned under some huge waves that transformed into the Pakihiwitahi hills in North Otago, while the kumara that fell from the canoe became the huge rocks known as the Moeraki Boulders. Rongo's canoe turned into a reef at

Matakaea. In the Gambier islands Rongo was symbolized by the rainbow, and in Hawaii, as Lono, it was said that he instituted the five-day harvest festival of Makahiki. During this period food was shaken from a net known as the Net of Maoleha; if no food remained in the net, provisions would be plentiful in the coming year.

### WORSHIP

*At planting times in New Zealand, carved images known as godsticks, bound with sacred cord, were traditionally thrust into the ground as Maori priests chanted prayers to Rongo for a good harvest.*

# DEITIES OF LOVE, CHILDBIRTH, AND THE HOME

Love, which can strike at random and engender a range of emotions – from ecstasy to despair, and anxiety to contentment – is often attributed to the capricious nature and powerful influence of the gods. For this reason the love deities are fervently worshipped and widely feared. More caring deities were called upon to look after the hearth and home.

**D**eities of love often began as fertility gods, beings who could encourage growth in plants and animals as well as enhance desire in humans. The mythologies of the earliest civilizations, such as that of ancient Mesopotamia, produced complex figures like the Sumerian goddess Inanna, a goddess of fertility, love, and war. In a warrior society the love goddess could extend her role. Xochiquetzal, the Aztec love goddess, welcomed into her paradise any woman who had died giving birth to boys (future warriors). The role of the goddess was often tailored to the needs of a particular society.

**Roman homes** usually featured a Lar (household god) who was prayed to daily for protection.

## CAPRICIOUS LOVE

A common aspect of love gods and goddesses is their ability to inspire love or desire instantly and unpredictably. One way is by shooting arrows at their victims: the Greek Eros, his Roman equivalent Cupid, and the Indian god Kama all share this power. Many myths relate the chaos and emotional havoc these deities cause among the gods. Humans would make offerings to them in the hope of achieving their own desires.

## HOMELY LOVE

Some love deities are less troublesome. These are the goddesses who help women through the dangerous time of childbirth and who guard over the home. They often stand slightly to one side of the rest of the pantheon, because they were as likely to be given offerings in small shrines in people's homes as in grand temples. Bes, the dwarf-like Egyptian god of the home, for example, was found all over people's houses – carved into beds, door-posts, or wherever his protective powers might be needed.

# Vesta

**Ancient Rome**   **Hestia (Greece)**

Goddess of the hearth and home, Vesta was an important deity in ancient Italy. She became increasingly significant to the Romans as a guardian of their city and was worshipped in a state temple in the capital.

The Romans believed that the cult of Vesta was introduced to their city by Romulus, Rome's founder. Vesta's main shrine was in Rome's Forum, housed in a round building. This circular form was said to recall the round huts that the first settlers lived in, reflecting Vesta's role as goddess of the home. Unlike other Classical temples, the shrine of Vesta contained no statue of the goddess to whom it was dedicated. Instead there was a sacred flame symbolizing her presence. The temple's attendants, the Vestal virgins, had to keep this flame permanently burning; its extinction was thought to spell disaster for Rome.

**The Vestal virgins** were chosen when young and expected to serve for at least 30 years (*see box, p.86*).

The shrine also contained a number of cult objects, including a sculpture of a phallus, which was said to ward off evil. Like her Greek ancestor Hestia, Vesta was regarded as a virgin, yet she represented the home and familial responsibility. The worship of Vesta was hugely important to the Romans; they believed their city would perish if the cult ended. Sixteen years after the shrine closed in 394 CE, barbarian invaders sacked Rome.

## WORSHIP

*If Vesta's sacred fire went out, the Vestal virgins were whipped by the high priest, and forced to rekindle the fire using a fire-drill.*
*• A Vestal virgin who broke her chastity vows was cruelly punished by being buried alive.*

# Aphrodite

**Ancient Greece**  **Venus (Rome)**

The Ancient Greek goddess of erotic love and fertility was known not only for her great beauty but also for her cruelty and capriciousness. She had many affairs with both gods and mortals.

Aphrodite's unusual birth took place after the war between the gods and the Titans (*see p.38*), when either the severed penis of Uranus, or a drop of his blood, fell into the sea. As this happened the sea frothed up and Aphrodite arose from the foam (*aphros*). Through her own love affairs, her support of many human couplings, her vanity and bad temper, and in countless other ways, Aphrodite was the cause of all kinds of conflicts. She bribed Paris to name her the most beautiful Olympian goddess, which led ultimately to the Trojan War (*see pp.70–71*). And she was ruthless: when the women of Lemnos neglected to worship her, she commanded them to kill their husbands as punishment.

# Hestia

**Ancient Greece**  **Vesta (Rome)**

Hestia, daughter of the Titans Cronos and Rhea, was an Olympian, and the goddess of the hearth, home, and family. Unlike most Ancient Greek deities, she remained a virgin, spurning advances from Apollo and Poseidon. She stayed forever on Mount Olympus, preferring not to travel the cosmos like the other gods. This rooted stability gave her a special status as a sacred focus on Mount Olympus, and led to her being worshipped in every temple. Domestic hearths were treated as her shrine in all Greek households.

# Cupid

**Ancient Rome**  **Eros (Greece), Cupidor**

Cupid was the Roman equivalent of the Greek Eros, and the names of the two gods have the same meaning: desire. The Romans often portrayed Eros as a small child, whereas the Greeks saw him as a boy or young man. His mother, Venus, was jealous of a beautiful mortal woman – Psyche – and sent Cupid to make Psyche fall in love with a hideous creature. Instead, Cupid and Psyche fell in love. In Virgil's *Aeneid*, Venus orders Cupid to make Aeneas fall in love with Dido, with tragic results.

## Eros

📖 Ancient Greece  ⚱ Cupid (Rome)

There are two different accounts of Eros, the Ancient Greek god of desire. An early myth places him at the beginning of creation, mating with Chaos to produce the primal egg from which the cosmos originated. But the more familiar story portrays him as the son of Aphrodite and another of the Olympians (usually Ares or Zeus). A charming but mischievous winged youth, Eros carried a bow and arrows, and whoever he shot fell in love straight away. Other gods often persuaded him to target the objects of their affection.

## Kamrusepa

📖 Hittite  ⚱ Kamrusepas

Kamrusepa, the goddess of healing and spells, plays a key role in the Hittite myth of Telepinu, the agricultural god who vanishes in a sulk, making the world infertile. Enlisting the help of a mortal man, Kamrusepa performs an elaborate ritual to purge Telepinu of his anger. While reciting her spell, she soothes the angry god with cedar essence, sap, chaff, grain, sesame, figs, olives, grapes, ointment, malt, honey, cream, and oil. She then sacrifices 12 of the sun god's rams, and re-directs Telepinu's anger into the Underworld.

## Inanna

📖 Mesopotamia  ⚱ Inana, Ishtar, Astarte, Ashtoreth

Inanna was by far the most significant Mesopotamian goddess, worshipped throughout the area that is now the Middle East. Her principal shrine was at the Sumerian – later Babylonian – city of Uruk (southeastern Iraq), said to have been built by the predecessor of the Mesopotamian hero Gilgamesh.

Inanna is often, for ease of reference, called the goddess of love, and the art of lovemaking is one of her sacred skills. But she is also a goddess of war, and the ruler of Earth and heaven. In one myth (*see p.149*) she descends to the Underworld ruled by her sister Ereshkigal, dies, and is revived to return to the world and claim her rightful power. As a result she becomes the most psychologically complete and potent of all the gods.

The myths do not agree on who Inanna's father was, variously naming him as An (Anu), Nanna, Enlil, or Enki. Inanna plays an important role in the story of Gilgamesh (*see pp.144–7*), whom she punishes for spurning her

**A carved ivory plaque,** thought to represent Inanna, found in the Assyrian palace at Nimrud.

sexual advances by letting loose Gugalanna, the bull of heaven, who was Ereshkigal's husband. Inanna's own marriage to the shepherd god Dumuzi (Tammuz) is highly erotic and symbolic; in the end, when Dumuzi does not humble himself to the ascended goddess, Inanna allows demons to drag him down to the Underworld.

### WORSHIP

*According to Herodotus, every Babylonian woman was required to prostitute herself at least once in the temple of Inanna; some women devoted their lives to the sacred service of the goddess as temple prostitutes.*

## Kama

📕 India      ♂ Kamadeva

Kama is the Indian god of love and desire. One version of his story says that he existed at the beginning of time, when desire was needed to begin the process of creation. Another story makes him the son of Lakshmi, goddess of good luck. When one deity fell in love with another, they would sometimes send Kama out on a mission to arouse desire in the object of their passion. Uma sent Kama to inspire desire in Siva, but the god was meditating and when he came out of his trance, he turned his powerful "third eye" on Kama. The fire from Siva's glance burned Kama and reduced his body to ashes, but the god of love and desire continued to exist in an invisible, bodiless form.

**Like Cupid,** Kama shot arrows of desire from his bow, which is decorated with flowers.

## Zao Jun

📕 China      ♂ Tao Chün, Tsao Jun

Zao Jun was widely worshipped in China because of his special role as messenger of the gods. It was his job to make a yearly report to the Emperor of Heaven on the conduct of every family member. At the beginning of each year, the family put up a picture of Zao Jun above the stove in the kitchen – for this reason he was often known as the Kitchen God. In some homes they would "feed" sticky cakes or honey to Zao Jun's image in the hope that this would sweeten his report. At the end of the year, the householder took down the image and ceremoniously burned it. Sometimes straw was added to the fire for the god's horse, as well as some alcohol, to put the god in a good mood. As the smoke rose towards heaven, it carried Zao Jun's report with it.

## Xochiquetzal

📕 Aztec, Mexico

Xochiquetzal, "Flower Quetzal", was the goddess of female sexuality, flowers, and pleasure. She was also responsible for taking care of women during pregnancy and childbirth. Always shown dressed luxuriously and bedecked with gold jewellery, she became the patron of weavers, embroiderers, goldsmiths, and other crafts. At her festival a young woman was sacrificed and a man would then "put on" her flayed skin, dress in her clothes, and pretend to weave at a loom, while the master craftworkers danced around in animal disguises.

## Chalchiuhtlicue

📕 Aztec, Mexico

Chalchiuhtlicue, "She of the Jade Skirt", was the Aztec goddess of lakes and streams. By association with amniotic fluid, she was also the goddess of birth, and is often depicted with a pair of male and female infants issuing from her in a birth-stream. Water sacred to Chalchiuhtlicue was also used in ritual bathing ceremonies for newborn infants, to purify the child of any pollution acquired from the parents. At these ceremonies the child was named and presented with tools felt to be symbolic of their future life.

## Hathor

📿 Ancient Egypt    🔥 Sekhmet

The cow goddess Hathor came to be associated with music, sexuality, and motherhood; pharaohs were called "son of Hathor", and depicted suckling from her udders. At Edfu, Hathor was the bride of Horus; she is also called the mother of Horus. In origin a sky goddess, Hathor's name means "the mansion of Horus", because she was the sky in which the falcon god flew.

## Bes

📿 Ancient Egypt

Bes and his hippopotamus consort, Taweret, helped women in childbirth. Bes was also the protector and friend of children. An unusual-looking deity, Bes was depicted as an ugly dwarf with a lion's mane, often sticking his tongue out and pulling faces. He was believed to frighten away demons, snakes, and harmful animals. As a protector of the home, his image was incorporated into domestic decorations and furniture. His long phallus indicated that he was also a god of sexuality. Bes's chambers at Saqqara have figures of the dwarf and a naked goddess on the walls; pilgrims spent the night there hoping to renew their sexual powers.

## Isis

📿 Ancient Egypt

Isis, consort of Osiris and the most significant goddess in Egyptian mythology, was worshipped as the ideal wife and mother. She was also the mistress of magic and, with her sister Nephthys, guardian of the dead.

The main myth of Isis tells of her search for Osiris after Seth murdered him. Her sister Nephthys (Seth's wife) joined her in her lamentations, and helped her gather up the pieces of Osiris's body, which Isis re-animated with her magic just long enough to conceive her son Horus. The widowed Isis then wandered the land in her grief, and at one point became a nursemaid in a royal household. There she tried to make the prince in her care immortal by setting him on fire to burn away his mortal parts. But she was interrupted and her plan failed. Instead, Isis found Osiris's corpse hidden in the palace, whereupon she uttered a cry so terrible that the baby was instantly killed.

### WORSHIP

*The most important sanctuary of Isis was at Philae near Aswan, but she was widely worshipped, with notable cults at Dendera and at Byblos. • Isis was worshipped at Philae until the sixth century CE and was a cult goddess of the Greco-Roman world too.*

# DEITIES OF FATE AND FORTUNE

Myths often exist to explain the inexplicable, and to provide a belief system that justified events with profound effects but no discernible cause. In ancient times, when the strange twists and turns of human life seemed hard to predict and difficult to comprehend, events were often attributed to the gods and goddesses of fate and fortune.

The deities of fate had great power to control lives, but they could sometimes be influenced by prayer or offerings. In Chinese mythology, the goddess Guan Yin would listen to people's prayers and help them through difficulties. She was considered the most compassionate of all the Chinese deities. Hindus about to start a new venture or needing help with a problem would turn to the elephant-headed god Ganesha, or Lakshmi, the goddess of good luck.

**The Fates** only once relented over the timing of a death, and agreed to take a wife in place of her husband (*see p.56*).

## CRUEL FATE

Not all the deities of fate and fortune paid attention to the wishes of mere mortals. In many cases they were detached, implacable powers, ruthlessly controlling the course of human life,

deaf to all appeals. Among these figures are the Greek Fates, a trinity of goddesses who spin the thread of human life and cut it when a person's time on Earth is over. The Norns of Norse mythology, another trio, had a similar role. They provided a tangible reason for the often seemingly arbitrary nature of human destiny.

But if one could not influence the actions of the gods, one could be forewarned through prophecy, and divination played a vital role in many cultures, including those of the Aztecs, the Etruscans, and the Greeks and Romans. However, prophecies could be hard to interpret, and those who commissioned them – from priests, oracles, or figures such as the Greek Sibyls – were often left none the wiser.

# Apollo

🏛 Ancient Greece and Rome

The god Apollo, son of Zeus and Leto, was always portrayed as a handsome young man with an athletic build. As god of the sun, medicine, music, poetry, and philosophy, he performed a wide range of functions.

Apollo was a powerful deity whose influence could be benevolent or malign. He possessed the gifts of prophecy and healing, which allowed him to do good and influence human fortune. But his affairs often went wrong, causing problems for those around him. When he fell in love with Cassandra, for example, he gave her the ability to see into the future. But when she spurned him, he ensured that no-one would believe her predictions. Apollo was close to nature and some of his partners were transformed into animals or plants.

**The god of music,** Apollo is often depicted with the lyre given to him by Zeus (*see p.49*), which he played with legendary skill and effect.

### WORSHIP

*Delphi, the most important Greek oracle, was a temple of Apollo founded by the god himself. • Apollo's oracular priestess, the Pythia, spoke in riddles from an underground chamber in which ethylene vapours naturally accumulated, inducing a prophetic trance.*

## The Fates (Moirae)

🏛 Ancient Greece 　 ⚱ Parcae (Rome)

The Fates were a trio of goddesses, all daughters of Zeus and Themis, who together controlled human destiny. The three made and kept a thread for each human life on Earth. The first Fate, Clotho, span the thread; the second, Lachesis, measured it out and wound it up; the third, Atropos, cut it, bringing its owner's life to an end in whatever manner she chose. No other deity could influence the Fates.

## The Sibyls

🏛 Ancient Greece, Ancient Rome

The Sibyls were priestesses who possessed the gift of prophecy. They were either mortals or the offspring of mortals and nymphs, and they usually lived to be very old. Two of the most famous were the Sibyl of Erythrae, who was dedicated by her parents to Apollo and lived the lifespan of nine men, and the Sibyl of Cumae in Italy, who had a long and agonizing old age after Apollo cursed her (*see p.88*).

# The Norns

**ℕ** Norse

The Norns were female figures who shaped human destiny, like the Fates of Ancient Greece. The Scandinavians thought of them in two ways: as a trio of individual goddesses called Urd, Verdandi, and Skuld (past, present, and future); and as three supernatural races of beings who controlled fate.

The three individual Norns lived in a hall beneath Yggdrasil, the world tree, and they watered its roots to keep it healthy. They wove a great tapestry of fate, which was never finished, because Skuld was forever tearing it to pieces so that it had to be begun again. The wider races of Norns were supernatural beings descended from the gods, the elves, and the dwarves, who would visit every newborn child to determine the course of its life. All parents hoped that a kindly Norn would visit their child and grant him or her a good life.

**In Wagner's** *Götterdämmerung*, the three Norns weave a rope of destiny, but as they sing of the fate of the gods, the rope breaks and they vanish.

> **WORSHIP**
>
> *The Viking Temple at Uppsala, Sweden, the centre of Norse worship, was said to have a huge evergreen tree, representing Yggdrasil, and a sacred pond symbolizing the well of Urd. Human sacrifices were thrown into the well – if the victim sank, the gods approved.*

# Gefion

**ℕ** Norse    **◑** Gefjon, Gefjun

The goddess Gefion, patron deity of ploughmen, could see into the future but could not change it. She had an affair with King Gylfi of Sweden and bore four sons to him. When she asked for land for her offspring, Gylfi said she could have as much land as she could plough in a day. So she turned her sons into four huge oxen and ploughed an enormous area, which she then tore away from Sweden, taking it to Denmark where it became the province of Sjaeland. The hole that was left in Sweden became Lake Vänern.

# Brigit

**ℕ** Celtic    **◑** Brigid, Brighit, Brid, Briid

Daughter of the Daghda, Brigit was a fertility goddess who became the patron deity of the Irish province of Leinster. She was also said to be a member of a trio of three fate-like goddesses: three sisters who all bore the name Brigit, and who were known for their ability to forecast future events. In the Christian era the Celtic goddess Brigit became identified with St Brigit, also known as St Bride. This saint's feast day is on 1 February, which is the same date as the Celtic festival of Imbolc, celebrating the pagan Brigit.

# Lakshmi

🚩 India 　 ⚲ Shri, Ksirabdhitanya, Lokamata, Padma

One of the most popular of all the Hindu deities, Lakshmi is the goddess of good fortune. Always portrayed as a beautiful woman, she is the consort of Vishnu and is often shown beside him, usually gazing up at him lovingly.

Regarded as the goddess of happiness, marriage, family, wealth, beauty, and good health, Lakshmi is especially popular with women. She is often depicted with a lotus blossom, which is a symbol of fertility, purity, and spiritual perfection. Lakshmi was said to have the power to take on an infinity of separate forms, so that she could visit and dwell with every human being.

Sometimes she might appear by the threshold of a house, bringing good luck to the household. She might also settle in a person's body, and the part of the body she chose to dwell in would bring good fortune to a specific aspect of the person's life: if she chose your thigh, she would bring you wealth; if she chose your genitals, she would bring good luck in love, and so on.

# Ganesha

🚩 India 　 ⚲ Ganesh, Ganapati, Gajanana

The elephant-headed god Ganesha is the god of good luck and solver of problems. A popular domestic deity, he is often seen in homes and at crossroad shrines.

Ganesha acquired his striking elephantine head as the result of an argument with Siva (*see p.160*). He is usually depicted with one tusk missing. One explanation for this is that the sage Vyasa, when he was writing his epic poem the *Mahabharata*, took on Ganesha as his scribe, and removed one of the god's tusks to use as a pen. Ganesha is thus the god of literature as well as being the deity on whom devotees call whenever they start a new project or have a difficult problem to solve.

**Ganesha is** one of the most popular Hindu gods. He is usually depicted in the company of a mouse, which here sits at the base of the statuette.

## WORSHIP

*The Ganesh Chaturthi festival celebrates Ganesha's birthday in the Hindu month of Bhaadrapada each year. • In 1995, statues of Ganesha in temples around the world were said to be drinking milk offered on spoons.*

# The seven gods of luck

**Japan**    **Shichi Fukujin**

The seven gods of luck or good fortune are variously of Shinto, Buddhist, and Hindu origin. They are Benzaiten (identified with the Shinto goddess Benten), Bishomonten, Hotei-Oshu, Fukurokuju, Jurojin, Daikoku, and Ebisu.

Each of the seven gods of luck has their own realm of influence. Benzaiten is a goddess of love, music, and happiness. As goddess of everything that flows, she demonstrates her origin as the Hindu river goddess Saraswati. Bishomonten is a warrior, a protector of the righteous, and a figure of authority. Also of Hindu origin, he carries a lance and a miniature pagoda. Hotei-Oshu is the god of generosity and large families. Depicted as a laughing fat Buddhist monk, he is often accompanied by a child. Fukurokuju is the god of long life and wisdom, shown holding a long walking stick and accompanied by a stork; like Hotei-Oshu, he is of Chinese Buddhist origin.

Jurojin is also a god of long life and carries a long staff. He is shown with a stag or a tortoise, symbols of longevity. Daikoku is the Shinto god of wealth and trade, usually shown standing on two sacks of rice and holding another symbol of wealth: a hammer. Ebisu is the Shinto god of work, and is depicted carrying a large fish. The seven gods often travel as a group aboard their treasure ship *Takarabune*.

> **WORSHIP**
>
> *All seven gods of luck are extremely popular in Japan, and may be called on for help as appropriate, especially at New Year. Prayers to Benzaiten for money are fervent, as she is known to favour the eloquent.*

# Benten

**Japan**    **Benzaiten**

Benten, the goddess of love, happiness, and the sea, was said to be the daughter of the dragon king Ryu-wo, who lived in a palace under the sea. As the patron of geishas, dancers, and musicians, Benten always carried a stringed instrument called a *biwa*, and she would appear to musicians who played with all their soul. One myth tells how Benten appealed to a serpent king who was terrorizing the countryside. The repulsive serpent wooed Benten with silken words; when he agreed to stop his reign of terror, she agreed to marry him.

# Guan Yin

**China**    **Kuan Yin, Kwannon (Japan)**

The compassionate goddess Guan Yin is the Chinese equivalent of the Japanese Kwannon (*see p.290*). She is an important figure in Chinese Buddhism and is also one of the best loved deities in Chinese popular religion, in which she is revered especially by women. Guan Yin is regarded as a bringer of children to childless couples, a comforter of the distressed, a healer of the sick, and a protector of seafarers and travellers.

**Guan Yin** is generally depicted as a beautiful woman in flowing white robes holding a bottle of pure water.

# Eshu

**⚑** Yoruba, Nigeria    **⚒** Esu

Eshu is a trickster god of supreme cunning, who also acts as a messenger and mediator between gods and men. As the god of Ifa divination (a Yoruba form of fortune-telling), Eshu is more important to human affairs than the supreme god Olodumare or the creator Obatala. He is, essentially, the god of Fate.

Eshu is related to the benevolent gods, the *orisha*, and the malevolent gods, the *ajogun*, and because of this he can be benign or malicious. As one Yoruba poem puts it, "Eshu turns right into wrong, wrong into right." When Eshu is angry, he internalizes his emotions, weeping tears of blood, or hitting a stone until it began to bleed. Offerings are made to Eshu before the start of any ceremony, to keep him happy.

## ESHU'S APPEARANCE

It was said that Eshu could assume 256 different forms, appearing one moment as a giant, then a dwarf, then a cheeky boy, and then as a wise old man. Eshu could also speak all languages. Carvings of Eshu, which Eshu priests wore hooked over their shoulders, often show him with two faces: one looking into the world of men, and the other looking into the world of the spirits.

## MAGIC MEDICINE

Eshu's magical powers enabled the thunder god Shango to spit lightning bolts. Shango asked Eshu for a weapon even more powerful than his

thunder. Eshu prepared a medicine for him that would grant his wish, and Shango sent his wife Oya to collect it. Doubting its strength, she tasted it. When she arrived home and opened her mouth to greet Shango, fire flashed out of her mouth and burned her husband. Shango was furious and tried to kill her with his thunderstones, but she hid from him. Then Shango tried the medicine himself, and so much flame leaped from his mouth that it burned the city of Oyo to the ground.

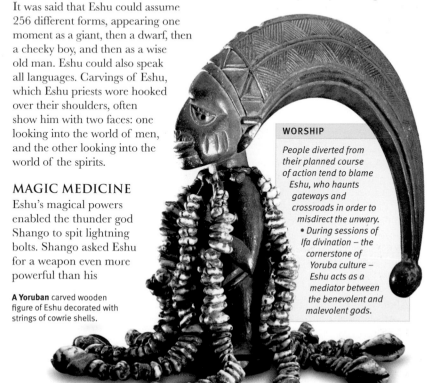

**A Yoruban** carved wooden figure of Eshu decorated with strings of cowrie shells.

### WORSHIP

*People diverted from their planned course of action tend to blame Eshu, who haunts gateways and crossroads in order to misdirect the unwary.*
*• During sessions of Ifa divination – the cornerstone of Yoruba culture – Eshu acts as a mediator between the benevolent and malevolent gods.*

# TRICKSTER DEITIES

Even for the gods, life can be unpredictable. There are some mythological figures who exist to cause confusion and disruption in the heavens. These tricksters take part in some of the most entertaining myths; they start arguments or even wars between gods, but they also have redeeming features that make them essential to many mythologies.

Tricksters are often shape-changers who also bring about transformations in the things around them. They sometimes use this power to take part in the creation of humanity, to bring natural forces like the winds into being, or to put right the problems that they have caused with their trickery. Tricksters are often associated with phenomena that are transient or unstable: it was the Greek Prometheus, for example, who gave fire to humanity.

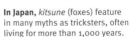

In Japan, *kitsune* (foxes) feature in many myths as tricksters, often living for more than 1,000 years.

## ANIMAL TRICKSTERS

Tricksters frequently take the form of animals, like the North American Coyote or the African spider deity Anansi. Their roles are many and varied. Coyote, for example, is a creator figure, but in some stories he also invents suffering and death. As with other tricksters, his ability to change his shape makes it easy for him to travel between the worlds of humans and gods as a messenger.

## HERO OR TRICKSTER?

The roles of hero and trickster are often surprisingly close. Today we might think of a hero as someone who exhibits special strength or bravery. But a hero also needs intelligence or guile, and figures who come up with ingenious schemes to fox their enemies, like the Greek hero Odysseus, may also be regarded as tricksters. Even destructive figures such as the Norse god Loki, who caused many episodes of mayhem among the gods and will finally cause the last battle and the end of the world, are not necessarily seen as evil. Loki and his like are regarded as necessary forces, taking their place in the scheme of things.

# Prometheus

**Ancient Greece**

Prometheus was a Titan and a cousin of Zeus who was closely associated with the origins of fire. Some traditions portray him as the creator of humanity; in others, he is the supreme trickster who stole fire from Zeus for mankind.

The myths about Prometheus describe how he tricked Zeus into choosing the inferior part of an offering and stole fire from the gods, carrying it in a fennel stalk, as Greek islanders used to do, to give to humanity (*see p.37*). As punishment for this trickery, Zeus had the Titan chained to a rock, where an eagle continuously pecked away at his liver. The hero Heracles, who was Zeus's son, rescued Prometheus by shooting the eagle and releasing the Titan. Zeus's reaction to this rescue was mixed. He was pleased that his son had performed a heroic deed, but he still wanted Prometheus to be reminded of his wrong. So Zeus forced the Titan to wear a ring made from the metal of his chains and always to carry a piece of the rock.

Prometheus later had a mortal son, Deucalion, whom he saved from a great flood unleashed by Zeus (*see pp.26–7*) by telling him to take refuge in a wooden chest.

## THE LEGACY OF PROMETHEUS

Prometheus's creative intellect, great cunning, and fearlessness has appealed to many writers. In Ovid's *Metamorphoses*, he is credited with the creation of humanity from clay. Some writers, such as the Greek playwright Aeschylus, depict him as a culture hero who brought important skills to humankind and defied the tyranny of Zeus.

Later European writers, such as Goethe and Shelley, portrayed him as the embodiment of noble suffering, resourceful and defiant in spite of his dreadful punishment.

**Tricksters often bring** about a change in the world as a result of their disregard for law and order. Prometheus's trickery ultimately made him a hero.

### WORSHIP

*At Athens in Greece, Prometheus was worshipped by potters, perhaps because they used both clay and fire in the making of their pots. They held a torch-race – a kind of relay passing a flaming torch – in his honour.*

# Dionysus

**Ancient Greece**　　**Bacchus, Liber Pater (Rome)**

The Greek god of wine and the vine was also famous for the ecstatic frenzy he could induce in both himself and his followers and for the trouble this drunkenness often caused.

Dionysus was the son of Zeus and Semele, a mortal woman. Semele wanted Zeus to appear before her in all his glory, but when he did so, she was struck dead by the blinding light around him. The god removed the unborn Dionysus from her womb and sewed the child inside his thigh until it was time for him to be born. Some versions of the myth say he was brought up by nymphs, while some say the Maenads raised him. These were a group of wild women who always travelled with him, carrying out alcohol-fuelled, frenzied rites. Dionysus is best known through Euripides's play *The Bacchae*.

### WORSHIP

*The Theatre of Dionysus, built in the fifth century BCE, stood at the southeast foot of the Acropolis in Athens. It served as the prototype for Greek theatres. The central chair was reserved for the High Priest of Dionysus.*

# Kurent

**Slovenia**　　**Korant**

Kurent is the Slovenian Dionysus, a god of revelry, drunkenness, and unrestrained pleasure. According to folklore, Kurent used to tour Slovenian villages in the spring to drive out the winter, welcome the spring, and encourage the Earth to awaken. The spring fertility festival of Kurentovanje is still celebrated: Kurent is represented by groups of men dressed in sheepskins wearing Kurent masks, who go from house to house scaring away evil spirits. People smash clay pots at the men's feet for good luck and to ensure abundant crops.

# Lemminkäinen

**Finland**

A combination of fertility god and trickster, Lemminkäinen is one of the heroes of the Finnish tales collected together in the *Kalevala* (*see pp.128–31*). He is a sorcerer, with a magical singing voice more powerful than any conventional weapon. An adventurer and womanizer, Lemminkäinen was always searching for love. As one of the suitors of the Maid of the North, he had to complete a number of tasks to win her, including shooting a swan in Tuonela, the Finnish Underworld. But it was there that he met his death.

# Loki

Norse

The trickster Loki is one of the most complex figures in Norse mythology, a character who could do good or evil, and who could move between the worlds of the gods and giants. He is famous for playing tricks on the gods – some of them malicious – but then devising ingenious ways of putting things right.

Although described as handsome, Loki could change his appearance at will, impersonating at various times a flame, a puff of smoke, an insect, and a bird. He was said to be one of the oldest of the Norse gods; in some accounts he is the most ancient of all. In the myths he is sometimes hero, and sometimes villain – but nearly always humorous. With the coming of Christianity, however, this changed, and Loki began to be portrayed as the Devil.

**Loki with his lips** sewn up as punishment from dwarves for cheating them (*see p.124*).

# Ahriman

Persia    Angra Mainyu, Dregvant

Ahriman is the destructive spirit in Zoroastrian dualism, the twin and opposite of the creative spirit of Ahura Mazda. Ahriman at first pretended to be Ahura Mazda, but their parent Zurvan recognized him and rejected him.

In Zoroastrianism, the ancient, pre-Islamic religion of Persia, Ahriman is the personification of evil, darkness, and death. He did everything he could to spoil Ahura Mazda's perfect creation, including poisoning the first man, Gayomart ("Dying Life"). In one of the sacred texts of Zoroastrianism, the *Gathas*, Ahriman is named Dregvant, "the deceitful one"; bad people are also called "dregvant", while the good – the followers of the truth – are "ashavan". Ahriman also killed the primal bull,

from whose seed new plants and life grew. He was aided in his wickedness by various demons, such as Az, the female demon of greed and lust, and Azi Dahaka, a storm demon with three heads and six eyes. Ahriman created evil and lies within his own Endless Darkness; he is ruler of the Underworld. The myths say that ultimately the world will be redeemed from his evil by the saviour Saoshyant, the purification of humanity, and the Frashokerti or Frashgerd – the renewal of the world.

# Coyote

**Native American**

The trickster Coyote is the subject of many myths from the Native American nations. Known for his irrepressible curiosity and voracious sexual appetite, he is always in trouble, but escapes to transgress another day.

Sometimes Coyote is a creator or co-creator. He helps Wolf create the world in Paiute myth, while in Mandan mythology the First Creator turns into Coyote once his work is done. The Pima say that Coyote was the child of the sun and the moon, and assisted Earth Doctor and Elder Brother in the creation. The Maidu, however, tell how Coyote constantly marred Earthmaker's perfect creation. Coyote is also a culture hero and transformer. The Apache tell of how he sneakily won fire from Squirrel as they danced, and the Wishram of how he freed the salmon.

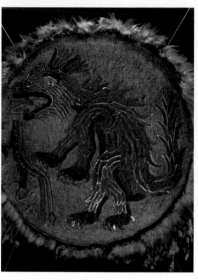

**The word "coyote"** is derived from the Aztec word *coyotl*, and the figure – shown here on an Aztec shield – seems to be part of Aztec mythology too.

## WORSHIP

*The Diné (Navajo) healing ceremony of Coyoteway takes nine days to perform. During the ceremony a chantway singer mediates with the divine Coyote People for the recovery of a patient who has offended them.*

## The Hero Twins

**Maya, Mesoamerica**

Hunahpu and Xbalanque are the Hero Twins of the Quiché Maya (*see pp.209–11*). Using bravery and trickery, they broke the power of the gods of death and destroyed the monstrous bird Vucub Caquix, with its shiny metal eyes and jewelled teeth. They shot at the bird as he perched in a fruit tree, knocking out his teeth, but he still tore off Hunahpu's arm. Pretending to be healers, they replaced his teeth with white corn, and filed the metal from his eyes. His greatness gone, Vucub Caquix died, and Hunahpu reclaimed his arm.

## Tezcatlipoca

**Aztec, Mexico    God K (Maya)**

Tezcatlipoca, "the smoking mirror", was the god of rulers, sorcerers, and warriors. Mirrors of obsidian were used in Aztec sorcery, and the surface of the Earth itself was also called a smoking mirror. Tezcatlipoca lost a foot battling with the Earth-monster at the creation, and he is usually shown with a smoking mirror in its place, from which a serpent-foot emerges. As god of the Earth, Tezcatlipoca is the enemy of the wind god Quetzalcoatl, and this enmity also raged in their human incarnations as king and sorcerer in Tollan, Mexico.

# Anansi

🏛 Ashanti, Ghana   ⚱ Nancy, Ture

Anansi the spider-man is the trickster god of the Ashanti (or Asante). His wiles managed to win the world's stories from the sky god Onyankopon (Nyame), and ever since then they have been called spider-stories. In the Caribbean, the spider-trickster is often called Nancy. Among the Zande he is called Ture, a culture hero as well as a trickster, who secured food, water, and fire for the people.

# Maui

🏛 Polynesia

The trickster Maui, who fished up the islands of Polynesia using the magic fish-hook Manai-a-ka-lani ("Come-from-the-heavens"), met his match when he tried to force himself upon the sleeping goddess of death Hine-nui-te-po; she woke, and crushed him. Maui had an odd birth: his mother was impregnated by putting on a man's loincloth and gave birth to a fetus that she wrapped in her top-knot and sent out to sea.

# Seth

🏛 Ancient Egypt   ⚱ Set

Seth is one of the oldest and most complex of the Egyptian gods. Commonly called the chaos god, he is a trickster figure comparable to the Aztec Tezcatlipoca or Japanese Susano. From about 800 BCE Seth was viewed as altogether evil, and many of his statues were recarved into statues of Amun.

Seth is represented with the head of an imaginary animal that features a long curved snout. He was the god of the desert – the arid, dangerous Red Land as opposed to the fertile Black Land. He was associated with everything that the Egyptians feared from the desert, including thunder and storms; but he was also the god of the oases that made it possible to survive the desert's dangers. Seth was married to his sister Nephthys, but he also had two warlike western Semitic goddesses, Anat and Astoreth, as consorts. Seth's violent and ruthless nature is described in three myths. In the first he kills his brother, the sky god Blind Horus, aided by the seven major stars that make up the constellation of the Great Bear. In the second he murders and dismembers his other brother, the wise ruler Osiris. In the third he has a bitter battle with Osiris's son, the reborn Horus, who represents order. Yet Seth was vital to the continuance of the world, for it was he who stood each night in the prow of Ra's night barque and speared the chaos serpent Apophis, so that Ra could rise again to bring light to the world each dawn.

## WORSHIP

Seth's cult centre was at Naqada, near Luxor, Egypt, in the pre-dynastic era.
• Carvings at the temple of Horus at Edfu show Horus spearing Seth in the form of a hippopotamus.

**This basalt stone** carving of Seth alongside his wife and sister Nephthys dates from c.1200 BCE.

# GODS OF WAR

All over the world, people have traditionally invoked their gods before going to war, and relied on divine assistance in battle. It is no surprise that many high gods, such as the Norse god Odin, are also gods of war. These gods were also inspirational: Odin inspired the Viking warriors through his runes, while Zeus could move men to bravery in battle.

**H**owever, in many cultures there were specific gods of war, such as the Greek god Ares and the Roman god Mars. Attar was the god of war and protection in battle in ancient southern Arabia. Called "he who is bold in battle", the morning star was his consort. Vahagn was the Armenian sun god and god of war. He had hair of fire, a beard of flame, and eyes like suns. Goddesses, too, had a role in war. In ancient Canaan, Anat was the goddess of both fertility and war. She would adorn herself with rouge and henna and then gleefully slaughter her enemies, cutting off their heads and hands before wading in their blood up to her knees.

**The traditional** symbol for the planet Mars derived from the spear and shield of the war god Mars.

## WAR AND SACRIFICE

Andraste, or "Invincible", was worshipped as the goddess of victory by the Iceni tribe of Celtic Britain. The Iceni leader Boudicca sacrificed Roman women to her in a sacred grove. Before fighting, Boudicca invoked Andraste and released a hare, her sacred animal. After a victory, Andraste was celebrated with sacrifices, feasting, and sexual licence.

The Aztecs developed a method of warfare known as "flowery war", in which the object was to capture rather than slay the enemy. Those captured were then ritually sacrificed, and their still-beating hearts offered to the god Huitzilopochtli.

## PEOPLE OF PEACE

There have been few cultures who have no words for war or quarrel, and whose myths reinforce a peaceful way of life. One notable exception is the Chewong people of Malaysia, whose society is rooted in non-violence. Their myths contain no legends of warfare, but instead reinforce egalitarian values. In one Chewong myth the culture hero Yinlugen Bud teaches the most important rule of all: food must always be shared.

# Ares

⚑ Ancient Greece

*Ares, the strife-loving son of Zeus and Hera, was the Greek god of battle. However, in the* Iliad, *he sides with the Trojans against the Achaian Greeks, filling them with bravery, and on one occasion even fighting on their side. He was cruel and violent: his own father called him "the most hateful of gods".*

Ares is considered to be similar to the Roman god Mars, although not his equivalent, being more brutal and less civilized. Ares was disliked because he gloried in fighting for its own sake. His unfortunate love of conflict was not accompanied by the strategic wisdom of Athena, and, strangely for a war god, Ares is frequently depicted on the losing side of an argument. He was defeated by Athena, Diomedes, Heracles, and even Poseidon's sons Otos and Ephialtes, who imprisoned Ares in a bronze jar for 13 months, before he was rescued by Hermes, another son of Zeus.

## MURDER AND TERROR

Ares was the first being to be tried for murder, after he killed Poseidon's son Halirrhothios for raping his own daughter, Alcippes. He was tried and acquitted before a jury of 12 gods, on a hill to the west of the Acropolis in Athens, known as the Areopagos, where the Athenians later held all murder trials. Ares also fathered three children with Aphrodite: Harmonia, Phobos, and Deimos (Harmony, Terror, and Fear), but even his love for Aphrodite (who was married to Ares's brother) was a jealous love. When Aphrodite bore a daughter to Adonis, a prince of Kypros, Ares took the guise of a boar and gored him to death.

### WORSHIP

*A temple to Ares used to stand in the sacred wood on the road from Akiai in Lakonia, Greece. • A statue of Ares in the town of Tegea, Greece, commemorated a time when the women alone fought for the city.*

**Ares was** a single-minded god, who would rush into battle, unconcerned about who won or lost as long as blood was shed.

# Mars

**PU** Ancient Rome    ♂ Mars Invictus, Mars Pater, Marspiter, Maris

The god of war, Mars, son of the goddess Juno, was important in the
Roman pantheon: as father to Romulus and Remus, the founders of Rome,
he was one of a triad of supreme gods worshipped on Rome's Capitoline
Hill, along with Jupiter and Quirinus, the Sabine war god.

Mars was married to the goddess Nerio
("Strength"), who is sometimes equated
with the Roman war goddess Bellona.
Mars developed from an Etruscan god,
Maris, whose role was more agricultural
than military; Mars retained an
association with agriculture, especially
when worshipped as Mars Silvanus or
as Mars Pater (Father Mars). As Mars
Pater he protected the crops from
disease and bad weather, enabling them
to grow and ripen.

### WORSHIP

*The main temple of Mars in Rome was on the
Via Appia. • Mars also had an altar in the
Campus Martius (the Field of Mars), which
was a training ground for Roman soldiers.*

**Mars developed from** the guardian of the land into a
more warlike deity as the Roman state itself grew in
aggression and territorial ambition.

# Mithras

**PU** Ancient Rome/Persia    ♂ Mithra, Sol Invictus

Mithra was a Persian god of light, and the relation of the
Persian Mithra to Roman Mithras is controversial. Mithras,
as the *kosmokrator* (ruler of the cosmos), was popular with
Roman soldiers, who propagated his cult of Mithraism.

In cave-like underground temples
called *mithraea*, found all over the
Roman Empire wherever the Legions
travelled, worshippers sacrificed bulls
to Mithras. The god's alternative name,
Sol Invictus, meaning unconquered sun,
was a term for the Syrian sun god
Elagabal (*see p.275*).

Mithraism was a mystery religion,
whose initiates were sworn to keep the
secrets they learned as they passed
through the seven grades of initiation –
Raven, Bridegroom, Soldier, Lion,

Persian, Courier of the Sun, and Father.
Each grade had its own protective deity,
and wore special clothes. A Raven
(Corax) wore a raven-headed mask,
under the protection of the god
Mercury. Mithraism made great use
of astrology, and its protective gods are
those associated with the planets. The
tauroctony (bull-slaying) scene in every
mithraeum (*see p.95*) was a coded
image of the night sky as Taurus set
in the west for the last time before the
spring equinox.

## Athena

📖 Ancient Greece    ♀ Minerva (Rome)

Wise Athena is the goddess of strategy and victory, and also of handicrafts. Zeus swallowed her mother Metis and the unborn Athena, and she was born from his head, springing out fully-armed and shouting her war cry. In the Trojan war she sided with the Achaians; she also helped and supported heroes such as Perseus, Bellerophon, and above all Heracles. The name of her mother Metis means "intelligence", and Athena inherited her mother's wisdom. Her sacred bird was the owl.

## Nike

📖 Ancient Greece    ♀ Athena Nike

The winged goddess Nike was said to be the daughter of the Titan Pallas and the Oceanid Styx. She helped the gods in their battle against the Titans, and Zeus made her goddess of victory as a reward. In Athens, she had her own temple on the Acropolis, where she was worshipped as an aspect of Athena. At Olympia she was depicted in a colossal statue by Pheidias as the companion of Zeus, dancing at his feet while the god held a miniature Nike of ivory and gold in the palm of his hand.

## Castor and Pollux

📖 Ancient Rome/Greece    ♀ Castor and Polydeuces (Greece), the Castores, the Dioscuri

Castor and Pollux were the Roman names for a pair of twins who originated in Greek mythology. They were identified with the Penates (gods of the household), and with the Cabiri, Phrygian gods of fertility and the protection of sailors.

Castor and Pollux, the Dioscuri, are usually thought to have been fathered by Zeus (in the form of a swan) on Leda, the queen of Sparta, and then hatched from an egg. However, some sources claim that Castor was in fact the son of Tyndareus, king of Sparta, and was therefore mortal, while Pollux is immortal. After death the brothers shared the one immortality between them, being alive and then dead on alternate days. Renowned as boxers and horsemen (they are often portrayed mounted), the Dioscuri were patrons of the Roman cavalry. Their sisters were Clytemnestra and Helen of Troy.

### WORSHIP

*The Temple of the Dioscuri in Rome (see p.89) was used not only for religious ceremonies, but also for political meetings and as a safe deposit for monies from the treasury.*

**The twins are often** depicted attending a goddess. The downturned torch may indicate that the small female figure in this grouping is Persephone.

## Tyr

🏳 Norse

Tyr was the Norse god of war; our word Tuesday recalls his earlier incarnation as the Germanic war god Tiw or Tiwaz. In Norse mythology, Tyr is eclipsed in importance by Odin, whose Valkyries (the "Choosers of the Slain") ride into battle and allot victory or defeat. Tyr was the only god brave enough to feed the terrible wolf Fenrir, and sacrificed his sword hand so that the monster could be bound. His noble act will lead to his death at the last battle of Ragnarok.

**This medieval illustration** shows the selfless Tyr, having lost his hand to the wolf Fenrir.

## Celtic Mars

🏳 Celtic, Europe

Many of the Celtic peoples of the Roman Empire worshipped Mars, but this god differed from the Roman Mars. The Celtic Mars was a much less warlike being than his Classical counterpart. He was associated with the goose, a bird that was seen as a protector because of its alarm call, and he was also worshipped as a god of healing. He was part of a group of native Celtic deities that included the hunting god Cocidius, the horse god Rudiobus, and the healing gods Mullo, Nodons, and Olloudius.

## The Mórrigan

🏳 Celtic, Ireland    ♂ Mor-Riogain, Morrigu

The Mórrigan was the early Irish goddess of war who, instead of fighting in person, changed the outcome of a conflict by appearing on the battlefield and terrifying one side or the other, either with her fearsome looks or by casting spells. Her warlike qualities were linked in a powerful way with her sexuality.

The Mórrigan was associated with a number of goddesses, including the war deities Badb and Macha, who either form a kind of martial trinity with her or appear as aspects of the Mórrigan herself. The sinister Morgan Le Fay of Arthurian legend (*see pp.110–11*) may also be considered as one of her aspects by some. A prolific shape-changer, the Mórrigan often appeared as a crow, arriving to prophesy the outcome of a war or descending on to a battlefield to peck at the corpses. The Irish banshee, envisaged as a sinister woman washing bloody garments at a ford, also derives from the Mórrigan. She allied herself to

different sides in different wars. For example, after sleeping with the Daghda (*see p.100*) she agreed to take the side of the Tuatha Dé Danaan (a magical people) at the battle of Mag Tuired, chanting spells that drove the Fomhoire into the sea. However, in a later conflict she was a supporter of the men of Connaught.

### WORSHIP

*The Mórrigan is thought to have lived in the cave of Cruachain in County Roscommon, Ireland.* • *A pair of hills near the Neolithic tombs of Newgrange in Ireland is called "the breasts of Mórrigan".*

# Durga

**ᴘᴜ India**

The Great Goddess Devi in her warlike incarnation is called Durga, a name that means "impenetrable" or "hard to approach". She is portrayed as an attractive woman, but she rides a big cat as a reminder that she defeats demons.

Durga can emerge from the gentle goddess Parvati when she is angry, or she can appear when a number of gods combine their power. This happens when the stability of the cosmos is threatened by demons. On one occasion, a group of gods called the Devas were harassed by a demon called Mahisha, who disguised himself as a buffalo. When the Devas told Siva and Vishnu about the problem, the two gods grew angry, which made Durga appear. Mahisha kept changing shape, from buffalo to man to lion to elephant, but Durga defeated him. With her foot on his neck, she forced the spirit from his mouth, and cut off his head. As he died, all the gods and all the creatures of the world shouted "Victory!"

**The multi-handed Durga** rides a fierce tiger and uses many weapons to defeat the demon Mahisha, who has taken the guise of a water buffalo.

## Skanda

**ᴘᴜ India     ♂ Karttikeya, Senapati, Kumara**

The six-headed Skanda is the Hindu god of war. In different Vedic texts he is said to be the son of either Agni or Siva. He was brought up by the Krttikas – the six stars of the Pleiades. He was often tasked with fighting evil demons, such as the demon Taraka, whom he killed with weapons made from the sun's rays.

**Skanda transformed** a Titan he had defeated into a peacock, and thereafter rode around on him.

## Guan Di

**ᴘᴜ China     ♂ Kuan Ti, Guan Yü, Kuan Yü**

Guan Di started out as a humble seller of bean-curd but became one of the famous Brothers of the Peach Orchard, a trio of adventurers similar to the Three Musketeers. Guan Di was considered such a military hero that in 1594, during the Ming Dynasty, he was officially elevated to the rank of war god. Soldiers in particular venerated him, but he continued to be the patron of bean-curd sellers.

# Hachiman

Japan

Hachiman was a fertility god who granted children to his devotees and encouraged the growth of their crops. As well as being a protector of agriculture he was also the defender of Japan, and so became god of war.

In the native Shinto religion of Japan, Hachiman is seen as a historical figure who was deified. He began life as the emperor Ojin, who died in around 394 CE. Ojin was renowned as a military leader and was said to have been able to influence the tides to throw invading ships off-course. When the Minamoto clan-hero Yoshi-iye and his soldiers were dying of thirst, he prayed to Hachiman before shooting an arrow into a rock, and was rewarded with an inexhaustible fountain of water. One of Japan's most popular gods, Hachiman is also a divinity within Buddhist belief.

**WORSHIP**

*The temple of Hachiman is at Kamakura, Japan. • Half of all Shinto shrines are dedicated to Hachiman. • At the age of 20, young Japanese men celebrate their coming-of-age at a Hachiman shrine.*

## Zi-yu

China    Ch'ih Yu

One of the culture heroes of China, Zi-yu was the first metalworker. He used his ability to shape metal to make the first weapons and armour, and so became the primeval Chinese god of war. He is portrayed as a fearsome creature with the head, horns, and hooves of a bull, which are so strong that they seemed to be made of metal. Zi-yu was said to show his strength by eating pebbles. He was prone to terrifyingly violent rages, during which he attacked his enemies by butting them with his horns.

## Huitzilopochtli

Aztec, Mexico

Huitzilopochtli was the chief cult god of the Aztecs, a deity of sun and fire who demanded human hearts as nourishment. Huitzilopochtli led the Aztecs in war in order that they might capture sacrificial victims to feed his hunger. Born, like Athena, fully-armed, Huitzilopochtli's first act was to kill and dismember his sister Coyolxauhqui, who was plotting to kill their mother. His cult centre was Tenochtitlan, where a double pyramid comprised his Great Temple together with that of Tlaloc, the god of rain and lightning.

## Morning Star

📖 Native American

Morning Star is the most powerful of all the beings placed in the sky by the creator Tirawahat (the sun). He is dressed like a warrior, painted with red dust and carrying a war club. When a Pawnee war chief was dressed by a priest in the ceremonial regalia of war, he was imitating Morning Star, and asking his blessing. In historical times the Pawnee sacrificed girls to Morning Star at the culmination of a four-day ritual. The girl was made to face east (towards the morning star), then shot repeatedly with arrows.

## Sekhmet

📖 Egypt

When humankind plotted against the sun god Ra, he sent his Eye in the form of the goddess Hathor to exact vengeance. The peaceful Hathor transformed into the lion-headed Sekhmet, who laid waste to humankind in an ecstasy of slaughter. When Sekhmet awoke the next day, Ra made her drunk with beer mixed with red ochre to look like blood, sating her blood-lust and saving humanity.

## Tu

📖 Polynesia    🔱 Ku, Tumatauenga

Tu (Ku in Hawaii), one of the sons of Rangi and Papa (sky and Earth), is the Polynesian god of war, known as Tu-of-the-angry-face. His name means both "to stand" and "to strike". Human sacrifices were made to him.

In his most warlike aspect, Tu/Ku was known as Ku-kaili-moku. The wooden image of this god, with a headdress of yellow feathers, was said to utter cries that could be heard over the sound of the fighting when carried into battle. The traditional Haka war dance, in which the dancers imitate Tu, has been adopted by the All Blacks rugby team and New Zealand's soldiers.

In Maori myth, Tu's warlike nature is evident at an early stage – when he suggests to his brothers that they kill their parents even before he and his brothers are born. His youngest brother Tawhirimatea decides to stay with his mother the Earth, and becomes buried under her stomach, to become the god of earthquakes and storms. Tu is the only god to withstand his attacks, and thus considers his other brothers to be his inferiors. To demonstrate his loss of

respect for them, he begins using their children – the fish, the birds, the plants that grow from the land – as food and materials, and in doing so, he allows humankind to do the same. Thus he became also a god of husbandry and abundance.

Tu/Ku is a complex god, and his responsibilities are wide. He is also a god of sorcery and of healing. In Hawaii, Ku was the principle of male generative power, paired with Hina, the principle of female fecundity. The rising sun is known there as Ku, and the setting sun as Hina.

### WORSHIP

*As Ku-of-the-abundance-of-the-seas, the god lived in human form on East Maui, at a place known as Leho-ula on the side of the hill Ka-iwi-o-Pele. • Prayers for the sick are said to Tu and Hina as the parents of humanity.*

# DEITIES OF THE UNDERWORLD

The idea of the Underworld came into being to explain one of the key questions of existence: what happens when we die? Most mythologies developed the idea of another world as the dwelling-place of the souls of the dead. Each of these worlds had its own deities, shadowy beings who oversaw our passage from life to death and ruled over the departed.

S ome cultures were closely concerned with death and with the soul's passage to the next world. Their myths, like those of Ancient Egypt for example, feature many gods who preside over the funerary rites, question the soul about its life on Earth, and admit it to the kingdom of the dead. The Egyptians saw their whole lives as preparation for this process, while the Ancient Chinese also saw the next world as in some ways more real than our fleeting, mortal life on Earth.

## SHADY FIGURES

The god of the Underworld was often a shadowy figure held in awe by humans. The Greek god Hades, unlike other Greek deities, was never depicted by artists: he was invisible, which added to the dread and mystery he inspired. The Romans saw his counterpart, Pluto, as a king who was assisted in his kingdom by deities such as the Furies. This trio of goddesses supervised the torments that were meted out to those who had behaved wickedly.

**An Ancient Egyptian** cat mummy, wrapped in highly decorated bandages.

## GRUESOME COMPANIONS

Myths often tell of the ruler of the Underworld's grisly attendants. The entrance to the Classical Underworld was guarded by Cerberus, a three-headed dog. The Celtic king of the Underworld, Arawn, was followed around by a band of demons; and Tuoni, ruler of the Finnish Underworld, was accompanied by a host of hideous children, diseases, and monsters. Many lands of the dead in the myths of Eastern civilizations were also populated by demons. Although these myths helped to explain what might happen after this life, they did not provide much comfort.

# Hades

**Greece**    The Other Zeus, the God Below, Pluton, Pluto

The grim brother of Zeus and Poseidon, sinister Hades was the ruler of the Greek Underworld, the dark realm to which mortals believed their souls would go after death. He was a much-feared god, most famous for his abduction of the girl who would become his consort, Persephone (*see p.54*).

Hades was invisible, either because of his dark realm or because of his helmet, which made the wearer disappear. He invoked such dread that many would not even utter his name, preferring phrases like "the Other Zeus" or just "lord". He was said to be indifferent to people's prayers, but his character also had a positive side, expressed by an alternative set of descriptions, such as Pluton ("wealth") and Polyxeinos ("host to many"). In this guise he was, with Persephone, the subject of worship.

**When Hades** abducted Persephone, he rode in a golden chariot drawn by black horses, according to the Roman poet Ovid.

# Hel

**Norse**

The Norse goddess Hel was ruler of the Underworld, a region (also known as Hel) found near a root of the world-tree Yggdrasil in the cosmic region of Niflheim. The upper half of Hel's body was flesh-coloured and alive, but the lower half was black and difficult to see in the darkness where she lived.

Hel, daughter of Loki and the giantess Angrboda, was a frightening figure but also a sad one, condemned by the god Odin to rule her dark kingdom. The names of her home and her various possessions provide clues to her unhappy character: her hall was known as Eliudnir ("damp"), and her threshold was Fallanda Forad ("stumbling block"). On her table were the dish Hungr ("hunger") and the knife Sultr ("famine"). Her bed was known as Kör ("sick-bed"). All those whose lives ended in illness and old age had to pass through one of the fortified gates into her dark, chilly realm. Here they are doomed to wait with the goddess until Loki arrives to call his daughter to join the final battle of Ragnarok — the one that will bring the world to an end.

# Arawn

📖 Celtic, Wales

The Welsh Otherworld was ruled by a pair of rival gods, Arawn and Hafgan, who fought each other every year for supremacy. Arawn longed to be the sole king of the Otherworld, and so made an alliance with the shape-changer Pwyll. Arawn and Pwyll changed places for a year, during which Pwyll killed Hafgan, allowing Arawn to take the kingdom on his return. In one myth, the divine ploughman Amaethon stole a dog and a deer from Arawn, and the ruler of the Otherworld had to fight to get them back. But Amaethon's ally, the magician Gwydion, turned trees into soldiers and so defeated him.

# Tuoni

📖 Finland

The ruler of Tuonela, the Finnish Underworld, was called Tuoni. He was a figure shrouded in darkness. With his consort Tuonetar, Tuoni ruled a dim, silent, forested kingdom surrounded by an icy river. As well as the souls of all the dead, both good and bad, Tuonela was populated by the many gruesome monsters fathered by Tuoni.

## WORSHIP

*Tuoni and his dreaded daughters, the goddesses of suffering, could be held at bay by magical formulas and spells, such as: "All pains, all troubles/go into a hole in brown rock/from which you also emerged."*

# Yama

📖 India, Tibet    ♂ Yima, Yanluo, Emma-O

Yama is the Hindu god of death. The son of Surya, the sun god, he was originally the first man to live and the first to die. In early Vedic mythology, Yama is a beneficent figure, ruling from a heavenly palace with his sister-wife Yami. But over time he became a terrifying lord of the dead. In Hindu myth it takes a soul nearly five hours to reach Yamapura, Yama's city. Once at his palace, souls have to venture past two ferocious dogs to reach Yama himself. Then Chitragupta, the dead's registrar, reads out the record of their deeds, and Yama judges them, sending them either to heaven or to one of the 21 hells, or back to Earth to live again.

# Kali

📖 India

Among the most terrifying of all the Hindu deities is Kali, goddess of death. She is usually shown as a ferocious naked woman, her tongue hanging out as if to lap up the blood of her victims. In one of her four hands she holds

a club or a sword; in another, a severed head. She wears a garland of skulls and a skirt of severed arms. Although Kali is a terrifying figure, she has positive aspects. She destroys demons who threaten cosmic order; her nakedness symbolizes her power to strip away illusions; and in the wake of her destruction comes the possibility of new life.

**The Hindu goddess** of death and destruction, Kali has a dark, fearsome appearance.

# Ereshkigal

🏛 Mesopotamia     ♂ Allatu

Ereshkigal was the dreaded queen who ruled the Sumerian and Babylonian Underworld. The main myth about Ereshkigal is that in which her sister Inanna (Ishtar) descended to visit her, ostensibly to attend the funeral of Ereshkigal's husband Gugalanna, the Bull of Heaven, but really to challenge her power. Ereshkigal was pitiless and cruel to Inanna. Her one weakness was her enormous sexual desire; in the Assyrian myth of Ereshkigal and Nergal, they made love for six days and nights but she was still not satisfied.

# Mot

🏛 Canaanite (Ugaritic)

Mot was the god of death and sterility. Some scholars translate the Bible's line in Psalm 48, "He will be our guide, even unto death", as "He will lead us against Mot." The main myth about Mot describes his battle for supremacy with the fertility and storm god Baal. Mot initially overcame Baal and killed him, but Mot was then killed by Baal's sister Anath. Both Baal and Mot came back to life and carried on fighting until the sun goddess Shapash persuaded them to accept separate kingdoms, above and below the Earth.

# Di Zang

🏛 China     ♂ Dizang Wang, Ti-tsang

Di Zang is a Chinese Buddhist god of the Underworld. He is a benevolent deity, devoted to helping others, and he is usually portrayed sitting cross-legged with an expression of compassion or repose on his face. Di Zang is said to travel around the Underworld, talking to all the human souls he meets and explaining Buddhist law to them. When he encounters a soul who repents of his or her sins, he visits one of the judges of the Underworld and asks for the soul's sentence to be reduced. His mission is to see all the chambers of hell emptied, and he is especially revered because he offers his compassion to everyone, whether they are rich or poor.

# Mictlantecuhtli

🏛 Aztec, Mexico     ♂ Tzontemoc

Mictlan was the Aztec Underworld, and its lord and lady were Mictlantecuhtli and his wife Mictecacihuatl. The god was represented as a skeleton, often wearing an owl-feather headdress and a collar of eyeballs. The principal myth featuring Mictlantecuhtli is that in which Quetzalcoatl tricks him into giving up the bones of previous eras of humankind in order to create a new race. Every 260 days, a man dressed as Mictlantecuhtli was sacrificed at night in the temple of Tlalxicco, the navel of the world. The victim may then have been eaten by the priests, in an act of communion.

**Mictlantecuhtli,** the Aztec god of all the dead, is traditionally portrayed as a blood-spattered skeleton with protruding teeth and eyes.

## The Mayan death gods

ᛈ Maya, Mesoamerica

Images of various death gods are found at Mayan temples. Many of these are known to scholars only as "Death God A" or "Death God L". "Death God D" was also known as Itzamna; "Death God N" was also known as Pauahtun.

In the Mayan epic the *Popol Vuh*, when the heroes Hunahpu and Xbalanque descend to Xibalba, the Underworld, they greet each of the lords of Xibalba by name: One Death, Seven Death, House Corner, Blood Gatherer, Pus Master, Jaundice Master, Bone Sceptre, Skull Sceptre, Wing, Packstrap, Bloody Teeth, and Bloody Claws. The pair knew their names because they had sent a mosquito ahead of them to bite each death god and learn their name. For this service the mosquito was rewarded with the freedom to suck the blood of people on the roads.

Xibalba was thought of as a place of foul smells, and the death gods are often shown with foliated scrolls emerging from their bodies that represent vile farts. One skeletal god was sometimes named Cizin ("farter") as well as Yum Cimih ("Lord of Death").

One characteristic of Mesoamerican death gods is that although they are terrifying and ruthless, they can also be tricked. Hunahpu and Xbalanque fool the Mayan gods of death into eagerly volunteering to be sacrificed; in the Aztec culture, too, Quetzalcoatl outwits Mictlantecuhtli to retrieve the bones from which a new race of humans can be created.

The importance of death in Mesoamerican culture is manifested today in the ritual feasting of the souls of the dead in the period between Halloween and All Saints' Day.

### WORSHIP

*In one form of Aztec sacrifice the lower jaw was torn away from a living man. The Death God of the Number Zero was often drawn with his hair bound like a sacrificial victim, and a hand gripping his jaw, ready to tear it away.*

## Xipe Totec

ᛈ Aztec, Mexico    ♂ Seven Rain (Mixtec)

The name Xipe Totec means "our lord the flayed one". This god was the deity of the season of spring and of goldsmiths. Images of Xipe Totec show a human inside the flayed skin of another man, which was supposed to represent the "new skin" of the Earth in springtime. At the 20-day festival of Tlacaxipehualiztli ("flaying of men") held in his honour, victims were killed by removing their hearts, and then young men impersonated the god by dressing in their skins. The skins were dyed yellow to become "golden clothes".

## Gédé

ᛈ Haiti    ♂ Ghede, Baron Samedi

Originating in Benin, Gédé, the lord of death, is one of the most important voodoo *lwa* (gods or spirits). Devotees possessed by Gédé act in a lascivious manner, demonstrating by their sexual vigour that Gédé is also a lord of life. Gédé is identified with the Catholic St Expedit, and takes various forms: Brave-Gédé, Gédé Nibo, Gédé Fouillé, and Gédé Loraj. Some regard these forms as a family of gods, with Baron Samedi at their head. All Gédés dress in black, with a funereal appearance, but act with unseemly merriment.

## Osiris

📕 Ancient Egypt

The god Osiris was the first king of Egypt. He taught the early Egyptians how to live, how to cultivate the wild wheat and barley, and how to make and use tools. After he was killed by his brother Seth, he became the king of the Underworld. Osiris was shown as a mummified king, holding the crook and flail of kingship and wearing a crown. His symbol was the *djed*-pillar, a stylized sheaf of corn. The cult centre of Osiris was at Abydos, where for more than 2,000 years the Mysteries of Osiris were celebrated in the last month of the Nile inundation.

## Anubis

📕 Ancient Egypt

Said to be the illegitimate son of Osiris and his sister Nephthys, Anubis was the canine god of the dead, often depicted as a jackal-headed man. Anubis created the first mummy by wrapping up the dismembered corpse of Osiris, and so became the patron of embalmers. He was also the guardian of the necropolis, and supervised the weighing of the souls of the newly deceased.

**Anubis is usually** shown with black skin, mimicking the colour of corpses after mummification.

## Ma'at

📕 Ancient Egypt

The Egyptian word *ma'at* means "that which is right, true, just, and proper", and it was the duty of the pharaoh to maintain *ma'at* in the kingdom. This subtle, abstract concept was personified as Ma'at, a goddess with an ostrich plume; it was against this feather that the heart – soul – of each Egyptian was weighed after death. Ma'at represents the divine order that came into being at the moment of creation. The rites that took place daily in Egyptian temples were repetitions of mythical acts that laid the foundations of *ma'at*. This repetition, done by or in the name of the king, secured those foundations, and therefore maintained the balance of the cosmos.

**Ma'at ensured** the continued existence of the ordered world, and held off an ever-threatening chaos.

## Hine-nui-te-po

📕 Polynesia     ♂ Hine-titama

*Hine* or *hina* simply means "young woman", and the many goddesses whose name begins with Hine are sometimes regarded as simply different aspects of a great goddess. Hine-nui-te-po, the Maori goddess of death, was originally Hine-titama, the Dawn Maiden; she killed herself in shame and took refuge in the Underworld when she realized she had unknowingly committed incest with her father Tane, the forest god. The blending of life-giving and devouring aspects in these goddesses reflects Polynesian taboos and fears about menstruation and childbirth. The lore of the Maoris holds that while all life comes from the womb, death comes from "the *mana* [power] of the female organ". Death is a return to the womb of the great mother.

# INDEX

Page numbers in **bold** refer to
main entries; numbers in *italics*
refer to illustrations and captions

# ACKNOWLEDGMENTS

### Publisher's acknowledgments

The publishers would like to thank: Carolyn Walton, Judy Barratt, and Peter Bentley for editorial assistance; Hilary Bird for the index; and Charles Wills and Jenny Siklos for Americanization. Thanks also in particular to Antony Gormley for allowing us to use the photograph on p.173, and to Paul Robishaw and the Save Tikopia project ( http://home.netcom.com/~yellowrose/tikopia/) for assistance in obtaining the pictures for pp.260–1.

### Picture credits

The publisher would like to thank the following for their kind permission to reproduce their photographs:

(Key: a-above; b-below/bottom; c-centre; f-far; l-left; r-right; t-top)

1 Corbis: Bob Krist (t). 2-3 Corbis: Dallas and John Heaton/Free Agents Limited (c). 4 Alamy Images: ArkReligion.com (c). 5 Alamy Images: Jon Arnold Images (c). 6-7 Corbis: Jacky Naegelen (c). 9 The Art Archive: Palazzo del Te Mantua / Dagli Orti (t). iStockphoto.com: jason walton (bl). 10 Alamy Images: Zevart Collection (ca). 10-30 iStockphoto.com: Ryan KC Wong (ftl). 11 Corbis: Archivo Iconografico (c). 11-31 iStockphoto.com: Ryan KC Wong (ftr). 12-13 Alamy Images: Peter Horree (tc). Corbis: Reuters (cb). 14 Alamy Images: Deco Images (ca). 15 Corbis: Atlantide Phototravel (tr). iStockphoto.com: Matthew Scherf (tr). 16 Corbis: Paul A. Souders (c). iStockphoto.com: Alan Tobey (clb). 17 Corbis: Burstein Collection (tc). 18 Corbis: Asian Art & Archaeology, Inc. (bl). 19 iStockphoto.com: Robert Churchill (tr). 20 The Bridgeman Art Library: Dinodia (bl). 21 Alamy Images: Peter Horree (tr). 22-23 Alamy Images: Christian Kapteyn (bc). 23 Alamy Images: Visual Arts Library (London) (tl). 24 Alamy Images: Black Star (tc); David Sanger Photography (bl). 25 Corbis: Sandro Vannini (br). 26 Alamy Images: The Print Cullector (ca). 26-27 iStockphoto.com: Chuck Babbitt (b). 27 akg-images: (tc). 28 The Bridgeman Art Library: Royal Library, Copenhagen, Denmark (bl). 29 Corbis: Gianni Dagli Orti (br); John Roddam Spencer Stanhope (tr). 30 Alamy Images: David Sanger Photography (br). 31 Alamy Images: Tibor Bognar (bc); Mary Evans Picture Library (tr). 32-33 Alamy Images: Tibor Bognar (cb); Jack Sullivan (tc). 34 Corbis: Roger Wood (br). 34-94 iStockphoto.com: George Cairns (ftl). 35 Corbis: Richard T. Nowitz (cb). 35-95 iStockphoto.com: George Cairns (ftr). 36 iStockphoto.com: Sue McDonald (tr). 37 Alamy Images: Peter Horree (bc). 38 Mary Evans Picture Library: (c). 39 Alamy Images: Iain Masterton (tc). 40 Alamy Images: Visual Arts Library (London) (tl). 40-41 akg-images: Erich Lessing (bc). 41 akg-images: Jean-Louis Nou (tr). The Bridgeman Art Library: Lauros/Giraudon, Louvre, Paris, France (cla). Corbis: Mimmo Jodice (clb). 42 iStockphoto.com: Tina Lorien (bl). 43 Alamy Images: Visual Arts Library (London) (tc). Corbis: North Carolina Museum of Art (bc). 45 The Bridgeman Art Library: Thomas Brod and Patrick Pilkington, Private Collection (cla). 46-47 The Art Archive: Palazzo del Te Mantua / Dagli Orti (c). 48 The Bridgeman Art Library: National Gallery, London, UK (br). 49 The Bridgeman Art Library: Giraudon, Louvre, Paris, France (bc). 50 iStockphoto.com: Sean Locke (b). 51 iStockphoto.com: David Kent (ca). 52 The Art Archive: Museo Nazionale Palazzo Altemps Rome /Dagli Orti (c). 52-53 Getty Images: George Grigoriou (b). 53 Alamy Images: Fan Travelstock (tr). 54 The Bridgeman Art Library: Birmingham Museums and Art Gallery (cb). 55 The Bridgeman Art Library: Bibliothèque des Arts Décoratifs Paris/Dagli Orti (bl). iStockphoto.com: Kent Weakley (cra). 56 Corbis: North Carolina Museum of Art (cla). 57 iStockphoto.com: Darrell Scott (b). 58 iStockphoto.com: kristian sekulic (c). 59 Corbis: Araldo de Luca (cra). 60 The Art Archive: Dagli Orti (b). 61 iStockphoto.com: Tomasz Resiak (tr). Mary Evans Picture Library: (br). 62 Corbis: Bettmann (tr). 63 The Art Archive: National Archaeological Museum Athens / Dagli Orti (bc). The Bridgeman Art Library: Fitzwilliam Museum, University of Cambridge, UK (cra). 65 The Art Archive: Musée du Louvre Paris / Dagli Orti (bc). The Bridgeman Art Library: Museumslandschaft Hessen Kassel, Gemaeldegalerie Alte Meister, Kassel, Germany (cra). 66 The Kobal Collection: Universal (b). 67 The Art Archive: National Archaeological Museum Athens/Dagli Orti (bc). Corbis: Richard T. Nowitz (cra). 68-69 Alamy Images: Roger Bamber (bc). 70 The Bridgeman Art Library: Meta and Paul J. Sachs, Fogg Art Museum, Harvard University Art Museums, USA (b). 71 The Kobal Collection: Warner Bros. (br). 72 Getty Images: Ray Massey (c). 73 Corbis: Araldo de Luca (cra). 74 Corbis: Alexander Burkatovski (b). 75 Alamy Images: The Print Collector (bc). The Kobal Collection: Warner Bros. (tr). 76 akg-images: Columbia Pictures/ Album/ Akg (tc). 76-77 Alamy Images: Robert Harding Picture Library Ltd (b). 78 iStockphoto.com: Bill Grove (tc). 78-79 Alamy Images: Visual Arts Library (London) (b). 79 iStockphoto.com: Hedda Gjerpen (tr). 80 The Bridgeman Art Library: National Museum and Gallery of Wales, Cardiff (c). 81 The Bridgeman Art Library: Lauros/Giraudon, Louvre, Paris, France (b). 82 Alamy Images: Tibor Bognar (br). 83 Alamy Images: Travelshots.com (tc). 84-85 Corbis: Araldo de Luca (b). 86 Corbis: Christie's Images (br). 87 Werner Forman Archive: (tr). 88 The Bridgeman Art Library: The Detroit Institute of Arts, USA (b). 89 Alamy Images: Stock Italia (br). 90 akg-images: Nimatallah (tc). 90-91 Corbis: Gianni Dagli Orti (b). 91 akg-images: (tc). 92 Alamy Images: ImageState (tr). 93 The Bridgeman Art Library: Ferens Art Gallery, Hull City Museums and Art Galleries (tr). 94 The Art Archive: Archaeological Museum Milan/Dagli Orti (br); Museo Capitolino Rome / Dagli Orti (A) (b). 95 The Art Archive: Museo Capitolino Rome/Dagli Orti (crb). 96-97 Alamy Images: tbkmedia. de (bc). iStockphoto.com: Cindy England (tc). 98 Corbis: The Art Archive (b). 98-134 iStockphoto.com: Martin L'Allier (ftl). 99 Alamy Images: Visual Arts Library (London) (tc). Corbis: Gianni Dagli Orti (br). 99-135 iStockphoto.com: Martin L'Allier (ftr). 100 Alamy Images: The Print Collector. 101 Alamy Images: AA World Travel Library / Alamy (b). iStockphoto.com: Gertjan Hooijer (tr). 102 Alamy Images: Ian Leonard (c). 102 103 Alamy Images: David Lyons. 104 Mary Evans Picture Library: (c). 105 Corbis: Herbert Spichtinger (br). 106 Werner Forman Archive: National Museum, Copenhagen (cl). 107 Alamy Images: Aguilar Patrice (br). 109 Alamy Images: The Photolibrary Wales (b). Werner Forman Archive: Dorset Nat. Hist. & Arch (c). 110 The Bridgeman Art Library: Bradford Art Galleries and Museums, West Yorkshire, UK (c). 110-111 Corbis: Skyscan (b). 111 The Kobal Collection: Touchstone Pictures/Jerry Bruckheimer Films/ Jonathan Hession (tr). 112 Alamy Images: Visual Arts Library (London) (tl). Werner Forman Archive: Statens Historiska Museum, Stockholm (c). 113 Mary Evans Picture Library: (tr) (tl). Werner Forman Archive: Statens Historiska Museum (c). 114 Werner Forman Archive: (c). 114-115 Alamy Images: britishcolumbiaphotos.com (bl). 115 Alamy Images: Renee Morris (cr). 116 Werner Forman Archive: (bl). 116-117 Werner Forman Archive: (b). 118-119 Corbis: Ted Spiegel (c). 120 iStockphoto.com: Serdar Uckun (bl). Werner Forman Archive: Statens Historiska Museet, Stockholm (cr). 121 Werner Forman Archive: (br). 122 Corbis: Ted Spiegel (br). 123 Corbis: Charles & Josette Lenars (cr). 124 Werner Forman Archive: Viking Ship Museum, Bygdoy (r). 125 Werner Forman Archive: Statens Historiska Museum, Stockholm (c); Stofnun Arna Magnussonar a Islandi (br). 126 The Art Archive: Oldsaksammlung Oslo/Dagli Orti (c). Werner Forman Archive: Upplandsmuseet, Uppsala (bl). 126-127 Alamy Images: Brian Harris (b). 128 Corbis: Hans Strand (c). 129 Alamy Images: Esa Hiltula (tr). 130 Alamy Images: Blickwinkel (bl). 131 Central Art Archives, Finland: Hannu Aaltonen (t). Getty Images: AFP (br). 132 The Bridgeman Art Library: Tretyakov Gallery, Moscow (c). 133 akg-images: (tc). 134 Corbis: Pablo Sanchez (b). 135 Getty Images: Lonely Planet/ Martin Moos (c). 136-137 Alamy Images: Chad Ehlers (b). iStockphoto.com: Benoist Sébire (t). 138 Alamy Images: Mireille Vautier (c); Visual Arts Library (London) (bl). 138-139 Corbis: Jose Fuste Raga (b). 138-188 iStockphoto.com: 300dpi (ftl). 139-187 iStockphoto.com: 300dpi (ftr). 140 Getty Images: Bridgeman Art Library/Sumerian (bl). 140-141 iStockphoto.com: Damir Cudic (b). 141 akg-images: Erich Lessing (c). 142-143 Alamy Images: Images&Stories (c). 145 akg-images: Erich Lessing (r). 146 Corbis: Gianni Dagli Orti (tr). 146-147 Alamy Images: Eitan Simanor (b). 147 akg-images: (c). 148 Corbis: Rob Howard (b). 150 akg-images: Gérard Degeorge (br). Werner Forman Archive: Christie's, London (tr). 151 The Bridgeman Art Library: Museum of Latakia, Latakia, Syria, Peter Willi (br). 152 iStockphoto.com: Willi Schmitz (c). 153 akg-images: Erich Lessing (c). iStockphoto.com: Jason Lugo (b). 154 Corbis: (bl). 155 Corbis: Gianni Dagli Orti (tc). 156 iStockphoto.com: Joe Ho (cr); millsrymer (br). 157 iStockphoto.com: Phil Date (br). 158 Corbis: Jayanta Shaw/Reuters (b). 160-161 Corbis: Jayanta Shaw/Reuters (b). 162-163 Alamy Images: ArkReligion.com (b). 163 Corbis: Lindsay Hebberd (tl). 164 Corbis: Jack Fields (c). 165 akg-images: Jean-Louis Nou (r). 166 Corbis: Lindsay Hebberd (bl). 167 Corbis: Brooklyn Museum (tc). 168-169 Corbis: Baldev (b). 169 Alamy Images: Samantha Nundy (tr).

170 Alamy Images: Dinodia Images (b). 171 Alamy Images: Wolfgang Kaehler (t). 172 Mary Evans Picture Library: (c). 173 White Cube Gallery: Antony Gormley (b). 174 Corbis: Andy Rain/epa (c). 175 Alamy Images: Dennis Cox (b). 176 Alamy Images: Mary Evans Picture Library (c). 176-177 Getty Images: Luis Castaneda Inc (b). 177 Alamy Images: Felix Stensson (tc). 178-179 Corbis: Free Agents Limited (c). 181 The Bridgeman Art Library: Museum of Fine Arts, Boston, Massachusetts, USA, William Sturgis Bigelow Collection (b). 183 Corbis: Michael S. Yamashita (tc). Getty Images: Orion Press (b). 184 Corbis: Norris/PhotoCuisine (bl). 185 iStockphoto.com: Can Balcioglu (bc); Robert Churchill (b). 186 akg-images: akg-images (tl). Corbis: Araldo de Luca (c). 186-187 Getty Images: Klaus Nigge (b). 188 Alamy Images: Bruno Barbier/Robert Harding Picture Library Ltd (c). 189 Corbis: Michele Falzone/JAI (t). 190 191 Corbis: Randy Faris (b). iStockphoto.com: Joy Fera (t). 192 Corbis: Burstein Collection (c); Hulton-Deutsch Collection (b). 192-220 iStockphoto.com: Kemie (ftl). 193 Getty Images: Michael J P Scott (b). 193-221 iStockphoto.com: Kemie (ftr). 194 Alamy Images: Stephen Frink Collection (c). 195 Corbis: Richard A. Cooke (r). 196 iStockphoto.com: Gerald Blair (tr). 196-197 Corbis: Craig Tuttle (b). 197 Alamy Images: Chuck Place (tr). 198 Corbis: Scott T. Smith (b). 199 Corbis: Kevin Fleming (c). iStockphoto.com: Loretta Hostettler (t). 200-201 Alamy Images: Visions of America, LLC (c). 202-203 Corbis: George H. H. Huey (b). 203 Getty Images: Nick Nicholson (tr). 204 Corbis: Arthur Morris (cr). iStockphoto.com: Jeremy Sterk (b). 206 Corbis: Michael Maslan Historic (c). 206-207 iStockphoto.com: Roman Krochuk (b). 208 Alamy Images: Siegfried Kuttig (b). 209 Alamy Images: Mireille Vautier (tr). 210 Corbis: Macduff Everton (tr). 210-211 Getty Images: Frans Lemmens (b). 212 Alamy Images: North Wind Picture Archives (c); Visual Arts Library (London) (bl). 213 Alamy Images: Annette Price - H2O Photography (b). 214 Corbis: Bettmann (c). 214-215 Corbis: Danny Lehman (b). 215 Alamy Images: Visual Arts Library (London) (c). 216 Corbis: Keren Su (b). 217 Corbis: Julio Donoso (c). Getty Images: Ira Block (br). 218-219 Alamy Images: Jon Arnold Images (c). 220 Alamy Images: f1 online (b). 221 iStockphoto.com: IMPALASTOCK (cr). 222-223 Corbis: Roger De La Harpe/Gallo Images (b). iStockphoto.com: Phooey (t). 224 Corbis: Anthony Bannister/Gallo Images (c). 224-242 Alamy Images: Steven Poe (ftl). 225 Corbis: Jose Fuste Raga (tr); Jacky Naegelen/Reuters (b). 225-243 Alamy Images: Steven Poe (ftr). 226-227 Getty Images: Adam Jones (b). 227 Alamy Images: The Print Collector (c). 228 The Bridgeman Art Library: John Bethell (c). 229 Alamy Images: Corbis Premium Collection (b). 230-231 Getty Images: Harvey Lloyd (c). 232 Alamy Images: Visual Arts Library (London) (c). 232-233 iStockphoto.com: Vladimir Pomortsev (c). 233 Corbis: Thomas Hartwell (tr). 234 Alamy Images: The Print Collector (tr). 235 iStockphoto.com: Anthony Dodd (t). 236 Alamy Images: Chris Howes/Wild Places Photography / Alamy (b). 237 iStockphoto.com: Nico Smit (b). 238-239 Corbis: Caroline Penn (c). 240 Alamy Images: Black Star (b). 241 Corbis: Kevin Fleming (c). 242-243 Corbis: Eduardo Munoz/Reuters (b). 243 Alamy Images: Jenny Matthews (c). Getty Images: Terry O'Neill (tr). 244-245 Corbis: Charles & Josette Lenars (c). 246 akg-images: akg-images (bl). 246-262 iStockphoto.com: Akivi (ftl). 247 Alamy Images: Jon Arnold Images (b). 247-263 iStockphoto.com: Akivi (ftr). 248 Werner Forman Archive: Art Gallery of New South Wales, Sydney (b). 249 The Bridgeman Art Library: Heini Schneebeli (cr). 250 Corbis: Danny Lehman (b). 251 Alamy Images: WaterFrame (b). 252 Alamy Images: Visual Arts Library (London) (c). 253 Corbis: Paul Chinn/San Francisco Chronicle/Corbis (bl). 254 iStockphoto. com: Jay Spooner (b). 255 Alamy Images: Douglas Peebles Photography (c). 256-257 Getty Images: Walter Bibikow (c). 259 Corbis: O. Alamany & E. Vicens (cr). 260 Paul A Robishaw: (c) (bl). 261 Paul A Robishaw: (b). 262 Alamy Images: Douglas Peebles Photography (b). 263 Corbis: Jack Fields (cr). 264-265 Alamy Images: TNT Magazine (b). Corbis: Ted Streshinsky (t). 266 akg-images: (c). 266-342 iStockphoto.com: Pronesis (ftl). 267 Corbis: Jon Hicks (b). iStockphoto.com: Pete Smith (t). 267-343 iStockphoto.com: Pronesis (ftr). 268 Corbis: Stapleton Collection (b). 269 Alamy Images: Russ Merne (br). Corbis: Araldo de Luca (tl). 270 Corbis: Araldo de Luca (t). 271 Alamy Images: Visual Arts Library (London) (tl). The Bridgeman Art Library: Bibliotheque des Arts Decoratifs, Paris, France, Archives Charmet (b). 272 The Art Archive: Centre Archéologique de Glanum Saint-Rémy-de-Provence/Dagli Orti (t). 273 akg-images: Erich Lessing (c). 274 Corbis: Bettmann (bl). Werner Forman Archive: (tl). 275 The Art Archive: Musée du Louvre Paris/Dagli Orti (tr). 277 Alamy Images: Mary Evans Picture Library (bl). The

Art Archive: Marc Charmet (c). 278 Corbis: Peter Harholdt (tl). 279 iStockphoto.com: Hanne van der Velde (tl). 280 Corbis: Nik Wheeler (br). 281 Alamy Images: Tina Manley (tl). 282 Werner Forman Archive: Dallas Museum of Art (formerly Schindler Collection) (b). 283 akg-images: François Guénet (b). iStockphoto.com: Vladimir Pomortsev (tl). 284 Alamy Images: Mary Evans Picture Library (b). The Art Archive: Egyptian Museum Cairo/Dagli Orti (tl). 285 Alamy Images: Rachael Bowes (cr). 286 Corbis: Mimmo Jodice (b). iStockphoto.com: Kativ (t). 287 Alamy Images: Craig Lovell / Eagle Visions Photography (tl); Mary Evans Picture Library (tr). 288 Corbis: National Gallery Collection; By kind permission of the Trustees of the National Gallery, London (br). Werner Forman Archive: Christie's, London (tc). 289 Mary Evans Picture Library: (br). 290 akg-images: Erich Lessing (tl); Jean-Louis Nou (cr). Corbis: Asian Art & Archaeology, Inc. (b). 291 akg-images: François Guénet (cl). 292 Alamy Images: Buzz Pictures (t). 293 akg-images: Erich Lessing (tl). The Art Archive: Museo del Prado Madrid/Dagli Orti (cr). 294 The Bridgeman Art Library: Nationalmuseum, Stockholm, Sweden (b). 295 Alamy Images: Mary Evans Picture Library (c). The Art Archive: Archaeological Museum Aleppo Syria/Dagli Orti (b). 296 Corbis: Lindsay Hebberd (b). 297 The Art Archive: Victoria and Albert Museum London Eileen Tweedy (cl). 298 Corbis: Gianni Dagli Orti (b). 299 Corbis: Gianni Dagli Orti (c). 300 Corbis: Archivo Iconografico, SA (bc). iStockphoto.com: Baldur Tryggvason (t). 301 Corbis: Mimmo Jodice (c). 302 akg-images: Nimatallah (tl). Alamy Images: Robert Preston (b). 303 Corbis: Staffan Widstrand (cr). 304 The Art Archive: Musée du Louvre Paris/Dagli Orti (c) (br). 305 Corbis: James L. Amos (tl). 306 Corbis: Ali Meyer (c). iStockphoto.com: Giacomo Nodari (t). 307 The Art Archive: Dagli Orti (tl). The Bridgeman Art Library: The De Morgan Centre, London (b). 308 Corbis: Araldo de Luca (c); Roger Wood (tr). 309 The Bridgeman Art Library: Bibliotheque Nationale, Paris, France, Archives Charmet (b). 311 Corbis: Werner Forman (cl). 312 iStockphoto.com: Vasiliki Varvaki (t). 313 Alamy Images: Visual Arts Library (London) (b). Corbis: Charles & Josette Lenars (tl). 314 Alamy Images: Russ Merne (r). Corbis: Araldo de Luca (b). 315 Corbis: Werner Forman. 316 akg-images: Jean-Louis Nou (c). 317 The Art Archive: Musée du Louvre Paris/Dagli Orti (br); Dagli Orti (cl). 318 The Art Archive: Musée du Louvre Paris / Dagli Orti (c). iStockphoto.com: Jodie Coston (t). 319 The Art Archive: National Archaeological Museum Athens / Dagli Orti (t). Getty Images: Italian School/The Bridgeman Art Library (cr). 320 Mary Evans Picture Library: Arthur Rackham (c). 321 The Art Archive: British Library (tl). Corbis: Jason Horowitz/zefa (br). 322 Alamy Images: Beaconstox (b); J Marshall - Tribaleye Images (tl). 323 The Bridgeman Art Library: Paul Freeman (b). 324 Corbis: Christie's Images (c). iStockphoto.com: William Casey (t). 325 The Bridgeman Art Library: Prado, Madrid, Spain, Index (br). Corbis: Jonathan Blair (tl). 326 Alamy Images: Peter Horree (tr). 327 The Bridgeman Art Library: Bibliotheque des Arts Decoratifs, Paris, France, Archives Charmet (cl). Corbis: Werner Forman (cr). 328 akg-images: (cr). iStockphoto.com: John Pitcher (tl). 329 The Art Archive: Musée du Louvre Paris/ Jacqueline Hyde (bc). 330 iStockphoto.com: Melody Kerchhoff (t). 331 Corbis: Mimmo Jodice (b). 332 Alamy Images: Visual Arts Library (London) (tr). Corbis: The Art Archive (bl). 333 Alamy Images: V&A Images (br). 334 Alamy Images: Visual Arts Library (London) (c). 335 akg-images: Jean-Louis Nou (bc). iStockphoto.com: eROMAZe (tl). 336 Corbis: Sakamoto Photo Research Laboratory (tl). 337 Alamy Images: Darroch Donald (cl). Corbis: Gianni Dagli Orti (tr). 338 iStockphoto.com: Kyle Froese (t). 339 The Bridgeman Art Library: Bibliotheque des Arts Decoratifs, Paris, France, Archives Charmet (c). 340 The Art Archive: Victoria and Albert Museum London / Eileen Tweedy (b). 341 Corbis: Werner Forman (b). 342 Corbis: Charles & Josette Lenars (tl). 343 The Art Archive: Musée du Louvre Paris / Dagli Orti (b). iStockphoto.com: Anthony Dodd (t). 344-352 iStockphoto.com: Ryan KC Wong (ftl). 345-351 iStockphoto. com: Ryan KC Wong (ftr)

Jacket images: Front: The Bridgeman Art Library: bl; Corbis: Christie's Images br; Macduff Everton c; G Richardson/Robert Harding World Imagery fbr; Herbert Spichtinger/Zefa t; Werner Forman fbl. Back: Corbis: Canadian Museum of Civilization cla; Free Agents Limited c; Stapleton Collection br; Summerfield Press cra; DK Images: British Museum bl, t. Spine: Corbis: Paul Almasy

All other images © Dorling Kindersley
For further information see: www.dkimages.com